DATE DUE

SEP 2 2 2006			

GAYLORD PRINTED IN U.S.A.

fP

Also by Michael McGerr:

The Decline of Popular Politics: The American North, 1865–1928

A Fierce Discontent

The Rise and Fall of the Progressive Movement in America, 1870–1920

Michael McGerr

Free Press
NEW YORK LONDON TORONTO SYDNEY SINGAPORE

fP

FREE PRESS
A Division of Simon & Schuster, Inc.
1230 Avenue of the Americas
New York, NY 10020

For information regarding special discounts for bulk purchases,
please contact Simon & Schuster Special Sales:
1-800-456-6798 or business@simonandschuster.com

Manufactured in the United States of America

1 3 5 7 9 10 8 6 4 2

Library of Congress Cataloging-in-Publication Data

McGerr, Michael E.
A fierce discontent : the rise and fall of the Progressive movement in
America, 1870–1920 / Michael McGerr.
p. cm.
Includes bibliographical references and index.
1. United States—Politics and government—1865–1933. 2. Progressivism
(United States politics)—history. 3. United States—
social conditions—1865–1918. I. Title.
E661.M415 2003
324.2732'7—dc21 2003048499
ISBN 0-684-85975-0

For Rosemarie

"So far as this movement of agitation throughout the country takes the form of a fierce discontent with evil, of a firm determination to punish the authors of evil, whether in industry or politics, the feeling is to be heartily welcomed as a sign of healthy life."

—THEODORE ROOSEVELT
APRIL 14, 1906

Contents

Acknowledgments

Three people inspired this book. I began it because of C. Vann Woodward's faith in my work and because I wanted to understand the country in which Rita and Gerald McGerr grew up. My one regret is that none of these people lived to see the end result.

A grant from the National Endowment for the Humanities and support from the Massachusetts Institute of Technology and Indiana University—Bloomington gave me precious time to work on this project. My research assistants, Suzanne Wurster and Kate Schroeder, simplified the labor of gathering sources, writing the manuscript, and bringing it to publication. Along the way, I received helpful comments and encouragement from many colleagues and friends, including Edward Ayers, John Bodnar, Jocelyn Bowie, William Cohen, James Madison, Bruce Mazlish, David Thelen, and David Ward. I am especially grateful for the advice and support of Casey Blake, Joanne Meyerowitz, James Oakes, and Kumble Subbaswamy.

Sheldon Meyer was exceptionally gracious when this book developed differently from the one we had originally envisioned. At the Free Press, Bruce Nichols's commitment and creativity helped me realize the full potential of the manuscript. I am grateful, too, for the work of Casey Reivich, Philip Metcalf, and others at the press.

The dedication acknowledges my greatest and happiest debt of all.

Michael McGerr
Bloomington
February 2003

Preface

We live in a politically disappointing time. No matter what our politics, the start of the twenty-first century is not what we hoped it would be. For liberals, the "American Century"—the *liberal* century—was the last one; and it ended early, in the 1960s and 1970s, with racial backlash, stagflation, and Vietnam. For conservatives, the "Reagan Revolution" of the 1980s ended pretty quickly, too; enough big government and economic uncertainty remain in the aftermath to make Americans wonder whether there was a revolution at all. For the handful of American radicals, the promise of the "Movement" of the 1960s is long gone: corporate America still stands powerful and the American "empire" looms larger than ever around the world. Despite sex scandals, financial scandals, and the worst terrorist attack in the nation's history, politics and government fail to engage the sustained interest of most Americans.

It is no wonder, then, that the Progressive Era remains so fascinating. The people and struggles of that age of "fierce discontent" a century ago still command our attention. There is Theodore Roosevelt himself, the energy glinting through his pince-nez, as he urges Americans to use the "movement of agitation throughout the country . . . to punish the authors of evil. . . ." There are the women suffragists marching in the streets to demand the vote. There are the determined anthracite coal miners of Pennsylvania quietly walking out en masse to demand recognition from their wealthy bosses. There is the crafty steel magnate Andrew Carnegie urging the families of the upper-class "plutocracy" to save themselves by giving their money to philanthropic causes. There is the calm courage of Jane Addams, crossing the social boundaries of urban Chicago to improve and change the lives of her new immigrant neighbors. There is the moral outrage of Carry Nation, smashing saloons to end the scourge of drink. These people provoke nostalgia and even jealousy; in one way or another, all of them felt the "fierce discontent" that Theodore Roosevelt described; all of them believed that progress was possible for their country.

The Progressive Era is more than a matter of nostalgia. It is the argument of this book that progressivism created much of our contemporary political predicament. The epic of reform at the dawn of the twentieth century helps explain the less-than-epic politics at the dawn of the twenty-first. Progressivism, the creed of a crusading middle class, offered the promise of utopianism—and generated the inevitable letdown of unrealistic expectations.

Those expectations were indeed remarkable. The progressives developed a stunningly broad agenda that ranged well beyond the control of big business, the amelioration of poverty, and the purification of politics to embrace the transformation of gender relations, the regeneration of the home, the disciplining of leisure and pleasure, and the establishment of segregation. Progressives wanted not only to use the state to regulate the economy; strikingly, they intended nothing less than to transform other Americans, to remake the nation's feuding, polyglot population in their own middle-class image.

This startling agenda had commonplace origins; it was rooted in the day-to-day lives of middle-class men and women in the Gilded Age of the late nineteenth century. Progressivism was the way in which these Victorian men and women came to answer the basic questions of human life that have confronted all people in all times and places: What is the nature of the individual? What is the relationship between the individual and society? What are the proper roles of men, women, and the family? What is the place of work and pleasure in human life? These are ordinary questions, but the middle class had to answer them at an extraordinary time. The Victorians lived in an industrializing society that generated dismaying extremes of wealth and poverty, tempting new pleasures, alien cultures, and frightening antagonisms. Threatened by these external developments, the Victorians lived with a private crisis of their own—the breakdown of the relationship between middle-class men and women. The result of these simultaneous public and private crises was a gradual but dramatic transformation: over the two generations from the end of the Civil War to the 1890s, the Victorians became progressives, with new views of the individual, society, gender, and pleasure. To make the world safe for themselves and their children, the progressive middle class sallied forth to reform the nation. In the face of spirited opposition from other groups, the progressives intended to build what William James sneeringly but accurately labeled the "middle-class paradise."

I believe progressivism was a radical movement, though not by the common measures of economic and political radicalism. More influenced by socialism than they liked to admit, progressives nevertheless shied away from a fundamental restructuring of the capitalist economy. They generally declined numerous opportunities to rethink the virtue of private property. Instead, progressives were radical in their conviction that other social classes must be transformed and in their boldness in going about the business of that transformation. As they themselves had been changed, so others should be changed, too. The sweep of progressivism was remarkable, but because the progressive agenda was so often carried out in settlement houses, churches, and schoolrooms, in rather unassuming day-to-day activities, the essential audacity of the enterprise can be missed. Progressivism demanded a social transformation that remains at once profoundly impressive and profoundly disturbing a century later.

Approaching progressivism in this way, I have shifted the balance of the conventional narrative.[1] The center of this book looks at four quintessential progressive battles: to change other people; to end class conflict; to control big business; and to segregate society. While I treat well-known laws and political events, this is also a book about less well-known, extrapolitical efforts to transform America and Americans, such as the antidivorce movement and the rise of Chautauqua. While I focus extensively on public life, this is very much a book about private, intimate life as well. Given its focus on the basic values of social groups, it is a book about parents and their children—John and Sarah Addams and their daughter Jane; the Russian immigrant tailor Golub and his rebellious daughter Rahel; the farming couple Richard and Belle Garland and their equally rebellious son Hamlin. It is in the relationships of these generations that we can most clearly see how the stresses of industrializing America fractured old ideologies and created new ones, including progressivism.

From its private and intimate origins, the progressive movement ultimately played out on a very public stage. Progressivism was an explosion, a burst of energy that fired in many directions across America. From the 1890s to the 1910s, the progressives managed to accomplish much of their ambitious agenda. World War I marked the high point of the progressive movement. As American soldiers fought overseas to make the world safe for democracy, the administration of Woodrow Wilson worked feverishly to create a wartime model for a peacetime progressive utopia. Against the backdrop of wartime struggle and sacrifice, reformers managed to outlaw alcohol, close down vice districts, win suffrage for women, expand the income tax, and take over the railroads. But the progressives had overreached. Winning the war abroad, the Wilsonians lost their war at home. The administration's war policies produced disorder instead of order, chaos instead of control. Amid race riots, strikes, high inflation, and a frenzied Red scare, Americans turned against the progressive blueprint for the nation. The climax of progressivism, World War I was also its death knell.

It is this story, this remarkable rise and cataclysmic collapse, that set the stage for the political life we now know so well. Americans' ambivalent attitudes toward politics and the state, our skepticism about reform, our fear of government's power, and our arm's-length relationship with political leaders have their roots before the ages of Franklin Roosevelt, Lyndon Johnson, and Ronald Reagan, in the few dramatic decades at the turn of the previous century. The New Deal, World War II, the Cold War, the Great Society, and now the war on terrorism have each entailed ambitious plans for America; and each has had dramatic impacts on policy and society. But the failure of the progressive movement set boundaries around the aspirations of all these efforts. None of them was as ambitious, as openly determined to transform people and create utopia, as the progressive movement. We have been scaling back our expectations ever since that age of bold reform. Chastened by his experience in the Wilson government, Franklin Roosevelt pursued a New Deal liberalism that was in many ways less radical than progressivism. Lyndon Johnson's Great Society fought the racial injustice that the progressives had shirked and even helped perpetrate in the first place; but Great Society liberalism avoided both the sharp attack on upper-class privilege and the optimistic faith in remaking individuals and creating utopia. And the New Right of Barry Goldwater and Ronald Reagan rose to power by condemning the powerful state that the progressives had worked to build and by celebrating the individualism that they had hoped to dismantle. For all of us, right, center, and left, the age of "fierce discontent" is long over.

PART ONE

The Progressive Opportunity

CHAPTER ONE

"Signs of Friction"

Portrait of America at Century's End

In one of Chicago's elite clubs on election night in November 1896, a group of rich men were euphoric. After a tense, uncertain campaign, their presidential candidate, the Republican William McKinley, had clearly defeated the Democratic and Populist nominee, William Jennings Bryan. As the celebration continued past midnight, a wealthy merchant, recalling his younger days, began a game of Follow the Leader. The other tycoons joined in and the growing procession tromped across sofas and chairs and up onto tables. Snaking upstairs and down-, the line finally broke up as the men danced joyfully in one another's arms.[1]

Their euphoria was understandable. McKinley's victory climaxed not only a difficult election but an intense, generation-long struggle for control of industrializing America. For Chicago's elite, the triumph of McKinley, the sober former governor of Ohio, meant that the federal government was in reliable, Republican hands. The disturbing changes that Bryan had promised—the reform of the monetary system, the dismantling of the protective tariff—would not pass. The frightening prospect of a radical alliance of farmers and workers had collapsed. The emerging industrial order, the source of their wealth and power, seemed safe.[2]

McKinley's victory certainly was a critical moment, but the election did not settle the question of control as fully as those rich men in Chicago would have liked. The wealthy could play Follow the Leader, but it was not at all clear that the rest of the nation was ready to follow along. Driven by the industrial revolution, America had grown enormously in territory, population, and wealth in the nineteenth century. The United States was not one nation but several; it was a land divided by region, race, and ethnicity. And it was a land still deeply split by class conflict. The upper class remained a controversial group engineering a wrenching economic transformation, accumulating staggering fortunes, and pursuing notorious private lives. Just three months later another party—this one in New York City—highlighted the precariousness of upper-class authority at the close of the nineteenth century.

While McKinley and Bryan battled for the presidency, Cornelia Bradley Martin had been plotting her own coup in the social wars of New York's rich. She and her husband, Bradley, were no newcomers to the ranks of wealthy Manhattan. Cornelia's father had been a millionaire merchant in New York; Bradley's, a banker from a fine Albany family. Though wealthy, their parents had lived by the old Victorian virtues. Cornelia's father, it was said, had been "domestic in his tastes"; Bradley's father, who early practiced "absolute self-denial," "never lost an opportunity of instilling" in his sons "ideas of the importance of work and one's duty towards others in every-day life." Cornelia and Bradley, married in 1869, had moved away from the old values. One sign of the change was their surname, which somewhere along the line borrowed Bradley's first name, occasionally added a hyphen, and doubled from "Martin" to "Bradley-Martin." Another was Cornelia's collection of jewelry, which included pieces from the French crown jewels, most notably a ruby necklace that had belonged to Marie Antoinette. Never "domestic" in their tastes, the Bradley Martins had become well known in New York social circles, especially for their renowned parties in 1885 and 1890.[3]

In the depression winter of 1897, Cornelia arranged a costume ball at the Waldorf Hotel that would, she hoped, eclipse not only her previous efforts but also Alva Vanderbilt's famous ball of 1883, widely recognized as the greatest party in the history of the city. Cornelia was not bashful about her intentions. For weeks before the ball, her secretary made sure that the papers got all the details. Yet the publicity was not quite what Cornelia had expected. Across the country, preachers and editorial writers argued over the propriety of a party that would cost hundreds of thousands of dollars amid the worst depression in the nation's history. At the fashionable St. George's

Episcopal Church in New York, rector Dr. William Rainsford urged his congregation, which included financier J. P. Morgan, to forgo the ball. "Never were the lines between the two classes—those who have wealth and those who envy them—more distinctly drawn," Rainsford warned. "[S]uch elaborate and costly manifestations of wealth would only tend to stir up . . . widespread discontent" and "furnish additional texts for sermons by the socialistic agitators." "Every thoughtful man," agreed a parishioner, "must have seen signs of friction between the upper ten and the lower. Whatever tends to increase it, as very elaborate social affairs may, can well be spared now." The pastor of Fifth Avenue Baptist Church, where John D. Rockefeller worshipped, preached that wealth should be used for philanthropy. Undeterred, Cornelia went ahead. Her supporters claimed that the expenditures for the ball would stimulate the economy.[4]

Some invited guests decided not to attend. But about six or seven hundred turned up, in costume, when the great night came on February 10. Bradley dressed as a member of the court of Louis XV. Cornelia, despite her Marie Antoinette necklace, dressed as another luckless queen, Mary Stuart. Like a queen, the hostess greeted her guests from a raised dais "beneath a canopy of rare tapestries." There were mirrors, tables laden with food, "a wild riot of roses," and "mimic woodland bowers." The scene "reproduced the splendour of Versailles in New York, and I doubt if even the Roi Soleil himself ever witnessed a more dazzling sight," Bradley's brother, Frederick Townsend Martin, remembered. "The power of wealth with its refinement and vulgarity was everywhere. It gleamed from countless jewels, and it was proclaimed by the thousands of orchids and roses, whose fragrance that night was like incense burnt on the altar of the Golden Calf." Royalty was everywhere, too—"perhaps a dozen" Marie Antoinettes came to the ball. Amid all the bewigged and bejeweled royalty, a reporter noted, there were hardly any American costumes. Only one or two George Washingtons reminded the guests of their republican origins. Outside, about 250 police closed the sidewalks to pedestrians and braced for trouble. While his wife danced inside, Police Commissioner Theodore Roosevelt directed his men as they watched for anyone "likely to prove dangerous from an anarchistic viewpoint."[5]

The revolutionary moment never came, but Cornelia's triumph turned into disaster anyway. Across the country, elite opinion condemned the Bradley Martins. The *Chicago Tribune* gave its verdict by quoting Shakespeare's

Puck: "What fools these mortals be." Worse, New York City itself suddenly became inhospitable. Municipal officials, noting Bradley's opulence, raised his property taxes. The members of the city's elite clubs pronounced the Bradley Martins' ball "magnificent" but "stupid." Unlike Marie Antoinette and Mary Stuart, Cornelia kept her head, but she and Bradley soon left the United States to begin a self-imposed exile. Selling their mansion in Manhattan, the Bradley Martins bought a new place in London, where their daughter had married Lord Craven a few years before. In 1899, they returned briefly to New York to give a defiant farewell dinner party at the Waldorf at the cost of $116 a plate. From then on, the Bradley Martins divided their time between London and Balmacaan, Bradley's estate in Scotland. They left behind a bemused Frederick Townsend Martin. Years later he still could not understand why all this had happened. After all, the ball had helped the economy because "many New York shops sold out brocades and silks which had been lying in their stock-rooms for years." "I cannot conceive," Frederick wrote sadly, "why this entertainment should have been condemned."[6]

If McKinley's victory emphasized the strength of the "upper ten," the Bradley Martins' ball epitomized their weakness. Absurd as it was, the affair highlighted the cultural isolation and internal division that plagued the wealthy. The industrial upper class upheld a set of values at odds with those of other classes. Approaching life so differently from the rest of America, the rich could not command respect from farmers and workers. Even among themselves, the "upper ten" disagreed how best to live their lives and secure their future. The party did not last very long at all.

Cornelia Bradley Martin staged her costume ball when class differences were more pronounced than at any time in the history of industrial America. The end of the nineteenth century saw more than just "signs of friction between the upper ten and the lower": wage workers, farmers, and the rich were alien to one another. That sense of strangeness was not only a matter of obvious differences in material circumstances. By choice and by necessity, America's social classes lived starkly divergent daily lives and invoked different and often conflicting values to guide, explain, and justify their ways of life. The classes held distinctive views on fundamental issues of human existence: on the nature of the individual; on the relationship between the individual and society; on the roles of men, women, children, and the family; and on the relative importance of work and pleasure. What would become the Progressive Era—an extraordinary explosion of middle-class activism—began as an unprecedented crisis of alienation amid the extremes of wealth and poverty in America.

In a land of some 76 million people, the "upper ten" were no more than a tiny minority, a mere sliver of the nation. Wealthy capitalists, manufacturers, merchants, landowners, executives, professionals, and their families made up not "ten," but only 1 or 2 percent of the population. These were the people who owned the majority of the nation's resources and expected to make the majority of its key decisions. They could be found in cities, towns, and rural estates across the country. Their ranks included the nation's roughly four thousand millionaires, fabulously rich by almost any standard. Their most visible and most powerful members were the two hundred or so families worth at least $20 million, fortunes with few parallels in history. Concentrated in the Northeast and especially New York State, theirs were the famous names of American capitalism—Vanderbilt, Whitney, Carnegie, Harriman, and Morgan. Probably the greatest fortune of them all—a billion dollars by 1913—belonged to John D. Rockefeller, the leader of Standard Oil.[7]

Membership in the upper ten was never only a matter of precise calculation in dollars; it was also a matter of origins, experience, and outlook. Wealthy Americans shared several attributes that made them a homogenous and distinctive group, similar to one another and different from the rest of the population. In an increasingly diverse nation of new and old immigrants, the upper class came mostly from English stock, from families long in America. In a largely Protestant land, they belonged, by birth or conversion, to the smaller, most fashionable Protestant denominations—Episcopalian, Presbyterian, and Congregational. With only occasional exceptions, they came from middle- and upper-class origins. Hardly any matched Andrew Carnegie's storied rise from rags to riches, from working-class bobbin boy in a textile factory to multimillionaire steel baron. While fewer than 10 percent of the population had even graduated from high school, many of the upper ten had gone to college or professional school.[8]

Above all, the upper ten shared a fundamental understanding about the nature of the individual. Glorifying the power of individual will, the wealthy held to an uncompromising belief in the necessity of individual freedom. To

Andrew Carnegie, "Individualism" was the very "foundation" of the human race. "Only through exceptional individuals, the leaders, man has been able to ascend," Carnegie explained. "[It] is the leaders who do the new things that count, all these have been Individualistic to a degree beyond ordinary men and worked in perfect freedom; each and every one a character unlike anybody else; an original, gifted beyond most others of his kind, hence his leadership." It was just this strong-willed sense of her "exceptional" individuality that inspired Cornelia Bradley Martin's idea for a ball; and it was just this sense of her right to "perfect freedom" that enabled her to stick to her plans in the face of so much condemnation.[9]

The upper ten attributed the hardships of the poor not to an unfair economic system but to individual shortcomings. The remedy was individual regeneration rather than government action. "[The] failures which a man makes in his life are due almost always to some defect in his personality, some weakness of body, or mind, or character, will, or temperament," wrote John D. Rockefeller. "The only way to overcome these failings is to build up his personality from within, so that he, by virtue of what is within him, may overcome the weakness which was the cause of the failure." Individualism, moreover, helped the wealthy resolutely deny the existence of social classes, despite all the signs of friction around them. "The American Commonwealth is built upon the individual," explained the renowned corporate lawyer and U.S. Senator Chauncey Depew of New York. "It recognizes neither classes nor masses."[10]

Upper-class individualism was more than just a crude version of "might makes right." These men and women had grown up in a land dedicated to individualism. In the Revolutionary era, the nation's sacred documents—the Declaration of Independence, the Constitution, and the Bill of Rights—proclaimed the dignity and worth of the individual. By the nineteenth century, that notion was so powerful and so distinctively American that the visiting French observer Alexis de Tocqueville coined the term *individualism* to describe it. The relentless spread of capitalism reaffirmed the individualist creed, but with a new emphasis on each person's ownership of his or her labor. By midcentury, this reworked individualism drove the abolitionist assault on slavery and spurred the Northern war against the South. Individualism justified the emerging factory system, built on individual workers' free exchange of their labor for wages. Individualism provided the core of the

Victorian culture that taught middle-class men self-discipline and self-reliance in the struggle for success. "Take away the spirit of Individualism from the people," warned Wall Street veteran Henry Clews, "and you at once eliminate the American spirit—the love of freedom,—of free industry,—free and unfettered opportunity,—you take away freedom itself."[11]

Ironically, the wealthy themselves challenged freedom and individualism by creating the nation's pioneering big businesses, the giant trusts and corporations that employed the first white-collar "organization men." There were even a few "organization men" among the upper ten. William Ellis Corey, the second president of United States Steel, "is part of the mechanism itself," wrote an observer early in the twentieth century. "He feels himself to be a fraction, rather than a unit. His corporation is an organism like a human body, and he is the co-ordinating function of its brain."[12]

Yet, men like Corey were unusual. For one thing, many of the wealthy did not share his familiarity with corporate life. In the industrial city of Baltimore, sixth largest in the nation in 1900, only about one-fifth of leading businessmen had made their careers as bureaucrats. Of the 185 leaders of the largest American firms between 1901 and 1910, just under half were career bureaucrats, men who had never had their own businesses. But even business leaders accustomed to bureaucracy tended to see themselves as individual units rather than fractions of some larger whole. Railroad executives, members of the nation's pioneering corporate hierarchies, still rejoiced in "competitive individualism" after decades of collective enterprise. Such people may have felt a special tie to their organizations, but that did not prevent them from feeling superior to everybody else. William Ellis Corey was, after all, United States Steel's "brain," rather than one of its lesser organs. James Stillman, the leader of New York's National City Bank, thought of his firm as a god and sometimes as "our mother." Yet, the obedience Stillman owed his god and his mother did not keep him from being "lordly in his manner."[13]

The aristocratic and even regal bearing, with its assumption of individual prerogative, came easily for the men and women of the upper ten. There were all those kings and queens at the Bradley Martin ball. There was the financier E. H. Harriman, who "had the philosophy, the methods of an Oriental monarch." His niece, Daisy Harriman, recalled visiting him in his library one evening. "Daisy, I have a new plaything," he told her. "I have just bought the Erie [railroad] for five million dollars. I think I will call them up now."[14]

J. P. Morgan, Harriman's sometime competitor in buying railroads and organizing the corporate world, shared that regal sense of individual entitlement. Although "a great gentleman," Morgan "was in his own soul, in his ego, a king; royalty." He exercised the royal prerogative not only in the male world of work on Wall Street but in the female domain of the home. Morgan, a family member related, "loved to display a frank disregard of the usual rules about babies and assert his entire independence of the mother's and the nurse's authority—he always took pleasure in doing that, not only with his own children but with his grandchildren." When his first child was born, Morgan had her crib taken out of the nursery and set next to his bed, "so that he could look after her himself and be perfectly sure that she was well covered up at night." An intensely religious man, Morgan nevertheless revealed his sense of individual authority even when he worshiped God in church. If Morgan did not like a hymn, he slammed his hymnal shut, an observer noted. "If he liked the hymn but not the tune, he would jingle the coins in his pocket quite audibly as a sign of his disapproval."[15]

Upper-class individualism was obviously self-serving and often self-deluding, but it was no sham. More than any other group, the upper ten carried individualism proudly into the organized and bureaucratized twentieth century. It was just this sort of individualism that their sons learned at home, at private school, and then at Harvard, Princeton, and Yale. And it was just this extreme individualism that set the upper ten apart from other classes and that guaranteed social tension and conflict in the new century.[16]

Despite their individualism, the upper ten had broken away from much of their Victorian heritage. Placing great emphasis on domesticity, Victorianism urged men and women to marry and create homes. A wife was expected to devote herself to making that home both a soothing refuge for her husband and a nurturing preparation for her sons' eventual immersion in the economic struggle. Unlike Cornelia Bradley Martin's "domestic" father, however, the upper ten were not so dedicated to the home. By the close of the nineteenth century, the wealthy had modified and contravened domesticity in striking ways.[17]

Of course, the rich typically married and created homes. Cornelia Bradley Martin and other wealthy women, shunning careers in business or politics, seemingly devoted themselves to the domestic ideal as wives and mothers. But these women artfully turned their domestic duty as hostesses into quite public roles that earned them fame and notoriety. Cornelia Bradley Martin was more of a public figure than her husband. Meanwhile, in a notable departure from Victorian tradition, upper-class parents thrust their sons out of the protective cocoon of the home at an early age. Rather than bring in tutors to school their boys at home as in the past, many of the wealthy began sending their male heirs off to Groton, Choate, St. Paul's, and other exclusive boarding schools in New England.[18]

The rich were also unusually willing to break up the home altogether. Before the Civil War, divorce had been as unthinkable for the wealthy as for middle-class Victorians. But with the rise of the industrial upper class after the war, May King Van Rensselaer of New York noted, society circles "began to sanction divorces. . . . All at once it became fashionable to divorce your helpmeet. . . ." In a nation where, as late as 1920, less than one percent of adults had been divorced, the marriages of the rich collapsed with notable frequency. Ten percent of the Americans worth $20 million or more who were born between 1830 and 1865 were divorced; of those born between the end of the Civil War and the turn of the century, 20 percent were divorced.[19]

The upper ten broke as well with the attitudes toward work and pleasure that underlay Victorian individualism. The Victorians of the mid–nineteenth century believed the individual could be free only because he was self-disciplined. Determined to accumulate capital and avoid dissipation, the nineteenth-century middle class had glorified hard work, limited leisure, and warily eyed consumption. As a boy in a Victorian household, Bradley Martin had duly learned about "the importance of work" and "absolute self-denial." But he and the rest of the upper ten, with so many millions of dollars, had no need to work, save, and deny themselves pleasure at the end of the nineteenth century. By and large, the upper ten agreed that life should be about pleasure as well as the accumulation of wealth. Daisy Harriman even contended that " . . . the Bradley Martin Balls that added to the gaiety of nations and set money in circulation were far more pious enterprises than unostentatious hoarding."[20]

Admittedly, some of the rich had to work hard to forget their Victorian maxims. "I have never in all my life done anything I wanted and cannot now," lamented James Stillman. Plagued by headaches, the banker nevertheless drove himself and others to work still harder. His handpicked successor at National City Bank, Frank Vanderlip, was much the same. "I had the work habit incurably . . . ," Vanderlip confessed. "I did not play. I did not know how to play. I never have learned to play." Nevertheless, Stillman and Vanderlip gradually found the time and money for a string of pleasures. Stillman had his fine mansion—"large, heavy, ornate, pillared"—on East Seventy-second Street; he had trips to Europe and Palm Beach, an art collection, and one of the earliest automobiles. "Like most men, Mr. Stillman wanted the best of everything," an early biographer explained almost apologetically, "but without extravagance." His protégé Vanderlip drew the line at buying a yacht but finally took up cigars and bought an estate up the Hudson River.[21]

Other members of the upper ten took much more quickly to a life of relaxation and pleasure. Morgan worked hard but enjoyed "frequent" vacations; Carnegie did not work full-time for most of his adult life. This liberation from work was one of the most distinctive features of the culture of the upper ten. To many Americans, the rich were, as Thorstein Veblen described them in 1899, *The Leisure Class.*[22]

The upper ten used their free hours, days, and months to enjoy a host of pleasures: mansions, yachts, private railway cars, horses, jewels, and art collections. The homes of the rich suggest how the old standards of restraint and frugality had decayed. The typical great mansion required a staff of about twenty-four servants and $200,000 or $300,000 a year to maintain. The houses of the four grandsons of Cornelius Vanderbilt illustrated the possibilities. The second oldest brother, Willie Vanderbilt, and his wife, Alva, had a $2 million "Gothic palace" on the corner of Fifth Avenue and Fifty-third Street; the oldest brother, Cornelius II, and his wife, Alice, had a $5 million house on Fifth Avenue between Fifty-seventh and Fifty-eighth Streets. At Newport, the Vanderbilt brothers had "cottages"—Willie's "Marble House," patterned after the Temple of the Sun at Baalbek, and Cornelius's 70-room residence, "The Breakers." Not to be outdone, the third brother, Frederick, had houses in Manhattan and Newport, and a stunning 54-room Italian Renaissance castle up in Hyde Park along the Hudson. The most extraordinary Vanderbilt home belonged to the youngest brother, George. "Biltmore," completed in the Blue Ridge Mountains of North Carolina in 1895, was a 250-room chateau on a feudal "barony" of 146,000 acres. Employing more workers than the United States Department of Agriculture, "Biltmore" included gardens designed by Frederick Law Olmsted, tree nurseries, dairies, reservoirs, schools, a hospital, and a model village.[23]

While many wealthy New Yorkers pursued pleasure, they kept the pursuit relatively private, hidden behind the walls of those mansions on Fifth Avenue. But part of Manhattan's upper ten sought the widest possible publicity. This was the "High Society" of the Bradley Martins. After the Civil War, Mrs. William Astor had tried to unify High Society by blending old and new wealth: in 1888, her aide Ward McAllister had drawn up his famous list of the "400" guests—actually 273—who would fit into the Astors' ballroom. With Mrs. Astor's gradual retirement in the 1890s, High Society fractured into factions led by Mrs. Ogden Mills, Mrs. Stuyvesant Fish, and other rival hostesses who staged extravagant and widely reported dinners, receptions, house parties, and cotillions.[24]

Why should the lavish life-style of the upper ten matter to us? As the Bradley Martins learned, the apparent trivialities of balls and parties counted for a great deal in turn-of-the-century America. The culture of the upper ten—half perversion and half repudiation of Victorianism—made their wealth and power all the more controversial. Elite values would repel the middle class enough to turn respectable Victorians into radicals and set off the progressive explosion.

The gulf between the upper ten and the working class was enormous. Of necessity, working men, women, and children lived by a different set of cultural rules that also challenged Victorianism and aroused both fear and sympathy in the middle class. The constraints and uncertainties of working-class life—low wages, lay-offs, accidents, limited opportunity, early death—made individualism at best a wasteful indulgence and at worst a mortal threat. Realizing that they had to depend on one another to survive, workers developed a culture of mutualism and reciprocity. At home and at work, they taught sometimes harsh lessons about the necessity of self-denial and collective action.

These were lessons that Rahel Golub learned painfully in the 1890s. Born in Russia, she came to America in 1892 at the age of eleven to help her father in a tailor shop in New York City. Rahel and her father lived in a one-room apartment in the crowded Jewish neighborhood of Cherry Street, not too many blocks from the Bradley Martins. But Rahel's world was far away from the lives of the Bradley Martins and their friends on Fifth Avenue. As she learned to baste pocket flaps and coat edges, she also discovered the rules of life in her new country.[25]

The center of Rahel Golub's world was her family. Everything revolved around the family's needs, above all the imperative of reuniting parents and children in America. Rahel and her father had to work and save to pay for the rest of the family's passage to the United States. Against that necessity, her needs and wishes, her chance for an education, did not matter at all. Rahel sometimes felt the tension between her family and her individuality. "One Saturday," she related, "while standing out on the stoop I saw one little girl show a cent to another and boasting that she was going to buy candy. . . . It occurred to me that I too would like to have a cent with which to do just as I pleased." So Rahel asked her father for the money. "He looked at me silently for a long moment," she recalled. "Then he rose slowly, took out his pocket book, took a cent from it, held it out to me, and said with a frown . . . , 'Here, and see that this never happens again.'" Rahel was stunned: "I felt as if the coin were burning my fingers. I handed it back quickly, left the room and walked about in the streets. I felt mortally hurt. I felt that I was working from morning till night like a grown up person and yet when I wanted one single cent—." When she would not eat that night, her father beat her with a twisted towel. "I felt the towel across my back again and again," she would write. "Finally he threw it down and said, panting for breath, 'Girl, I'll break you if you don't change.' And I said in my heart, 'My father, we shall see!'"[26]

Nevertheless, Rahel came to accept the self-denial at the heart of her life and her father's. "In the shop one morning I realised that he had been leaving out of his breakfast the tiny glass of brandy for two cents and was eating just the roll," she said. "So I too made my sacrifice. When as usual he gave me the apple and the roll, I took the roll but refused the apple. And he did not urge me." There were other sacrifices: Rahel avoided changing jobs because the loss of even one day's pay would slow her family's arrival.[27]

As a new "feller hand" in a tailor shop, Rahel worked as hard and as fast as she could to make the money needed to bring her mother and siblings to America. The work seemed to be worth her while because the shop owner paid by the piece—her output—rather than by the hour. But the older women in the shop turned on her for showing that it was possible to produce more goods in less time. They thought that her production would encourage the boss to lower the piecework rates he paid them. "I . . . knew that I had done almost as much work as the 'grown-up girls' and that they did not like me," Rahel realized. "I heard Betsy, the head feller hand, talking about 'a snip of a girl coming and taking the very bread out of your mouth.'" And so Rahel learned to obey the rules of a workplace "family," too.[28]

Rahel and her father discovered other collective bonds. "Each of you alone can do nothing," a member of the garment workers' union told them. "Organize!" They joined the union. Rahel's father also belonged to a mutual aid society; she remembered meetings in their apartment to discuss burial plots for the members.[29]

Rahel's self-denial paid off. Eventually, she and her father earned the money to bring her mother, brother, and sisters to America. But the reunion of the family did not end the demands on her. Plagued by poor health that kept her from working, Rahel knew she still had to help: she had to marry well. Her parents arranged a match for her with Israel, a young grocer. "It is true that you are young," her mother explained, "but you see, father is poor and you are not strong!" By then, Rahel understood the logic: "'It is clear then,' I thought, 'that I must marry. . . . My people could live near and get things at cost price, bread, butter, sugar, potatoes. It will be a great help.'" But she was reluctant to live with "the strange young man and his mother." So Rahel put off the decision. "At last," she remembered the scene, "I heard father lay down his spoon and push his chair away from the table a little. 'Well,' he asked in a 'by the way' tone, 'what have you decided?' It grew so still, even the breathing seemed to have stopped. And in this stillness I heard myself say, 'Yes.' I did not look up. I knew that every face had grown brighter. It was pleasant to know that I was the cause. I had been nothing but a sorrow so long."[30]

In one way or another, the story of Rahel Golub was repeated over and over in the United States at the turn of the century. This was, at least numerically, a working-class nation. In 1900, more than half the country, perhaps 36 to 40 million men, women, and children, made up the laboring class that performed manual work for wages. They toiled with their hands on docks, roads, and farms, in factories, mines, and other people's houses. They practiced ancient crafts such as tailoring and carpentry, and newer arts such as iron molding and metal cutting. They were machine tenders in mills and factories, unskilled laborers in towns, farm hands in the countryside, cowboys on the range, and domestic servants in Victorian houses. All of them, even the best-paid skilled workers, lived circumscribed, vulnerable lives, constrained by low pay and limited opportunity, and menaced by unemployment, ill health, and premature death.[31]

The central fact of working-class life was limited resources. In 1900, wage workers in manufacturing earned an average of $435 for the year; in contrast, middle-class clerical workers in railroad and manufacturing firms averaged $1,011, more than twice as much. The lowest working-class wages were low indeed: in 1900, anthracite coal miners averaged $340 for the year; domestics, $240; and agricultural laborers, only $178 with room and board.[32]

These numbers alone virtually guaranteed that Victorian individualism was impossible for the working class. Many workers simply could not make enough to support themselves, let alone a family. In cities, working-class women, crowded into less-skilled jobs and paid less than men, struggled to get by on their own. Even working-class men, generally better paid, had trouble making ends meet. In Buffalo, New York, where it took from $650 to $772 to support an Italian family of five for a year, a laborer could expect to earn only between $364 and $624. The calculus held true elsewhere. In Chicago, a typical packinghouse worker could make just 38 percent of the income needed to support a family of four in 1910. Meanwhile, in Pittsburgh, working-class fathers contributed only about three-quarters of average family income.[33]

Workers' wages were uncertain as well as low. Skilled and unskilled alike lived with the almost constant threat of unemployment. The cycles of capitalism produced regular upheavals, such as the depression of the 1890s that cost Rahel's father and hundreds of thousands of other workers their jobs. Even in prosperous times the working class could not count on year-round employment. Common laborers and dockworkers found their jobs measured in days or weeks; they had to hope that a boss or superintendent would choose them at the next "shape up" along the docks or at the factory gates. Every worker knew that a job might end at any time because of seasonal lulls, irregular supplies, and equipment problems.[34]

If workers survived the threat of unemployment, they still faced the twin specters of injury and early death. Every working-class occupation had its difficulties and dangers, from the explosions, fires, cave-ins, debilitating "miner's lung," and other notorious perils of hard-rock mining in the West to the "Monday morning sickness," asthma, byssinosis, tuberculosis, and maimings in the textile mills of the East. While the upper ten seemed to last into their sixties, hard labor and poor diets aged workers quickly. An iron puddler was "old at forty," ready for a helper on the job. In Detroit, life expectancy for children born to white-collar workers in 1900 was fifty-three years. Working-class children born that year could expect to live to forty-eight; the children of Polish immigrants, who were mostly unskilled workers, could expect to live only to forty-one.[35]

By the turn of the twentieth century, few workers had much hope of escaping this cycle of low wages, looming unemployment, frequent accidents, and early death. Only marriage delivered working-class women from dead-end jobs that seldom led to advancement. Most male workers could hope at best only to rise to more skilled manual jobs. With little chance of joining the middle class, workers could only interpret Andrew Carnegie's storied rise into the upper ten as an isolated miracle, a freak of nature. "The average wage-earner has made up his mind that he must remain a wage-earner . . . ," observed the trade union leader John Mitchell. "He understands that working men do not evolve into capitalists as boys evolve into men or as caterpillars evolve into butterflies. . . ."[36]

The constraints and dangers of labor decisively shaped gender roles, childhood, and family arrangements for the working class. When so few working-class men could support a family, working-class women had to make money. Most labored for pay at some point in their lives. Unlike nearly all middle- and upper-class women, working-class women typically took jobs before marriage. Many held semiskilled positions in textile mills, garment shops, and box factories. Others worked as domestic servants and field hands. However briefly, they entered the mostly male world of wage work that few middle- and upper-class women ever experienced. After marriage and childbirth, the wives and mothers of some particularly hard-pressed laboring families had no choice but to return to the workplace. Even stay-at-home working-class women contributed to family income by helping husbands with craft work, making jewelry and artificial flowers, taking in washing and sewing, keeping animals, or cooking and cleaning for paying boarders.[37]

Children worked as well. Although some ethnic groups, notably immigrant Jews, placed a high value on education, economic realities forced sons and daughters, like Rahel Golub, to leave school early. In the South, boys and girls as young as seven and eight labored in the textile mills, first as unpaid helpers for their parents and siblings, then as wage earners in their own right. In cities around the country, boys got their start on the streets as newsboys, peddlers, junkers, scavengers, even thieves. Girls occasionally worked as newsies and peddlers, but, not surprisingly, parents wanted their daughters off the streets and in the home, where they helped with cooking, cleaning, childcare, handicraft work, and boarders. In one way or another, most working-class children were contributing to family income by their midteens. Few went to high school.[38]

In one sense, then, working-class children grew up fast. "I was twelve years old but I wasn't," recalled Yetta Adelman, a Polish garment worker. "Compared to a child [born] here in the United States I was twenty."[39] In another sense, working-class children grew up quite slowly. Like Rahel's father, working-class parents made sure their sons and daughters did not think too much about independence. The crowded conditions of their homes made it that much harder for children to develop a sense of their individuality and autonomy. Wage work did little to change this reality. For the most part, working-class sons and daughters dutifully turned over their wages to their parents. They tended to live with those parents longer—even into their twenties—than did middle- and upper-class children. As Italian children in Pittsburgh put it, "you never left your mother and father."[40]

That sentiment was no doubt reassuring for working-class husbands and fathers, who were "old at forty." Yet, they lived with the discouraging knowledge that they could not match middle- and upper-class men. "A tailor is nothing," sighed a German immigrant, "without a wife and very often a child." "I left Europe and I was a man," a Russian Jew lamented, "and here I am a what?" America, Ukrainian men concluded, is "a woman's country." That frustrating thought led some working-class men to give up. In the South there were the "mill daddies," idle fathers who abandoned work in the textile factories and depended instead on the earnings of their wives and children. For many working-class men who continued to labor, life seemed to exact a toll in frustration, drink, and domestic violence. Perhaps that was why Rahel Golub's father, already dependent on his daughter's wages, beat her when she defied his order to eat dinner.[41]

Immigrant and migrant workers had an especially strong sense of the economic interdependence at the heart of working-class family life. Many immigrants came to America with some notion of a "family economy," in which each member of the family, under the direction of the male head, contributed his or her earnings and resources for the benefit of the whole. Like Rahel Golub's family, people came to America in chains of families, as relatives in the United States sent back news and steamship tickets to the next immigrants. Once in the New World, immigrants depended on relatives to show them the ropes, keep storekeepers from cheating them, and find and teach them work. Native-born migrants from the countryside also depended on kin to make the transition to mill towns and cities. At every step of the way—from Europe to America, from the country to the city, from childhood to adulthood—workers knew that strong mutual ties made life possible in America.[42]

They worked hard, but their attitudes toward work were far from Victorian. Most workers labored out of compulsion, need, ambition, and pride. But given the dangers and indignities of wage labor, there was little chance that laboring men would mimic the Victorians and glorify hard work. There was also virtually no chance for American workers to mimic the outlook of the upper ten and celebrate a life of leisure: laboring men and women spent far too much time on the job for that. "Father," asked Rahel Golub soon after her arrival in New York, "does everybody in America live like this? Go to work early, come home late, eat and go to sleep? And the next day again work, eat, and sleep?" Most workers did. At the turn of the century, employees in the blast furnaces of Pittsburgh's steel mills often toiled twelve hours a day, seven days a week. Around the country, live-in domestic servants labored eleven or twelve hours a day, with two half days off a week—and then remained "on call" at almost all hours. Only a privileged minority, such as unionized cigar workers, lived the dream of an eight-hour day, forty-hour week.[43]

Despite the limits on their free time and income, many laboring men and women did share with the wealthy a powerful attraction to pleasures and objects. Countless immigrant workers were drawn to the United States because the country held out the promise of consumer pleasures. "My godfather was in Detroit and wrote me that he had paper on the walls, shoes, meat every day, fresh bread, milk, water in the house, beer on the corner, soup, and plenty of money," a Polish immigrant recalled. "From that time I was crazy to come." But industrializing America proved to be an expensive place. Rents in Pittsburgh were twice as high as in the English manufacturing city of Birmingham. In order to save money or even get by in this expensive country, many working-class Americans typically had to deny their appetites, just as Rahel gave up her apple at breakfast and her father skipped his brandy. Yet, other workers felt that lack of money and opportunity made self-restraint irrelevant. Many wage workers, notably single men and Southern plain folk, saw little point in trying to save their dollars and deny themselves.[44]

As a result, a rich culture of release and expressiveness flourished. Some workers shared the upper-class obsession with fashion and display. Young laboring women spent precious dollars on flashy clothing intended to match or even outdo the upper ten. "If my lady wears a velvet gown, put together for her in an East Side sweatshop," a reporter in New York observed in 1898, "may not the girl whose fingers fashioned it rejoice her soul by astonishing Grand Street with a copy of it next Sunday? My lady's in velvet, and the East Side girl's is the cheapest, but it's the style that counts. In this land of equality, shall not one wear what the other wears?" The clothing of young working-class women was bold, unconventional, and overstated: "Does Broadway wear a feather? Grand Street wears two. Are trailing skirts seen on Fifth Avenue? Grand Street trails its yards with a dignity all its own."[45]

Workers were known for their boisterous observance of the Fourth of July and their noisy, demonstrative behavior in theaters. Public drinking was a further element of this expressive life. Amid Victorian abstemiousness, the saloon had emerged as a vital working-class institution by the late nineteenth century. The barroom served many functions—meeting place, reading room, music hall, ethnic preserve, and male bastion. The saloon was also the place where workers dropped the discipline of the workplace and loosened self-control.[46]

For many workers, sex offered a similar opportunity for expression and release. In towns and cities, working-class neighborhoods were associated with the public display of sexuality. Men and women made physical contact in the popular dance halls that featured such risqué steps as the hug me close, the shiver, the hump-back rag, and the lovers' walk. "[C]ouples stand very close together," a middle-class observer noted, "the girl with her arms around the man's neck, the man with both his arms around the girl or on her hips; their cheeks are pressed close together, their bodies touch each other."

Working-class neighborhoods were also the site of brothels and red-light districts. Most prostitutes were apparently working-class women desperate for a living wage.[47]

As it celebrated pleasure and release, the public culture of the working class still embodied the mutualism taught at home. The quintessential saloon custom was the practice of treating, in which a man bought a round of drinks for his mates and they bought drinks for him. On the giant wheat farms of California, rootless, single male migrant harvesters and threshers developed "a strong sense of confederation" out of shared coarse humor, hunting, banjo music, cards, and drinking binges. Single working women forged their own mutualistic communities in cities such as Chicago. Mutual aid associations, like the one Rahel's father had joined, pooled contributions so that individual workers and families could cope with unemployment, illness, and death. Trade unions, like the one Rahel and her father had joined, celebrated collective action and condemned upper-class individualism. "The organization of laborers into Trades Unions," wrote the labor reformer George McNeill, "recognizes the fact that mutualism is preferable to individualism." The middle-class journalist Herbert Croly saw workers' unions the same way. "[The] American laborer . . . is . . . far more aggressively preoccupied with his class, as contrasted with his individual interests, than are his employers," Croly observed. "He has no respect for the traditional American individualism. . . . His own personality is merged in that of the union."[48] It was a formula for labor strife; and it would help fuel the middle-class rebellion to come.

The nation's farmers also seemed to share little with the rich at the turn of the century. Like the working class, farmers lived precariously; they, too, valued cooperation and practiced a form of family economy. Like many workers, farmers had a practical, unromantic view of work, a restrained attitude toward leisure, and a wary skepticism about pleasure. But farmers were set apart from workers as well as from the rich. Unlike most of the working class, agrarians had not lost the chance for economic self-rule. Squeezed by competition and threatened by nature, American agrarians could aspire if not to wealth then at least to independence. Unlike workers, farmers ruled over their own domain, however small. On a far smaller scale, they could be as lordly as the Stillmans, Harrimans, and Morgans. America's farmers were a cultural hybrid, caught between independence and dire need.

The pressures of agrarian life and culture were starkly apparent in the story of Richard Garland and his family. This longtime farmer loved to hear his wife, Belle, sing his favorite song, "O'er the Hills in Legions, Boys," with its exuberant, imperial chorus: "When we've wood and prairie land,/ Won by our toil,/ We'll reign like kings in fairy land,/ Lords of the soil!" That song, Richard's son Hamlin wrote, "was a directing force in the lives of at least three generations of my pioneering race." In the 1850s, the dream of dominion and independence had directed Richard Garland's father to leave the Northeast and strike out west for Wisconsin. There, Richard had mortgaged a 160-acre farm of his own in Green's Coulee, a little valley along the LaCrosse River. His belief in that economic and political vision—the dream of a free man, lord of his agricultural domain, the equal of his fellow lords—was so strong that Richard, like millions of other Northern men, was ready to fight for it. The day he paid off his mortgage in 1863, Richard joined the Union Army and went to battle the slave-holding, freedom-denying South. After the Civil War, Richard's vision directed him farther and farther west on the nation's "Middle Border" to ever larger farms and better lands that would surely, he believed, make him a true "lord of the soil." Richard moved first to Winnishiek County, Minnesota, then to Mitchell County, Iowa, and then on to Brown County in the Dakota Territory in the 1880s.[49]

Richard's quest for independence depended on the labor of his family. He could not take care of his land alone: his Dakota wheat farm sprawled across nearly a thousand acres. Neither could he afford to hire all the laborers his land demanded. So Richard turned to his family for help. Hamlin remembered how hard his mother worked. "Being a farmer's wife . . . ," he noted, "meant laboring outside any regulation of the hours of toil." Belle not only managed the Garland household and fed her children and her husband; she also cooked and cleaned for his hired hands. As Richard's farms grew larger, Belle had only more "drudgery . . . cooking, sewing, washing, churning, and nursing the sick from time to time." As soon as they were old enough, Richard's children—Hamlin, Frank, Harriet, and Jessie—began to work on the farm. "My father believed in service," Hamlin explained. "[H]e saw nothing unnatural in the regular employment of his children." At seven, Hamlin had "regular duties." "I brought firewood to the kitchen and broke nubbins for the calves and shelled corn for the chickens," he remembered. "In summer Harriet and I drove the cows to pasture, and carried 'switchel' to the men in the hay-fields. . . ." Hamlin soon graduated to more demanding tasks, including dragging and plowing.[50]

Working hard for his father, Hamlin absorbed contradictory messages. On one hand, his father taught stern lessons about mutualism and self-denial that Rahel Golub would have found familiar. Richard schooled his children to obey his will, not their own. "We were in effect small soldiers . . . ," Hamlin recalled. Richard, the Civil War veteran, was their "Commander-in-Chief." Like Rahel, Hamlin had his first real confrontation with his father over the impulse to gratify an individual desire. In his teens, Hamlin wanted a fashionable lightweight yellow duster like the one owned by his friend John Gammons, who was known as "somewhat of a dandy in matters of toilet." Richard declined. "If you are too warm," he told Hamlin, "take your coat off." At first, Hamlin obeyed. But, "furious," the boy "rebelled" against "the Commander-in-Chief." "As I am not only doing a man's work on a boy's pay but actually superintending the stock and tools, I am entitled to certain individual rights in the choice of a hat," he told Richard. "You will wear the hat I provide," Richard insisted. "For the first time in my life I defied him," Hamlin reported. "He seized me by the arm and for a moment we faced each other in silent clash of wills." "Don't you strike me," Hamlin warned. "You can't do that any more." Richard, "[a]fter a silent struggle with himself," handed Hamlin two dollars. "Get your own hat," the farmer told his son, and walked off. Like Rahel, Hamlin had gotten his way. And like her, he was shocked at what he had done.[51]

In a sense, Richard's "silent struggle" and capitulation were not surprising. Unlike Rahel's father, Hamlin's wanted independence for his child. Richard wanted Hamlin to follow his own path, to grow up and become an independent "lord of the soil." So, teaching obedience on one hand, Richard taught Hamlin independence on the other. "Fight your own battles, my son," Richard instructed. "If I hear of your being licked by a boy of anything like your own size, I'll give you another when you get home." Hamlin got the message. His father's farms were, he concluded, "a stern school, the school of self-reliance and resolution."[52]

Across the continent, the nation's nearly 6 million farmers would easily have recognized that "school." Their farmsteads likely differed from Dick Garland's. Notably diverse, American agriculture ranged from the developing dairy farms of New England and the Mid-Atlantic states to the increasingly mechanized grain and hog farms of the Midwest, to the impoverished sharecropping cotton and tobacco plots of the South, and on out to the giant wheat farms and cattle ranches of the West. About two-thirds of American farmers, like Dick Garland, owned or mortgaged their land. The rest were renters, tenants, and sharecroppers who cultivated other people's land under a bewildering variety of agreements. In the North, renters were often young men who would purchase land eventually. In the South, tenants and sharecroppers, laboring on unfavorable terms, were less likely to become independent. The poorest of the sharecroppers, without animals and tools of their own, were virtually as dependent as wage workers. But for all the variations in land, crops, profits, and ownership, American agrarians generally shared the central practices and values Hamlin Garland learned on his father's farm.[53]

Hardly any man or woman could manage to do all the work of a farm alone; a farmer had to have help. But as late as 1910, American farmers' average annual income was only $652. This average concealed notable differences. Landowning agrarians—the "progressive" farmers of the North and the "yeomen" of the South—typically made more money than sharecroppers and tenants. Nevertheless, the great majority of farmers could not afford to hire all the help they needed. And all farmers, however wealthy, faced the same threats from nature—the droughts, wind storms, insects, illness, and other perils that could doom one harvest and then another. These economic and natural realities almost inevitably compelled farmers to develop various forms of mutualism.[54]

One was the stereotypical "family farm." "There is a co-operative unity in the farm family that is rather striking," an observer noted. "The whole family is engaged in work that is of common interest." Other rural wives and mothers worked as hard as Belle Garland did. Like her, they saw to the farmhands and sometimes took in paying boarders. By tradition, farm wives also raised chickens and tended garden plots. The cash these women earned from selling eggs, vegetables, and other products was often the only money a farm family saw before the harvest. Farm women frequently labored in the family's fields. Sometimes, they worked for pay off the farm.[55]

Children also played a critical role in the survival of American farms. "[E]very boy born into a farm family was," one farmer observed, "worth a thousand dollars." Girls were worth more than a little, too. That understanding helped to explain high rural fertility rates—the highest in the nation. Most farm women still had several children at the turn of the century. On the frontier farms of South Dakota and the poor white farms of the South, families with eight, nine, or ten children were not uncommon. Like working-class sons and daughters, the children of farmers had to grow up quickly. Like Hamlin and his siblings, other farm children helped out with the chores. Many did wage work. On Southern cotton farms, a nine- or ten-year-old was already reckoned a "halfhand," able to pick half as much as an adult. As in working-class households, education often had to give way to work. The school year was typically shorter in the countryside than in the city. Farm parents were more likely to take their children out of school. When Hamlin Garland wanted to stay in school rather than work full-time at the age of sixteen, it took his mother's determined intervention before Richard would agree. Even then, Hamlin had to wait until November before his father let him go back to his studies. In many farm families, a sixteen-year-old would never have gone back at all.[56]

At times, farmers needed more help than wives, children, and paid farmhands could provide. American agrarians had long cooperated with one another through a variety of formal and informal arrangements. To secure needed goods and services, rural neighbors established systems of borrowing and bartering. This tradition of mutual aid culminated toward the end of the nineteenth century in Midwestern threshing "rings," groups of farmers who rented expensive mechanical grain threshers together and then worked the large, complicated machines on one another's farms at threshing time. Immigrant farmers had their own forms of cooperation—the churches and mutual-benefit associations similar to those of the cities. In the 1870s, the Patrons of Husbandry, the farmers' organization known as the Grange, tried a number of cooperative efforts. For a couple of years in Mitchell County, Iowa, Richard Garland managed one of the thousands of local Grange grain elevators, cooperative ventures intended to net farmers better prices than those offered by commercial elevator operators. In the 1880s and 1890s, the Farmer's Alliance developed its own cooperatives for purchasing supplies and processing and marketing crops.[57]

There were limits to cooperation, however. Most of the farmers' cooperatives collapsed, partly because of mismanagement and competition. The cooperatives were also undermined by farmers' strong sense of individual self-interest and autonomy. One early supporter of the cooperatives traced their failure to "the inadaptation of rural life and character to the coöperative method of managing business." Farmers tended, he explained, "to gratify their whims" rather than support their own cooperatives. As Richard Garland angrily discovered when he managed the Grange elevator in the 1870s, many farmers would abandon the cooperative whenever they could get "a little more than the market price" for their grain somewhere else. "It only shows . . . how hard it will be to work out any reform among the farmers," he concluded bitterly. "They will never stand together." His lesson duly learned, Richard went back to farming—and his independent ways.[58]

Richard Garland was typical. "Completeness, individuality, self-dependence, is the ideal life which the country should stimulate—a state so desirable for the really developed man," an agrarian advocate maintained in 1890. Isolated by poor roads and poor mail service, farm families felt independent. Like Garland, agrarian parents prepared their children for the difficult life ahead by encouraging personal toughness and independence. Farmers' children obviously expected to help their parents, but it would have been unusual to hear a son or daughter echo the Italian children of Pittsburgh and say "you never left your mother and father." When Hamlin Garland decided to leave home, Richard did not beg or order him to stay. Instead, the "Commander-in-Chief" handed Hamlin some travel money.[59] More prosperous Northern farmers in particular tried to prepare their children for independence. Recognizing that their sons and daughters might well leave the land, mothers and fathers first provided adolescent children with a "room of one's own," a separate bedroom; next came livestock and plots of land, along with encouragement to make money and manage it for themselves.[60]

Unlike the upper ten, rural couples were highly unlikely to divorce. But this rather Victorian commitment to the permanence of marriage did not mean that agrarian husbands and wives were committed to the Victorian domestic ideal. Set amid barns, chicken coops, and fields, the American farmhouse was no refuge. Rural women contributed much to the family economy. Agrarian fathers spent a good deal of time supervising their sons and daughters. As Hamlin Garland and thousands of other hardworking farm children could testify, their fathers were hardly remote figures. Men and women mixed together more readily in sitting rooms, camp meetings, and picnics than did city dwellers. Joining the Grange and the Farmer's Alliance, women participated in discussion in both groups.[61]

Rural attitudes toward work and leisure were neither Victorian nor working-class. Farm labor was as difficult as any working-class occupation and often just as dull—hardly something to glorify. Even in the more prosperous North, agriculture was barely mechanized at the turn of the century. Farmers, unlike wage workers, could set their own pace much of the time, but that pace was demanding. Life on the farm, a commentator noted in 1896, was "drudge, drudge, drudge, from daylight to dark, day after day, month after month, year after year." Most farmers worked a six- or seven-day week and took no vacations. Yet, farmers took pleasure in work when they could and just accepted it for the rest. "They had always worked," the son of a ranch family recalled. "[T]hey assumed that work was a condition of life."[62]

Although American farmers worked hard, most of them seemed not to be particularly acquisitive. Well into the nineteenth century, many farmers, distant from the market, had lived fairly self-sufficient lives; they raised what they needed on their land, and bartered for much of the rest. By 1900, that self-sufficiency had largely ended. Whether they wanted to or not, most farmers now produced cash crops for the market. Caught up in a thoroughly commercial enterprise, they needed money to get by in turn-of-the-century America. That did not necessarily make them lust for capital, however. Farmers might work hard to buy their land and to see that it went to their children, but they had no great yearning for riches. The typical farm was no place to make a fortune, in any event.[63]

Agrarians were not entranced by leisure and pleasure, either. Obviously, hardworking farmers had little time for leisure. They tended to spend that time attending meetings and revivals, hunting and fishing, and just singing and talking at home. Some agrarians, Southern poor whites in particular, liked their liquor; but others practiced temperance or at least preached self-discipline. "My father did not believe in serving strong liquor to his men, and seldom treated them to even beer," Hamlin Garland remembered. "While not a teetotaler he was strongly opposed to all that intemperance represented." Agrarians were similarly restrained about sexual pleasure and personal affection. "Love was . . . a forbidden word," Garland recalled. "You might say, 'I love pie,' but to say 'I love Bettie,' was mawkish if not actually improper."[64]

This sense of restraint helped produce a growing divide between farmers and their hands, who zestfully embraced the working-class culture of expressiveness and pleasure. By the turn of the century, farmers talked about their wage-earning "labor" with suspicion and contempt. They derided these men as "hobos," "tramps," and "bums"—"men whose lives and aims are not on so high a plain." Farmhands, said Hamlin Garland, "are often creatures with enormous appetites and small remorse, men on whom the beauty of nature had very little effect." For them, time off meant "a visit to town and a drunken spree." Their talk of women and vice districts "shocked and horrified" the young Garland: "We had not known that such cruelty, such baseness was in the world and it stood away in such violent opposition to the teaching of our fathers and uncles. . . ."[65]

Farmers were similarly restrained about consumerism. Farmhouses ranged from Southern sharecroppers' pathetic one- or two-room shacks to Northern "progressive" farmers' framed, sometimes bricked houses, with two-gabled roofs. But they were all generally plain. Inside even the most prosperous farmhouses, there was not much in the way of objects—some factory-made furniture, perhaps a sewing machine, possibly a piano. Even prosperous farmers, proud of their houses, still disdained urban showiness. Instead of an ornate, overstuffed parlor, there was a simple sitting room with a plain rag carpet. Rural life was unadorned in other ways, too: children had few toys; parents had few good clothes. Farmers were simply reluctant to take money away from their barns and fields. Even when crop prices were good, Hamlin Garland recalled, "the homes in the neighborhood were slow in taking on grace or comfort."[66]

So alien in condition and outlook, farmers, workers, and wealthy almost inevitably came into conflict. The relentless development of the industrial economy, the increasing spread of news in papers and magazines, and the unceasing political contests of a democracy all made the different classes constantly aware of one another and generated the many signs of friction in late nineteenth-century America. It was an unstable situation—the more so because each group suffered from organizational weakness and internal divisions.

By 1900, farmers' largest cooperative endeavors, optimistically begun in the Gilded Age, had already waxed and waned. The once-mighty Grange numbered only about 98,000 families nationwide. Perhaps 30,000 or 40,000 agrarians belonged to other farmers' organizations. The vote totals of the People's Party, the greatest political expression of agrarianism, had lurched downward from a million in the presidential election of 1892 to a mere 50,000 in the national contest of 1900. In the South, Populism had provoked costly retaliation: powerful whites were making sure that virtually all African-Americans and even some poor white farmers lost the right to cast ballots in elections. At the start of the new century, any new agrarian political organization would have to draw from a greatly diminished bloc of voters.[67]

Agrarians were themselves partly to blame for their organizational weakness. Agrarians with different kinds of crops did not always care enough about one another's challenges. Well-to-do farmers often had little sympathy for the poorest agrarians. Ethnic and racial prejudice kept farmers divided from one another. In the 1890s, nativism ran through the countryside as the American Protective Association railed against the malign influence of foreigners and Roman Catholics on the nation. But at least farmers were fairly homogeneous ethnically. As late as 1910, immigrants—Canadians, Norwegians, Swedes, and, above all, Germans—made up only about 10 percent of farm operators. And the immigrants did not differ fundamentally in practices and outlook from native-born farmers.[68]

Race made a starker, more difficult divide across rural America. Only a couple of thousand Japanese and several hundred Chinese operated farms, mostly in the West, at the turn of the century. They faced substantial hostility and discrimination from whites. Meanwhile, about three-quarters of a million African-Americans operated farms, mainly in the South. White prejudice against black farmers had seriously weakened the Farmer's Alliance and the People's Party. In most cases across the South, white and black agrarians had formed separate alliances. When white elites moved to disfranchise Southern blacks, too many white farmers were unwilling to defend the African-Americans' right to vote. By 1900, agrarian leaders such as the old Populist Tom Watson of Georgia were whipping up racial hatred instead.[69]

Dogged by organizational weakness and internal division, agrarians also suffered from a more general sense of defeat and decline. Richard Garland was fairly typical in this respect. The hard work and hybrid rural culture of his family never quite made Richard the independent "lord of the soil" he wanted to be. Each year, harvests were too small, or prices too low. Chinch bugs—"pestiferous mites" with "ill-smelling crawling bodies"—ate up his crops two years running and drove him out of Iowa. Drought and low prices plagued him in Dakota. Death struck along the way, too: Harriet died in Iowa; Jessie died in Dakota. "Where are the 'woods and prairie lands' of our song?" Hamlin asked his brother Frank. "Is this the 'fairy land' in which we were all to 'reign like kings'? Doesn't the whole migration of the Garlands . . . seem a madness?"[70]

Hamlin was not the only agrarian asking such questions as the 1890s arrived. By the middle of that difficult decade, most farmers across the nation, however prosperous, had begun to feel diminished. Like Richard Garland, whose farms increased from 160 acres to 300 to 1,000 as he moved westward, American agriculture had grown in the late nineteenth century yet somehow deteriorated in the process. Despite increases in farms, population, and aggregate wealth, agricultural America was falling behind the nation's urban areas. "While rural conditions are actually no worse than they were thirty years ago, relatively they are worse," noted one observer in 1906. "The cities of the United States have moved forward by leaps and bounds." Though the number of agricultural workers increased, the number of nonfarm workers increased still faster. Agriculturalists, a majority of the gainful workforce as late as 1870, made up only 38 percent of the nation's labor by 1900. Farms, which accounted for about 40 percent of the nation's wealth before the Civil War, now represented only 16 percent. Even a rise in crop prices in the late 1890s did little to change the farmers' relative economic position: in 1900 nonfarm workers averaged $622 in income but farm workers averaged only $260.[71]

The sense of decline powerfully affected younger agrarians. As early as the 1880s and 1890s, rural sons and daughters were questioning farm life. Hamlin and Frank Garland did not care for all the hard, dull work on their father's land. For Hamlin, the human toll of farming was unbearable. He could not stand to see his mother worn down by all her labors and cares. The death of his sister Harriet left Hamlin feeling "like a wounded animal, appalled by weight of despair and sorrow. . . ."[72]

Meanwhile, Hamlin and Frank had glimpsed another, much more alluring way of life. When their father agreed to run the Grange elevator in Mitchell County, Iowa, he moved the family temporarily to the town of Osage. For the Garland children, Osage was "a new and shining world, a town world where circuses, baseball games and county fairs were events of almost daily occurrence." Without realizing it, Richard had critically weakened his hold on his children. The spectacle of Osage "had . . . far-reaching effects," Hamlin remembered. "It tended to warp us from our father's designs. It placed the rigorous, filthy drudgery of the farm-yard in sharp contrast with the carefree companionable existence led by my friends in the village, and we longed to be of their condition. We had gained our first set of comparative ideas, and with them an unrest which was to carry us very far away."[73]

Chief among those "comparative ideas" was the attractiveness of a life more devoted to pleasure. The Garland children raptly drank in the leisure and consumption of the well-to-do. "We had observed . . . how well Avery Brush's frock coat fitted and we comprehended something of the elegant leisure which the sons and daughters of Wm. Petty's general store enjoyed," Hamlin wrote. "Over against these comforts, these luxurious conditions, we now set our ugly little farmhouse, with its rag carpets, its battered furniture, its barren attick, and its hard, rude beds. —All that we possessed seemed very cheap and deplorably commonplace."[74]

By the time he reached the age of twenty-one, in 1881, Hamlin Garland was animated by a vision quite different from the one that had driven his father. Richard had been inspired to go west to live out the agrarian dream of independence; Hamlin was inspired to go east to live out an urban dream of consumer pleasures. Leaving the farm that year, Hamlin became a writer—a successful one, too, with the publication in 1891 of *Main-Travelled Roads,* a book of six stories about rural life on America's "middle border." The pattern of Hamlin's life was set: his career as a middle-class writer in Boston, Chicago, and New York City depended on the farm, but he would never be a farmer. Neither would Frank, who also left home for an urban life as an actor.[75]

The Garlands' exposure to a life-style of leisure and consumerism was not unique. By 1900, farm families did not have to move into town to glimpse another way of life. Since the Civil War, pioneering mail-order businesses had produced increasingly thick and beguiling catalogs filled with clocks, sewing machines, clothes, sporting goods, and other consumer pleasures. Beginning in 1872, John Montgomery Ward of Chicago built the first great mail-order business; by the end of the century, Sears, Roebuck and Company was successfully challenging Ward's hold on the rural market.[76]

Paging through the Sears and Ward catalogs, rural sons and daughters found more reasons to escape the relative decline of the American farm. Like Hamlin and Frank Garland, young people with "a desire for improvement, an ambition for wider success, an impulse to greatness," kept leaving for towns and cities. "Sons were deserting their well-worn fathers, daughters were forgetting their tired mothers," Hamlin concluded. "Families were everywhere breaking up."[77]

At the turn of the century, wage workers did not have to worry about the survival of their class. As long as industrial capitalism endured, there would be plenty of low-wage manual jobs. But workers, like farmers, suffered from organizational weakness and internal division. The union movement was still more a promise than a power. Hard times, hostile employers, and unfriendly courts handicapped organized labor in the 1890s. With the gradual return of prosperity, the total number of unionized workers shot up from 447,000 in 1897 to 1,125,000 in 1901. Nevertheless, unions claimed only a small fraction—less than 10 percent—of the American workforce. Unions had barely penetrated broad sectors of the economy and had left numerous working-class occupations almost alone—semiskilled factory workers, domestic servants, agricultural laborers. The most ambitious attempt to organize across occupational lines, the Knights of Labor, had grown astonishingly in the 1880s and then collapsed. The largest national labor organization at the turn of the century, the American Federation of Labor, consisted almost exclusively of craft unions of male, skilled workers.[78]

Working-class political organization was still less developed. Gilded Age ventures such as the Union Labor Party had come and gone. The most promising political vehicle, powered by a form of mutualist ideology, was socialism. But in 1900, Eugene V. Debs, the leader of the American Railway Union, won only 87,000 votes as the Social Democratic candidate for president. Third-party political action was controversial. Many trade unionists held back from partisan endorsements, let alone separate political action. And most politically active workers cast ballots for the Republicans and Democrats.[79]

One of the chief obstacles to political action and unionization was the striking diversity of American wage earners. In 1900, the majority of the 36 to 40 million members of the working class were Protestants. But most of the nation's 10 million Roman Catholics and several hundred thousand Jews were workers. In 1900, 26 million people, more than a third of the population, were immigrants or native-born Americans with at least one foreign-born parent; most of this minority belonged to the working class. And the immigrant population was surging as the economy revived: the 229,000 arrivals of 1898 were followed by 449,000 in 1900 and more than a million in 1905. The immigrants were becoming more diverse, too, as Southern and Eastern Europeans like Rahel Golub and her family increasingly supplanted the German, English, and Irish mainstays of nineteenth-century migration. Moreover, the predominantly white working class also included many of the nation's 10 million African-Americans, 103,000 Mexicans, 82,000 Chinese, and 25,000 Japanese.[80]

All these differences of race, ethnicity, and religion produced suspicion, antagonism, and conflict among workers. Irishmen harassed Rahel Golub's father and other Jews on the Lower East Side. Around the country, Irish, Polish, and Italian Catholics fought for control of churches, and trade unionists kept out blacks. Working-class children quickly learned to respect and perpetuate such divisions. In New York City, Jewish boys who strayed into Catholic or Protestant neighborhoods discovered what it meant to be "cockalized." "The enemy kids," a victim recalled, "threw the Jew to the ground, opened his pants, and spat and urinated on his circumcised penis while they shouted 'Christ killer.'" Racial, ethnic, and religious differences spilled over into occupational differences among workers. Skilled "labor aristocrats," prizing their high wages and specialized knowledge, often looked down on less-skilled workers. The leaders of the American Federation of Labor, mostly skilled craftsmen from German, Irish, or English stock, wanted nothing to do with the unskilled workers who came from Eastern and Southern Europe. And occupational differences in turn spilled over into gender differences. Despite Rahel Golub's experience, very few male unionists welcomed wage-earning women into their organizations around the country.[81]

Like farmers, workers also faced the loss of children enticed by other ways of living. Frank Capra, born in Sicily a few years after Rahel Golub, passed through New York City with his family on the way to Los Angeles early in the new century. Although the California city was three thousand miles from the Lower East Side, Capra found the same kind of working-class life that Rahel had come to know so well. But Capra could not stand it. "I hated being poor," he said. "Hated being a scrounging newskid trapped in the sleazy Sicilian ghetto of Los Angeles. . . . I wanted out. A quick out." Capra was sure that education would give him that out. His family, like most working-class families, believed jobs were more important than school. "To my family I was a maverick," he recalled. "I was jeered at, scorned, and even beaten." Finally, Capra's determination forced a compromise. As long as he made money for the family by selling papers and doing odd jobs, he could go to school. Daring to "think of myself as another Horatio Alger, the success kid, my own rags-to-riches hero," Frank Capra was on his way—to high school, to Cal Tech, and ultimately to wealth and fame as a film director.[82]

Rahel Golub's story illustrated another way that workers could lose hold of their children. Although Rahel submitted to her parents, she still felt the tension between the demands of family and her individuality. How captivating it was to think of one's self. She remembered the shock of reading a Hebrew translation of Charles Dickens's *David Copperfield:* "I turned to the first page of the story and read the heading of the chapter: 'I am born.' Something in these three little words appealed to me more than anything I had yet read. I could not have told why, but perhaps it was the simplicity and the intimate tone of the first person. I had not yet read anything written in the first person."[83]

For a long time, that sense of self, of life lived in the first person, was only a faint, private stirring within her. To meet her obligation to the family, Rahel continued to work hard when she could and then agreed to marry Israel when he asked. Nevertheless, she could not bear the prospect of life with this shopkeeper and his mother. Eventually Rahel had the courage to give him back his ring—and risk her family's reaction. "Mother cried bitterly," Rahel remembered, "and father, who had been so quiet, so silent all afternoon, went out into the street without saying a word." Powerful as they were, the old ties could not survive the revolt of too many Rahel Golubs and Frank Capras.[84]

Despite the weaknesses and internal divisions that plagued workers and farmers, the upper ten still could not manage to take the lead in a divided

America. By 1900, the rich had their own problems. The rising number of divorces and other danger signals warned of a basic instability in wealthy families. So many rich men and women seemed chronically unhappy. The sons of the upper class were particularly unfortunate. Inevitably measured against their famously successful fathers and grandfathers, wealthy boys found men like Rockefeller and Morgan a hard act to follow. Not only that, but the sons of the upper ten had to perform a tricky balancing act their fathers had been spared: these boys and young men had to be conscious of the responsibilities of wealth yet immune to its temptations; they had to be loyal to the family yet independent enough to lead it effectively in the future. To help meet these challenges, anxious upper-class parents confined Cornelius Vanderbilt IV and other boys in the fortresslike mansions and secluded boarding schools, safe from the lure to spend too much money or to meet unsavory strangers.[85]

Despite such efforts—or partly because of them—upper-class boys too often became miserable young men. "My life was never destined to be quite happy," said William K. "Willie" Vanderbilt, grandson of the Commodore. "It was laid out along lines which I could foresee almost from earliest childhood. It has left me with nothing to hope for, with nothing definite to see or strive for." That realization often led to indolence, incapacity, and even self-destruction. John D. Rockefeller, Jr., had a nervous breakdown at sixteen. The Bradley Martins' son Sherman was evidently an alcoholic with "an inordinate desire for liquor." "[He] had too much money to spend and too much time to spare," *The New York Times* reported. "His parents, with an indulgence that he had been accustomed to from childhood, permitted him to do pretty much as he pleased. . . ." Falling in with a "dissolute set" in fashionable London, Sherman, underage, married a music hall "ballet girl" without his parents' knowledge. In December 1894, he left a sanitarium in Hartford, Connecticut and went drinking with friends in Manhattan. Collapsing into unconsciousness in a café, Sherman died of "apoplexy of the brain" the next morning at the age of twenty-five.[86]

The plight of upper-class children helped turn key members of the upper ten against the frivolous life of High Society. Some businessmen, such as Morgan, avoided it as much as possible. One upper-class group, descendants of the Knickerbocker founders of New York, self-consciously offered an alternative public style. This so-called Faubourg–St. Germain set, including the Van Rensselaers and the Roosevelts, rejected ostentation and frivolity and emphasized intellectual culture and quiet home life instead. Decidedly "old money," the Faubourg–St. Germain set also objected to High Society's willingness to admit rich new members to its ranks. The Knickerbocker descendants believed the upper class would best survive by keeping out unsuitable nouveau riches. The values of the Faubourg–St. Germain set were the product of necessity: these people had the pedigrees but not the huge fortunes necessary to triumph in High Society. Yet, the Knickerbocker elite also acted out of a different sense of what life was all about.[87]

So did perhaps the two richest New Yorkers at the turn of the century. John D. Rockefeller and Andrew Carnegie, migrants to the city, certainly had the money to compete in Society, but both abhorred the world of the Bradley Martins. Neither was known for ostentation; indeed, Rockefeller was considered "poor in his pleasures." But both men were also critical of "unostentatious hoarding." Looking for another way of life, the two found it in philanthropy.[88]

Mostly for religious reasons, Rockefeller had long been a giving man. Driven by Protestant beliefs in the stewardship of God's gifts, he made charitable contributions as soon as he began earning money as a teenager in the 1850s. By the 1890s, Rockefeller's commitment to philanthropy also reflected his realization that the pursuit of money and pleasure was ultimately unsatisfying. "I know of nothing more despicable and pathetic than a man who devotes all the waking hours of the day to making money for money's sake," Rockefeller declared. The conversion of money into possessions was not very satisfying either. "The novelty of being able to purchase anything one wants soon passes, because what people most seek cannot be bought with money," he said. "As I study wealthy men, I can see but one way in which they can secure a real equivalent for money spent, and that is to cultivate a taste for giving where the money may produce an effect which will be a lasting gratification."[89]

Simply because Rockefeller had so much money, it was difficult for him to live up to his philanthropic ideals. With the aid of his son, John, Jr., and his adviser, Baptist minister Frederick Gates, Rockefeller increasingly made his giving more businesslike, "scientific," and grandiose. In fact, he began to dream of a giant philanthropic "trust" to manage his benevolences. With the establishment of the Rockefeller Institute for Medical Research in 1901, the General Education Board in 1903, the Rockefeller Sanitary Commission in 1909, and ultimately the Rockefeller Foundation in 1913, he realized that dream. Giving away hundreds of millions of his wealth to better society, Rockefeller believed that other rich men ought to do the same. "[We] have come to the period," he said, "when we can well afford to ask the ablest men to devote more of their time, thought, and money to the public well-being."[90]

Carnegie, meanwhile, had reached the same conclusion by a different route. More than Rockefeller, he presented philanthropy as an answer to the fundamental, perhaps intractable problems of the industrial upper class. Beginning with two famous articles published in 1889, Carnegie laid out what his British publisher titled "The Gospel of Wealth." While Carnegie defended the inequities of industrial capitalism, he recognized both the social isolation of the wealthy and the plight of their children. The Scot also freely criticized the lifestyle of Society. "Whatever makes one conspicuous offends the canon," he insisted. "If any family be chiefly known for display, for extravagance in home, table, or equipage, for enormous sums ostentatiously spent in any form upon itself—if these be its chief distinctions, we have no difficulty in estimating its nature or culture." Noting the hostility between classes in America, he called on the wealthy to use their money for the common good. "The problem of our age," the steel baron wrote, "is the proper administration of wealth, that the ties of brotherhood may still bind together the rich and poor in harmonious relationship."[91]

Carnegie also favored philanthropy for the sake of the rich themselves. If they spent their money on ostentatious pleasures, they were guilty of offensive selfishness. If they tried to pass it on to their offspring, they were making a terrible blunder. "Why should men leave great fortunes to their children?" Carnegie asked. "[The] parent who leaves his son enormous wealth generally deadens the talents and energies of the son, and tempts him to lead a less useful and less worthy life than he otherwise would. . . ." For the sake of their families, the rich should give their money away. "This, then, is held to be the duty of the man of wealth," Carnegie concluded: "To set an example of modest, unostentatious living, shunning display or extravagance; to provide moderately for the legitimate wants of those dependent upon him; and, after doing so, to consider all surplus revenues which come to him simply as trust funds . . . for his poorer brethren, bringing to their service his superior wisdom, experience, and ability to administer, doing for them better than they would or could do for themselves."[92]

In promulgating his Gospel of Wealth, Carnegie was not worried whether particular families managed to retain their money and upper-class status over the years. At bottom, the steel magnate doubted that wealth offered much of a basis for a self-perpetuating class. Unsurprisingly, perhaps, this rare example of rags-to-riches mobility insisted "that the greatest and best of our race have necessarily been nurtured in the bracing school of poverty—the only school capable of producing the supremely great, the genius." With no son to follow him, Carnegie wanted to promote turnover in the membership of the upper ten. Most sons of the rich, he thought, should not hold places of authority in their fathers' companies. Believing the industrial elite needed a steady influx of talented men from the lower classes, he made a special effort to elevate poor young workers to partnerships in Carnegie Steel. Philanthropy was one more way to ensure that the wealthy, relieved of their fortunes, would make way for new blood. To make sure the rich pursued philanthropy in life, Carnegie even favored the heresy of inheritance taxes at death: rather than lose their money to the government, wealthy men would likely prefer to give it away themselves for the public good.[93]

Carnegie himself gave his money away with huge donations for higher education, public libraries, hospitals, parks, meeting and concert halls, swimming pools, and churches. In 1911, he founded the charitable Carnegie Foundation to continue his work. Distributing 90 percent of his fortune before his death in 1919, Carnegie lived up to the prescriptions of the Gospel of Wealth. And like Rockefeller, he expected the rest of the upper ten to do the same.

In their way, Carnegie and Rockefeller were the revolutionaries of the upper ten. More than most other members of their class, these two men grasped its fundamental problems at the end of the nineteenth century. Carnegie in particular understood just how ill-equipped were the wealthy to win the battle for authority in America. Rejecting the acquisitive obsession of big businessmen, the ostentation of the Bradley Martins, and the genteel withdrawal of the Faubourg-St. Germain set, the Gospel of Wealth demanded a radically different approach to life. Carnegie tried to conceal his radicalism: philanthropy, he insisted, was only "the further evolution of existing conditions . . . founded upon the present most intense individualism." But, not unexpectedly, few wealthy New Yorkers were ready to follow Carnegie and Rockefeller. High Society held hardly any charitable functions at the turn of the century; rich men set up few foundations. Having earned or inherited their money, these New Yorkers were going to keep it. Whatever they thought of their sons and daughters, the wealthy intended to leave their fortunes to the next generation.[94]

Two generations had come and gone since the Civil War, but the fundamental problems of the upper class remained unresolved. Many of the rich, isolated as they were, did not understand that time had run out on their opportunity to take full control of industrializing America. The wealthy faced challenges, not only from workers and farmers; the Victorian middle class could no longer abide the alien cultures, class conflict, and violence of a divided industrial nation. By the turn of the century, middle-class men and women, radicalized and resolute, were ready to sweep aside the upper ten and build a new, progressive America.

As if to reassure the rich, the election of 1900 repeated 1896. Once again, McKinley and Bryan battled for the presidency; once again, McKinley won the White House. Yet, in September 1901, when the president traveled to the Pan-American Exposition in Buffalo, an anarchist, Leon Czolgosz, fired a concealed revolver twice and mortally wounded him. News of the president's assassination shocked the gay partygoers at a costume ball in Newport. As the crowd fell silent and the host pulled off his mask, the orchestra began to play the national anthem. "[T]hey felt, those bearers of America's 'greatest' names," wrote Cornelius Vanderbilt IV, "that from then on they would have to run as fast as they could in order to remain in the same place, in order that the nightmare of the future might not become the terror of the present." The Vanderbilts woke their children in the middle of the night, bundled them on board the family yacht, and steamed hurriedly to New York to consult bankers and lawyers. Cornelius realized what it all meant for his class. "The party," he knew, "was over."[95]

CHAPTER TWO

THE RADICAL CENTER

Jane Addams adored her father. Self-disciplined and self-contained, John H. Addams epitomized the Victorian virtues. To his admiring daughter, this former miller's apprentice was truly "the self-made man." Leaving his home state of Pennsylvania in 1844, John Addams had moved west to the young town of Cedarville, Illinois. By the time Jane, the last of his children, was born in 1860, Addams had made his mark. He owned mills, invested in lands and railroads, and presided over a local bank. Even in successful middle age, John Addams "still woke up punctually at three o'clock because for so many years he had taken his turn at the mill in the early morning." Comfortably well off, Addams nevertheless deplored excess and exhibition: Jane cringed when one Sunday he told her to wear an old cloak to church rather than stand out from the other girls in her pretty new one.[1]

A spur to Addams's success, individualism was not an excuse for selfishness. True to his Christianity, John Addams placed a high value on the worth of other human beings. Accordingly, he believed strongly in serving people, whether as a teacher in Sunday school or a senator in the state legislature. Addams joined the newly formed Republican party in its crusade for "Free Soil, Free Labor, Free Men," for individual economic opportunity, and, finally, for an end to slavery, the denial of that opportunity. Addams's political hero—"the greatest man in the world"—was Abraham Lincoln; Addams prized his letters from the president addressed to "My dear Double-D'ed Addams." After the assassination of the "Great Emancipator" in 1865, Jane wrote, "To my amazement I found my father in tears, something that I had never seen before. . . ."[2]

John Addams ruled his house like a gentle, tolerant patriarch; his wife Sarah submitted to him and dedicated herself to their family. An attentive father, John Addams was devoted to his children. And Jane was devoted to him, especially after Sarah died in 1862. Although she gained a stepmother when John Addams remarried six years later, Jane's focus was clear. John Addams was "the dominant influence" in her life, the object of her "great veneration and pride" and her "doglike affection." Jane wanted so much to be like John Addams. She read the books in his library so that she would think as he did and "understand life as he did." The young girl even wanted to look like her father. She yearned "desperately" to have his "miller's thumb," distinctively flattened by years of rubbing ground wheat between his fingers as it fell from the millstones.[3]

Hard as she tried, Jane Addams never could become like her father. Instead, she left his home and his world behind. At the age of seventeen, Jane went off to Rockford Seminary, a women's school in Illinois. During her four years at this "Mount Holyoke of the West," she pressed to make Rockford into a full-fledged college and had the satisfaction of earning one of its first bachelor's degrees in 1881. But, with her diploma in hand, she did not know where to go next. In the "sad August" of that year, John Addams died suddenly from a ruptured appendix. During "the black days" after his death, Jane found herself agonizingly unsure of what to do. Seemingly uninterested in marriage, the conventional Victorian choice, she was "absolutely at sea" for years to come. In the fall of 1881, she went to Philadelphia to become a medical student but soon ended up a patient, taking a "rest cure" in S. Weir Mitchell's Hospital of Orthopedic and Nervous Diseases. Out of the hospital, but still troubled, Addams had an operation on her spine: the procedure led to six months in bed and a breakdown. "The long illness," Addams related, "left me in a state of nervous exhaustion with which I struggled for years. . . ."[4]

Trying to cope, she made the conventional tour of Europe from 1883 to 1885. Jane responded to the poverty she saw there, but most of all she felt her own lack of purpose. Back in America, things did not improve; she lived with "a sense of futility, of misdirected energy, the belief that the pursuit of cultivation would not in the end bring either solace or relief." Jane had failed to marry and make a new home, yet she had also failed to make her way, hardy and self-sufficient, as her father had for years. For all her veneration of John Addams, Jane hardly seemed like her father's daughter.[5]

Jane Addams was one of many young Victorians who figuratively and literally left the comfort of home for an uncertain quest in the Gilded Age. Never in open rebellion against their parents, Addams and other middle-class Americans nonetheless had to reconsider and reject the lessons they had learned in their safe, gabled houses. The Victorians of the late nineteenth century found themselves caught in crises spurred by the development of industrial capitalism. Brought up on the conventions of domesticity, middle-class men and women felt increasingly dissatisfied with their lives together. Taught to revere individualism, the Victorians were trapped amid the "signs of friction," the class conflict generated by the economic, political, and cultural innovations of the intensely individualistic upper ten. Schooled in self-discipline and self-denial, the Victorians found troubling signs of self-indulgence in their homes. In some ways, the Progressive Era emerged from a middle class that could not cope with its own affluence.

Driven by these crises, Addams and other Victorians searched for new ways of living—and gradually found them. By the end of the nineteenth century, the middle class was giving distinctive new answers to the questions that confronted all social groups about the relationship between the individual and society, the nature of men, women, and the home, and the place of work and pleasure in daily life. These answers added up to a novel set of guiding values, a new ideology for the middle class: Victorianism gave way to progressivism. This ideological transformation not only drove middle-class people to change themselves and to make new homes; it also demanded that they change the world around them. Progressivism unleashed a powerful reforming dynamic across America, just at the time when farmers, workers, and the upper class were all too weak or divided to command the nation. Seizing the opportunity, the progressive middle class offered a radicalism at the center of American society, an ambitious program to halt the friction and conflicts of the industrializing nation.

Like other classes, the middle class covered a wide range of circumstances at the turn of the twentieth century. It was defined most obviously by occupation. Victorian fathers and sons—and sometimes wives and daughters—were small proprietors and professionals, clerks and salespeople, managers and bureaucrats. In 1900, the United States Census counted 5.1 million white-collar workers, male and female, aged fourteen and over. Among them were 1.2 million professionals, 1.7 million managers, officials, and proprietors, 1.3 million sales workers, and almost 900,000 clerical workers. A few hundred thousand of the professionals, managers, officials, and proprietors, wealthy and powerful, belonged to the upper ten; the rest of these white-collar workers—petty proprietors, more modest professionals, and salaried employees—made up the core of Victorian America. These men and women, along with their families, probably numbered between 12 and 16 million people in 1900. In all, about one American in five was middle-class at the turn of the century.[6]

Their white-collar positions clearly set the Victorians apart from the working-class families who lived by manual labor. But it was money more than occupation that divided the middle class from the upper ten, whose fathers and sons also performed white-collar work. Though Victorian families lived fairly well, they had nothing like the fabulous resources of the upper class. The middle class lived always with a sense of constraint, a mixture of comforts and limits.[7]

That was plainly true for the families of clerks and small shop owners, who with incomes of a thousand dollars or so a year might be little better off than the best-paid skilled workers. But it was also true for a prosperous bureaucrat such as Charles Spencer, an aide to the steel magnate Henry Clay Frick. Spencer and his family lived with their servants in a fine Queen Anne house on Amberson Avenue in Shadyside, an affluent neighborhood of Pittsburgh's East End. Yet, with seven children, the "roomy" house "nearly burst at the seams" and the Spencers had to scrimp and save. "We lived in a neighborhood where everyone had more money than we had . . . ," Spencer's daughter, Ethel, recalled. "[T]here was never enough money in our house for unconsidered expenditure and every spare penny had to be put aside for the future use of the children." The eldest of them had started out "in aristocratic fashion" with a governess and private schools, but the others had to go off to public school despite "a little social sacrifice." At home, Ethel's mother, Mary Acheson Spencer, "was thrift personified." Managing the household with a firm hand, Mrs. Spencer made clothes for her children. "Mother," wrote Ethel, "spent much of her life at the sewing machine." And she put her children to work making toilet paper from "bits of tissue paper salvaged from old dress patterns." "When her seven children were at loose ends and demanded something to do," Ethel remembered, "she would set them down with some old patterns or torn sheets of tissue paper and a pair of blunt scissors to cut the paper into pieces of suitable size and shape for the toilet-paper box."[8]

Making toilet paper, sewing clothes, and counting pennies, middle-class families like the Spencers had created a solid, seemingly enduring culture, one of the central facts of nineteenth-century America. Generations of Victorians had built successfully on the bedrock values of domesticity, hard work, self-restraint, and individualism. Middle-class men dedicated themselves to the world of work; middle-class women, by and large, devoted themselves to the home and motherhood. Although some wives took in boarders and some held paying jobs outside the home, Victorian families hardly resembled the mutualistic families of the working class. Middle-class children typically were not expected to contribute to family income; they needed to go to school in order to prepare for white-collar careers. Partly because nonworking children were so expensive to raise, the Victorians practiced family limitation more than workers and farmers did. Middle-class couples had fewer children—averaging between three and four to a household by the end of the nineteenth century. As a result, Victorian mothers lavished more attention on each child. Until well after the Civil War, middle-class domesticity seemed to pay off: self-controlled, individualistic sons, schooled in the virtues of hard labor and postponed gratification, and increasingly likely to have gone to high school, succeeded for the most part in following their fathers into white-collar jobs and small businesses. Victorian values seemed to dominate public life, from the "free-labor" individualism of the Northern war on slavery to the popular standard of female beauty—the restrained, demure "steel-engraving lady."[9]

Middle-class homes—Queen Anne, Gothic Revival, Colonial Revival, Shingle Style, and Romanesque—testified to the Victorians' values and achievements. Solid and sizable, situated in quieter neighborhoods in cities and towns, these houses shielded middle-class families from the noisy, competitive world of wage work and from the dubious examples of other classes. As more and more of the middle class left the cities for new suburbs toward the end of the century, Victorian houses served even better as idealized refuges from workplaces, workers, and wealthy. In these homes, mothers and fathers created the delicate balance of community and privacy that spawned individualistic children who would go their own way in adulthood. Even unusually large middle-class families such as the Spencers could afford to divide private from public, familial from individual. Sleeping quarters were upstairs, well away from the family and public rooms—the parlor, the sitting room, or the "library"—downstairs. With separate bedrooms for parents and children, and with the innovation of the bathroom, there was enough room and solitude for the sense of self—"the first person"—so hard to develop in farmhouses and crowded working-class apartments. In the evenings, the Spencer children gathered around their mother in the library downstairs; as they sat and knitted or sewed, they listened to her read Dickens and other acceptable authors. But when it was time for bed, the children retired upstairs to the privacy of their own rooms.[10]

From the outside, the world of the Spencers seemed safe, secure, and self-satisfied. But Victorianism was already a culture in crisis.

By the time Jane Addams earned her degree from Rockford, domesticity was in trouble. Inside their Queen Anne houses, Victorian men and women, eyeing one another uneasily, postponed marriage. In the 1880s and 1890s, the marriage rate for white Americans decreased. Jane Addams's failure to marry was not unique: the generation of women arriving at maturity became the least likely to marry in American history. Once married, couples postponed having their first child. Judging by an apparently large increase in prostitution, those couples did not always find sexual satisfaction together. Perhaps not surprisingly, there was an increase in the divorce rate as well. On a typically more modest scale, the Victorians echoed the marital travails of the rich. As the breakup of middle-class unions helped push the national divorce rate from 1.5 per 1,000 marriages in 1870 up to 4.0 in 1900, Victorians began to worry about a "divorce crisis" in their ranks.[11]

Women were the most clearly unhappy. Never divorced, Mary Acheson

Spencer never entirely cared for life in the big house on Amberson Avenue, either. "I do not think she ever liked domesticity . . . ," her daughter Ethel observed. Mrs. Spencer did not enjoy all that sewing. She kept her house well "because it was her duty."[12]

For some middle-class women, unhappiness turned to anguish, unbearable and uncontainable. At twenty-one, Charlotte Perkins met the artist Charles Walter Stetson, "the greatest man, near my own age, that I had ever known." When he asked her to marry him, she agreed instead to see him for a year. When that time was up, she demanded, unsuccessfully, a year of separation. Finally making the marriage, the new Mrs. Stetson was miserable. "Here," she confessed, "was a charming home, a loving and devoted husband . . . a highly competent mother to run things; a wholly satisfactory servant—and I lay all day on the lounge and cried." Like Jane Addams, she consulted S. Weir Mitchell, but his prescription—more rest and limited creative activity—was no help. Stetson was happy only, she found, when away from home. Her marriage ended in divorce. By the turn of the century, the distinctive unhappiness of Victorian women had been studied, deplored, and given a name—"neurasthenia."[13]

Changes in the art of homemaking were part of the problem. So preoccupying for many middle-class women, the job of running a home had become less demanding and less fulfilling for others. In the late nineteenth century, bakeries, laundries, washing machines, and improved stoves made life easier for Victorian wives and mothers; but women's work accordingly seemed to be less an art and a source of pride than before the Civil War. And perhaps middle-class women had more free time to ponder their lot. "Once work was so constant that married women did not realize their loneliness or the want of appreciation which befell them," Kate Gannett Wells contended in an essay titled "Why More Girls Do Not Marry":

> Now society and the middle class have leisure to examine their states of mental solitude, and to see just where husbands are wanting. Fifty years ago the woman was too busy to stop for the morning kiss as her husband went to work. Now she has time to think about the absence or infrequency of the greeting for half an hour before she reads the morning paper, in which she finds some fresh instance of man's wickedness.

It is hard to imagine Mary Acheson Spencer finding that idle half hour of reflection, but it is not hard to conclude that domesticity never absorbed all her powers.[14]

Domesticity failed to absorb Mrs. Spencer and other women partly because, like Jane Addams, they had more opportunity for education. Women's academies and colleges proliferated in the late nineteenth century: Smith was founded in 1872; Wellesley, in 1875; Bryn Mawr, in 1886. Many male institutions opened their doors to women. By 1900, there were 85,000 women enrolled in over a thousand institutions of higher education around the country. Away at school, a young woman had a taste of independence. In the company of other women, she had the chance to evaluate her life. For many, that was an exciting experience. Mary Acheson Spencer had been to the Pennsylvania College for Women. "She . . . loved it," Ethel Spencer related, "and she wanted the experience for her daughters." But college could set women apart in unsettling ways. Ethel's sister Adeline entered Bryn Mawr in 1902. "In those benighted days it was not socially the thing for a girl to go to college, and to go to Bryn Mawr College, which was regarded as extremely highbrow, was to damn oneself in the eyes of all right-thinking young males," Ethel wrote. "So for the two years Adeline spent in Bryn Mawr College she never once confessed her shame to any man. . . ." Receiving a proposal of marriage in 1905, Adeline happily left school. Other women stayed on until graduation, only to find that college had changed them. Female college graduates, the middle class discovered, were less likely to marry. Committing themselves to careers, college women learned that outside of a few callings, such as teaching and nursing, those careers were hard to find. "For a girl who was not a social success and did not get married, who had neither society, a husband, house nor children to occupy her, life was," Ethel concluded, "dull and meaningless." Jane Addams would probably have agreed.[15]

Marriage was unattractive, of course, because it meant intimacy with Victorian men. "The average young girl considers herself a finer product of humanity than the average young man," Kate Gannett Wells reported. "The girl starts with the notion that her father, just because he was a man, has made life hard for her mother, and that all men are more or less explosive. . . . The feminine mind is preoccupied with the original sinfulness of man." Too many middle-class men seemed to spend too much time away from home in the evenings, enjoying the masculine camaraderie of clubs and fraternal lodges. The double standard, which allowed men pleasure outside the marriage bed and the home, seemed intolerable. "How can men bear to live double?" asked twenty-one-year-old Annie Winsor. "How can they be gentlemanly, of pure speech and right behavior at home and with ladies, and go to drink and swear and think foul thoughts, to see ugly sights . . . do ugly deeds and cover them over." Winsor knew the answer: "[T]here is a code of honour which will protect them from exposure."[16]

Middle-class men had their own complaints about women. For Victorian males, life was a difficult balancing act. They had to be tough enough to succeed in the world of commerce, yet gentle enough to please at home. They could feel uncomfortable in the feminized parlor, where they had to keep their feet off the furniture, watch their tobacco, and generally mind their manners. They could feel uncomfortable, too, in the new office buildings, where more and more young women invaded the male preserve of white-collar work. A young man soon discovered that he could satisfy women only if he showed them he was not "like other men," that he did not live by the double standard.[17]

This combination of circumstances could make Victorian fathers an enigma for the women and children around them. "Father was a tense, nervous man," Ethel Spencer remembered. "When he came home in the evening tired, nerves on edge, he found his seven children hard to take, and we were too young to understand his irritability. It seems to me sad, now that I am older than our father ever became, that we understood him so little and that most of us gave so little of ourselves to one who was in truth devoted to his children." Charles Spencer's hobby of photography summed up his veiled, restrained relationship with his family. Spencer interacted most easily with the people he loved when, standing on the other side of the lens, he hid himself under the camera's shroud and took their pictures over and over. "Most of his fun," Ethel concluded, "he found in his darkroom in the cellar."[18]

The Victorian male driven into hiding, unable to deal directly with women and children, was one of the arresting images of late nineteenth-century middle-class culture. In *Looking Backward,* Edward Bellamy's best-selling novel of 1888, the protagonist, Julian West, cannot manage to marry the woman he loves, cannot build a new house for her, and cannot sleep. Like Charles Spencer, Julian is forced underground. In desperation, he constructs a basement bedroom with thick concrete walls in order to seclude himself in "the silence of the tomb."[19]

Looking Backward sold so many copies partly because the novel helped point the way out of that tomb. Put to sleep one troubled night by a hired hypnotist, Julian West slumbers in his bunker while, aboveground, a fire consumes his Victorian house. He sleeps on until finally discovered in the year 2000. Revived by his host, Dr. Leete, Julian finds that in the intervening decades, society has addressed the crisis of domesticity. "It seems to us that women were more than any other class the victims of your civilization," Dr. Leete tells Julian. "There is something which, even at this distance of time, penetrates one with pathos in the spectacle of their ennuied, undeveloped lives, stunted at marriage, their narrow horizon, bounded so often, physically, by the four walls of home, and morally by a petty circle of personal interests." Technology and the state have helped free women from their predicament by the year 2000. Thanks to new laborsaving devices and government services, there is no housework to keep women at home. Released from domestic confinement, they enjoy new rights and opportunities: they own property, hold paying jobs, and vote for their own officers. But women are not men's full equals and are still confined to separate spaces. Consigned to their own segregated industrial "army," they cannot hold society's most important public offices. Their freedom seems less the product of innate rights and power than the result of masculine indulgence. "We have given them a world of their own, with its emulations, ambitions, and careers," brags Dr. Leete, "and I assure you they are very happy in it."[20]

This transformation does not benefit women alone; men profit too. "Women are a very happy race nowadays, as compared with what they ever were before in the world's history," Dr. Leete declares, "and their power of giving happiness to men has been of course increased in proportion." Freedom, however qualified, makes twentieth-century women such as Dr. Leete's daughter Edith far more appealing than Victorian women. "Feminine softness and delicacy," Julian marvels, "were in this lovely creature deliciously combined with an appearance of health and abounding physical vitality too often lacking in the maidens with whom alone I could compare her." Because women no longer depend on men for financial support, relations between the sexes flourish. "The sexes," Dr. Leete points out, "now meet with the ease of perfect equals, suitors to each other for nothing but love."[21]

Whether or not they read *Looking Backward,* Victorians were undergoing their own conversion along the lines forecast in the novel. By the end of the nineteenth century, the middle class had drafted—but had only begun to ratify—a kind of tacit peace treaty between the sexes. Forced mainly by the individual and collective struggles of Victorian women, this rough agreement included three principal provisions: eliminating the double standard, easing women's domestic burdens, and increasing their public opportunities.

Any reconciliation between men and women demanded, first of all, a new standard of male behavior. Put simply, the middle-class man had to be reined in. While the double standard would endure, male conduct had to become more acceptable to women. At home, this meant endorsing the concept of "voluntary motherhood"—the right of wives to dictate when they would have sexual intercourse and children. That is, women would take control of their bodies. And men would have to have more regard for women's needs. In the pamphlet *Sexual Hygiene,* published in 1898, the Physicians Club of Chicago lectured men "that the God-given relation is two-sided, and that without harmony and mutual enjoyment it becomes a mere masturbation to the body and mind of the one who alone is gratified." As well, men would have to pay more attention to household chores and to their role as fathers. Outside the home, there had to be a crackdown on masculine "vice." In the late nineteenth century, middle-class women and men crusaded against alcohol, pornography, prostitution, and gambling. This "purity crusade" intended to create a world less enticing to men, less likely to seduce them from home.[22]

Voluntary motherhood was part of the broader effort to lighten the weight of domesticity for women, the second provision of the peace treaty. Housing reformers looked for ways to redesign dwellings and adapt new technologies to the home. The more radical of these reformers, echoing *Looking Backward,* called for the replacement of the traditional Victorian home altogether. The middle class should trade houses for more manageable apartments, they argued; mothers should be able to use the services of public kitchens and child care. But most housing reformers believed "the home will not pass away. . . ." Accordingly, an emerging "home economics" movement tried to help women by making their housekeeping more systematic, businesslike, and "scientific." "Home economics," a promotional slogan explained, "stands for: The ideal home life for to-day unhampered by the traditions of the past; The utilization of all the resources of modern science to improve the home life." Supporting the assault on the double standard, the home economics movement insisted, in the words of Marion Talbot, one of its leaders, that "men and women are alike concerned in understanding the processes, activities, obligations and opportunities which make the home and the family effective parts of the social fabric."[23]

Although home economics generally supported wives' and mothers' continuing role as homemakers, the movement hardly intended to confine women to the house. Instead, the pioneering home economists wanted to make it easier for them to venture out. Home economists such as Talbot and Ellen Swallow Richards insisted that women's very responsibility for the home required them to become involved in public affairs. As Talbot put it, "[T]he obligations of home life are not by any means limited to its own four walls. . . ." One of the purposes of the home economics movement was, in fact, "preparation of young women for higher leadership" outside the home; their emergence "as leaders of public sentiment" was, home economists agreed, a "necessity."[24]

By promoting women's role in teaching homemaking in schools, colleges, and other public venues, the home-economics movement helped hammer out the third provision of the treaty between the sexes. Across Victorian America, women demanded new opportunities outside the home. As more and more young women sought college degrees, other middle-class women, especially middle-aged ones, pursued informal education. Beginning in 1868 with the New England Women's Club in Boston and Sorosis in New York City, a new generation of women's clubs offered chances for "self-improvement," for learning about art, literature, and public issues. The women's-club movement grew rapidly around the country and spawned the National Federation of Women's Clubs in 1890. Meanwhile, the Chautauqua movement, inaugurated on the shores of Lake Chautauqua in western New York in 1874, served a similar educational purpose. In annual assemblies at the lake and in similar gatherings in more than a hundred other communities by the turn of the century, thousands of Victorians studied religious questions, foreign languages, literature, science, and public issues. The Chautauqua Literary and Scientific Circle, a series of structured home-study courses leading to diplomas, diffused educational opportunity still more widely. Although Chautauqua was open to men, women played an especially prominent role as students and eventually as speakers. "The Chautauqua idea is the predominance of the feminine . . . ," an observer reported. "Man has a subdued look, no matter his pounds or whiskers, at Chautauqua."[25]

Victorian women sought political opportunity as well. The women's suffrage movement, largely led by such middle-class women as Susan B. Anthony, Elizabeth Cady Stanton, and Carrie Chapman Catt, slowly expanded in the Gilded Age. In 1890, the leading suffrage organizations—the National Woman Suffrage Association and the American Woman Suffrage Association—united to form a single, stronger body, the National American Woman Suffrage Association (NAWSA). That year, Wyoming entered the Union as the first state giving women the right to vote. Colorado adopted women's suffrage in 1893; Utah followed in 1896.[26]

In addition to educational and political opportunities, middle-class women successfully sought work outside the home. Increasingly, Victorian families in need of income allowed daughters to take positions as clerks or teachers. Some of these young women dared to justify employment on personal, rather than familial, grounds. "I do not plead poverty, but ambition," declared Lizzie Shannon, as she applied for a federal clerkship in 1893. "I am tired of being dependent." The number of women employed in white-collar positions, including teaching, office work, and sales, reached nearly a million by 1900. Still others advanced the broader middle-class program by working as reformers.[27]

For most of these working Victorian women, marriage meant the end of employment. But some stayed on the job after wedding. Ellen Swallow Richards, after marrying another professor on the faculty at the Massachusetts Institute of Technology, continued to work at the institute and led the home-economics movement. After marrying George Gilman in 1900, Charlotte Perkins Gilman continued to work as a writer and lecturer in the cause of domestic and social reform. Some working Victorian women never married at all. One of the most important aspects of the sexual peace treaty was the tacit acceptance that these women could escape conventional domesticity altogether by performing useful work. After a career as an educator in the 1860s and 1870s, the unmarried Frances Willard became a public figure as the driving force of the Women's Christian Temperance Union (WCTU), the most powerful organization of the purity crusade. In essence, the Victorians equipped domesticity with a safety valve, just in case the various reforms of the Gilded Age had not lowered the pressure in the middle-class household enough.[28]

Jane Addams finally solved her domestic crisis by claiming the opportunity to do useful work. In 1887, she set off with her friend Ellen Gates Starr to see Europe again. This time, visiting Toynbee Hall, the People's Palace, and other philanthropic missions to the poor of London, she recognized a solution to her problems: " . . . I gradually became convinced that it would be a good thing to rent a house in a part of the city where many primitive and actual needs are found, in which young women who had been given over too exclusively to study, might restore a balance of activity along traditional lines and learn of life from life itself. . . ." Returning to the United States, Addams and Ellen Starr moved to Chicago early in 1889 to work on "the scheme" for a "settlement." Later that year, they rented part of the first floor and all of the second of a house in a working-class section of Chicago. "Hull-House," named for its original occupant, was "a fine old house standing well back from the street, surrounded on three sides by a broad piazza which was supported by wooden pillars of exceptionally pure Corinthian design and proportion." There, living between a saloon and an undertaker, Addams gradually found a new purpose trying to help the Russian Jews, Italians, Greeks, and Bohemians who made up that working-class neighborhood. She had found a home.[29]

Addams was singular in her achievements but symptomatic in her ambitions. As she and other Victorians transformed domesticity, the middle class grew stronger and more aggressive. Increasingly, a troublesome rift between men and women became a dynamic source of social energy. The sexual peace treaty freed and even compelled Victorians to turn outward to engage other Americans over issues of personal behavior. As women joined men in carrying out the extensive Victorian public agenda, the middle class augmented its ranks for the whole range of social and political battles ahead. Such organizations as Hull-House, the WCTU, the NAWSA, and the home economists' annual Lake Placid Conference, created in the struggle to change domesticity, substantially increased the middle class's organizational strength. Finally, as activist women moved from conventional domesticity to the front lines of the middle-class public struggle, they brought a useful ideological weapon—ironically, the rhetoric of domesticity itself. Frances Willard, for instance, wanted "to make the whole world Homelike."

Swathing aggressive intentions in the reassuring warmth of home and hearth, this rhetorical device would become a key means of advancing the middle-class agenda in the new century.[30]

Jane Addams's arrival at Hull-House did not finish her journey. Although she had a new home, she had not moved completely out of her father's ideological house. In the 1890s, amid economic depression and social turmoil, she finally abandoned John Addams's individualism. Jane Addams already understood that individualism was an inadequate approach to life. As her experience in the 1880s had taught her, even privileged men and women could not stand alone: she had needed Ellen Starr to set up Hull-House, and she had needed the poor of the Hull-House neighborhood to give her life purpose and form. But it was only in the troubled Chicago of the 1890s, riven by class conflict, that Addams fully recognized individualism as a selfish, destructive creed, a threat to an industrializing society.

Class conflict was fundamental to the Victorians' experience of industrial capitalism. Profoundly affected by the class differences and antagonisms all around them, they gradually became more willing to see and explore what the rich preferred to deny—the truth, as economist Richard T. Ely put it, that "men exist in classes. . . ." "We do not like to acknowledge that Americans are divided into two nations," Jane Addams observed. For her and for other Victorians, those "two nations" were the working class and the upper class. After the turn of the century, middle-class reformers would pay more attention to farmers, but in the last decades of the nineteenth century, it was wage earners and the rich who preoccupied the Victorian imagination.[31]

To the Victorians, the two classes were threatening because of their economic power, their alien cultures, and their mutual hostility. The economic power was obvious: the Victorians were ever more dependent on big business for processed foods on the table, for rail trips to work, and even for work itself. Always risky, small business had become more difficult. Some petty proprietors, driven to the wall by larger firms, had to choose between selling out to the competition and going out of business. Middle-class business owners also had to worry about the demands of workers and unions. "The small business man," complained a grain dealer in Providence, Rhode Island in 1898, "is the most heavily oppressed man there is to-day, for capital grinds him on the one hand and labor on the other." With diminishing prospects in small business, more young middle-class men traded independence for subordinate, salaried white-collar jobs. From 1880 to 1900, the ranks of male clerical workers more than tripled, from 153,000 to 550,000. Some of these jobs were already being degraded. As organizations grew, clerical positions often became routinized, simplified, and lower paid.[32]

The upper ten and the working class were all the more disturbing because of their alien values and practices. The rich had their mansions and lavish entertainments, their divorces, yachts, and all the other trappings of consumerism and self-indulgence. Workers had their slums, saloons, and festivals, their supposedly freer sexuality and expressiveness. To many Victorians, each class was defective. "In your day," Dr. Leete tells Julian West in *Looking Backward,* "riches debauched one class with idleness of mind and body, while poverty sapped the vitality of the masses by overwork, bad food, and pestilent homes." Edward Bok, editor of the *Ladies' Home Journal,* contrasted "unrest among the lower classes and rottenness among the upper classes." Workers and the rich lived, Dr. William Rainsford contended, by "jungle law." Moreover, the practices of these classes had an insidious cultural appeal. On one hand, after the Civil War, fashion seemed to turn from the middle-class ideal of the "steel-engraving lady" to the more working-class, frankly sexual "voluptuous woman." On the other hand, the upper-class divorce habit was catching.[33]

Finally, workers and the rich seemed inclined to selfishness and conflict. " . . . I witnessed with sorrow and alarm," recalled Washington Gladden, the well-known Congregational minister from Columbus, Ohio, "the widening of the breach between these classes; the deepening tendency, in each of them, to erect its own social group into a separate principality, ignoring the solidarity of society, and pushing its own claims at the cost of all the rest." To some Victorian onlookers, the defects of each class led inevitably to economic clashes and physical violence. "The rich become effeminate, weak, and immoral," explained James Weir, Jr., a physician from Kentucky, in 1894, "and the lower classes, taking advantage of this moral lassitude, and led on by their savage inclinations, undertake strikes, mobs, boycotts, and riots." The Gilded Age offered a litany of class conflict: the great railroad strike of 1877, the strike against Jay Gould's Missouri-Pacific Railroad in 1886, the Haymarket Bombing in Chicago the same year, the Homestead strike of 1892, the Pullman strike of 1894, and countless other battles.[34]

These and other strikes dramatized the Victorians' plight as a true middle class, trapped in no-man's land. Never completely comfortable with either side, they were caught in the crossfire between rich and poor. Middle-class consumers and business owners had to put up with the disruption of supplies and services. Protestant clergymen watched their churches suffer because of the bitter division between rich and poor in the cities and towns.[35]

Trying to respond to these calamities, Victorians found that their individualistic values were of no help. In fact, individualism had clearly spurred the crisis in the first place. By the 1880s and 1890s, the middle class had to face the painful irony that it was upwardly mobile men, living the individualist creed, who had built big businesses and stood ready to take on their workers. Moreover, the rich had perverted individualism itself. The Victorians balanced individual freedom with self-control, hard work, and domesticity. The rich had seemingly cast aside those balance weights. In the hands of the upper ten, individualism became an excuse for complete autonomy, a legitimization of indulgence and inequality, and a rationalization of the troubling national status quo.

It was the tumultuous Pullman strike of 1894 that drove home these truths for Jane Addams. "Before it," she said, "there had been nothing in my experience to reveal that distinct cleavage of society, which a general strike at least momentarily affords." Now she saw how the exalted sense of personal prerogative of George Pullman, the famous builder of the railway sleeping car, led to wrenching, destructive "class bitterness." With much fanfare, Pullman had built a model company town just south of Chicago to house his workers. Named after the industrialist, the community of Pullman had been enveloped by the expansion of Chicago. In the middle of the depression of the 1890s, Pullman cut his workers' wages without reducing their rents. The result was conflict and chaos: the workers struck in May; the American Railway Union boycotted trains with Pullman cars around the country in June; and the federal government called out the army at the start of July. In Chicago, hundreds of freight cars burned and thirteen people died. By mid-July, Eugene V. Debs, the leader of the railway union, was in jail and the strike had collapsed.[36]

For Addams, the Pullman strike was a personal and professional calamity. With ties to both the workers and the wealthy of Chicago, Hull-

House had "opportunity for nothing but a realization of the bitterness and division along class lines." Addams's efforts to arbitrate the strike failed. Meanwhile, she felt the quintessential middle-class sense of helplessness amid class conflict. When Addams's eldest sister, Mary Linn, lay gravely ill in a hospital near Chicago, Addams managed to reach her. But then Addams sat helplessly as the disruption of the railroads kept Mary Linn's husband and children from reaching her before she died. This "very intimate and personal experience" left Addams with "constant dread of the spreading ill will." She understood how episodes like this could draw the Victorians themselves into class hatred and warfare. "[H]ow many more such moments of sorrow and death were being made difficult and lonely throughout the land," she asked, "and how much would these experiences add to the lasting bitterness, that touch of self-righteousness which makes the spirit of forgiveness well-nigh impossible."[37]

The strike—"this great social disaster"—forced Addams back to first principles, to the values she had learned from her father. During the battle, Addams walked "the wearisome way" to Chicago's Lincoln Park "in order to look at and gain magnanimous counsel . . . from the marvelous St. Gaudens statue" of John Addams's great hero, Abraham Lincoln. In the aftermath, she was determined to salvage something from the debacle. "It sometimes seems," Addams observed, "as if the shocking experiences of that summer . . . can only be endured if we learn from it all a great ethical lesson." And so she began to write an article, "A Modern Lear," that became a farewell to her father's creed, so twisted and distorted in Pullman's hands.[38]

Trying to assess the conflict between the industrialist and his workers, John Addams's daughter thought of the tragedy of a Shakespearean father and daughter, King Lear and Cordelia. Because Lear was king, she noted, he was "unique" in his ability either to help or to hurt the people dependent on him. Pullman, the wealthy employer, was very much like a king. Even though he had not acted out of ill will, Pullman had failed to recognize his special power and obligation. Just as Lear had not understood his daughter's thoughts and feelings, this modern upper-class man had not understood the mutualism of his workers, whose "watchwords were brotherhood, sacrifice, the subordination of individual and trade interests to the good of the working class. . . ." Instead, Pullman blindly asserted the prerogatives of upper-class individualism. "He stood throughout pleading for the individual virtues . . . ," Addams noted, "those which had enabled him and so many of his contemporaries to rise in life, when 'rising in life' was urged upon every promising boy as the goal of his efforts. Of the new code of ethics he had caught absolutely nothing." Worse, Pullman had acted on his individualism in provoking the strike: Addams pointed out "the unusual part played in it by the will of one man." Trapped by his own egotism, Pullman became like Lear, disowning a daughter whom he did not understand. "So long had he thought of himself as the noble and indulgent father," Addams maintained, "that he had lost the faculty by which he might perceive himself in the wrong."[39]

Criticizing Pullman, Addams was also critical of his workers. With their newer mutualistic values, they forgot "the old relationships" with employers. Like Cordelia with her father, Pullman's workers seemed not to acknowledge what the industrialist had done for them. Addams emphasized "the similarity of ingratitude suffered by an indulgent employer and an indulgent parent." Still, it was Pullman's values, not the workers', that Addams condemned most strongly. Since this rich man's individualism had produced as much "failure" as good, "we are forced," Addams concluded, "to challenge the ideal itself. . . ." Individualism would have to go. As Addams wrote on another occasion after the strike, "A large body of people feel keenly that the present industrial system is in a state of profound disorder, and that there is no guarantee that the pursuit of individual ethics will ever right it."[40]

This was no easy conclusion for Addams. "A Modern Lear" was clearly and uncomfortably about her relationship with her father, which may help explain why editors rejected the article for more than a decade. Explaining Cordelia's behavior toward Lear, Jane Addams seemed to defend her abandonment of John Addams's ideas. There was no "disrespect to her father," she wrote plaintively. "The virtues of one generation are not sufficient for the next. . . ."[41]

Perhaps no other Victorian explored and discussed her renunciation of individualism so candidly. But many members of the middle class, traveling by a host of separate paths, arrived at the same ideological destination. Protestant ministers made perhaps the most notable journey. Their inherited Christian faith was intensely individualistic: they preached the worth of each individual human being; they presented salvation as an individual matter, the result of self-reformation. Yet, after the Civil War, many of these men began to condemn individualism in impassioned terms. Noting the social conflict that the doctrine was producing in America, the well-known Congregationalist Lyman Abbott, editor of *The Outlook* magazine, insisted, "individualism is the characteristic of simple barbarism, not of republican civilization." Because of the power of big business, the Baptist minister and reformer Walter Rauschenbusch argued, "individualism means tyranny." "I do not believe," Washington Gladden admonished, "that political society or industrial society or any other society will endure on a purely individualistic basis."[42]

Similar condemnations of individualism rang out almost everywhere in middle-class culture by the end of the nineteenth century. In *Looking Backward*, Dr. Leete blames the crises of the Gilded Age on "excessive individualism." As the individualistic United States industrialized, E. A. Ross lamented, "The community has become too often the prey of individuals." A new generation of economists, led by Richard T. Ely, Henry Carter Adams, Edmund J. James, John Bates Clark, Simon N. Patten, and others, attacked the long-dominant "English" school of political economy that demanded the individual's utmost freedom from external interference. Troubled by the power of big business and the plight of workers, the new economists insisted that the individual pursuit of self-interest did not necessarily serve the interests of society. Meanwhile, Francis Peabody, professor of Christian Morals at Harvard, blamed divorce on the "reactionary force of self-interested individualism." Commentators decried the "exaggerated individualism" of the Victorian home. Architects, home economists, and housing reformers called for less individual, more homogeneous family dwellings.[43]

A turning point in the life of the middle class, the condemnation of individualism was also a critical development in the contest for authority in America. In questioning their longtime creed, the Victorians completed the cultural isolation of the upper ten. Increasingly, the fundamental values of the wealthy, deprived of middle-class endorsement, appeared selfish and destructive. And, as would become clear, the Victorians' ideological emancipation, like their reworking of domesticity, unleashed a powerful new dynamic in American society.

As the Victorians reconsidered domesticity and individualism, they also had to reevaluate the place of work and pleasure in their lives. Industrial capitalism seemed to eat away at the ascetic discipline of Victorianism, especially its emphasis on hard work, thrift, and self-denial. As the American economy grew, leisure, abundance, and pleasure beckoned seductively to the middle class.

In the Gilded Age, the work ethic lost its iron hold on the Victorian conscience. The middle class began to entertain the notion that one could work too hard. After all, it was hard work that had produced the upper ten and the consequent horrors of industrial America. And certainly the continued growth of the national economy appeared not to require quite as much labor—at least from middle-class white-collar workers. As in so many other areas, Bellamy's *Looking Backward* pointed hopefully toward change. Utopian Boston does not worship work: in fact, men and women labor short hours, take "regular" vacations, and look forward to an early retirement at forty-five. "Know, O child of another race and yet the same," Dr. Leete bombastically addresses Julian West, "that . . . labor . . . is by no means regarded as the most important, the most interesting, or the most dignified employment of our powers. We look upon it as a necessary duty to be discharged before we can fully devote ourselves to the higher exercise of our faculties, the intellectual and spiritual enjoyments and pursuits which alone mean life."[44]

This was a view many Victorians were eager to accept. Like Bellamy, the middle class envisioned a world with less work and more leisure. That world seemed to be emerging. As early as 1883, most federal clerks had achieved a forty-two-hour week and thirty days' annual leave. By the turn of the century, the middle class looked forward to a shortened work week and perhaps a week-long annual vacation. But the middle class still clung to the work ethic. The Victorians justified their leisure by linking it to work. Without labor, a Methodist minister reminded his flock in 1892, play became "dissipation." "There can be no recreation without previous toil," the parson declared. "There are thousands who spend their summers at Newport . . . who don't know what recreation means." Although the Victorians wanted to work less, they were not about to endorse the values of the wealthy "leisure class."[45]

That was apparent as well in middle-class attitudes toward the uses of leisure. Generally, the late-nineteenth-century middle class placed more emphasis than before on enjoyment and satisfaction. One sign was the gradual demise of the pious "Puritan Sunday," given over to devotions rather than recreations. By the turn of the century, much of the middle class devoted the Sabbath to carriage rides, visits to museums, and other pleasures, as well as traditional church services. For those fortunate enough to have a vacation, there might be a stay at the shore or a camping trip. An ideal vacation was a trip to Chautauqua, which blended self-improving lectures and classes with concerts, tennis, baseball, and walks in the woods. Another, more subtle sign of the importance of pleasure was the way in which married couples seemed to expect more from each other in the Gilded Age. Increasingly, middle-class husbands and wives judged their spouses by the pleasures they provided—the quality of the home and its objects, the happiness of the marriage. The failure to meet those increased expectations was a principal reason for the increasing breakup of Victorian marriages.[46]

Despite this greater emphasis on pleasure, the middle class was not ready to tighten its embrace of all forms of enjoyment. Rather than celebrate sexual pleasure, the Victorians tried to contain sexual desire. The single standard of sexual conduct that middle-class women had in mind was their own, not the looser standard of many men. The Gilded Age witnessed, as Charlotte Perkins Gilman put it, "a fine, earnest movement toward an equal standard of chastity for men and women, an equalizing upward to the level of women." So the Victorians tried to rein in male sexuality by combating prostitution and encouraging voluntary motherhood, women's control of their own bodies.[47]

The Victorians were much more open to other forms of pleasure. Never wholly given to asceticism, the middle class had always bought inessential services and objects, of course. Consumption and hard work went together in capitalism; products had to be purchased. For the Victorians, a certain amount of consumption and display had also been a basic part of class identity, a means of differentiating themselves from wage workers. Still, the antebellum Victorians did not equate life with an unceasing pursuit of pleasure and the loss of self-control. But something happened to this Victorian attitude after the Civil War. In Washington, D.C., federal clerks strained their budgets and took out loans to pay for such necessities as fine clothes, servants, and singing lessons. Many Victorian men spent freely for cosmetics and other "toiletries," athletic uniforms and equipment, tobacco and alcohol, and sumptuous dinners and entertainments at their clubs and fraternal orders. Middle-class weddings became increasingly lavish. Couples needed costly gifts from family and friends to get started in marriage. Some new husbands and wives even put their presents on display for visitors.[48]

This changed attitude was especially apparent in the gradual corruption of the Victorian house. By the Gilded Age, the middle class tended to copy features of upper-class mansions and install them—often incongruously—in its own more modest dwellings. Victorian householders, anxious to demonstrate artistic individuality, filled their formal front rooms with a riot of possessions. Overwhelmed by clutter, parlors became known as "thickets." Homemade objects and decorations gave way to mass-produced goods; horsehair, to fine upholstery; carpets, to rugs; painted rooms, to fabric-covered or papered walls. The colors turned exotic—vermilions, russets, bottle greens. Advances in woodworking machinery allowed still more garish ornamentation, inside and out. The Victorians ordered beaded and floral moldings and shingles shaped like fish scales and snowflakes.[49]

Even as they drowned their homes in ornaments, the men and women of the middle class began to worry about materialism. The Victorians were so angry with the hedonism of the wealthy and the working class precisely because they themselves felt so much temptation. "Love of money, faith in money, devotion to material things, has become the prevailing distemper of the time," Washington Gladden warned. "It is not the rich or the prosperous alone who hold this creed; . . . those of us who are not wealthy, according to modern standards, have our qualms about the enjoyments which we allow ourselves." Noting "the wanton luxury of our period," economist Richard T. Ely admitted, "it is not merely the rich who stand condemned, but the disposition which is found in all social classes. . . . The disease is, indeed, widespread."[50]

In response to these concerns, middle-class attitudes toward the pleasure of consumption stabilized as the century came to an end. There was no celebration of asceticism, but the Victorians tried to hold themselves more in check. Tellingly, in Bellamy's utopia, there is an almost impossible balance of pleasure and restraint: twentieth-century Bostonians freely enjoy shopping yet feel no need for accumulation and ostentation. Edith Leete is an "indefatigable shopper," but somehow, as her father explains, "[W]e have as little gear about us at home as is consistent with comfort. . . ." Bellamy's middle-class readers tried to attain this balance. Once more, the Victorian house, so central to the life of the class, symbolized the change. By the turn of the century, the middle class was rejecting the aesthetic of the upper ten. Deriding "The Poor Taste of the Rich," Herbert S. Stone of the *House Beautiful* declared, "Costly ugliness is a crime." Wanting to make homes simpler and less ornate, middle-class men and women undertook campaigns to reform housing. Edward Bok of the *Ladies' Home Journal,* urging his readers to "the simple life," condemned "repellently ornate" Victorian houses, with "useless turrets" outside and "useless bric-a-brac inside." "No child," he warned, "can develop a true simplicity of nature when the home of his parents is stuffed by shams." In kitchens and bathrooms, and even in dining rooms and living rooms, lively colors and wallpapers gave way to plain white paint. Fashionable furniture now had clean, spare lines; parlors, less cluttered, no longer seemed like "thickets." These reforms were also intended to curb the lust for pleasure in another way. By making the home less "feminine," architects and housing reformers hoped to keep men happily at home. The parlor, that domain of the middle-class woman, began to go out of fashion, eventually to be replaced by the "living room." And some new houses included a "den," furnished as a lair for the Victorian man.[51]

As they restrained their desires, the Victorians also labored to make themselves physically stronger for the battles of industrial America. The preoccupation with the body, so basic to Victorian culture from the beginning, was especially evident in its last days. By the 1890s, the middle class was caught up in a cult of fitness. Educators stressed the importance of physical culture for the young; success required not only sound values but sound bodies. There was a rage for cycling. Men lifted weights. Women, swinging "Indian clubs" and riding cycles, also took part in the toughening of the middle class: women's colleges included athletics in their curricula.[52]

Toward the end of the century, new standards of masculine and feminine beauty reflected the strengthening of the middle class. Men and women alike admired Eugene Sandow, the great strong man whose arrival in the United States from Europe in 1893 set off a frenzy. To admiring Americans, he was both "the perfect man" and "the perfect gentleman." In the 1890s, the woman depicted in the drawings of Charles Dana Gibson enjoyed enormous popularity. The "Gibson girl," like the sexual treaty she represented, was a compromise. In some ways, she was a conservative figure—a "girl," after all, not a "woman" or a "lady" like her predecessor, the "steel-engraving lady." But the Gibson girl was lithe, tall, strong, athletic, and dignified; she conjured up the healthy Edith Leete rather than the demure "steel-engraving lady" or the blatantly sexual, working-class "voluptuous woman." Charlotte

Perkins Gilman praised the Gibson girl for representing "the new women . . . a noble type, indeed . . . honester, braver, stronger, more healthful and skilful and able and free, more human in all ways."[53]

By the turn of the century and the approach of Queen Victoria's passing, the American Victorians were no longer Victorians. Rethinking domesticity, rejecting individualism, reconsidering work and pleasure, and redesigning the body, middle-class men and women had cast off much of their old identity. Strengthening themselves, they were becoming new people. But what sort?

The new identity of the middle class became plain as men and women considered how to end class conflict and create a safe society for themselves and their children. With individualism in disrepute, the middle class needed another doctrine to guide them in the world. Amid the poverty of Halstead Street and the social division of Chicago, Jane Addams felt that need acutely. When she and Ellen Starr moved into Hull-House in September 1889, they had no clear course of action. "I . . . longed," Addams wrote, "for the comfort of a definite social creed, which should afford at one and the same time an explanation of the social chaos and the logical steps towards its better ordering."[54]

Socialism was an obvious possibility. In the 1880s and 1890s, impassioned discussions of socialism spilled across the pages of magazines and rang through lecture halls and the rooms of Hull-House. For middle-class Americans repelled by individualism, socialism offered an appealing insistence that society's needs were more important than those of selfish individuals like George Pullman. Socialism also provided an intriguing example of the willingness to use the power of the state to regulate society. Numerous middle-class reformers and even politicians acknowledged their interest in socialism, especially in the reassuring form offered in *Looking Backward* and in the writings of the antimonopolist reformer Henry George. A few middle-class reformers declared themselves socialists outright. Some softened their socialism with a qualifying term, such as the "Christian Socialism" advocated by the Reverend George D. Herron and the Reverend William Dwight Porter Bliss. The need for that qualification suggested the uneasiness produced by an ideology imported from Europe. Rejecting "the narrow and rigid 'economic determinism' of Marx," Charlotte Perkins Gilman explained, "My socialism was of the early humanitarian kind. . . ." A socialist only "[f]or working purposes," Walter Rauschenbusch favored just as much socialism as was necessary, such as state ownership of natural monopolies. But a thoroughgoing socialism that turned the nation into "a colossal machine" posed too great a threat, the minister and reformer believed, to the family, religion, freedom, creativity, and civic peace. Rejecting socialism and individualism alike, the great majority of the middle class wanted something in between the two doctrines, which Richard T. Ely labeled "the golden mean."[55]

Despite her yearning for a creed, Addams could not endorse socialism either. "I should have been most grateful at that time to accept the tenets of socialism," she explained with her customary politeness. But, like Gilman, Addams disliked Karl Marx's seemingly deterministic version of socialism, which she did not want confused with what really mattered—"the growing sensitiveness which recognizes that no personal comfort nor individual development can compensate a man for the misery of his neighbors. . . ." It was that sense of neighborliness, of connection to those around her, that drove Addams. At first, she and Starr seemed to envision the settlement as a seat of middle-class culture, a place for art shows, lectures, and readings of George Eliot's *Romola* that would uplift the working-class people of the area. But sympathy for the difficult lives of their neighbors soon made Hull-House something more. "We were asked to wash the newborn babies, and to prepare the dead for burial, to nurse the sick, and to 'mind the children,'" Addams recalled. " . . . [W]e were ready to perform the humblest neighborhood services." This willingness to serve led to the establishment of a nursery, a kindergarten, a variety of clubs and classes for women and children, and a boardinghouse for working women. The settlement tried a number of experiments in consumer cooperation, including a coal-purchasing scheme for the neighborhood. With all these activities, the settlement grew beyond the original house into a complex of thirteen interconnected buildings. By the early 1900s, up to seventy men and women lived and worked with Addams in Hull-House.[56]

The lesson of the development of Hull-House was obvious, especially against the backdrop of the Pullman strike. The settlement, the neighborhood, and Addams herself benefited from the growing web of human connections. However tentative, however flawed, a feeling of community grew in and around Hull-House for Addams in the 1890s, even as Pullman's blind individualism tore apart the community he had built. "[W]e are passing from an age of individualism to one of association . . . ," Addams concluded. "[W]e must demand that the individual shall be willing to lose the sense of personal achievement, and shall be content to realize his activity only in connection with the activity of the many." That was what Addams herself had done; that was what she urged others to do as well. "Our thoughts, at least for this generation," she counseled, "cannot be too much directed from mutual relationships and responsibilities."[57]

Addams was not alone in calling for "association." As they condemned individualism, Lyman Abbott, Washington Gladden, Walter Rauschenbusch, Josiah Strong, and other protestant ministers preached instead what became known as the "Social Gospel." They exhorted Christians to seek salvation by reaching out to others in industrial America. "The next great principle . . . ," Rauschenbusch announced in 1896, "is *association.*" "Now men are free, but it is often the freedom of grains of sand that are whirled up in a cloud and then dropped in a heap, but neither cloud nor sand-heap have any coherence," he observed. "New forms of association must be created. Our disorganized competitive life must pass into an organic cooperative life." Gladden, too, saw life in terms of "interdependencies and co-operations," rather than individualism. "For this human personality, whom we wrongly name an individual, finds its life only in vital union with other lives," Gladden maintained. "To live is not to separate ourselves from our fellows, but to unite with them in multiform ministries of giving and receiving. We are parts of a whole. . . ."[58]

The new economists likewise called for some form of "association" in place of individualism. For instance, Richard T. Ely, who was influential in the Social Gospel movement as well, used the term *social solidarity* to signify "the dependence of man upon man, both in good things and in evil things." "Social solidarity means that our true welfare is not an individual matter purely, but likewise a social affair," Ely clarified: "our weal is common weal; we thrive only in a commonwealth; our exaltation is the exaltation of our fellows, their elevation is our enlargement."[59]

Association and *social solidarity* were broad, vague terms; their meaning would need to be worked out more concretely in the years ahead. But it was clear from the beginning that Addams, Ely, and the other advocates of association had in mind a distinctive approach to life. Obviously antithetical to upper-class individualism, association also differed fundamentally from the working-class and agrarian brands of mutualism. Workers helped one another out of a sense of common class identity, a sense of shared viewpoints, circumstances, and hazards. Association, on the other hand, grew out of a sense of difference; for the middle class, it meant crossing class lines to bring together people of diverse identities and conditions. Mutualism was a strategy of self-preservation, a way to keep a class going. Association was at once more modest and more aggressive than mutualism. Addams and other Victorians admitted that they could not survive except through contact with other classes. Yet, as would become clear, the Victorians also insisted on cross-class contact in order to change other groups, to make individualistic rich people like George Pullman behave, and to reshape workers' and farmers' lives.

Even as the middle class began to explore the implications of association and social solidarity with others, it also looked to a more coercive replacement for individualism—state power. Despite her interest in socialism, Jane Addams did not begin at Hull-House with any grand idea of the state. Instead, her experience in the settlement gradually moved her toward political action and regulatory government. To protect the interests of Hull-House and the neighborhood, Jane Addams participated in three campaigns "against a powerful alderman . . . notoriously corrupt." When she recognized the health problems caused by inadequate garbage collection, she tried to educate the neighborhood about waste disposal, setting up an incinerator at Hull-House and urging the city to enforce its sanitation laws. Her efforts were unsuccessful. As she discovered, legislation was not enough; administration mattered. "In sheer desperation," Addams herself tried to win the contract for garbage removal. Turned down on a technicality, she persuaded the mayor of Chicago to make her the garbage inspector for the ward.[60]

Addams learned further lessons in a campaign against child labor and the so-called sweating system, in which laboring families did piecework in their crowded, poorly lit apartments. Hull-House resident Florence Kelley, appointed factory inspector for the state bureau of labor, investigated the sweating system in Chicago. She and Addams lobbied first for an Illinois factory law and then for federal legislation. "Even in our short struggle with the evils of the sweating system," Addams wrote, "it did not seem strange that the center of the effort had shifted to Washington, for by that time we had realized that the sanitary regulation of sweatshops by city officials, and a careful enforcement of factory legislation inspectors will not avail, unless each city and State shall be able to pass and enforce a code of comparatively uniform legislation." Such perceptions pushed Addams toward a cautious but firm justification of more powerful government. "[A]s the very existence of the State depends upon the character of its citizens," Addams explained, "therefore if certain industrial conditions are forcing the workers below the standard of decency, it becomes possible to deduce the right of State regulation."[61]

Other middle-class Americans deduced that right, too. As the economist Henry Carter Adams of the University of Michigan observed in 1887, "There is at the present time a growing clamor for more government. . . ." The Social Gospel movement called for an activist state. So did the new economists. "We . . . need," said Simon Patten, "a new society and a state whose power will be superior to that of any combination of selfish individuals, and whose duties will be commensurate with human wants." In *Looking Backward,* the "nation" and its vast, anonymous governmental bureaucracy have taken over from the "selfish individuals" of big business and dominate utopia. Writing in *The Chautauquan* magazine in 1888, economist Edmund J. James expressed the increasingly common wisdom. "Government," he said, "should interfere in all instances where its interference will tell for better health, better education, better morals, greater comfort of the community."[62]

With this resolve, the Victorians' new identity became clear. By the end of the 1890s, the middle class had not only rejected its longstanding individualism; it had also adopted a new "creed," the will to use association and the state to end class conflict and the other problems of industrial capitalism. This imperative to turn outward, combined with the reform of domesticity and the reconsideration of work and pleasure, made the Victorians a new class. By the turn of the century, they had become "progressives." The term had not yet been coined, of course; in the 1890s, sympathetic observers talked about "the social movement" instead, without much acknowledgment of its class basis. Pointing freely to the "two nations" of workers and wealthy, the middle class was often coy about its own existence. It would be a while before the middle class, let alone society as a whole, understood just what the Victorians had become and what they were creating.[63]

The 1890s were, Jane Addams modestly observed, a "decade of discussion" and "preliminary argument" at Hull-House. In truth, the residents of the settlement and the middle class as a whole did more than talk during this tumultuous decade. Troubled by internal and external crises, the middle class had already succeeded in the 1880s in imagining a better world, such as the utopian Boston that Edward Bellamy conjured up in *Looking Backward.* In the 1890s, middle-class men and women began to create real versions of their utopia in the controlled, contained environment of small communities. Hull-House was one such place. As Addams had hoped, the settlement's Victorian staff mixed with people from other walks of life, lived a different kind of domesticity in a different kind of home, absorbed new associational ways of feeling and thinking, and earnestly threw themselves into aspects of the broader middle-class project. In short, the settlement community created progressives. "Although . . . diversified in social beliefs," Addams contentedly reported, "the residents became solidly united through our mutual experience in an industrial quarter, and we became not only convinced of the need for social control and protective legislation but also of the value of this preliminary argument."[64]

The same process occurred in the sylvan summer world of Chautauqua. Visiting the community for one or two weeks a year, thousands of Victorians escaped domestic routine, relaxed without fear of conflict or violence, lived out new gender relations in the temporary setting of tents and dining halls, enjoyed responsible leisure, and absorbed progressive ideas from such speakers as Jane Addams, Richard T. Ely, Charlotte Perkins Gilman, Washington Gladden, and Frances Willard. "It was largely through Chautauqua that I was able to exercise my greatest influence," Ely, the well-published author and much-honored university professor, admitted.[65]

Lecturing at Chautauqua in 1896, William James, the renowned Harvard philosopher and pioneer of psychology, quickly grasped the meaning of the summer community. Chautauqua was, he said, "Utopia," "the realization—on a small, sample scale of course—of all the ideals for which our civilization has been striving: security, intelligence, humanity, and order." As he strolled the grounds and attended the classes, James found only progress. "You have no zymotic diseases, no poverty, no drunkenness, no crime, no police," he testified. "You have culture, you have kindness, you have cheapness, you have equality, you have the best fruits of what mankind has fought and bled and striven for under the name of civilization for centuries." In short, James concluded, this was "the middle-class paradise." And so the

Harvard professor, acolyte of high culture and admirer of the "antique spirit of English individualism," could not bear the place. The summer community was, he fumed, "this unspeakable Chautauqua," the "quintessence of every mediocrity." After a week, James had to get away. "Let me take my chances again," he begged, "in the big outside worldly wilderness with all its sins and sufferings."[66]

James underestimated the middle class. In particular, he failed to acknowledge how much the denizens of Chautauqua were in fact worried about "the big outside worldly wilderness with all its sins and sufferings." Jane Addams and the other progressive lecturers made the long trip to western New York precisely in order to talk about that "worldly wilderness." Their audiences made the same long trip in part because they wanted to hear about "sins and suffering" even as they enjoyed a happy sojourn. Chautauqua, Hull-House, and so many turn-of-the-century middle-class households certainly were refuges from a troubling outside world. But they were also preparations for that world. Progressivism inexorably pushed the middle class out into American society. The challenge for the progressives was to make the hothouse environment of Chautauqua and Hull-House a day-to-day reality in society as a whole.

This was an ambitious, radical undertaking. The middle-class project demanded attention "to the entire life of man, individual and social," a Methodist minister in Indianapolis explained in 1901; "to the home, to social customs, to the organization of industries, to education, to government, to diplomacy, to literature and the fine arts, to the correction of social evils, etc., as well as to the eternal welfare of human hearts." Given the fundamental differences among social classes, the "middle-class paradise" would require revolutionary changes in the ways Americans imagined and lived their lives. Progressives, so troubled by violence and conflict, never liked the term *revolution.* Precisely because their intentions were so radical, these middle-class men and women seldom risked arousing the fears of other Americans with aggressive, revolutionary talk. Washington Gladden put the undertaking in safer terms in a commencement address at the University of Michigan in 1902. "A great work of reconstruction, social, industrial, political, ecclesiastical, has got to be done . . . ," he told the graduating class.[67]

In some ways, the progressives were ill-equipped for such a job of "reconstruction." At the turn of the century, the middle class lacked the money and power of the upper ten; it lacked as well the sheer numbers of farmers and wage workers. Although the progressives had created a shared approach to life, their ideology did not dictate specific policies. The middle class had not worked out common answers to some large questions: Should big business be broken up or preserved? Should trade unions be banned or encouraged? Should divorce be abolished or allowed? "The social movement on the whole seems at best a tuning of the orchestra," observed the sociologist Albion Small in 1897. "Many are the doubters whether there will be any symphony."[68]

Moreover, progressivism, like any ideology, contained ambiguities and contradictions. The middle class, despite its renewed efforts at self-discipline, was clearly uneasy about the place of pleasure in life. There was as well a contradiction between the justifications for two key progressive goals—curbing the autonomy of the wealthy and improving the status of women. In response to the rich, the progressives condemned individualism. But individualism was central to middle-class women's rebellion against domesticity. Elizabeth Cady Stanton, for instance, invoked the "isolation of every human soul and the necessity of self-dependence"; she spoke of the female "birthright to self-sovereignty." "In discussing the rights of women," Stanton averred, "we are to consider, first, what belongs to her as an individual, in a world of her own, the arbiter of her own destiny, an imaginary Robinson Crusoe with her woman Friday on a solitary island." Such language was problematic at a time when the middle class resolutely denied the "self-sovereignty" of the rich and dreamed of "association" rather than solitude. Understanding the danger, younger activist women learned to talk less about individual rights and more about the maternal female role in making "the whole world Homelike." Nevertheless, the enemies of progressivism would exploit the persistence of individualism within the middle class.[69]

Despite their weaknesses, the progressives had important advantages. Especially in comparison with other classes, the middle class had a notable unity. Potential fault lines of gender and generation, race and religion, never split wide open. The rift between men and women was being healed. Despite the break with inherited Victorian values, the young were not notably bitter or antagonistic toward their elders. Obviously troubled themselves, middle-class parents probably did not make inviting targets. Further, the middle class was almost as overwhelmingly white and Protestant as the upper class. Middle-class African-Americans, Roman Catholics, and Jews, who could maintain a strong sense of connection to working-class brothers and sisters, were not very numerous. With their own separate Chautauquas and women's clubs, these minorities still had little influence on the middle class as a whole.[70]

The middle class also avoided occupational fissures. Clerks and other relatively low-paid white-collar workers might well have concluded they had more in common with the working class than with well-to-do professionals, bureaucrats, and store owners. In the 1880s, some retail clerks explored unionization and affiliation with the American Federation of Labor. But to nearly all members of the middle class, the distinction between manual and nonmanual labor remained vitally important. For many clerical and sales workers, their jobs represented upward mobility across a critical class divide. For many sons and daughters of struggling petty proprietors, clerical work was a preferable, still middle-class alternative to the increasing insecurity of small business. The middle class was not about to become "proletarianized."[71]

Similarly, the "new" middle class of managers, bureaucrats, and professionals and the "old" middle class of petty proprietors, despite differences in occupation, shared important bonds. Shopkeepers and white-collar workers alike found themselves caught up in the conflict of labor and capital. Clerks, managers, and engineers may have found opportunity in the large-scale corporation, but these members of the middle class, like small-business men, knew they all had far fewer resources than the upper ten. And whether their occupations were "new" or "old," the great majority of the middle class shared Victorian origins, domestic culture, gender roles, attitudes toward work and pleasure, and hostility toward individualism. Social scientists and historians have made much of the differences between "new" and "old," but, at least at the turn of the century, there was one middle class, not two.[72]

In addition to social and occupational unity, the middle class also enjoyed real ideological advantages. More than any other major group in American society, the progressives had a clear and aggressive agenda by the end of the 1890s. The upper ten had helped to unleash powerful economic changes across the country, but the wealthy had trouble articulating a set of ideals for themselves, much less for society. Workers offered a clear cultural alternative to Victorianism, but the working class was internally divided, split by conflicting mutualisms and threatened by the defection of the young. Farmers, their power waning for decades, were caught between individualism and mutualism. The middle class, in contrast, had responded to a period of internal and external crisis with a dynamic set of new ideas and a driving desire to reform society. The progressive cause may have suffered because those ideas did not necessarily translate directly into specific policies. But the progressives also benefited from the very breadth of such fundamental commitments as reworking domesticity, fostering association, and developing the power of the state. Since there were many ways to accomplish these ends, progressives could pursue their particular reforms without stepping on one another. Rather than turn into a nineteenth-century symphony orchestra, they became like a musical innovation of their own time, the jazz band, in which each instrumentalist improvised a unique melody on top of a shared set of chords. Some middle-class activists could focus on drinking and gambling, others on monopolies and railroad freight rates, others on child labor and juvenile justice, and still others on poverty and housing—and all would advance the progressive cause. Further, the progressives' fundamental approach, this powerful blend of reworked domesticity, restrained pleasure, antiindividualism, association, and state power, managed to seem rather reassuring: it was an ideology of the center, in a society seemingly torn between "two nations" or between individualism and socialism.

Despite the enormity of the undertaking, there were good reasons, then, for the progressives to begin their "great work of reconstruction" with optimism. Even William James, despite his contempt for the "middle-class paradise" of Chautauqua, thought it foreshadowed the future of the nation. The United States was caught up in "a social process which in the long run seems everywhere tending towards the Chautauquan ideals," James admitted dispiritedly. "The whole world . . . is . . . obeying more and more just those ideals that are sure to make of it in the end a mere Chautauqua Assembly on an enormous scale." Modest and restrained, Jane Addams would never allow herself to make such bold predictions. But other progressives were not so shy about the power and mission of the middle class. "If it were not for the restraining influence of the sober, level-headed middle classes,—the true police of the world," Dr. James Weir, Jr., insisted in 1894, "—civilization would be swept from the face of the globe, and men would become savages like the communal tribes of the Aleutian Islands." The reformer Henry

Demarest Lloyd expressed the progressive spirit of self-assurance in 1903, when he foresaw "the aggrandisement of the middle class" not only in America but all around the world. "The middle class," he prophesied, "is not to be exterminated, but is to absorb the other classes."[73] Lloyd perfectly captured the progressives' mission.

PART TWO

Progressive Battles

CHAPTER THREE

Transforming Americans

After breaking her engagement with Israel, the grocer, Rahel Golub was in poor health again. One day, as she lay weakly on the couch at home, she felt a hand touch her wrist. "It was a doctor's touch," Rahel recalled. "I opened my eyes and saw a woman, . . . sitting beside the couch. Neither in looks nor in dress had I ever seen any one like her in our neighbourhood. She was also beautiful and distinguished." The woman spoke: "How do you feel[?]" She smiled, Rahel noted, "but her eyes remained almost sad." Speaking German to Rahel's mother, the woman handed over a card and left. Rahel "spelled out the printed name on the card, Lillian D. Wald, 265 Henry Street."[1]

That touch began an effort to change Rahel Golub's life. Like Jane Addams in Chicago, Lillian Wald was the founder of a settlement house—the Nurses' or Henry Street Settlement in lower Manhattan. She too believed in the necessity of "association," of stepping across the social boundaries of industrial America. Determined to help Rahel, Wald urged the Golubs to let their daughter go to Presbyterian Hospital. Now Rahel, like Wald, had to cross the boundary lines of New York City. It was a terrifying prospect; hospitals were a place to die, a place to be feared. And Presbyterian Hospital seemed far away from the self-contained neighborhood of Cherry Street. But Rahel agreed to go. "Late one afternoon then, with a change of clothing in a little bundle under my arm and a letter from Miss

Wald in my hand, I started out for the part of the city we called 'uptown,' as strange to me as if it were in a different country," she would recall. "And now a great experience was to be mine. Never again could I look upon the life I was leaving in the same way, for I was to have a glimpse into a different world." As Rahel rode on the streetcars, it was as if she had never been in the United States at all. "Although almost five years had passed since I had started for America," she said, "it was only now that I caught a glimpse of it."[2]

Because of Lillian Wald and other social workers, Rahel caught many more glimpses of the United States in the next few years. She was in and out of the hospital. She went to programs at the Nurses' Settlement. She stayed at White Birch Farm—"a summer house run for needy city children" in the country outside New York City. In all these places, she had new experiences. In the hospital, she ate "trafe . . . cattle [that] had not been killed in accordance with Jewish law." She met what she called "Americans"—native-born, white, middle- and upper-class men and women. There were the doctors and nurses. "They looked so different from us, the people I had been accustomed to see all my life," Rahel observed. "They were tall, healthy men and women, so well dressed with such fine quiet manners!" There were Protestant missionaries: one praised Judaism; another tried to convert Rahel to Christianity. There were other visitors whose mission was harder to understand: the "charming young girl," back from college, who asked "eager questions"; the "daughter of one of the biggest millionaires in the United States"; and the "beautiful woman" who "wore a bunch of violets tied with a purple cord" that made "the air about my bed . . . sweet." "I had never dreamed there was anything like her beauty," Rahel would recall, "her blue-black hair, her blue-gray eyes, her teeth, her smile." Rahel, "so ignorant of life," nevertheless "understood at once, somehow, that much of this woman's beauty was due to the care she had received all her life, and her mother before her, and perhaps even her grand mother." But Rahel could not understand why she had all these visitors. "I did not know," she wrote, "that the part of the city where I lived was called the East Side, or the Slums, or the Ghetto, and that the face of the East Side, or the Slums, or the Ghetto was still new and a curiosity to the people in this part of the city, a sight to cheer any unhappy person." Of course Rahel was unhappy, too; and these educated, well-to-do women were "new and a curiosity" for her as well. She became friends with some of them. "They and their lives still fascinated me," Rahel admitted.[3]

All these contacts were profoundly unsettling. Rahel left Presbyterian Hospital with "a feeling of dread." Having had "a glimpse of the New World, a revolution took place in my whole being," she confessed. "I was filled with a desire to get away from the old order of things. And I went groping about blindly, stumbling, suffering and making others suffer." Rahel felt much the same when she came back from White Birch Farm. "It was hard to get used to the old life again when I came home," she said. "It was all stranger than ever, the home, my people; their ways."[4]

Rahel Golub's encounter with "uptown" was one episode in the vast struggle over how men, women, and children should live their lives in the twentieth century. This struggle reflected the many differences over fundamental values, over the nature of the individual, the family, gender roles, work, and pleasure, that divided Americans. The conflict embroiled the whole nation—town and countryside as well as metropolis, south and west as well as north. It was not one battle but many battles, fought by different people with different beliefs and interests. But the progressives, driven by their project to transform relations between men and women, end class conflict, and make the nation more middle-class, were almost always in the thick of the fighting.

The progressives' agenda required an impressive host of reforms. To reshape adult behavior, middle-class reformers fought to ban liquor, eradicate prostitution, and limit divorce. To change other classes, the reformers attacked the life-style and fortunes of the upper ten, tried to improve the living conditions of workers, and attempted to modernize the agrarian way of life. To ensure a better future, progressives sought to reconstruct childhood. Together, these campaigns added up to a bold effort to remake Americans, to create new people living by new codes of conduct. Just as the middle class itself had been remade, now other classes would be remade as well.

This effort was fundamental to progressivism. Traditionally, the struggle to control big business organizations has been seen as the quintessential progressive crusade. Almost inevitably requiring the authority of the federal government, the battle against corporate power thrust a flamboyant president to the fore and produced landmark national legislation. Yet, intense and substantial as it was, the legislative and political struggle constituted only one phase of the effort to reform big business, and certainly not the entirety of progressivism. Progressives feared the upper ten not only for its management of corporations. "The plutocracy in politics, the plutocracy in business, the plutocracy in society, the plutocracy in the home—in its own homes—that is our 'peril,'" insisted the best-selling author David Graham Phillips. Progressives aimed at people more than institutions; they wanted to change big-business men as well as big businesses. "It is idle to imagine that changes in our governmental machinery, or in the organization of our industries will bring us peace . . . ," Washington Gladden observed; "the trouble lies deeper, in our primary conceptions. What we have got to have . . . is a different kind of men and women. . . ." Walter Rauschenbusch, so strongly influenced by socialism, put more faith in state activism than did Gladden. But Rauschenbusch, too, emphasized the fundamental importance of transforming individual human beings. "The greatest contribution which any man can make to the social movement is the contribution of a regenerated personality . . . ," Rauschenbusch maintained. "Such a man will in some measure incarnate the principles of a higher social order in his attitude to all questions and in all his relations to men, and will be a well-spring of regenerating influences." Even Theodore Roosevelt, the president who did so much to focus attention on the struggle over big business, shared this fundamental progressive concern with the reform of individuals. "It is only by a slow and patient inward transformation such as . . . laws aid in bringing about that men are really helped upward in their struggle for a higher and a fuller life," Roosevelt maintained. More than anything else, progressivism, "the great work of reconstruction," was the attempt to reconstruct the individual human being.[5]

The various campaigns to reshape values and behavior sprang from an optimistic belief that heredity's power was not absolute, that people were malleable. Progressivism drew strength from a powerful current of environmentalist thought flowing through turn-of-the-century America. A broad range of social scientists argued that human beings responded to their environment: people changed when their surroundings changed. "The striking aspect of the recent development of thought is the changing concept concerning the part heredity plays in life," economist Simon N. Patten summarized. "[R]ecent discoveries in biology . . . are establishing a new equilibrium between natural or inherited qualities and those acquired after birth. Many qualities are inherited, but the number is smaller than it was thought to be, and many of them may be readily suppressed by the action of environment in which men live." Reformers, among them settlement workers such as Jane Addams and preachers of the Social Gospel such as Josiah Strong, eagerly grasped the implications for the middle-class project. "It is found," observed Strong, "that there is an intimate relation between a bad environment and bad habits; that bad sanitation has not a little to do with bad morals; that bad ventilation and bad cooking are responsible for much drunkenness." Mainstream politicians such as Robert La Follette of Wisconsin accepted the environmental argument as well. As an aggressive county prosecutor in the 1880s, the future progressive leader held criminals individually responsible for their crimes. By the 1900s, La Follette thought differently: "I see that the individual criminal is not always wholly to blame; that many crimes grow directly out of the sins and injustices of society." Presumably, then, progressives could stop crime by stopping sins and injustices; they could end drunkenness by improving ventilation and cooking; they could reshape character by reshaping the environment. Armed with what Patten called "man's power over heredity," the progressives set out confidently on their many campaigns.[6]

Not all the contact across social boundary lines was as gentle as the touch of Lillian Wald. On the morning of June 6, 1900, in the town of Medicine Lodge in southwestern Kansas, Carrie Nation gathered up brickbats and bottles of Schlitz-Malt. With these "smashers" loaded in her buggy, she drove, nervous and praying, to the nearby town of Kiowa. A respectable Christian woman in her sixties, known as Mother Nation for her compassion, Carrie Nation was angry nevertheless. Saloons had been outlawed in Kansas since the passage of an amendment to the state constitution in 1880. But the "joints" and "dives" still flourished with the connivance of police and local government. Carrie Nation was going to Kiowa to do something about that. The next morning, armed with the brickbats and bottles, she strode into Mr. Dobson's saloon. "I don't want to strike you," she told the proprietor, "but I am going to break up this den of vice." She hurled her "smashers" at Dobson's liquor bottles; she hurled some more at the mirror behind his bar. "Mr. Dobson . . . ," she noted with satisfaction, "jumped into a corner, seemed very much terrified." Leaving Dobson behind, Carrie Nation attacked three more saloons that morning in Kiowa. Passersby, she observed, "seemed to look puzzled." Dive owners, the town marshal, and the mayor confronted her. But these men were puzzled, too. When they decided not to arrest Nation, she stood in her buggy and lifted her hands to the sky. "Peace on earth," she called to the people of Kiowa as she rode out of town, "good will to men."[7]

It was a stunning episode. In unladylike fashion, Carrie Nation had crossed the boundary between respectable women's place and men's public preserve. This unusual act was the work of an unusual woman who had lived a particularly difficult life. From Kentucky to Missouri, to Texas, and then, in the 1890s, to Kansas, Carrie Nation had faced poor health, unhappy marriages, straitened circumstances, and the sad illnesses of her daughter. Forced to support herself and her family, Nation had taught school and run a hotel. Her first husband had been an alcoholic; her second husband, a failed lawyer and minister, had "deceived" her "in so many things." Driven by her powerful faith, Nation had served as a jail evangelist for the WCTU—and "learned," she said, "that almost everyone who was in jail was directly or indirectly there from the influence of intoxicating drinks." So she had become determined to confront the saloon, the cause of so much misfortune. In 1899, she had gone into Mort Strong's joint and forced him to close. Carrie Nation had found the calling that would take her to Kiowa in 1900.[8]

Her confrontation with the saloon did not end there. Nearly seven months later, only days after Christmas, she went to Wichita with "a rod of iron" in her valise. There she smashed the bar in the Carey Hotel, the "finest" in town. This time there was no puzzlement: she was arrested, tried, found guilty of "malicious mischief," and packed off to jail. Her sanity questioned, Nation had to remain there for nearly a month before getting out. Undaunted, she continued her confrontation with the saloon: in Enterprise, a cow town, people threw rotten eggs, beat her, kicked her, and tore her hair; in Topeka, the state capital, she used a hatchet to attack the dives, raised her own "army" of "Home Defenders," and, predictably, went to jail more than once.[9]

Nation's violent encounter with the saloon had many consequences. Across Kansas, people attacked more than a hundred dives. At Winfield, the battle to close the saloons led to mass meetings, the deployment of cannon, and a raid against prohibitionist women and children huddled for protection in a church. A column of ministers, businessmen, college students, and women suffered injuries but managed to reduce one of the town's joints to nothing "except the smell." These conflicts persuaded officials to enforce prohibition more seriously in the state of Kansas. There were consequences for Carrie Nation, too. Although her second husband divorced her, she felt happy for the first time in memory. "I have never had so light a heart or felt so well satisfied," she said, "as since I smashed those murder mills." Famous across the United States, she looked beyond Kansas. By altering the spelling of "Carrie" and using her middle initial, she turned her name into an advertisement of her new mission—"Carry A. Nation." To fulfill that mission, she went on to the lecture circuit. In the 1900s, Nation passed out miniature hatchets and got herself arrested from Coney Island to Los Angeles. She had become a spectacle of contradictory images, of violence and compassion, of Christian humility and blatant self-advertisement.[10]

An odd figure, Carry A. Nation was nevertheless quite representative. Her "smashings" laid bare much of the logic and passion that spurred the progressive crusades to reshape adult behavior. Nation's action may have been extreme, but the things that drove it were typically progressive: changing middle-class values and a profound sense of urgency. Like the scourge of the male-dominated saloon, the progressives wanted to regulate pleasure and alter masculine behavior. Like the traveling lecturer and professional reformer, the progressives accepted a new role for women outside traditional domesticity. Like the general of the Home Defenders, the progressives tended to wrap their worries about a host of problems in a consuming fear for the fate of the home. They went into battle waving the flag of domesticity. Fittingly, Rahel Golub's experience with Lillian Wald began at home, because for the middle class, it was fundamentally the home that was at issue. This was a struggle, as a book by reformer Jacob Riis put it, over *The Peril and the Preservation of the Home.* "[B]rethren, upon the home rests our moral character; our civic and political liberties are grounded there; virtue, manhood, citizenship grow there," Riis declared. "For American citizenship in the long run will be, *must be,* what the American home is." And the home, as Carry Nation felt acutely, seemed to be disappearing. "[T]here is," said Josiah Strong, "an increasing population, which, though by no means shelterless, is really homeless. . . ."[11]

Carry Nation also displayed a typically middle-class religious fervor and an insistence on action. Like the Christian who prayed on the road to Kiowa, the progressives were inspired by an emotional, evangelical Protestantism. Like the partisan of the brickbat and hatchet, they had lost faith in attempts to convert individuals by exhortation alone. "Moral suasion!" Nation snorted. "If there's anything that's weak and worse than useless it's this moral suasion. I despise it. These hell traps of Kansas have fattened for twenty years on moral suasion." Many reformers agreed. In the new century, they were increasingly interested in compelling, not cajoling, people to change and behave.[12]

Nation's obsession with the saloon was typical as well. Early-twentieth-century battles over adult behavior touched on a number of suspect practices—card playing, gambling, horse racing, Sabbath breaking, pornography, dance halls, contraception. But the problem of alcohol outweighed all these concerns in the 1900s. Liquor, said the moderator of the Presbyterian General Assembly, was "the open sore of this land . . . the most fiendish, corrupt and hell-soaked institution that ever crawled out of the slime of the eternal pit." Many people believed that alcohol contributed to a second major problem—prostitution. Drink appeared to be a spur to illicit sex; the saloon was a venue for harlots. Together, liquor and prostitution, the saloon and the brothel, seemed to be the very heart of "vice" in the United States. A third issue, divorce, also commanded major attention. For many Americans, the legal dissolution of marriage posed an obvious mortal threat to the home. In large part, then, the attempt to reshape adult behavior centered above all on campaigns to remove the trinity of temptations—drink, prostitution, and divorce—from the social environment.[13]

This was not an irrational crusade against a purely imaginary enemy. Alcohol, prostitution, and divorce loomed large in turn-of-the-century America. After some success in the 1880s, the war on drink had gone badly in the 1890s. Like Kansas, the handful of states with legal prohibition saw the law defied. As the new century began, the repeal of prohibition in Vermont and New Hampshire left only Kansas, Maine, and North Dakota with statewide bans on drink. In addition, the per capita consumption of beer and hard liquor was on the rise. Americans had drunk 590 million gallons of beer and other malt liquor in 1885; in 1900, the figure reached 1.2 billion gallons. The saloon, the public symbol of alcohol, was more visible than ever.

In the twenty years from 1880 to 1900, the number of retail liquor establishments had nearly doubled, from 150,000 to 250,000.[14]

The extent of prostitution was harder to judge, but the "social evil," as it was called in polite company, also seemed to be spreading. Despite vice crusades in the late nineteenth century, prostitution had become quite open, above all in urban "vice" or "red light" districts across the country—the Tenderloin in Manhattan, Hooker's Division in Washington, Gayosa Street in Memphis, the Levee in Chicago, Storyville in New Orleans, the Barbary Coast in San Francisco. As medical science revealed the consequences of venereal disease, prostitution became a much more urgent issue in the early 1900s. Contemplating the horrors of congenital and tertiary syphilis, the specter of birth defects, paralysis, and insanity, many Americans feared for the home. Venereal diseases, declared a leading expert, Dr. Prince Morrow, in 1908, "are directly antagonistic to all that the family stands for as a social institution. . . ." And prostitution, people believed, was chiefly responsible for the spread of these diseases and therefore for their introduction into innocent homes.[15]

Divorce, too, was still on the increase. In the 1890s, the middle class had read lurid tales about the "divorce mills" of the West. Supposedly, such places as Sioux Falls, South Dakota, Fargo, North Dakota, and Guthrie, Oklahoma, attracted married men and women who, after a short period of residence, received quick and easy "migratory" divorces. Progressives had noticed also that states were accepting more grounds for divorce; in particular, "cruelty," expansively defined, had become a popular justification for marital dissolution. And some religious denominations, notably Episcopalians, seemed more willing to sanction divorce. As a result, the divorce rate had risen from 3.0 divorces per thousand marriages in 1890 to 4.0 per thousand in 1900. At the start of the new century, the United States had the highest rate of legal marital dissolution in the world.[16]

Although the increase of drink, prostitution, and divorce troubled a range of Americans, the crusades against these "vices" appealed more to the middle class than to others. Hoping to promote progressive values and practices, ministers, settlement workers, white-collar workers, and small-business men played prominent roles in the campaigns to reshape adult behavior.[17] Reformers saw in vice the loss of self-control and the celebration of selfishness. Divorce represented, as Anna B. Rogers put it in 1909, "the latter-day cult of individualism; the worship of the brazen calf of Self." Although progressives regretted the consequences of such individualism for the drunkard, the divorcée, and the prostitute, now more than ever, the middle class deplored the impact of vice on innocent people. "The drunkard and the drunkard's interests are not the chief consideration," observed a Southerner in 1908, "though these are not lost sight of. It is the drinker as a husband, a father, a voter, a worker, and a citizen—the man as a social factor, who is being considered."[18]

As this identification of drunkenness with masculinity suggests, the attempts to regulate adult behavior also sprang from the progressive concern about the relationship between the sexes. To vice reformers, prostitution, alcohol, and other vices grew from male desire and victimized women above all. At the Carey Hotel in Wichita, Carry Nation attacked an oil painting of a nude woman, a typical bar decoration of the period. "It is very significant that the pictures of naked women are in saloons," she explained. "Women are stripped of everything by them. Her husband is torn from her, she is robbed of her sons, her home, her food and her virtue, and then they strip her clothes off and hang her up bare in these dens of robbery and murder. Well does a saloon make a woman bare of all things!" Some middle-class men also believed that vice sprang from what a professor at Oberlin College called "the sinister hypocrisy of men in their relations to women." "Observation shows that men are the responsible authors of these social crimes—women the victims," said Prince Morrow. "The root of the evil is grounded in the double standard of morality." Not surprisingly, then, women played an especially prominent part in the struggle to reform adult behavior. The crusades against vice became in large part an assertion of female authority, one more element of the emerging treaty between middle-class men and women. Carry Nation decried "the idea that woman is a toy, pretty, doll, with no will power of her own, only a parrot, a parasite of a man." Standing outside the joints barricaded against her on lower Kansas Avenue in Topeka, she became a dominating mother figure for the infantilized men inside: "Aren't you going to let your mother in, boys?" she called with a sneer. "She wants to talk to you."[19]

The campaigns against drink, prostitution, and divorce found less support among farmers and still less among urban workers and the upper class. None of these groups fully embraced middle-class values; none unequivocally welcomed government interference in private life. For all the drudgery in the lives of working-class and agrarian women, they never revealed the intense discontent that spurred so many middle-class women to demand changes in male behavior, including drinking. Given their views on pleasure, many agrarian men and women did strongly advocate prohibition or temperance. And, to be sure, there were some workers, like the Protestant Swedes of Worcester, Massachusetts, who supported prohibition as well. But there were more workers who believed in the freedom to drink and who defended their saloons against outside interference. The controversies over prostitution and divorce seemed to have still less impact on agrarian and working-class communities. Prostitutes came primarily from the working class; vice districts flourished, thanks to the police, in poor urban neighborhoods. Yet, workers did not conspicuously lead or resist the attack on the "social evil." Many workers, of course, were Roman Catholics, whose church condemned divorce, but the divorce crusade appeared not to arouse much support among the working class. For workers and farmers alike, divorce was a remote phenomenon, a luxury of the well-to-do.

Some members of the upper ten did play prominent roles in the campaigns to regulate behavior. There were still big-business men who wanted to encourage more temperance and self-discipline in the workforce. But some of the wealthy made a great deal of money by financing breweries and distilleries and by renting rooms to brothels and saloons. Rich women, increasingly well educated, certainly did share some of the unhappiness of middle-class women. Yet, the wives and daughters of the upper class, whatever they thought privately of male dissipation, represented and generally enjoyed a culture built on pleasure, on public drinking and easy access to divorce.[20]

The crusades against drink, prostitution, and divorce would be contested, then. But reformers pushed their causes aggressively. Combining the old Protestant fervor with businesslike efficiency, prohibitionists developed an especially strong network of pressure groups. The small Prohibition political party, formed after the Civil War, gave way to more effective organizations. The potent WCTU, to which Carry Nation belonged, continued to press legislatures for better liquor laws and "scientific temperance instruction" in the schools. The Anti-Saloon League, which began in Ohio in the 1880s, emerged as the great power of the prohibition crusade in the

1900s. Rooted in the Protestant churches, the league envisioned nationwide prohibition. But rather than condemn all drinking, the group wisely focused attention on the saloon, the ultimate symbol of public vice. In the short run, the league also wisely concentrated on campaigns for local option, the right of individual communities to choose whether to close their saloons.[21]

Well organized, the prohibitionists nevertheless confronted significant obstacles. The liquor interests were just as well organized; many people, workers in particular, resented the assault on the saloon; and the authorities, bribed or simply sensitive to public opinion, did not always enforce the laws. In Kansas, things soon went back to normal after Carry Nation's campaign against the dives. Around the country, prohibitionists pressed for local option. Failing that, they harassed the saloons with a phalanx of laws restricting selling hours, forcing Sunday closings, banning side and rear entrances, raising license fees, and mandating one- and two-mile "dry zones" around schools, military bases, and crossroads.[22]

It was hard going. Even politicians sympathetic to progressivism recoiled from so controversial an issue. With so many evangelical Protestants in their ranks, the Republican Party came under heavy pressure to back prohibition. But Republican leaders feared alienating the rest of the electorate. The politicians' caution in the face of a divided country was most apparent at the highest level of government. The three presidents of the Progressive Era, Theodore Roosevelt, William Howard Taft, and Woodrow Wilson, all sought middle-class support. But all three did their best to avoid taking a public stand on liquor. Believing "such hideous misery does come from drink," Theodore Roosevelt said privately that "I cordially sympathize with any successful effort to do away with it or minimize its effects." McKinley's successor favored local option but opposed broader prohibition laws as unenforceable. It was a sensible—and convenient—position for a national leader. Mostly, Roosevelt wished the whole matter would go away. "My experience with prohibitionists . . . is," he confided, "that the best way to deal with them is to ignore them."[23]

During the Progressive Era, however, it became harder and harder to do that. The prohibitionists began to demonstrate real political power. In 1905, the Republican governor of Ohio, opposed by the Anti-Saloon League, lost his bid for reelection. Around the country, the drive for local option went forward. In the South, an alliance of rural evangelicals and the middle class spurred campaigns for statewide prohibition. In 1907, Georgia and Alabama went dry. Oklahoma, with the help of Carry Nation, entered the union as a dry state that year. Mississippi and North Carolina adopted prohibition in 1908; Tennessee followed the next year. The South was, a writer declared, "well-nigh puritanized." Kansas also went emphatically dry in 1909, with even a ban on the sale of liquor in drugstores, a longtime loophole in prohibition. By then, 90 of Connecticut's 168 towns had gone dry. In Illinois, over a thousand townships had banned the saloon. Responding to the increasing power of the prohibitionists in 1913, Congress passed the Webb bill, which banned the shipment of liquor into dry states. Taft vetoed the measure, but Congress voted to override the President.[24]

Like the campaign against drink, the prostitution crusade also surged ahead in the 1900s. Never as imposing as the Anti-Saloon League, the American Purity Alliance and the Society for the Prevention of Crime, founded in the late nineteenth century, organized against the "social evil." So did a newer organization under the leadership of Prince Morrow, the American Society of Sanitary and Moral Prophylaxis, which urged men to avoid sexual intercourse outside of marriage. But the most influential antiprostitution group was probably New York City's Committee of Fifteen, established by reformers, clergy, and wealthy men in 1900. The committee investigated prostitution and published the results as *The Social Evil* in 1902. In 1905, settlement workers and members of the Anti-Saloon League organized the Committee of Fourteen, which worked for better enforcement of New York City's vice laws. The two committees became a model for similar vice investigations in cities around the country.[25]

Nevertheless, the prostitution campaign did not make quite as much headway as the battle against the saloon. In one sense, that was surprising. Prostitution was far less controversial than alcohol; hardly any American thought of publicly justifying the "social evil." Theodore Roosevelt was much more willing to speak out against prostitution. And the federal government acted more quickly than it did on alcohol. By proclamation of the President, the United States joined an agreement of European countries promising cooperation to abolish the "White slave trade," the alleged transnational traffic in women. The federal immigration acts of 1903 and 1907 put penalties on the importation of women for purposes of prostitution. The latter act not only made alien prostitutes liable to deportation up to three years after entering the United States; the measure also made the importers and employers of alien prostitutes subject to fine and imprisonment. But that was too much for the Supreme Court, which ruled in *Keller v. United States* in 1909 that the provisions against importers and employers were an unconstitutional assumption of police powers reserved for the states.[26]

The prostitution campaign faced other, more serious obstacles. Like the liquor interests, prostitution had police and political connections. Moreover, the antiprostitution forces had unique difficulties. While prohibitionists could condemn all impulses to drink as morally wrong and biologically unnecessary, prostitution crusaders could not make similar claims about sexual appetites: marital intercourse was still legal and necessary for the continuation of the species. The unwillingness to deny at least male sexual urges may have contributed, in turn, to a noticeable reluctance to penalize the men who patronized prostitutes. Most important, perhaps, the prostitution crusaders confronted public and private reticence about sexual matters. As the use of the euphemism "the social evil" suggests, many Americans were still uncomfortable with the open discussion of sexuality. "[S]ocial sentiment," Prince Morrow observed in frustration, "has decreed that the 'holy silence' upon everything relating to sex or its diseases must not be broken." That reticence made the campaign against prostitution much more difficult.[27]

Nevertheless, the campaign made progress. Reformers won enactment of criminal statutes aimed at the pimps and brothel keepers who employed prostitutes. In Iowa in 1909, the legislature approved the Injunction and Abatement Act, an important innovation that allowed a permanent injunction against any brothel and an abatement closing the property for up to a year and permitting the sale of its contents. The law, a strong blow to landlords who rented to brothel keepers, appeared to be a promising means of wiping out red-light districts.[28]

As the prohibition and prostitution crusades grew stronger in the face of resistance, the divorce movement, in contrast, seemed to wane. Antidivorce crusaders never organized effectively. The leading divorce activist was Samuel W. Dike, a Congregational minister from Vermont who had lost his church in 1877 after refusing to preside at the wedding of a divorced parishioner. Inspired to make a study of divorce, Dike served as secretary of the New England Divorce Reform League, which evolved into the National

Divorce Reform League in the 1880s and then the National League for the Protection of the Family in the 1890s. Never very powerful, Dike's organization mainly collected statistics and lobbied Congress.[29]

Dike and other reformers did not expect to wipe out divorce completely; they wanted only to limit it. But even that goal eluded them. Much as drinkers evaded local option by going to another town or city, men and women seeking to dissolve marriages traveled to states where divorce was easier to obtain. Under public pressure, states with renowned "divorce mills" increased the period of residence required before a couple could obtain a divorce. South Dakota, for example, imposed a one-year residency requirement that went into effect in 1909. Despite these restrictions, migratory divorce continued. The solution, reformers believed, was uniform state divorce laws or even a national divorce statute. But it was impossible to persuade state legislatures to accept a uniform code. In fact, it was impossible for reformers even to agree on such a code themselves. Meeting in Washington in 1906, the National Conference on Uniform Divorce Law could not arrive at a binding list of grounds for divorces. Only Delaware, New Jersey, and Wisconsin followed the conference's recommendations.[30]

In light of these difficulties, reformers looked to the federal government. In 1906, Roosevelt warned against "dangerously lax and indifferently administered" state divorce laws and urged the federal collection of statistics on marriage and divorce. As a result, the Department of Commerce and Labor issued an extensive report two years later. But not much else happened in Washington. Observers believed that a national divorce law would be unconstitutional. And an amendment to the Constitution seemed unpopular and unlikely. Even Roosevelt, who advocated congressional authority over marriage, had to concede "how difficult it is to pass a constitutional amendment."[31]

The fundamental problem was that the divorce movement did not attract enough support. Not only did Dike and his colleagues fail to engage workers, farmers, and the rich; the antidivorce cause also failed to win over much of the middle class. In part, the arguments for the cause were often unappealing and ineffective. Instead of ending their marriages, unhappy couples should content themselves, a writer advised in 1904, with the "purging, purifying influence of suffering." The cause also suffered when social scientists argued that stricter laws would not necessarily decrease the divorce rate.

Above all, Dike and other reformers failed to convince middle-class women that divorce was as much a threat to them as the saloon and the brothel. For many wives, divorce offered the only refuge from male misbehavior. "Liberal divorce laws for oppressed wives," Elizabeth Cady Stanton had long maintained, "are what Canada was for Southern slaves." Progressive women were hardly enthusiastic about divorce, but they considered it preferable to the alternatives. "I do not favor divorce," said Carry Nation, "but it is better to separate, than bring up children of drunkards or licentious fathers." Some middle-class men felt the same way. "No one," said Prince Morrow, "can condemn a self-respecting woman for separating from a man who has dishonored her with a shameful disease."[32]

So the antidivorce movement stalled. Instead of falling, the divorce rate continued to rise. From 4.0 divorces per thousand marriages in 1900, the rate reached 4.5 per thousand in 1910. By then, divorce crusaders seemed to be losing heart. Even Samuel Dike agreed that "lax laws" had not caused the increase in divorce and that legal change would not likely bring much improvement. Going further, some social scientists suggested divorce was a good thing. To George Elliot Howard, historian and sociologist at the University of Chicago and perhaps the leading academic authority on divorce, the legal dissolution of marriage was a "remedy" rather than a "disease"; divorce was "a healing medicine for marital ills." Better education of young men and women before marriage, Howard contended, was more important than trying to ban divorce. Samuel Dike did not go that far, but he too began to feel that divorce reform might not be the answer to domestic problems. Instead he looked, in typical progressive fashion, to a broader transformation of the social environment. "The instructions of the church and the school, better industrial conditions and an improved social sentiment must be," Dike concluded, "our chief reliance for reform."[33]

These were not the only second thoughts about the crusades to reshape adult behavior. The prohibition and prostitution campaigns also raised troubling reflections. To some reformers, the repression of human instinct seemed an impossible, self-defeating enterprise; fundamental drives had to be acknowledged. Realizing saloons catered to more than the desire for liquor, the Boston cleric Raymond Calkins contended that prohibition would not work unless reformers found "substitutes for the saloon." Alcohol-free clubs and dance halls were needed to fulfill people's desire to meet and socialize; libraries and gymnasiums were needed to fulfill the desire for stimulation. In short, the transformation of individuals required a more sweeping transformation of their environment. Meanwhile, Jane Addams expressed another developing doubt about the campaigns against vice. "The love of pleasure will not be denied . . . ," she declared. Accordingly, repression was ineffective and perhaps even counterproductive. "In failing to diffuse and utilize this fundamental instinct of sex through the imagination," Addams explained, "we not only inadvertently foster vice and enervation, but we throw away one of the most precious implements for ministering to life's highest needs." This would not be the last time that the middle-class ambivalence about pleasure made progressives hesitate.[34]

The campaigns against drink and prostitution raised another troubling concern. Some progressives recognized that vice was at least partly the product of social class. Extremes of income seemed particularly to sustain the saloon and the brothel. The Social Gospel leader Washington Gladden traced prostitution in part to middle- and upper-class affluence. "Young men say that they will not marry until they are able to support a wife in good style," Gladden observed, "and as the wealth of the land increases and their neighbors live more and more luxuriously, the phrase 'in good style' is constantly undergoing changes of meaning. Young women become accustomed in their parental homes to a certain amount of comfort and of leisure, and they do not relish the thought of beginning to live more plainly and more laboriously in a home of their own." When these people postponed marriage, Gladden affirmed, "one of the inevitable consequences is the increase of social immorality": young men, single for too long, would seek sexual satisfaction with prostitutes. The attack on the brothel, then, might not get at the real problem that threatened the home. "I do not believe that there is any remedy for this social disease but the restoration of a more wholesome sentiment concerning this whole subject of family life," Gladden concluded. "The morality of what we call our respectable classes needs toning up all along this line."[35]

More commonly, progressives recognized that poverty and economic constraint led to vice. Before the turn of the century, Frances Willard of the WCTU had already presented drunkenness as the result of economic hardship. Simon Patten offered the same conclusion in 1907. "Drinking and the new sedative pleasures of smoking and saloon card-games are," he wrote, "the vices of a faulty economic system. . . ."[36] The crusade against the brothel led to similar reflections. By the early twentieth century, most reformers no longer believed that women turned to prostitution because they were innately immoral. To some observers, it was plain that inadequate incomes, among other circumstances, led young working-class women to become prostitutes. In the short run at least they could make a better living from the "social evil" than from the low-paying, legal jobs typically open to them. Economic need, it seemed, produced prostitution. "The one most effective way to lessen the social evil . . . ," said Anna Garlin Spencer of New York, "would be to make every young girl self-supporting with a living wage."[37]

Even as progressives continued their campaigns against vice, not a few of them understood that the transformation of adults required more than attacks on the saloon, the brothel, or the divorce mill. To preserve and perfect the home, reformers had to confront the economic environment as well. They would have to address the particular needs and flaws of the different classes.

The effort to deal with the economic environment of the home underscored the essentially middle-class character of the movement to remake Americans. Progressives seldom suggested that middle-class status itself was problematic. Instead, the problems belonged to the other classes—wealthy, workers, and farmers. Progressives believed that the rich and workers led especially troubled domestic lives. "In the city," Josiah Strong observed, "the home is disappearing at both social extremes." "The American family is out of gear in two strata, in both of which pretty much everything else is out of gear," said sociologist Albion Small. "On the one hand is the stratum of the over-wealthed, over-leisured, over-stimulated, under-worked, under-controlled. . . . Only miracles could save this stratum from rot." Small found conditions little better among workers. "On the other hand," he continued, "is the stratum of the over-worked, under-fed, under-housed, under-clothed, under-hygiened, physically and morally, under-leisured, under-stimulated except by the elemental desires. Nothing in their lot is right."[38]

The transformation of the rich was no easy matter. Progressives could not very well seek "association" with the upper class by starting settlement houses on Fifth Avenue. Lillian Wald could travel to Cherry Street and straightforwardly offer to help a working-class girl like Rahel Golub; but Wald could not knock on the door of a Fifth Avenue mansion and make the same offer to help the household's debutante. Instead, progressives most often had to wait for the wealthy to come to them. Some did. In Chicago, the heiress Louise de Koven Bowen, active in charity work, heard Jane Addams compare George Pullman to King Lear in a speech. Bowen visited Hull-House, then contributed some money, and eventually accepted Addams's artful invitation to join the settlement's Women's Club. Drawn ever more deeply into the affairs of Hull-House, Bowen began to change and accept the importance of association. "To come in contact constantly with the people of that neighborhood certainly gave one a new impression of life in a great city," Bowen wrote, "and I began to feel that what was needed more than anything was an acquaintance between the well-to-do and those less well off."[39]

Of course, most of the rich did not turn up at the doors of Hull-House or the Nurses' Settlement. The progressives could reach them, then, only through public exhortation and public policy. Throughout the 1900s, the middle class leveled trenchant fire at the upper-class world of highly publicized divorces, lavish parties, and extravagant expenditures. That world was explored with insight and subtlety in the novels of Edith Wharton and the sociology of Thorstein Veblen and Simon Patten. It was exposed with sensationalist caricature in the fiction and nonfiction of the popular David Graham Phillips. In *The Reign of Gilt,* a blistering nonfiction tirade published in 1905, Phillips surveyed the "mighty cataract of extravagant ostentation." The upper-class mansion was, he claimed, "a true palace—the dwelling-place, but in no sense the home, of people of great wealth." Family members, each wrapped up in "his or her separate social life," hardly ever met at meals. The millionaire's wife fought so hard at "prolonging youth" that "you would not suspect from her looks or her conversation that she is a mother." The family's college-educated son had inherited "his father's supreme contempt for the ordinary moral code." In all, Phillips concluded, it was "a sordid life."[40]

In their crusade against the life-style of the upper ten, the progressives had a potent ally in Theodore Roosevelt. As his handling of the liquor question underscored, Roosevelt was a politician, ready to disappoint the progressives, if necessary, in order to maintain his popularity and power. And the President, born to wealth in a Manhattan mansion in 1858 and graduated from Harvard College in 1880, was certainly an upper-class man. But Roosevelt, in the course of his remarkable life, had broken free from the conventions of the upper ten and repeatedly remade himself. His stunning résumé of vocations—naturalist, cowboy, author, hunter, state legislator, government bureaucrat, soldier, governor, and vice president—had awakened him to the diversity and division of turn-of-the-century America. Uncomfortably aware of the "very ugly manifestations of antipathy between class and class," Roosevelt wanted urgently to reform his own. A member of the cultured Faubourg-St. Germain set, proud of his Knickerbocker heritage, Roosevelt instinctively held back from the new money in big business and High Society. The namesake of a charismatic father renowned for devotion to charity and philanthropy, the President disdained mere moneymaking. And this impassioned advocate of the "strenuous life, the life of toil and effort," who turned himself from a "sickly," asthmatic boy into a tough, "rugged man," had only contempt for the life of the leisure class. "Too much cannot be said against the men of wealth who sacrifice everything to getting wealth," Roosevelt declared in the 1890s. "There is not in the world a more ignoble character than the mere money-getting American, insensible to every duty, regardless of every principle, bent only on amassing a fortune, and putting his fortune only to the basest uses—whether these uses be to speculate in stocks and wreck railroads himself, or to allow his son to lead a life of foolish and expensive idleness and gross debauchery, or to purchase some scoundrel of high social position, foreign or native, for his daughter."[41]

Many among the upper ten wanted to ignore the indictment leveled against them by Roosevelt and the progressives. Despite the example of the Bradley Martins, they could not learn to tone down their public behavior. In 1902, Charles M. Schwab, the president of United States Steel, made a well-publicized visit to the casinos of Monte Carlo. Back in the United States, lurid reports of gambling and debauchery earned him the private hostility of Andrew Carnegie and the public censure of *The New York Times.* J. P. Morgan came under pressure to remove the steel man from his post, but Schwab's behavior was hardly the sort of thing that offended the captain of American finance. Still, Schwab had to learn his lesson. Returning to New York, he visited Morgan's great house on Thirty-seventh Street. "I did indeed gamble at Monte Carlo," Schwab confessed, "but I didn't do it behind closed doors."

"That's what doors are for," Morgan shot back. It was good advice for the upper ten, but not enough of them took it. The bad publicity continued. In 1908, *The New York Times* still had to deplore "the frequent evidence of the lack of discipline and respect for moral conventions among very rich Americans. The disregard of ordinary prudence in the conduct of their domestic relations, the willful neglect of the proprieties, among rich people . . . tend to increase the volubility of the agitators against existing social conditions." Certain that "we have reached something like a social crisis in the United States," the paper lashed out at the wealthy. "Within a year we have had far too many marital scandals, and other results of moral turpitude in our 'high life'—that is to say, among the rich Americans—and there is not enough intellectual force, artistic appreciation, or public spirit among people of that quality to compensate the country for the bad influence of their misdeeds."[42]

The rhetoric was all well enough. But translating the critique of the upper ten into results proved difficult, as the controversy over "race suicide" made clear. Naturally, Theodore Roosevelt took center stage in this debate about the falling birthrate among the well-to-do. "Surely it should need no demonstration," he told Congress in 1906, "that willful sterility is, from the standpoint of the nation, from the standpoint of the human race, the one sin for which the penalty is national death; a sin for which there is no atonement; a sin which is the more dreadful exactly in proportion as the men and women guilty thereof are in other respects, in character, and bodily and mental power, those whom for the sake of the State it would be well to see the fathers and mothers of many healthy children, well brought up in homes made happy by their presence." Rather than settle the issue, Roosevelt's statement provoked a round of finger-pointing. Some observers blamed selfish, college-educated women for the small families of the well-to-do; educated women refused to take the blame. "Men are more responsible than women for the decline in the birth-rate," insisted Marion Talbot, the home economist. "[Q]uite as many American homes are suffering from the incapacity of husbands and fathers to contribute their share to family life as from the attempt of wives and mothers to develop their individuality." None of this compelled the men and women of the upper class to become parents.[43]

Even as they tried to shame the rich into behaving themselves and having more children, the progressives used their remaining weapon: public policy. If wealth made the upper ten behave so poorly, then perhaps government should take some of that wealth away. Public support for taxes on huge incomes and inherited fortunes had been growing for some time. In the 1890s, fifteen states instituted taxes on large inheritances; more than forty states had inheritance taxes in place in the 1910s. The federal government itself adopted a temporary inheritance tax to help pay for the Spanish-American War. In 1894, Congress included a 2 percent tax on annual incomes over $4,000 as part of a new tariff bill. When the Supreme Court declared the tax unconstitutional, sentiment built for a constitutional amendment authorizing an income tax. In his annual message to Congress in 1906, Roosevelt called for graduated taxes on incomes and inheritances. "The man of great wealth owes a peculiar obligation to the State, because he derives special advantages from the mere existence of government," the President maintained. "Not only should he recognize this obligation in the way he leads his daily life and in the way he earns and spends his money, but it should also be recognized by the way in which he pays for the protection the State gives him." Roosevelt particularly objected to the inheritance of great fortunes. In his annual message in 1906, he justified placing "a constantly increasing burden on the inheritance of those swollen fortunes which it is certainly of no benefit to this country to perpetuate." Bowing to public opinion, Congress approved an income tax amendment to the Constitution in 1909. Easily ratified by 1913, the Sixteenth Amendment paved the way for Congress to enact the next year a modest but path-breaking 1 percent tax on annual incomes from $4,000 to $20,000, with an additional surtax on larger incomes. In 1916, Congress raised the income tax rates and enacted the first permanent inheritance tax, which included a maximum levy of 10 percent on estates over $5 million. Over the long run of the twentieth century, federal income and inheritance taxes would pose a serious threat to the wealth of the upper ten. Over the short run of the 1910s, these measures powerfully revealed the depth of popular hostility toward the rich.[44]

The effect of taxation, condemnation, and association on the upper ten was difficult to assess. Certainly the wealthy did not become new people, with safely progressive values, in the 1900s and 1910s. Very few of the rich joined Andrew Carnegie in endorsing inheritance taxes. Hardly any of the rich could welcome the vituperative assault on their values and life-styles; but the upper ten surely felt the sting of the attack. "I remember, even in my own lifetime, a period when the people of this country looked up with admiration and respect to their wealthy classes," sighed Frederick Townsend Martin, brother of the exiled Bradley Martin, in 1911. "To-day how great the change! . . . America has learned to hate great wealth . . . public opinion is relentless." Frederick Townsend Martin and some of his colleagues did recognize the danger posed by progressivism. "I take it for granted that the wiping out of the idle rich is to be one of the first steps in a programme of national advancement . . . ," he said. "The idle rich are an obstacle in the way; therefore they must be eliminated or destroyed."[45]

Martin believed that many of his class were at least waking up to their predicament. But, as before, they did not agree on how to proceed. Carnegie, Rockefeller, and some others still relied on philanthropy to win over the public. Yet, some of the wealthy, including Martin, doubted the philanthropic strategy would work. Meanwhile, too many of the rich refused to accept reality. As Martin put it, "[S]till within the gates of gold there dwells a great host of people barely roused." Precisely because they had not become new people along progressive lines, the rich were fated for destruction, Martin concluded. "That grim truth is that we as a class are condemned to death," he lamented. "We have outlived our time." And only time would tell whether he was right.[46]

Reformers took a less fevered, more creative approach to the problems of the working class. From Jacob Riis's pioneering study of New York tenement life, *How the Other Half Lives*, published in 1890, to Robert Hunter's *Poverty*, published in 1904, to a host of surveys, studies, and magazine articles, the literature on the poor was far more compassionate than the writings about the upper ten. As in the vice crusades, the older emphasis on individuals' shortcomings had given way to a focus on the impact of environment. Reformers no longer quickly concluded that the poor were individually responsible for their plight. Simon Patten exemplified the new environmentalist understanding: the character flaws of the urban poor were, he wrote, "in reality a short-lived product of the unwholesome food, bad air, debilitating climate, and other preventable conditions that rob men of vigor and of forethought." Urban "segregation" exacerbated the problem, Patten believed. "The poorer the family the lower is the quarter in which it must live," he observed, "and the more enviable appears the fortune of the anti-social class, which has found a way to easy incomes, to irresponsible extra-marital relations, and to glittering unwholesome pleasures." Moreover, the rigors of city life overwhelmed working-class mutualism, the attempt of the poor to help one another. If the poor could not save themselves, progressives concluded, then it was up to compassionate outsiders to remake the working class.[47]

The first, crucial instruments of this effort were the settlement houses and church programs established in workers' neighborhoods. Settlements multiplied rapidly: there were only six in the early 1890s, over a hundred by 1900, and more than four hundred by 1910. Most numerous in the Northeast and the Midwest, the settlements covered urban America nevertheless—from Andover House in Boston, Union Settlement in Providence, and Greenwich House in New York, west to Kingsley House in Pittsburgh and Hull-House in Chicago, south to Neighborhood House in Louisville, Wesley House in Atlanta, and Kingsley House in New Orleans, and still farther west to College Settlement in Los Angeles. Like Hull-House, the settlements offered lectures, classes, plays, pageants, kindergarten, and child care. Like Hull-House, the settlements tried to respond flexibly to neighborhood needs. So Lillian Wald, a trained nurse concerned about children's health, found her way to Rahel Golub's home on Cherry Street.[48]

In addition to sponsoring some settlements, Protestant churches had their own programs in working-class communities. By the end of the late nineteenth century, the churches still employed a battery of tract societies, Sunday schools, revivals, settlements, and city missions to appeal to the urban poor. But the results were disappointing: the churches had not reached most nominally Protestant workers, let alone the entire working class. Organizations without direct denominational ties, such as the Young Men's Christian Association (YMCA) and the Salvation Army, fared better. The army, an English import, developed an especially effective program of soup kitchens, secondhand stores, and simple faith. At the start of the new century, many Protestants, especially advocates of the Social Gospel, felt a renewed commitment, as Washington Gladden expressed it, "to comprehend the full meaning of the Parable of the Lost Sheep, and to put forth the kind of effort in seeking and saving the lost which Jesus expects of his disciples." The "institutional church" movement, which had begun in New York City in the 1890s, seemed particularly promising. As Josiah Strong explained, the institutional church, much like a settlement, took on "educational, social, recreational, and charitable" functions. "It finds that the people living around it have in their homes no opportunity to take a bath; it therefore furnishes bathing facilities," Strong observed. "It sees that the people have little or no healthful social life; it accordingly opens attractive social rooms, and organizes clubs for men, women, boys, and girls. . . . They are ignorant of household economy; the church establishes its cooking-schools, its sewing-classes, and the like. In their home the people have few books and papers; in the church they find a free reading-room and library. The homes afford no opportunity for intellectual cultivation; the church opens evening schools and provides lecture courses." By the early 1900s, there were enough churches involved in the movement to maintain an Institutional Church League. In all, the YMCA, the Salvation Army, and the institutional churches, like the Social Gospel, reflected a "social" vision of Christianity. They understood that environmental factors shaped individuals, that material conditions influenced the human spirit. As Josiah Strong insisted, these organizations "recognize the whole man, body as well as soul."[49]

Along with Jane Addams, most progressive activists realized that they had to provide more than the programs of the settlements and the institutional churches. In addition to teaching and helping workers, reformers needed to reshape the material environment. The obvious place to start was the home itself. Beginning in the 1890s, the tenement house reform movement worked to improve the dwelling places of the urban poor. In New York City, Jacob Riis, Lawrence Veiller, and others were horrified by the squalor of working-class neighborhoods. Riis, a Danish immigrant and former police reporter, used pen and camera to dramatize, and even exaggerate, the overcrowding, darkness, and miserable sanitary facilities of the city's tenement buildings. The tenement, said Riis, was "a cancer . . . the enemy of the commonwealth." In 1900, Veiller, a former relief worker and city buildings official, helped persuade then-governor Theodore Roosevelt to support the creation of a Tenement House Commission. Named secretary of the commission, Veiller pushed the state legislature to enact a housing code that raised standards for light, ventilation, sanitation, and safety in existing and future tenements. As in the prostitution campaign, the New York experience became a model for the rest of the country. In Chicago in 1900, Jane Addams helped found the City Homes Association to investigate and publicize tenement conditions. As a result, the city accepted a tenement house ordinance the next year. Elsewhere, there were investigations, conferences, and legislation. But the laws had the usual loopholes, and city officials did not always enforce the laws anyway. Nevertheless, tenement house reform was under way nationwide.[50]

The shortcomings of the working-class dwelling made it all the more important that workers have access to public parks, baths, gymnasiums, swimming pools, and auditoriums. Settlement workers and other reformers campaigned for such facilities to help workers and to change them. There was no ambiguity on the last point. Bathhouses, insisted a New York State commission, had a "favorable effect . . . upon character." Parks, said a reformer, promoted "desirable types of humanity." As they transformed old institutions and established new ones, reformers began to talk ambitiously about city planning. Worried by urban overcrowding, Lillian Wald, Florence Kelley, and Mary Simkhovitch of Greenwich House joined together in 1907 to help launch the Committee on Congestion of Population in New York. This body, dedicated to the dream of a more controlled, regulated urban environment, in turn aided in the creation of the National Association for City Planning at Washington, D.C., in 1909.[51]

Certainly the progressives were taking tentative first steps on the road to the regulated utopia of *Looking Backward.* But we should not overestimate the middle-class commitment to crass manipulation and coercion in the first years of the twentieth century. The progressives had compassion for workers and at least some respect for their culture and values. In 1900, for instance, Jane Addams and Ellen Starr set up the Hull-House Labor Museum to preserve and commemorate immigrant handicrafts. Self-conscious about their relationship with the poor, some reformers set limits on their intrusion into working-class life. When Rahel Golub asked for a copy of the New Testament at the Nurses' Settlement, Lillian Wald's colleague, Mary Brewster, declined. "I am afraid . . . we can not give it to you," Brewster replied. "You see your father would think, 'True, the nurses have been kind to my daughter but they have led her away from our faith.' And that would never do for the Settlement. Do you see?"[52]

Still, the settlement workers and other reformers intended to change working-class life. Mary Brewster spoke out of self-interest as well as compassion; she wanted to preserve the settlement's influence on the neighborhood. She and her associates had a real impact. To be sure, many of their efforts were ineffective. Some were almost laughable: Rahel, barely able to read English, once sat through an absolutely incomprehensible lecture on Shakespeare at the Nurses' Settlement. But the reformers, often unintentionally and unknowingly, transformed working-class people like Rahel Golub. Sometimes the smallest acts of "association" had unforeseen consequences. When Mary Brewster declined to give Rahel a New Testament, the settlement worker handed the immigrant "a sweet love story" instead. Of course, the idea of choosing a mate on the basis of romantic love was about as inflammatory as Christianity in Cherry Street, as Rahel's rejection of Israel the grocer made clear. Along with the books, lectures, hospitals, and summer outings, Rahel observed middle-class values and living standards. That exposure began to tear her away from her own culture and her own people.[53]

Rahel understood what was happening to her. "I was hearing good English, I was reading and with the trait of my race for adaptability I was quickly learning the ways of this country," she related. "But at home and in the shop life became harder and harder." The apartment on Cherry Street became more inadequate than ever. "The rooms seemed smaller and dingier than they had been," Rahel reported. "In the evening the lamp burned more dimly. And there was a general look of hopelessness over everything." The gap between working-class and middle-class life depressed her: "I saw the years stretching ahead of me, always the same, and I wept bitterly. I had never been so aware of it all." Rahel did not get along with her parents. Her father did not care for her reading. When he found the word *Christ* in one of her books, he threw it out the window. For her part, Rahel no longer accepted her parents' authority. She and her father often refused to speak to each other. "My only thought now," she said, "was of myself and the whole world outside of home and Cherry Street."[54]

Work became intolerable as well. After discovering the fine manners of middle-class men at the hospital, the settlement, and the summer camp, she could not abide the behavior of working-class males in the tailor shops. "To the little insinuating jokes and stories I listened now, not with resignation as before but with anger," Rahel recalled. "'Why should this be? Why should they talk like that?' And I was filled with a blinding dislike for the whole class of tailors." At one shop, a male tailor "talked of the most intimate relations of married people in a way that made even the men exclaim and curse him while they laughed. We girls as usual sat with our heads hanging. . . . His eyes were on my face and they were hurting me." Furious, Rahel threw her work aside and denounced the men. "You have made life bitter for me," she wept. "I pray God that rather than that I should have to go into a tailor shop again I may meet my death on my way home." She quit her job that day.[55]

Rahel Golub could not endure such unhappiness forever. Gradually, she found some peace. Staying at White Birch Farm, Rahel realized, to her surprise, that she could not stop thinking about Cherry Street. Back in the city, she discovered, "I felt strangely glad to be home and share the good and the bad with my people." Rahel was happy again, but she was no longer the same person who had felt the touch of Lillian Wald. Rahel never again fit easily into the world of Cherry Street; but she did not fit easily into "uptown" either. Wald and the reformers had created a new person, but not necessarily another member of the middle class. "I was able to see that the Old World was not all dull and the new all glittering," Rahel concluded. "And then I was able to stand between the two, with a hand in each."[56]

Rahel Golub was unusual: most immigrant workers did not eventually publish a book about their experiences, and most did not have sustained exposure to reform in the early 1900s. The settlements and the institutional churches remained on the edges of working-class life. Typically, these institutions reached women and children more easily than proud men who held back from such seemingly feminized charity. "The social settlement here meant nothing to us men," said an immigrant. "We went there for an occasional shower, that was all." But clearly the reformers could stir some workers, especially those like Rahel Golub—curious, ambitious, young, and yearning for freedom. How many more Rahels were there? What would they become? There were no answers in the first decade of the twentieth century.[57]

Almost reluctantly, reformers began to turn their attention to farmers during the Roosevelt administration. The middle class, wrestling with the problems of urban vice and inequality, tended to romanticize rural America. "The ideal, always in my mind, is that of a man with his feet upon the soil and his children growing up there," said Jacob Riis. "So, it seems to me, we should have responsible citizenship by the surest road." But reformers slowly realized that the rural road was no longer so sure. In the 1900s, they discovered the relative decline of rural America, the increase of farm tenancy, and the flight from the land. To preserve and improve the rural "ideal," reformers launched the Country Life movement.[58]

The campaign to save rural America began in the cities, not on the land. The participants in the Country Life movement were mainly urban, middle-class activists, state and federal agricultural officials, and academics from land-grant colleges. The leaders were such men as Kenyon Butterfield, sociologist and president of the Massachusetts State College of Agriculture, and Liberty Hyde Bailey, writer, horticulturist, and dean of Cornell University's agricultural college. Butterfield, Bailey, and the rest had a high opinion of rural people. Indeed, Butterfield bestowed the highest accolade on the "frank, virile, direct, clean, independent" men and women of the countryside. "Farmers are essentially a middle class . . . ," he insisted. "In the country there is little of large wealth, luxury, and ease; little also of extreme poverty, reeking crime, unutterable filth, moral sewage."[59]

Farmers had not, however, kept up with the changes in middle-class culture. As the countryside lagged behind the city, farmers clung to their old individualism. Kenyon Butterfield deplored "the intense individualism of the country, and the lack of co-operative spirit" that threatened the rural family and its members. "There is neighborliness in the country," Butterfield allowed; "there is intense democracy; there is a high sense of individual responsibility; there is initiative; but this over-development of the individual results in anemic social life, which in turn reacts powerfully upon the general life of the family." Butterfield and other Country Life reformers did not attribute rural shortcomings to farmers' character flaws. Instead, the Country Life movement focused on the influence of the rural environment. "Perhaps the one great underlying social difficulty among American farmers," Butterfield declared, "is their comparatively isolated mode of life." Isolation encouraged individualism and discouraged cooperation and institutions. "[R]ural isolation is a real evil," Butterfield concluded. "Present-day living is so distinctively social, progress is so dependent upon social agencies, social development is so rapid, that if the farmer is to keep his status he must be fully in step with the rest of the army. He must secure the social view-point."[60]

That conclusion, with its echoes of Edward Bellamy and his utopian army, spurred the usual conferring, fact-finding, and organizing. Butterfield convened a conference on rural life at Michigan Agricultural College in 1902. Over the next several years, further conferences followed around the country.

Soon there were such organizations as the Rhode Island League for Rural Progress and the Pennsylvania Rural Progress Association. Inevitably, Theodore Roosevelt became interested in the issue. In 1908, Roosevelt appointed the Country Life Commission, chaired by Liberty Hyde Bailey, to report on rural conditions. The commission, which included Kenyon Butterfield, articulated the emerging consensus of reformers. In addition to improved farming methods, rural America needed telephones, better mail delivery, and better roads to diminish isolation. Rural women, beset by drudgery, needed more appliances, more help from family members, and more organizations. In general, farmers needed to trade their individualistic ways for organized cooperation. The countryside also needed better sanitation and health care, more active churches, and, to safeguard the future, better education. Eager to exchange the one-room school for larger, consolidated schools with better teachers, the Country Life reformers also wanted a curriculum that would ennoble agriculture and persuade youth to remain on the land.[61]

The Country Life Commission stimulated considerable interest. Rural organizations, such as village-improvement societies and "people's clubs," began to appear in the 1900s. But the Country Life movement seemed stronger in the Northeast than in the rest of rural America, and stronger among prosperous farmers than among the rest of the agrarian population. Rural people were not always receptive to an essentially urban, middle-class, Northeastern crusade to remake their lives. Farmers wanted paved, macadam roads, but they resisted paying higher taxes for the benefit of urban cyclists and drivers, and yielding their independence to government. "The tendency and drift of public sentiment and all legislation is toward centralization and consolidation," wrote "Hawkeye Subscriber" to a farm journal in 1904, "when it ought to be in the other direction, to distribute power and divide honors, and make the individual more responsible, instead of the township, the county, or the mass of the people."[62]

The rest of the Country Life movement's progressive agenda met similar suspicion and hostility. One agrarian dismissed the movement as "pure rot." Others felt that rural problems stemmed from a more fundamental environmental factor—the lack of money. "The reason [the farmer] does not provide for better sanitation, for better social privileges," a correspondent told Liberty Hyde Bailey, "[is] he does not get his due and cannot afford it." Farmers had no need for a lot of outside advice. "Give us a chance to make money," declared one of Bailey's correspondents, "and let the spending to us." The movement to change rural America, to transform what *The New York Times* called the "whole soggy mass of rural conservatism," had a long way to go.[63]

The Country Lifers' emphasis on children and education was neither surprising nor unique. Confronting so many difficulties in changing adult behavior and transforming established social groups, reformers naturally found childhood an inviting target. Certainly young people should be more malleable than their elders. "A far-sighted policy, such as the training of the young, is," E. A. Ross wrote, "preferable to the summary regulation of the adult."[64]

Reformers saw danger as well as opportunity among the young; they were disturbed by just how far childhood in America diverged from the middle-class ideal. Jane Addams and other progressives worried particularly about rural and working-class children taken prematurely out of school and put to work. At the turn of the century, the middle class was stunned by the reality of child labor. "Walking up the long, orderly building, deafened by the racket," reported a visitor to a Southern textile mill, "you become suddenly aware of a little gray shadow flitting restlessly up and down the aisles—a small girl, and with bare feet and pale face. She has a worn and anxious aspect, as if a weight of care and responsibility rested already on her baby shoulders. . . . A thread breaks first at one end of the long frame, then at the other. The tiny fingers repair the damage at the first place and she walks listlessly to the other. . . . With a great shock it dawns on you that this child is working." Reformers refused to believe that any circumstances in working-class homes, any form of mutualistic family economy, truly justified sending such children out to wage work. "We know the curse of child labor," said Jacob Riis. "Experience has taught us that it is loss, all loss, ever tending downward. . . . Child-life and citizenship are lost; for the children of to-day are the men of tomorrow." To reformers, it was clear that all American children should have what Simon Patten called "the enormous advantage of prolonged childhood." Every working-class and agrarian child, that is, should have a more middle-class youth.[65]

The same was true for upper-class children. Progressives relentlessly blasted the upbringing of the wealthy. Upper-class families, David Graham Phillips complained, "educate their children to folly and superciliousness and economic helplessness or at best give them a training not in business, in useful labor, but in the truly aristocratic chicanery of high finance." Elite colleges only made matters worse for the typical rich man's son. "In place of a brain," Phillips lamented, "the boy acquired at college and elsewhere a lump of vanities, affectations and poses." As president of Princeton, Woodrow Wilson feared that universities were failing to educate the children of the upper class. "Colleges must not be mere country clubs in which to breed up a leisure class," Wilson warned in 1909. If the "sideshows" of leisure and pleasure were taking over for the education in the university's "main tent," he said in a revealing image, "I don't know that I want to continue as ringmaster. . . ."[66]

Worrying about other classes' children and also their own, middle-class adults focused their fears on adolescence, the crucial period from the mid- to late teens when middle-class children should be preparing for adulthood. In his influential book, *Adolescence*, published in 1904, G. Stanley Hall, the president of Clark University in Worcester, Massachusetts, argued that youth recapitulated the stages of human evolution. Adolescence, corresponding to humanity's transition from savagery to civilization, was accordingly a difficult period. Progressives fretted over teenage sexuality, especially because puberty arrived increasingly earlier. They feared the dangers of sexual experimentation for adolescent girls. And they feared for adolescent boys, so much more likely than girls to leave school for the streets. Once again questioning the wisdom of individualism, some middle-class observers wondered whether mothers and fathers had allowed their children too much freedom. "We have removed from the single pair and their children all the props and discipline of the patriarchal family, and now we are rapidly democratizing the family," said Anna Garlin Spencer. "[W]e are even afraid of controlling effectively our own children lest we check their growth toward self-government." Fortunately, a solution was at hand in the nature of adolescence itself. This was, as reformers noted, "the period of childhood when character is plastic and can be moulded for good or evil as clay in the potter's hands."[67]

To mold childhood "for good" and allow it to serve the progressives' transformative purpose, reformers had to make sure children were out of work, off the streets, in school, and under control. That meant, first of all, the passage of laws limiting child labor. Naturally many employers, particularly Southern mill owners, resisted such legislation. Many working-class families, so dependent on income from their sons and daughters, also opposed this threat to their livelihood. But settlement workers and other middle-class reformers pressed hard for legislation. They had allies in organized labor, who believed that child labor forced down adult wages. In 1903, the child labor crusaders demonstrated their power. In New York, a child labor committee, formed by Florence Kelley and other settlement workers, led the drive for a model state law. In Illinois, settlement workers, women's clubs, and the state federation of labor helped to push a child labor bill through the legislature. In Alabama, the state's Child Labor Committee, sparked by Edgar Gardner Murphy, an Episcopal rector in Montgomery, won a law setting twelve as the minimum age for industrial work. Similar laws passed elsewhere, but loopholes and hostile courts limited their impact. Turning in frustration to federal power, Murphy, Kelley, Jane Addams, and Lillian Wald joined to form the National Child Labor Committee in 1904. But any kind of federal legislation faced strong opposition from employers, workers, Catholics hostile to state intrusion into family life, romantic defenders of the work ethic, and states-rights Southerners suspicious of Washington. In 1916, Congress finally enacted the Keating-Owen Child Labor Act, a modest measure that applied to less than 10 percent of wage-earning children. Ruling two years later in *Hammer v. Dagenhart*, the Supreme Court struck down the law as an unconstitutional violation of the limits of federal power over interstate commerce. Despite progressives' efforts, child labor was still pervasive in rural and urban America.[68]

In addition to getting children out of work, reformers had to get them into school. Obviously education was crucial to any effort to reshape young Americans. "A child that came to this country and began to go to school had taken the first step into the New World," Rahel Golub affirmed. "But the child that was put into the shop remained in the old environment with the old people, held back by the old traditions, held back by illiteracy." Others put the promise of education more bluntly; E. A. Ross called it "'breaking in' the colt to the harness."[69]

Around the country, progressives mounted a host of campaigns to improve public education and make it mandatory. Along with efforts to replace one-room country schools with "consolidated" schools, there were attempts to raise spending, lengthen school terms, increase attendance, improve school buildings, raise teacher salaries, strengthen vocational training for working-class children, and add high schools. In the South, where education lagged behind the rest of the country, the drive for education was especially fervent. In 1901, the Southern Education Board, with Edgar Gardner Murphy as executive secretary, formed to publicize the need for reform and for increased taxes and appropriations. Southern education became one of John D. Rockefeller's favorite causes: from 1902 to 1909, the oil man put $53 million into the General Education Board, which in turn funneled resources to various campaigns in the South.[70]

Many Americans rejected education reform. Farmers and workers resisted compulsory attendance for their older children; immigrants, wary of coercive attempts to "Americanize" their children, maintained their own private schools; white Southerners worried about high taxes, Yankee interference, and the specter of educated African-Americans. Agrarians particularly sniffed out and resented the progressive assault on their values. "Individuality will be lost . . . ," a rural critic of education reform complained. The one-room schoolhouse withstood the progressive attack. Nevertheless, the campaigns for education had a clear impact. From 1900 to 1909, the enrollment rate for children aged 5 to 19 in all types of schools rose from 50.5 per 100 to 59.2; public secondary-school enrollments grew from 519,000 to 841,000; expenditures per pupil in public schools increased from $14 to $24; and the average public school term lengthened from 144.3 days in 1900 to 155.3 days in 1909.[71]

As Ross's remark about the colt suggests, an aura of compulsion and coercion hung over the many campaigns for education across the country. There were the compulsory attendance laws, passed mainly in the North, that compelled children to stay in school at least to age fourteen. There was the increased centralization of authority in the hands of teachers and, above all, school boards. There was the obvious intent to transform pupils into dutiful, hardworking, loyal citizens.

The coerciveness of education reform can be overemphasized. As Southern whites clearly realized, a little education for blacks was a dangerous, liberating thing. Certainly some progressives wanted to encourage children's independence and individuality. "The most precious moment in human development," Jane Addams contended, "is the young creature's assertion that he is unlike any other human being, and has an individual contribution to make to the world." This point of view was especially apparent in the work of Addams's friend, philosopher John Dewey. From 1896 until 1904, Dewey ran an experimental "Laboratory" School at the University of Chicago. Through the school and such books as *School and Society* and *The Child and the Curriculum,* Dewey helped to launch what would be known as "progressive" education. Believing that children should become full, individual participants in a democratic society, he wanted school to be a true participatory community for students.[72]

Given the progressives' condemnation of individualism, their support of the child's individuality seems paradoxical. But there were limits to that support. Dewey did not think students should develop just as they pleased; they had to be guided. He warned against "the danger of the 'new education' that it regard the child's present powers and interests as something finally significant in themselves." Moreover, the progressives supported the child's individuality because it served their interests in the struggle to change the values and behavior of other classes. When they endorsed "the young creature's assertion that he is unlike any other human being," they were encouraging the child to break free from his parents' way of life. Working to reform the education of wealthy students at Princeton, Woodrow Wilson expressed the progressives' intentions with particular candor. "Our problem is not merely to help the students to adjust themselves to world life," he told an audience. "Our problem is to make them as unlike their fathers as we can." Further, some progressives expected schools to teach values other than individualism. Arguing for educational opportunities for African-Americans, the reformer Edgar Gardner Murphy enumerated the four key "disciplines" of the Southern common school: *"punctuality," "order," "silence,"* and, beloved of progressives, *"association."*[73]

In addition to transforming children's education, progressives knew they needed to transform children's leisure. In the 1900s, reformers generally accepted what Addams termed "the insatiable desire for play." They realized that adventurous youth had to be diverted from dance halls, saloons, and brothels, from criminal and sexual experimentation. "To fail to provide for the recreation of youth, is not only to deprive all of them of their natural form of expression," Addams insisted, "but is certain to subject some of them to the overwhelming temptation of illicit and soul-destroying pleasures." This recognition led to the expansion of "girls' work" and, especially, "boys' work" in the 1900s. There were rural clubs, encouraged by county agents of the United States Department of Agriculture, for farm youth; Federated Boys' Clubs for the urban working-class; and the junior departments of the YMCA and then the Boy Scouts for the sons of the middle class. Developing since the 1880s, the movement for urban playgrounds surged forward, with settlement workers in the lead, in the 1900s. The Playground Association of America, with Jane Addams as a vice president, formed in 1906. By 1909, 267 municipalities were managing 1,537 playgrounds. Adults also encouraged organized sports, particularly baseball. In New York City, money from Rockefeller and J. P. Morgan helped to launch the Public Schools Athletic League in 1903. Churches and settlements also sponsored ball teams.[74]

In all these endeavors, there was an emphasis on combining release and control, freedom and supervision. Children were encouraged to play—and to change in carefully guided ways. The playground movement stressed the importance of adult supervision; the progressives wanted professional playground supervisors who would schedule and regulate children's activity. Reformers wanted working-class youth to learn middle-class rules of deportment or, at least, just to keep out of trouble. A playground supervisor, according to a Chicago handbook, "should praise every tendency of a boy or girl to sacrifice himself or herself for the good of the team. Show them that this is the only way to succeed—by unity of action. If you can develop this spirit, you have laid the foundation of cooperation, politeness, and good morals." Marion Lawrence, an upper-class woman of Boston, maintained the North Bennet Street Boys' Club for "underprivileged," mainly Irish and Italian, adolescent boys; the club rules said that members "mustn't get excited, chew gum, spit, swear, cheat or talk Italian." Catering to middle-class youth, the YMCA and the Boy Scouts emphasized the drive for individual achievement but also the necessity of team play.[75]

Finally, progressivism addressed the special problem of orphaned and delinquent children. Here, especially, reformers blended compassion with a desire to transform young people. Opposed to the longtime practice of keeping orphans cooped up in asylums, progressives preferred to allow the inmates of orphanages to leave these "barracks" during the day to go to school and to participate in YMCA and other extracurricular programs—

that is, to enjoy the transforming experiences devised for other children. Similarly, homes for young, unwed mothers increasingly emphasized rehabilitation in the Progressive Era. Although the progressives articulated a clear critique of nineteenth-century institutions, they did not simply have their way. The managers of asylums such as the Chicago Nursery and Half-Orphan Asylum resisted change. Moreover, the network of institutions in a city as large as Chicago grew so rapidly in the 1890s and 1900s that progressives could not readily control it.[76]

Progressives achieved their goals more quickly in the courts. Passionately against the traditional treatment of young delinquents as criminals, they did not want youthful offenders tried in adult courtrooms. Instead, reformers wanted to create specialized juvenile courts. Yet one more progressive innovation with roots in Hull-House, the new approach emerged when Edith Abbott, Sophonisba Breckinridge, and other settlement residents helped lobby successfully for an Illinois state law authorizing the creation of special courts for youthful offenders in 1899. By 1909, twenty-two more states had passed laws authorizing juvenile courts. Denver was home to the most famous juvenile court, presided over by the charismatic reformer Judge Ben B. Lindsey. Regarding youthful offenders as "the victims of environment," Lindsey and the juvenile courts sought to rehabilitate rather than punish. Typically, juveniles brought before the court for one offense or another found themselves placed on probation. To lessen the influence of unfit parents and a troubling urban environment, juvenile courts frequently prohibited young people from drinking, going to dance halls, and staying out late. To maximize progressive influences, the courts prescribed enrollment in an industrial school, participation in settlement-house programs, and, especially for sexually delinquent girls, placement in foster homes. "The old process is changed," Lindsey concluded. "Instead of coming to destroy we come to rescue. Instead of coming to punish we come to uplift. Instead of coming to hate we come to love."[77]

The crusades to remake childhood took place largely at the local and state levels. Once again, the federal government was only belatedly and weakly involved. By 1908, Roosevelt was calling for better funding for the National Bureau of Education, but he conceded the primacy of state and local initiatives. Sensitive to the issues of childhood, the president listened to Lillian Wald's idea for a federal children's bureau. But he did not summon a

White House Conference on the Care of Dependent Children until January 1909, shortly before he left office. Congress eventually established a Children's Bureau in the Department of Commerce and Labor in 1912. Its first head was Julia Lathrop, a former resident of Hull-House, who thus became the first woman to lead a federal bureau. Although precedent-setting in various ways, the Children's Bureau was nonetheless a fairly weak instrument, charged mainly with collecting and disseminating information.[78]

Like the other campaigns to remake Americans, the drive to refashion childhood was difficult to evaluate. By the 1910s, reformers had articulated a vision, established organizations, and launched campaigns. Although it was too early to judge the outcome, there were already clear signs of resistance. The pupils did not necessarily learn their lessons or like their teachers. In Worcester, an eleven-year-old boy declared, "I can't go to the playgrounds now. They get on me nerves with so many men and women around telling you what to do." Once again, reform produced unintended results. After equipping her Boys' Club for baseball, Marion Lawrence thought a game against the young gentlemen of the Groton boarding school would offer her Irish and Italian boys some useful lessons in manners and values. She demanded "one essential thing" of her team—"a clean, sporty, gentlemanly game." But, to the "disgust and surprise" of the boys, the students from the boarding school cheated; the Groton first baseman purposely tripped a North Bennet Street runner. "So that's what you call gentlemanly playing!" the boys told Miss Lawrence. Reshaping youth was not an easy business.[79]

For that matter, the entire attempt to transform Americans was not an easy business. Nevertheless, Lillian Wald and other progressives had set in motion a powerful dynamic. In different ways, through different activities, they had begun to push other classes toward "the middle-class paradise," toward the imaginary Boston of the future and the real Chautauqua of the present, with more safety for the home, more justice and power for women, more uniform opportunities and experiences for different classes, more external control and regulation. That was a considerable achievement in so short a time.

Along with this progress went some troubling possibilities. Ironically, reform could destroy what it was intended to preserve. Crusading in the name of the home, reformers were supplanting the very thing they wanted to protect. As outside agencies supervised children in and out of school, ordered the material environment of tenements and parks, and regulated adult behavior, the family and the home became less important. "As in the human organism, when one organ fails, its functions are often undertaken and more or less imperfectly performed by some other organ," Josiah Strong noted; "so in the great social organism of the city, when the home fails, the church sometimes undertakes the functions of the home." A host of other "organs"—settlements, playgrounds, Boys' Clubs, schools, courts, municipalities, state governments, the federal government—were undertaking those functions as well. But even the most reflective progressive activists appeared oblivious to the actual impact of their reforms on many homes.[80]

Some observers did have second thoughts about the denigration of individualism that ran through so many reform causes. Watching the elaboration of regulatory laws and institutions, the occasional reformer worried about the diminished emphasis on individual self-control. Washington Gladden and E. A. Ross feared a Bellamyite society in which external regulation replaced inner restraint. "The entire stress of the demand for reform has been laid upon changing the environment, rather than upon strengthening the character," Gladden observed. "The efforts of the great multitude of philanthropic laborers in this field have been concentrated upon the problem of getting temptation out of the way of men, rather than upon the problem of equipping men to resist temptation. . . . The impression made by the popular presentation of any of these reforms upon the mind of a drunkard or a gambler or a libertine would be that the community or the public officials or the purveyors of vice are to blame for his degradation; that he is a victim, more than a sinner; that there is no very loud call on him to be a man so long as there are opportunities of being a brute."[81]

From the perspective of social Darwinism rather than the Social Gospel, Ross saw a similar problem. "Too much consideration for moral weakness would fill the world with moral weaklings," he insisted. "To abolish temptation is to deprive the self-controlled of their natural right to outlive and outnumber those who have a cotton string for a backbone." While Gladden worried about character, Ross worried about heredity. "If social pressure inhibits drinking, those born with the liquor appetite live out their days and plague our descendants with their ill-constituted offspring," Ross predicted. "If society attacks prostitution by repressive methods that do not go to the core of the individual conscience, it simply poisons the family. . . . [T]he abnormal . . . rear children in their own image." Fearing "race degeneration," Ross rejected the whole premise of the campaigns to remake Americans. "The shortest way to make this world a heaven," he suggested, "is to let those so inclined hurry hell-ward at their own pace."[82]

A few did not worry about the decline of the old values. Simon Patten believed that the abundance of America would make struggle and self-discipline irrelevant. "In a society . . . which is conscious of ample resources and is learning that coöperation can abolish poverty by saving men instead of spending them, the philosophy of the disciplinary values of hardship rings false," he suggested. "The opulence and triumphs of powerful young nations like America make hearts recoil from the barren energies of misery." Abundance, Patten argued, would bring the transformation of character and behavior that reformers desired. "In a rich environment . . . men become idealistic, artistic, and moral," he proclaimed. Abundance would create "a new type of man."[83]

Of course, abundance would also create a new type of question: How should riches be distributed? Here the fashionable environmentalist thinking could suggest unfashionable and radical answers. If material well-being shaped character and behavior, then a broad redistribution of wealth and income might be necessary to remake Americans. That was something most progressives refused to countenance. Ross, with characteristic sweep, dismissed any thoroughgoing transformation of capitalism in the Western or "Occidental" world: "If there is any means whereby the Occidental with his private property and free enterprise can escape acute economic contrasts, he has not yet discovered it." Gladden, the advocate of the "great work of reconstruction," declined to consider radical measures. "Society," he said flatly, "cannot be pulled down and rebuilt successfully." For all their interest in using governmental power to change society, reformers had firm limits in mind. "Shall the state," asked George K. Holmes, "treat the family as a child, enforce saving, invest its wealth, guarantee the deposits, establish postal savings banks, the solvency of which will be protected by the wealth of the nation?" Holmes hardly even wanted to ask, let alone respond. "These questions," he pontificated, "need not be answered in the affirmative until great social necessity requires such answers, and need not receive consideration at all until self-help, with neighborly encouragements, has failed."[84]

Other people were already giving these and other questions a good deal of "consideration." Progressives were not the only Americans to see that income and assets had a great deal to do with culture and behavior. Rahel Golub "often got into arguments" with one of her middle-class friends. "She defended her people and I defended mine," Rahel reported. "She talked of refinement and culture. I was at a loss. What was refinement and culture?" Her friend answered, "When for generations you live in a beautiful home, you are surrounded by beautiful pictures, you listen to beautiful music, you eat good food, you are taken care of. Do you see?" Rahel "saw," but she was troubled. "It seems to me," she said, "that when a man, my father, works all day long, he ought to have a beautiful home, he ought to have good food, he too ought to get a chance to appreciate beautiful music. All day my father is making coats yet his own is so shabby, and my mother, if you ever saw her hands! Why should she know of nothing but scrubbing and scrimping?" Then it was the middle-class woman who was troubled: "her pretty forehead would pucker up; she moved closer to me, if we were on the couch, her hand would clasp mine. 'Yes, it does seem so,' she would say thoughtfully."[85]

CHAPTER FOUR

Ending Class Conflict

The "greatest conflict between capital and labor ever waged in the history of the world" began in stillness on the morning of May 12, 1902. That day, at a call from the United Mine Workers (UMW), more than 140,000 laboring men abandoned their jobs in the anthracite coal fields of northeastern Pennsylvania. In mine after mine across the Wyoming, Lehigh, and Schuylkill districts, the hard, noisy work of blasting, digging, and hauling coal gave way to "absolute quiet."[1]

The stillness in the coal fields testified to the power of working-class mutualism. For years, anthracite workers had tried and failed to unite against the owners of the mines. Since the Civil War, the Miners' Benevolent Association, the Molly Maguires, and the Knights of Labor had come and gone. Since the 1880s, the arrival of Poles, Hungarians, Lithuanians, and Italians—the "Slavs" who took the place of the English, Irish, Scots, Welsh, and Germans—had tested the miners' unity. Like workers elsewhere in America, the anthracite workers were divided by nationality, religion, and culture; by skill, income, and standard of living. Yet, whatever their differences, the anthracite miners shared the vulnerabilities of working-class life: long hours, low pay, poor health, and periodic unemployment. In 1899, the UMW, growing strong in the nation's bituminous coal fields, had sent organizers into the anthracite region. In 1900, a strike led by the UMW had failed to win recognition for the union but had forced a pay raise for the anthracite workers. With that success, membership in the union soared. Now, bound together in the UMW , the workers—"Anglo-Saxons" and "Slavs," skilled miners and less-skilled laborers—dared to bring the anthracite business to a standstill in 1902.

The miners acted to win more power over work and its rewards. Laboring long hours, they demanded an eight-hour day. Struggling to make ends meet, they demanded a 20 percent increase in pay. Doubting their employers' honesty, they wanted coal production measured more fairly. In addition, the anthracite workers wanted the UMW , the expression of their mutualistic ethic, recognized by the operators.[2]

Mutualism appalled the upper-class men who ran the mines. In 1902, nine railroads, including the Erie, the Pennsylvania, and the Reading, owned most of the anthracite fields. Like other members of the upper ten, the railroad bosses clung to an individualistic worldview. They preferred to deal with individual employees, not a union. According to the owners, labor organizations stole a worker's loyalty and restricted his "individual exertions." Moreover, unionists struck unfairly because they envied other workers' success. "Strikes began with Genesis," declared George Baer, president of the Reading and chief spokesman for the anthracite operators. "Cain was the first striker, and he killed Abel because Abel was the more prosperous fellow." To Baer, organized labor meant "terrorism, tyranny and lawlessness." He and the other operators believed that the capitalist should be left free to deal with his employees and his property. The operators still bitterly resented pressure from Republican politicians, worried about William McKinley's reelection, that had helped force the settlement of the strike in 1900. The mine owners were determined not to be thwarted again in their battle against mutualism.[3]

There could be no compromise, then. The operators rejected the miners' demands; a meeting of UMW delegates voted to make the strike permanent on May 16. "They have no tangible grievances," said the president of the Lackawanna Railroad. "We will let them fight it out." "It will be a fight to the end," promised John Mitchell, president of the UMW, "and our organization will either achieve a great triumph or it will be completely annihilated."[4]

That apocalyptic language hardly seemed out of place in 1902. The anthracite coal strike was one of the soaring number of work stoppages that made the United States the most strike-torn nation in the world. In 1898, there had been 1,098 strikes and lockouts across the country. The number jumped to 1,839 in 1900 and jumped again to 3,012 in 1901. These battles testified to the intensity of class conflict in industrial America. With the return of prosperity, with the continuing mechanization of the workplace, with the growth of labor organization, workers and employers naturally continued their ongoing struggle to control manual labor and its rewards. The deep ideological divide between the two sides, the chasm between individualism and mutualism, intensified the conflict. In the 1900s, no one knew what the outcome would be.[5]

Inevitably, the progressives tried to stop the battle between labor and capital. It was, after all, the sense of being caught in the middle of class conflict that helped spur the emergence of progressivism in the first place. In the long run, middle-class reformers hoped that their projects to transform farmers, workers, and the wealthy would produce interclass harmony. But the progressives had to find a more immediate way to resolve the anthracite strike and other potentially bloody confrontations. The progressives also had to shape the day-to-day struggle over the nature of wage work, which was producing so much antagonism between workers and employers.

None of these tasks was easy. With so much at stake, neither workers nor employers readily welcomed the alien views of middle-class reformers and their political allies. In order to succeed, the progressives needed to mobilize the authority of the state on their behalf. But courts and presidents did not automatically support progressive solutions either. Progressives made surprising headway in the years before World War I; even so, conflict between labor and capital remained a threat to the middle-class paradise.

The onset of the anthracite coal strike posed difficult questions for both the upper ten and organized labor. Within each camp, there were sharp divisions over strategy. While the mine owners sought a showdown with labor, some wealthy men favored moderation. Deploring open social warfare, they preferred a pragmatic recognition of organized labor. As Senator Mark Hanna of Ohio, a veteran of the coal business, put it, "A man who won't meet his men half-way is a God-damn fool!" Capitalists like Hanna did not much care for working-class mutualism, but they understood that unions of the right sort could control workers and help to stabilize labor relations. "[M]y plan," said Hanna, "is to have organized union labor Americanized in the best sense, and thoroughly educated to an understanding of its responsibilities, and in this way to make it the ally of the capitalist, rather than a foe with which to grapple." Hanna's approach had found expression in the National Civic Federation, formed in Chicago at the turn of the century to confront the large problems of industrial society. With an imposing roster of leaders drawn from capital, labor, and the "public," the NCF had established an "Industrial Department" to advocate collective bargaining and to conciliate disputes. In 1902, the department, headed by Hanna, stood ready to bring the anthracite owners and workers together.[6]

The NCF approach posed a dilemma for workers. Was cooperation with the NCF an opportunity or a threat? Some working-class leaders thought the latter. Mother Jones, famed organizer of the coal fields, rejected any association with the NCF. Eugene Debs, leader of the American Railway Union and the Socialist Party, urged miners "to cut loose from the Civic Federation, and to stand together to a man and fight it out yourselves." To many workers it was obvious that the anthracite strikers should widen the war instead of talk peace. Rather than treat with the NCF, the UMW should call out the nation's bituminous coal miners in a sympathy strike.[7]

Powerful labor leaders did not agree. Samuel Gompers, president of the American Federation of Labor, served as a vice president of the National Civic Federation. So had John Mitchell, head of the UMW. A complex, charismatic man in his early thirties, Mitchell had gone into the bituminous coal fields at thirteen, joined the Knights of Labor, and risen quickly to a vice presidency in the AFL. A "new type of labor leader," Mitchell was not "a demagogue; a haranguer; a typical agitator" but rather "a business man in the labor movement" who "leads organized labor as our 'captain of industry' manages a great commercial or industrial combination." Although committed to unionism, Mitchell had a hunger for money that would lead him to dubious business dealings with coal operators and to secret payments from the NCF. He had no patience with socialism or radicalism. "I believe in progress slowly,—by evolution rather than by revolution," the UMW chief would say. Like Gompers, Mitchell wanted capital to recognize organized labor; he wanted collective bargaining to replace conflict; he wanted the negotiated trade agreement to supplant employers' lockouts and workers' walkouts. "The trade agreement is the bridge between labor and capital,"

Mitchell would declare. "It restores, as far as it is possible to do, the personal relationship, the mutual interest which existed prior to the advent of the factory system." So, like Gompers, he was ready to meet Hanna "half-way" in the NCF. To do that, Mitchell knew, he had to prevent the sympathy strike in the bituminous coal fields that would break existing trade agreements and make organized labor appear untrustworthy. The UMW president, well read, well dressed, and well out of the mines, did not trust his own members. "They remind me very much," he wrote privately, "of a drove of cattle, ready to stampede when least expected. . . ." In the spring of 1902, Mitchell was determined to head off the stampede of a sympathy strike and herd his cattle into the NCF fold.[8]

Mitchell's strategy prevailed: there was no sympathy strike. Instead, the UMW cooperated with the NCF—but the mine owners refused to go along. Contemptuous of the federation and all "outside interference of whatever nature," the anthracite interests stood resolute on the high ground of individualism. "In my judgment . . . ," a member of the Erie's board of directors announced, "the operators are only doing their plain duty in declining to arbitrate a question which . . . involves the personal liberty of individuals."[9]

The mine operators had miscalculated. For one thing, the bonds of the miners' mutualism held firm. Despite the operators' attempts to exploit ethnic differences, the workers remained unified. Here, working-class mutualism showed its coercive side. Scabs, brought in to work on the mines, were terrorized: strike sympathizers hanged and buried them in effigy; stores, threatened with boycotts, refused to sell to them. But the miners mostly avoided violence that would have alienated middle-class opinion around the country.[10]

While the miners controlled themselves, the owners did not. Unable to grasp middle-class dismay over individualism and class conflict, the capitalists won only "public disgust and resentment" with their "unreasonable bullheadedness." "'The public be damned' appears to be their motto," declared an Illinois paper. The unfortunate Baer, "a cold-tempered man" with "little magnetism," particularly inflamed opinion. "The rights and interests of the laboring man," Baer announced, "will be protected and cared for—not by the labor agitators, but by the Christian men to whom God in His infinite wisdom has given the control of the property interests of the country, and upon the successful Management of which so much depends." "God's viceregent at the mines," scoffed the *New York Tribune.* "[The] doctrine of the divine right of kings was bad enough," declared another paper, "but not so intolerable as the doctrine of the divine right of plutocrats. . . ."[11]

As fall came on, the price of coal rose sharply in the Northeast, from five or six dollars a ton up to fifteen and even twenty dollars. On New York's East Side, the poor cooked food with oil-soaked asbestos and heated apartments with coconut shells. Pneumonia increased, factories closed, schools stayed shut. A miserable winter loomed for the poor, for the middle class, for business—and for the Republican Party. "The country was on the verge of a vast public calamity," wrote Social Gospel leader Walter Rauschenbusch. "A sudden cold snap would have sent Death through our Eastern cities, not with his old-fashioned scythe, but with a modern reaper." Amid calls for government management of the mines, conservative men such as Theodore Roosevelt's friend Senator Henry Cabot Lodge of Massachusetts fumed privately at "the insensate folly . . . of the operators."[12]

The President was growing angry, too. Roosevelt had reservations about organized labor, as he did about any potentially radical force in American life. But, unlike the mine operators, he could accept workers' mutualism. "I strongly favor labor unions," he said. "If I were a wage worker in a big city I should certainly join one." Early in the strike, Roosevelt had doubted his authority to intervene. But the pressure to act increased. Social Gospel leader Washington Gladden led a petition drive urging Roosevelt to arbitrate the strike. By fall, the President, privately contemplating "the coal famine impending, with untold misery as the result, with the certainty of riots which might develop into social war," felt he had to take action. Accordingly, Roosevelt invited Mitchell and the operators to an unprecedented tri-cornered meeting of capital, labor, and state on October 3.[13]

The conference, held at Jackson Place while the White House underwent repairs, did not go well. The operators refused arbitration, denounced Mitchell, and "insulted" the President. George Baer told Roosevelt, who was confined to a wheelchair by one of his frequent accidents, "not to waste time negotiating with the fomenters of this anarchy and insolent defiance of law. . . ." The mine owners had blundered again. Whatever doubts Roosevelt had about organized labor, he also had an underlying disregard for most businessmen. The President was livid over the operators and their backers, "the men . . . in the narrow, bourgeois, commercial world . . . still in a condition of wooden-headed obstinacy and stupidity and utterly unable to see the black storm impending." As always, Roosevelt was swayed, too, by his reading of individual character. John Mitchell's "great dignity and moderation" left the President with "a very uncomfortable feeling that" the operators "might be far more to blame relatively to the miners than I had supposed." Most important, the President now saw himself as the representative of a public interest that the owners refused to accept. "The operators forget that they have duties toward the public, as well as rights to be guarded by the public through its governmental agents," Roosevelt observed. "It is amazing folly on their part. . . ." "Do they not realize," he told a friend, "that they are putting a very heavy burden on us who stand against socialism; against anarchic disorder?"[14]

News of the meeting stirred resentment of the operators' "insolent defiance of public sentiment and disregard for public rights and interests." At mass meetings and at least one Democratic convention, there was approving talk of "state socialism," of public ownership or management of the mines. As fuel supplies declined, as politicians and business leaders scurried about, as Roosevelt considered sending in the United States Army to run the mines, a solution emerged. On October 11, the secretary of war, Elihu Root, met secretly with J. P. Morgan on the financier's yacht in New York to produce a proposal: the operators would call for a presidential commission to review the facts of the situation and offer a binding solution. Morgan himself went down to Washington to give the proposal to Roosevelt on the thirteenth. There was still room for comedy: the operators refused to have a representative of organized labor on the committee and insisted on dictating the occupations of the committee members—an engineer, a sociologist, and so forth. Roosevelt bridled at such restrictions. Then, at a late-night meeting with Morgan's associates on the fifteenth, the President hit on the "utter absurdity" of appointing a labor leader as the "sociologist" and adding a Roman Catholic bishop for good measure. The next morning, the White House announced the settlement. The miners went back to work.[15]

It was a signal defeat for capital. To the public, the operators' obstinate individualism looked like "hallucinations" or some "mental disease." The arbitrated settlement was a partial victory for labor. After hearing from more than five hundred witnesses, Roosevelt's commission reported in March

1903. Although the UMW did not win official recognition or a change in the weighing of coal, the anthracite workers generally received a 10 percent wage hike and a reduction of the workday from ten hours to nine. The coal strike was a victory, too, for progressives. Their middle-class interests had been successfully subsumed and depoliticized in a broader "public" interest, and linked effectively to the power of the state to stop class conflict. The strike was a victory as well for Theodore Roosevelt, the agent who forged and symbolized the linkage between the "public" interest and state power. Drawing "the permanent lesson of the strike," Roosevelt declared, " . . . it was essential that organized capital and organized labor should thoroughly understand that the third party, the great public had vital interests and overshadowing rights in such a crisis. . . ." This was not necessarily the worst thing for the upper ten, Roosevelt insisted. "I wish that capitalists would see," he said a bit plaintively, "that what I am advocating . . . is really in the interest of property, for it will save it from the danger of revolution."[16]

The anthracite strike offered a progressive model for labor relations in modern America. Ultimately, this state-sanctioned acceptance of organized labor, collective bargaining, and trade agreements, all in the name of stability and the public interest, would win out in the twentieth century. But in the short run of the Progressive Era, not everyone, not even Theodore Roosevelt, was ready to accept the "permanent lesson" of the strike. The struggle had been unusual for several reasons. The mine owners had been notably inept; the miners, notably disciplined. Because an unusual state law required miners to earn a license with two years of work, the mine owners had been unable to bring in enough licensed strikebreakers to run the mines. Further, anthracite's importance for the Northeastern cities had focused unusual public attention on the strike. All these circumstances had given Roosevelt an unparalleled opportunity to intervene. But circumstances would often be different. The anthracite coal strike did indeed point to the future of labor relations in the United States, but it was a more distant future than many recognized.[17]

Employers generally backed away from collective bargaining after the anthracite settlement. Although the NCF established a "Trade Agreement Department" in 1904, the federation's approach lost momentum. Mark Hanna, chief upper-class exponent of the trade agreement, died that year.

Meanwhile many businessmen, frightened by workers' success in the wave of strikes, opposed the recognition of organized labor and the practice of collective bargaining. Working-class mutualism seemed to give workers, especially skilled craftsmen, far too much power over the workplace. Through the enforcement of "working rules" on the job, machinists, carpenters, and dock workers too often determined the hours, the methods, and, most ominously, the rate of production: in 1907, a federal study concluded that workers substantially restricted industrial output. By controlling the training of apprentices, organized workers could limit the labor supply of the future. Worse, by insisting on a "closed shop" that hired only union members, workers could seize the right to determine the labor force in the present.[18]

Dwelling on these horrors, many employers aimed to destroy, rather than accommodate, the mutualism of the trade union. Even as the NCF lauded the trade agreement, a powerful antiunion campaign took shape. In 1901, the executives of the newly created United States Steel Corporation, facing a walkout by the Amalgamated Association of Iron and Steel Workers, broke the strike and crippled the union. The steel men declared that "we are unalterably opposed to any extension of union labor." Repudiating trade agreements, employers organized to push vigorously for the "open shop" across the United States. Old and new trade associations, such as the National Founders' Association, provided members with legal and technical help and with strikebreakers and company guards. In 1903, the National Association of Manufacturers dedicated itself to the crusade in the name of individualism. "The keynote of the open-shop plea is 'liberty,'" cried David M. Parry, president of the NAM. "Organized labor takes no account of the varying degrees of natural aptitude and powers of endurance displayed by individuals and seeks to place all men in each particular trade on the same dead level as respects his daily output and his daily wage." Although Theodore Roosevelt accepted unions, his strong sense of individualism led him to dislike the coercion of individual workers that was an inevitable feature of the closed shop. The President lent encouragement to the open-shop cause in 1903 by upholding the reinstatement of a worker in the Government Printing Office who had been dismissed because he no longer belonged to the International Brotherhood of Bookbinders.[19]

In addition to the open-shop drive, employers tested other strategies. A number of businesses pursued what became known as "welfare capitalism," the provision to employees of services and benefits not mandated by the state. Workers at the National Cash Register Company in Dayton, Ohio, and other large firms might be offered company housing, kindergartens, nurseries, libraries, adult education, playgrounds, baseball teams, clubs, field days, medical care, churches, or YMCAs. The Pennsylvania Railroad provided its employees east of Pittsburgh with no fewer than thirty-two baseball diamonds, thirty-three tennis courts, seven running tracks, and a golf course. United States Steel, Procter & Gamble, Standard Oil, and International Harvester tried such innovations as employee stock ownership, profit sharing, or pensions. A handful of firms even allowed employees some token participation in management. The Boston department store magnate Edward Filene, a leader in welfare capitalism, initiated the Filene Cooperative Association Council, which mimicked the federal government with a "house of representatives" elected by workers, a "senate" chosen by the company president, and a "cabinet" composed of top-ranking company officers.

A range of motives spurred welfare capitalism. Certainly some employers felt real concern for their workers' well-being. Welfare capitalism also reflected the influence of the progressive passion for remaking other Americans. Through the American Institute of Social Service, Social Gospel leaders Washington Gladden and Josiah Strong had pioneered the concepts of welfare capitalism at the end of the nineteenth century. At the Toledo factory of progressive politician Samuel "Golden Rule" Jones, a slogan on a fence captured the optimistic reformist faith at the heart of welfare capitalism: "PRODUCE GREAT PERSONS, THE REST FOLLOWS." Businesses also turned to welfare programs to produce more goods, of course. But most of all, the proponents of welfare capitalism intended to weaken unions by winning over workers. Naturally, the National Civic Federation, so committed to harmony between labor and capital, helped lead the crusade for corporate welfare programs.[20]

While some capitalists tried to beguile the workforce into submission, other businessmen moved more aggressively to break labor's power over production. Already in the late nineteenth century, a group of manufacturers and engineers, troubled by workers' restriction of output, had begun experimenting with new managerial techniques. These pioneers of "systematic management" particularly favored piece-rate schemes that would encourage workers to defy their formal and informal "working rules" and increase production.[21]

By the 1900s, the most prominent advocate of managerial reform was Frederick Winslow Taylor. Born in 1856 into a wealthy Quaker family in Philadelphia, Taylor, like Theodore Roosevelt and Jane Addams, had managed to step across the boundaries between social classes. When eye trouble kept Taylor from attending Harvard, he became an apprentice machinist and pattern maker in Philadelphia. At the Enterprise Hydraulic Works and then at Midvale Steel, Taylor had a rare opportunity to observe the working-class world of the shop floor. But he was not going to remain in that world. Taylor earned an engineering degree, produced a number of machine tool innovations, and moved into management and ownership. By the depression of the 1890s, he was a wealthy man and a consulting engineer—"systematizing shop management and cost systems a speciality." At Bethlehem Iron Company and other firms, he and his associates began to install a new system of "scientific management." Retiring to his splendid Georgian estate, Boxly, in Philadelphia's Chestnut Hill, Taylor astutely broadcast his system in the 1900s by giving lectures to visitors, placing his disciples in jobs, and publishing an important statement, *Shop Management.*[22]

Despite his experience on the shop floor, Taylor remained emphatically an upper-class man—a member of the Young America Cricket Club and the first doubles champion of the United States Lawn Tennis Association. His creed was conventional individualism—"energy, grit, pluck, determination, ability to stick to it, character." Like Roosevelt, Taylor could be sharply critical of big-business men, particularly those who did not listen to engineers. But unlike Addams and even Roosevelt, Taylor had little sympathy for workers.[23]

That lack of sympathy became clear as he refined "scientific management." Taylor had no interest in welfare capitalism: it was a "joke," he said, " . . . of distinctly secondary importance." Instead, Taylor wanted passionately to revolutionize work itself. He aimed his most important innovations squarely at workers' control over production. Influenced by systematic management, Taylor had evolved his own incentive wage system in the 1880s and 1890s: the "differential piece rate" would reward highly productive workers with increases while stimulating or driving away their less productive mates with pay cuts. Taylor and his disciples also tried to wrest the secrets of production away from workers. Scientific management used "motion study"—the detailed observation of each minute aspect of a task—to make labor more efficient.

"Time study"—measurements with a stopwatch—supposedly established the optimal time a job required. There was little "science" in scientific management, however. For all Taylor's boasting about "the art of shoveling earths," for all his mathematical formulas, scientific management came down to arbitrary production standards set by "rule of thumb," by the needs and interests of managers.[24]

Like the progressives, Taylor believed human beings could be remade. He promised "momentous changes in the men"—a "complete revolution in their mental attitude toward their employers and their work." Realizing their common interests with management, workers would boost output and prosper. They would not need to strike. Of course, wage earners would have to sacrifice a great deal. "Each man," Taylor insisted, "must learn how to give up his own particular way of doing things, adapt his methods to the many new standards, and grow accustomed to receiving and obeying directions covering details, large and small, which in the past have been left to his individual judgment." Taylor intended to take any intelligence and creativity out of manual labor. Supervisors, he explained, would "do the thinking for the men. . . ." Ultimately, Taylor's system rested on coercion, not science and harmony: the threat of wage cuts, temporary layoffs, fines, and dismissal hung over troublesome or inefficient workers. The yard laborers at Bethlehem Iron, subjected to time study and piece rates, were not fooled: men balked and were fired; other workers did not want to replace them. Scientific management spread only gradually, as workers in other factories resisted. Relatively few employers adopted Taylor's whole system, but his approach, so clearly rooted in progressivism, became widely influential.[25]

Unwilling to accept the "permanent lesson" of the anthracite strike, employers had responded in both antediluvian and creative ways. The bludgeon of the open-shop drive contrasted with the progressive aura of welfare capitalism and Taylorism. The American Federation of Labor was equally unwilling to accept the anthracite strike's "lesson." But the federation did not respond nearly as creatively. In the years after the strike, the AFL focused on its fundamental, craft-based strategy. The results were disappointing.

Since the late nineteenth century, the AFL had drawn together an impressive array of city labor councils, state labor federations, national unions, and international unions. But these organizations contained mostly skilled workers—carpenters and molders, cigar makers and printers. The United Mine Workers, an "industrial" union of the skilled and the less skilled, was exceptional: by and large, the AFL represented autonomous trade unions of highly trained craftsmen. Most of these workers were men born in the United States or Western Europe. For all its growth, then, the federation did not reflect the increasing diversity of the workforce, which was female as well as male, black as well as white, Eastern and Southern European as well as Western European, less skilled as well as skilled. Clearly, the long-term power of the working class depended on organizing the wide range of American labor. Yet, the craftsmen of the AFL, fighting off Taylorism and the open-shop drive, had little energy and still less enthusiasm for broader organization. Although the UMW reached out to the Slavs of the anthracite coal fields, the federation preferred to keep Eastern Europeans and Italians out of the country. Samuel Gompers and other trade unionists strongly supported immigration restriction in the 1900s and 1910s.[26]

The federation also had a woeful record with black labor. In its early days in the 1880s, the AFL had forbidden member unions to bar African-American workers. This was more a pragmatic than an egalitarian stance: Gompers and other leaders contended that drawing African-American workers into the federation was the best means of avoiding economic competition between blacks and whites. But with the collapse of prosperity in the 1890s, a different point of view prevailed. To many in the AFL, black workers were dangerous competitors, scabs who threatened white jobs and white unions. Blacks had, Gompers declared, "so conducted themselves as to be a continuous convenient whip placed in the hands of the employers to cow the white men and to compel them to accept abject conditions of labor." The solution to black competition was to keep African-Americans out of craft unions—and out of skilled jobs—as much as possible. By the early 1900s, the AFL was even admitting unions that openly denied admission to blacks. Not surprisingly, many African-Americans were ambivalent about unionism. "They hang the negro in the South," a black paper in Kansas bitterly observed, "but they are not so bad in the North; they just simply starve him to death by labor unions." The African-American sociologist W. E. B. Du Bois found that hardly any AFL unions had more than a few black members; some craft organizations had no African-American membership at all. Gompers and the AFL leadership did try to encourage the formation of separate black local unions, but even then the hostility of white locals limited the organization and recognition of these African-American unions.[27]

Black-and-white mutualism was not impossible. By the 1900s, Du Bois and other African-Americans argued in favor of black unionization. Where black workers were numerous, organized, and aggressive, the white labor movement would have to incorporate them, even in the South. "It is only a question of time when white working men and black working men will see their common cause against the aggressions of exploiting capitalists," Du Bois promised in 1907. "The economic strength of the Negro cannot be beaten into weakness, and therefore it must be taken into partnership, and this the Southern white working man, befuddled by prejudice as he is, begins dimly to realize." In Alabama, where many coal miners were African-American, the UMW was perhaps half black and half white during the Roosevelt years. Many African-Americans labored on American docks; the International Longshoreman's Union, unwilling to risk competition with those black stevedores, longshoremen, and screwmen, accepted them as members. In New Orleans, where white and black dockworkers had agreed to share jobs half-and-half, the two races stood together in a notable strike in 1907. White employers, who at first refused even to meet with black workers, caved in to the union's demands. It was an extraordinary moment—and a rare one, too.[28]

If anything, the federation was even more reluctant to incorporate female workers. The skilled tradesmen of the AFL felt strongly that women belonged in the home. Further, the male craft unionists labored under the impression that women worked to earn unnecessary "pin money" for luxuries, rather than essential income for themselves and their families. Most seriously, the AFL considered working women, like African-Americans, an economic threat. By accepting poor wages and working conditions, female wage earners jeopardized the hard-won achievements, and even the jobs, of laboring males. "It is the men who suffer through the women who are employed in the manufacture of clothing," said a male garment worker in 1903. "[T]he girls . . . can afford to work for small wages and care nothing about the conditions of the trade." "Every woman employed displaces a man," the AFL's journal argued, "and adds one more to the idle contingent that are fixing wages at the lowest limit." The reduction of men's earnings, in turn, increased the unnatural employment of women outside the home. The circular reasoning of the AFL was simple. "We stand for the principle that it is wrong to permit any of the female sex of our country to be forced to work, as we believe that the man should be provided with a fair wage in order to keep his female relatives from going to work," proclaimed a member of the federation. "The man is the provider and should receive enough for his labor to give his family a respectable living." To shore up male wages, the AFL favored equal pay for women. Of course, if men and women received the same wages, then men were more likely to get the jobs. But the AFL had little interest in organizing women workers. After appointing a lone female organizer for several months in 1892, the federation failed to name a replacement until 1908. Meanwhile, craft unions tended to reject individual female members and the AFL tended to reject organizations built by women.[29]

The organization of female, black, and immigrant labor lagged only partly because of sexual, racial, and ethnic divisions; skill differentials continued to inhibit working-class mutualism as well in the new century. Women, African-Americans, and new immigrants held mostly semiskilled and unskilled jobs. The craftsmen of the AFL, looking down on such employment, had little interest in organizing separate unions for the less skilled. In the early 1900s, the federation did try to form federal labor unions of unskilled workers, but the initiative died quickly. Firmly committed to craft autonomy, the AFL certainly did not want to transform its own trade unions, each dedicated to a single occupation, into industrial unions embracing all the occupations in a particular business. When the United Metal Workers Industrial Union tried to draw together all the members of the metal trades, Gompers and his associates forced the union out of the federation in 1905. When the United Brewery Workers tried to form an industrial union, the AFL expelled them, too, in 1907. That year, the AFL did set up industrial departments to coordinate craft unions in the same industries, but the federation was not going to unite the skilled and the less skilled.[30]

The strategies of capital and labor posed a difficult challenge for progressives eager to influence the course of labor relations. Neither employers nor unions typically welcomed intrusions from well-meaning reformers. Such progressives as Jane Addams and fellow Chicago settlement leader Graham Taylor offered their services as mediators in labor disputes, but obviously they had to be invited by the opposing sides to have any chance to shape events. Progressives did use settlement houses and other forums to draw workers and employers into discussion of labor issues. And progressives were free to study labor conditions and report the results. Hull-House resident Mary McDowell investigated the Chicago stockyards; fellow resident Florence Kelley analyzed sweatshops and child labor; the progressive economist John R. Commons of the University of Wisconsin pioneered the field of labor economics.[31]

As in the effort to transform the upper ten, it was especially difficult for the middle class to inject itself into the affairs of big-business men. The leaders of the open-shop drive, intensely committed to individualism and the rights of property, were the least likely members of the upper ten to want to listen to progressive ideas. Welfare capitalism, the deepest penetration of progressives and progressive ideas into business, was a satisfying development that engaged a good deal of reformers' energy. In its early days, Taylorism was an enigmatic development, wrapped in at least some progressive language, whose implications were difficult for progressives to discern.

The middle class certainly did share Taylor's interest in transforming work. To progressives, the workplace, like every other sphere of American life, needed improvement. No longer so confident of the joys and rewards of labor, settlement workers, Social Gospel leaders, and other progressives sympathized with the hard lives of working-class wage earners. In the 1900s, more and more middle-class Americans understood that factories were stealing the sense of pleasure and purpose from manual labor. Observers lamented the passing of what one writer called "the old all-round craftsman who knew his craft as a whole and saw, in each task which came to him, a challenge to his knowledge and capacity."

In response, a number of progressives envisioned a utopian transformation of labor, quite different from Frederick Taylor's intended revolution. An emerging handicrafts movement, centered in Boston, New York, and Chicago, sought a return to an older way of work. The Boston Arts and Crafts Society and the Society of Arts and Crafts, inspired by William Morris, John Ruskin, and the English Pre-Raphaelites, discovered an exemplary combination of pleasure, creativity, beauty, and labor in the Middle Ages. Architects Frank Lloyd Wright and Louis Sullivan, along with Jane Addams, celebrated the cooperative work of medieval craft guilds and the organic quality of Gothic art and architecture as guides to the industrial future. "The present factory, with its monarchical order and intense division of labor, will give way," promised a leader of the handicrafts movement, "to the guild or small co-operative society, which shall be integral as to its work, human as to its motives, artistic as to its ends." For all their obvious nostalgia, the members of the arts and crafts societies did not reject mechanization and industrialization. But, like so many other progressives, they would not consider just how drastically capitalism might have to be altered in order to create a new kind of work. The handicrafts movement never got very far. Yet, it dramatized the reformist understanding that workers needed imaginative power over their labor. "A new industrialism . . . ," contended Louis Sullivan, "means the exercise of a higher form of intelligence upon the part of the workman."[32]

Fascinated by medieval guilds and repelled by capitalist individualism, middle-class reformers mostly endorsed workers' collective efforts to control labor. When they saw the working class as the underdog in the struggle with powerful, insensitive capital, the progressives were sympathetic to organized labor. Yet, there was almost always some qualification in the progressives' endorsement. Progressives were generally quick to deplore any tendency to selfishness and confrontation in the union movement. Jane Addams, for instance, praised "the ring of altruism" in the union movement, but chided its pursuit of "negative action." "Unions use their power to frustrate the designs of the capitalist, to make trouble for corporations and the public, such as is involved, for instance, in a railroad strike," Addams observed. "A movement cannot be carried on by negating other acts; it must have a positive force. . . . A moral revolution cannot be accomplished by men who are held together merely because they are all smarting under a sense of injury and injustice. . . ."[33]

For all Addams's sincere sympathy with workers, her words subtly emphasized the gulf between the middle and working classes. The progressive middle class wanted a "moral revolution"; reformers most wanted workers and the upper ten to become different people, the sort who would not pursue their own interests exclusively. In calling for "association" and "fellow-feeling," the progressives and such political allies as Theodore Roosevelt wanted other Americans to transcend class differences. Labor organizers, on the other hand, wanted to draw the working class together and set it apart from other classes. When the resolution of a Chicago teamsters' strike led to higher prices and less service for customers, progressive journalist Ray Stannard Baker expressed middle-class consternation. "We have been sighing for labor and capital to get together; we have been telling them they are brothers, that the interest of one is the interest of the other," Baker commented. "Here they are together; are we any better off?" And so, even as they leaned more toward workers than employers, progressives kept a wary eye on the union movement. "It is clearly the duty of the settlement," Addams concluded with a characteristic tinge of middle-class condescension, "to keep [the union] to its best ideal. . . ."[34]

This determination was clearly in evidence when progressives assessed the organizing efforts of the AFL. So driven by the determination to expand female opportunities, some reformers could not ignore the federation's grudging approach to organizing women. In 1903, AFL representatives, female labor activists, and settlement house workers met in Boston to form the Women's Trade Union League. The new organization was a natural undertaking for such working-class women as bookbinder Mary Kenney O'Sullivan, who had served as the AFL's pioneer female organizer, and shirtmaker Leonora O'Reilly, who had taught her craft to Rahel Golub in classes at the Nurses' Settlement. The WTUL was also a logical step for settlement workers who pondered the economic inequities that troubled Rahel. "As I became more familiar with the conditions around me, I began to feel that while the Settlement was undoubtedly doing a great deal to make the lives of working people less grim and hard, the work was not fundamental," said Grace Barnum, a veteran of Hull-House and founder of the WTUL. "It . . . did not raise their wages or shorten their hours."[35]

Hoping to do something "fundamental," the league confronted the usual difficulties of labor organizers—the hostility of employers, the ethnic and cultural differences of workers—and some special obstacles as well. Although the league pledged allegiance to the AFL, the federation gave little in return. Men like Gompers found the WTUL doubly suspicious: it included both women and the well-to-do. Moreover, wage-earning women were difficult to organize. Planning to work only until marriage, most single young women did not necessarily see the need to join a union. Many wage-earning women were immigrants from countries with little tradition of labor organization. The WTUL also suffered from internal tensions between working-class women and the middle- and upper-class members known as "allies." While the wage earners intended to wed, many of the allies never married. Labor could seem like liberation to allies and hard necessity to working-class women. The allies tended to trace the plight of impoverished female wage earners above all to sexual exploitation; the working-class leaders of the WTUL looked more often to class differences. To Leonora O'Reilly, even the association with middle- and upper-class reformers might be a mistake for working-class women. "Contact with the Lady does harm in the long run," O'Reilly maintained. "It gives the wrong standard." Allies, in turn, recoiled at the idea that class differences could override gender unity. "Before I was unconscious about this class and that class and this stupid difference and that stupid difference," an ally told O'Reilly. "Girls were just girls to me and now you people are putting all sorts of ideas in my head and making me timid and self-conscious."[36]

Despite these obstacles, the WTUL had some success. With support from Jane Addams and Lillian Wald, and with funds from Margaret Dreier Robins and other well-to-do women, the league opened branches in cities from Baltimore to Los Angeles. The WTUL did particularly well among the more than 350,000 working girls and women of Rahel Golub's New York City. There the capmaker Rose Schneiderman and other activists organized effectively on the Lower East Side. Nevertheless, the proportion of organized women workers across the United States actually declined: perhaps 3.3 percent of female industrial labor belonged to unions in 1900; a decade later, only about 1.5 percent were organized.[37]

Progressives did find common ground with the AFL on the issue of protecting working women. Demanding the prohibition of child labor, a number of progressives also wanted the state to limit the hours and even the occupations of wage-earning women. While those women should be free to work, their labor, it seemed, should not be too demanding. The AFL agreed: special protection for women workers would make it harder for them to compete with men and would lessen the need for female labor organization. By the turn of the century, a number of states had legislated maximum hours for women workers, especially in manufacturing. But these laws were usually found ineffective in practice or unconstitutional in court. An eight-hour provision in the Illinois factory law advocated by Florence Kelley and Hull-House had been thrown out by the state supreme court in 1895. Nevertheless, ten states passed new or improved hours laws during the 1900s; typically, wage-earning women were restricted to ten hours of work a day or sixty hours a week. Moreover, a number of states kept women from serving liquor, laboring in mines, delivering messages, and grinding metals.[38]

In general, the courts seemed willing to accept such restrictions: after all, judges reasoned, women and children were dependent beings, clearly weaker than men. "The employer and the laborer are practically on an equal footing, but these observations do not apply to women and children," the Nebraska Supreme Court explained in 1902. "Women and children have always to a certain extent been wards of the state." Thus, government had the right to regulate their labor. That principle received the highest sanction in 1908, when the United States Supreme Court upheld an Oregon law stipulating maximum hours for wage-earning women. There were, the majority opinion in *Muller v. Oregon* explained, "inherent differences between the two sexes": "That woman's physical structure and the performance of maternal functions place her at a disadvantage in the struggle for existence is obvious. . . . [A]s healthy mothers are essential to vigorous offspring, the physical well-being of women becomes an object of public interest and care in order to preserve the strength and vigor of the race."

Protective legislation was clearly a mixed blessing for women and the working class. Maximum-hours laws could safeguard the health of wage-earning women, but at considerable cost. Women had to give up their freedom of contract. Worse, they were defined as weak and dependent, the inferiors of men. Special protective legislation also widened the sexual divide within the working class: male and female wage earners had still less reason to recognize their common plight; male unionists had still less incentive to organize laboring women.

Some progressives justified special protection for women as an "entering wedge" that would open the way for legislation shielding all workers. But the wedge did not work very well in the 1900s and 1910s. Legislatures and courts believed that wage earners, whether male or female, required special protection in some occupations. Because all government employees did not have a clear right to strike, their ability to protect themselves was limited. Accordingly, eight states from New York to Oregon passed so-called public works laws, which limited hours for government workers. Legislatures and courts also favored the restriction of hours for wage earners in some dangerous occupations. During the 1900s, several states limited the workday for miners. Recognizing the threat to public safety posed by fatigued railroad workers, fifteen states and then the United States Congress passed laws stipulating maximum hours and mandatory rest periods for railroad employees. But more general protection for workers was unacceptable. In *Lochner v. New York* in 1905, the Supreme Court set aside a state law prescribing maximum hours for bakers. The court denied that the New York legislature had the right to protect male wage earners who "are in no sense wards of the state." Protective laws like this one, the court complained, were "mere meddlesome interferences with the rights of the individual."[39]

With the hostility of courts and employers, the campaign to regulate work made slow progress in the 1900s and 1910s. Despite mounting public concern about workers injured on the job, no state adopted anything like the systems of workmen's compensation in place across Europe. In 1902, Maryland passed a measure providing benefits for miners, quarrymen, and railway workers who contributed to a state fund, but the law was soon declared unconstitutional. In a special message to Congress in January 1908, Roosevelt called the plight of injured federal workers "an outrage"; the House and Senate responded with a modest bill covering only a minority of federal employees.[40] There was more progress during the administration of Woodrow Wilson. In 1914, the La Follette-Peters Act, pushed by the National Consumers' League, mandated an eight-hour day for most women workers in the District of Columbia. The next year, the administration supported passage of the La Follette Seaman's Act, which regulated the hours and working conditions for American sailors. In 1916, the Adamson Act mandated the eight-hour day for railway workers for the sake of public safety. That year, too, Congress passed, with Wilson's support, the Keating-Owen Child Labor Act, but the Supreme Court invalidated the measure.[41]

Surveying the resistance of employers and government, some workers were ready to strike a much more confrontational stance in the 1900s. Labor radicalism posed an obvious challenge to progressive efforts to end class conflict.

Like the UMW in the East, the Western Federation of Miners had been growing robustly out West. Unlike the coal miners' union, the WFM, tested in the raw industrial conflict of the 1890s, had left the AFL. The leaders of the WFM did not share Mitchell and Gompers's more accommodating view of capitalism. "There can be no harmony between organized capitalists and organized labor," said Ed Boyce, president of the WFM. Instead, Boyce looked to "the overthrow of the whole profit-making system." Eager to organize outside the mines, the WFM began unionizing smelters in Colorado City, 225 miles south of Denver, in August 1902. But the Standard refining company fired workers who joined the new WFM local. To retaliate, the federation went out on strike against the Standard and two other mills in February 1903. In turn, the employers persuaded Governor James H. Peabody to send in state troops. By then the WFM wanted to settle the strike, but the Standard would not. The conflict escalated: in April, Colorado businessmen formed "Citizens' Alliances" to combat the WFM; in August, the miners' union struck mines in the Cripple Creek district that shipped ore to the mills of Colorado City. In response, Governor Peabody ordered state troops back into Colorado City under the command of General Sherman Bell, one of Roosevelt's old Rough Riders. Invoking "military necessity which recognizes no laws, either civil or social," Bell declared, "I came to do up this damned anarchistic federation." Although there was no violence of significance, Bell's men ignored courts and public officials to arrest miners illegally. "To hell with the constitution," said one of the general's officers, "we aren't going by any constitution."[42]

At the same time, west of Colorado City, the WFM and the Citizens' Alliance squared off in the mining region of Telluride. When the miners struck to defend an eight-hour day and a minimum wage, Governor Peabody directed militia to arrest strikers as vagrants. In November, back at Cripple Creek, company detectives secretly tried to wreck a train of nonunion miners in order to focus public anger on the WFM; soon after, a mysterious mine explosion left two men dead. Seizing on these events, Peabody declared "a state of insurrection and rebellion," suspended habeas corpus, and used his vagrancy trick again. Bell's troops refused to allow citizens to sell food or give aid to miners' families. By the spring of 1904, the strikes were shattered: WFM members had gone back to work, been "vagged," left town on their own, or been deported. The last act began in June, when a bomb blew up a train of nonunion miners in Cripple Creek. The Citizens' Alliance took vigilante action, closed down WFM headquarters, and deported union members with the help of state troops. Several days later, mobs destroyed WFM cooperative stores and General Bell stranded seventy-nine more miners in other states.[43]

Roosevelt sent investigators but declined to intervene. Washington Gladden also took a trip out to Colorado: the conduct of both sides offended him. The anthracite formula apparently did not apply when unions were aggressive and the population centers of the Northeast were not threatened. "Colorado," wrote a WFM sympathizer, "it is of thee, / Dark land of tyranny, / Of thee I sing; / Land wherein labor's bled / Land from which law has fled / Bow down thy mournful head, / Capital is king."[44]

Radicalized by its experiences in Colorado, the WFM was ready to expand the boundaries of working-class mutualism by starting a broader labor organization. But the federation's creations—the Western Labor Union and the American Labor Union—did not have much success. Then, at the initiative of the miners' federation, twenty-one people, including Mother Jones and representatives of the reorganized United Metal Workers Industrial Union, met secretly in Chicago in January 1905 to discuss the formation of "a general industrial union embracing all industries." In its manifesto, the meeting bitterly criticized the Gompers–Mitchell brand of unionism. "Craft divisions hinder the growth of class consciousness of the workers, foster the idea of harmony of interests between employing exploiter and employed slave," the "Industrial Union Manifesto" insisted. "They permit the association of the misleaders of the workers with the capitalists in the Civic Federation, where plans are made for the perpetuation of capitalism, and the permanent enslavement of the workers through the wage system." In any case, craft unions of the skilled were irrelevant now that machines could "wipe out whole trades and plunge new bodies of workers into the ever-growing army of tradeless, hopeless unemployed. . . ." And so, the manifesto invited workers to a convention in Chicago in June. "[U]nion smashers," growled Samuel Gompers.[45]

The Industrial Workers of the World convened anyway. Mother Jones, Eugene Debs, and Daniel DeLeon, leader of the Marxist Socialist Labor Party, were in the hall. At the rostrum was William D. "Big Bill" Haywood, secretary-treasurer of the Western Federation of Miners. "Fellow Workers,"

Haywood proclaimed. "This is the Continental Congress of the Working Class." For days, the delegates discussed the formation of what would be called "one big industrial union." They drew up a "Preamble" that made clear their rejection of the AFL's values. "The working class and the employing class have nothing in common," the "Preamble" announced. "There can be no peace so long as hunger and want are found among millions of working people and the few, who make up the employing class, have all the good things of life." Industrial unionism, then, would not be linked with the accommodating strategy of the trade agreement and collective bargaining. "We have been naught," the delegates sang, "we shall be all."[46]

Launched with song, the IWW nearly foundered in the next few years. The Wobblies, as they were called, did not have enough money to pay organizers; their first leadership was corrupt and incompetent. And soon their organization was notorious. On December 30, 1905, a drifter named Harry Orchard killed the former governor of Idaho, a bitter opponent of the WFM, with a bomb at his home in Caldwell. Law enforcement officials quickly induced Orchard to blame a so-called Inner Circle of the WFM for instigating the crime. With dubious legal authority, Bill Haywood was taken from a brothel in Denver and sent, along with two associates, to prison in Boise. The episode aroused strong passions: Margaret Dreier Robins of the WTUL marched with four thousand workers through the streets of Chicago to protest the treatment of Haywood and the others. But Theodore Roosevelt denounced these "undesirable citizens." Despite the President's condemnation, Haywood was acquitted in 1907, an associate was acquitted in 1908, and the third defendant was never brought to trial. Still, the affair damaged the IWW: to many Americans, including much of the middle class, the Wobblies were branded as lawless, bomb-wielding revolutionaries.[47]

In those years, the IWW organized from one end of the country to the other. There were notable successes—followed by equally notable failures. In December 1906, the IWW conducted what seems to have been the first sit-down strike in American history: workers at the General Electric Works in Schenectady, New York, sat down at their places, rather than walk out, and forced the rehiring of three fired Wobblies. In Bridgeport, Connecticut, the IWW organized Hungarians and native-born skilled workers to contest the management of the American Tube and Stamping Company. Wobblies organized textile workers in Paterson, New Jersey, and then built the

National Industrial Union of Textile Workers with representatives from mill towns around New England. Back out West, a growing IWW industrial union was "LAW" in the Nevada mining town of Goldfield until businessmen struck back in March 1907. President Roosevelt was induced to send federal troops to keep a peace that had not been disturbed; the soldiers helped intimidate miners who faced wage cuts and infamous "yellow-dog" contracts forswearing union membership. By the time the troops left Goldfield in 1909, the IWW local was destroyed. In the Northwest, the Wobblies organized lumber workers, the "bindlestiffs" who had to carry their own bedding—their "bindles"—from job to job. But in March 1907, a strike against a Portland lumber mill was crushed. By 1908 the IWW still had only about thirty thousand members nationwide.[48]

During these battles, the Wobblies struggled to define the purpose of their union. While some members favored political action through socialist parties, others championed "direct action" through uncompromising use of the strike weapon in the workplace. According to an IWW manifesto on direct action, "The worker on the job shall tell the boss when and where he shall work, how long, and for what wages and under what conditions." The advocates of direct action won out: the socialists drifted away; the WFM, growing conservative, withdrew in 1907; and Daniel DeLeon was expelled in 1908. By then, the IWW had new and more effective leaders: the president was "Big Bill" Haywood, who left the WFM; the general organizer was "the Saint," Vincent St. John, who fought at Telluride, allegedly belonged to the old WFM "Inner Circle," and had his right hand crippled by a gunshot at Goldfield. Calling for radical action in the workplace to overturn capitalism, these men held out a syndicalist vision of a nation managed, not by a state, but by industrial unions of workers. "It is the historic mission of the working class to do away with capitalism," ran a new version of the "Preamble." "By organizing industrially we are forming the structure of the new society within the shell of the old." Despite the Wobblies' violent reputation, the IWW placed much more emphasis on peaceful measures—strikes and the passive resistance of the sit-down at Schenectady. Nevertheless, this was a revolutionary ideology, fully comparable to European syndicalism. Committed to industrial unionism, confrontational tactics, and a utopian social vision, the IWW could become a potent force in America. "It is not even a house of cards," Samuel Gompers sneered, a bit nervously, "they have not even made the cards stand." But the IWW was already changing the nature of working-class mutualism. Some progressives would go along; the great majority would not.[49]

The radicalism of the IWW provoked retaliation from the state. After the anthracite coal settlement, Theodore Roosevelt and the executive branch of the federal government had not done much to help or hurt labor. Congress and state legislatures had not done much, either. William Howard Taft also made little attempt to enforce the "permanent lesson" of the anthracite strike. Instead, as in other matters, he preferred to defer to the courts. And it was the courts, both state and federal, that struck blow after blow against the IWW and the rest of organized labor in the 1900s. It was not only that the judiciary refused to extend protection to all workers on the job. At the same time, judges were disarming labor by tearing away the vital weapons of mutualism.[50]

The courts were a longtime enemy of organized, assertive wage earners. Drawn mostly from the upper class, justices naturally defended the interests of property against labor. Moreover, courts rightly saw working-class mutualism as a threat to their authority and to the individualist values embedded in the American common law. Robert F. Hoxie, a political economist at the University of Chicago, summed up the ideological conflict between courts and unions: "As the law in spirit is individualistic, as it makes the freedom and sacredness of individual contract the touchstone of absolute justice, and as the unions are formed to escape the evils of individualism and individual competition and contract, and all the union acts in positive support of these purposes do involve coercion, the law cannot help being in spirit inimical to unionism."[51]

Courts attacked mutualism in several ways. In 1904, judges in Illinois and Wisconsin overturned the closed shop: there could be no restriction, they ruled, on the right of employers to hire nonunion labor. In 1905, the state supreme court in Colorado upheld the suspension of habeas corpus in the WFM strikes. In 1908, the United States Supreme Court, overturning a ban on yellow-dog contracts in the railroad business, seemingly left employers free to discharge workers who joined unions. Worse, judges frequently issued injunctions to stop wage earners' collective action. It was difficult to deny the right to strike: courts seldom enjoined primary strikes by workers against their own employers. But the injunction could be readily deployed against other weapons in labor's arsenal, particularly secondary, sympathetic strikes and boycotts. Workers responded with bravado. "A strike isn't looked upon as a real strike . . . ," boasted a machinist, "until there is an injunction against it." But the results were devastating. A judge could enjoin thousands of workers at a time; he could tell them not to picket, not to march, not to meet, not to shout "scab" at strikebreakers. "No weapon has been used with such disastrous effect against trade unions as the injunction in labor disputes," John Mitchell observed. "It is difficult to speak in measured tone or moderate language of the savagery and venom with which unions have been assailed by the injunction. . . ."[52]

During the early twentieth century, the courts' hostility to boycotts turned into a threat to the very legitimacy of unions. In Danbury, Connecticut, in 1902, Dietrich Loewe, a hat manufacturer, refused to recognize the United Hatters of North America. Loewe's workers went on strike; he hired scabs. The union then did what workers often did when they could not effectively control the workplace: the hatters started a boycott on the purchase of Loewe's hats. The boycott became far-reaching when the AFL added Loewe to the federation's official "We Don't Patronize" list and sent out representatives to block distribution of his hats around the country. But Loewe had recently helped found the American Anti-Boycott Association. Striking back in federal court, the association argued that the United Hatters had violated the Sherman Anti-Trust Act's prohibition against "conspiracy in restraint of trade or commerce among the several States." Accordingly, Loewe, under a provision of the act, should be able to sue his workers for triple damages. Anticipating a suit, the Anti-Boycott Association attached the homes and bank accounts of 248 hatters. In February 1908, the United States Supreme Court unanimously reached the extraordinary conclusion that the anti-trust act did indeed cover organized labor as well as big business: the hatters had unconstitutionally restrained trade. Not only was the boycott in grave jeopardy; so, presumably, was the right of workers to organize and strike.[53]

The AFL did not back down in the face of hostile courts. John Mitchell argued that "when an injunction . . . forbids the doing of a thing which is lawful, I believe . . . it is the duty of all patriotic and law-abiding citizens to resist, or at least to disregard, the injunction. It is better that half the workingmen of the country remain constantly in jail. . . ." But the courts were ready to punish defiance. In 1906, the AFL called a boycott of the Buck's Stove and Range Company of St. Louis, whose president, J. W. Van Cleave, was also president of the National Association of Manufacturers and a vice president of the Citizens' Alliance. When the supreme court of the District of Columbia enjoined the AFL, Samuel Gompers and other federation leaders continued to call publicly for the boycott. In December 1908, the court found Gompers, Mitchell, and another AFL official in contempt for their "unrefined insult, coarse affront, vulgar indignity" and sentenced them to jail.[54]

Meanwhile, on the other side of the country, the law further demonstrated its willingness to violate the right of free speech in order to suppress mutualism. In the Northwest, the IWW could not easily reach migrant workers who labored in mines, forests, and farms; so the Wobblies began to organize in the cities where these wage earners hired out for work. In Spokane, Washington, in 1908, Wobblies spoke out on street corners against the "sharks"—employment agencies that funneled itinerant, unskilled workers into short-term jobs in the countryside. The sharks snapped back: in March 1909, the Spokane city council banned street speaking by "revolutionists." When Wobblies continued to speak out, they were hauled off to prison. Soon the IWW filled the jails to overflowing. Unable to lie down, given only bread and water twice a day, the prisoners sang the "Red Flag" and the "Marseillaise."[55]

The Wobblies got no help from the federal government, but Gompers and the AFL received some support, at least. A provision of the Clayton Act of 1914 exempted unions from the threat of prosecution under the Sherman Anti-Trust Act. Saved from the threat of the Danbury Hatters' and Buck's Stove and Range cases, Gompers enthusiastically labeled the new law labor's "Magna Carta." But the Clayton Act, full of loopholes, was hardly that. As the general counsel of the American Anti-Boycott Association smugly explained, the measure had only "slight practical importance."[56]

By the 1910s, conservative courts, intransigent employers, radical Wobblies, and obdurate trade unionists had undone the "permanent lesson" of the anthracite strike. Even though the number of strikes and lockouts nationwide fell from a high of 3,648 in 1903 to 1,204 by 1914, progressives' hopes for an end to class conflict had dimmed. Reformers had made some strides, especially in promoting special protection for women workers. As the crusade for special protection and the rise of welfare capitalism indicated, progressives could sometimes make common cause with employers and union leaders. But, overall, middle-class reformers had little success in shaping the outlook and behavior of workers and the upper ten. Worse, the progressives' great hope, the power of the state, had proved unreliable. Presidents were fickle, legislatures ineffectual, judges individualistic. Instead of ending in a state-sanctioned entente between capital and labor, the battle over work seemed more likely to continue on the shop floor and the picket line, and in the legislature and the courtroom.[57]

CHAPTER FIVE

Controlling Big Business

Ann Bassett grew up on a ranch in northwest Colorado in the late nineteenth century. As a girl, she knew the Utes and other Native Americans who lived around the Little Snake, the Elk, and the Yampa Rivers; she encountered the outlaw Butch Cassidy and the bounty hunter Tom Horn. Her family, like other small cattle owners in Brown's Park, grazed their herd on land owned by the federal government. And like those cattlemen out on the frontier, she still clung to individualist values as a young woman in the Roosevelt years. Hers was a world of equality and opportunity. "It was a privilege to live in a new free land," she recalled, "where real democracy existed in a wholesome atmosphere, where people were accepted on their individual merits, and background or great wealth had small importance." There was, she insisted, "[e]qual opportunity for development on all sides in an uncluttered America, before collectivism got a stranglehold on the nation." More than anything else, Bassett valued freedom and independence. "All I asked of life," she declared, "was to be perpetually let alone, to go my way undisturbed."[1]

Ann Bassett was not let alone, however. Like other small cattle owners, her way was disturbed by wealthier ranchers. The big cattlemen intended to keep the range for themselves; they were determined to drive the small ranchers out and to keep sheep raisers from coming in. Ann Bassett loathed "the grasping cattle barons . . . the biggest thieves of all time." She especially hated the Two Bar Ranch, owned by Ora Haley and managed by Bill Patten, two self-styled "rolling juggernauts." Despite her individualism, she applauded federal regulation of the government land in Brown's Park—first its inclusion in the new, 757,000 acre Park Range Forest Reserve in 1905, and then the levy of a grazing fee that ensured access for all cattle owners, large and small, in 1906. "The common people being overrun and struggling to live under adverse conditions, welcomed forest control with its legal protection," she remembered years later.[2]

Haley, Patten, and the rest of the "Two Bar outfit" would have none of that. As the "bleaching bones" of dead sheep made clear, these were ruthless men. They would not pay the grazing tax. They would not even let the Forest Service count their cattle. Unable to bribe the forest rangers, the Two Bar outfit scattered their herds across the vast range of Brown's Park. When forest ranger Harry Ratliff rounded up the cattle, Haley's men stampeded the herd in the dead of night. Then the "rolling juggernauts" went after Ratliff. They tried threatening him; they tried hauling him before a judge on trumped-up horse-theft charges. Then they tried more desperate measures. Just across the state line in Baggs, Wyoming, on the northern edge of the reserve, the Two Bar outfit installed a new marshal, Bob Meldrum, who was, Ann Bassett reported, "a professional strike breaker" and "killer" with "several killings to his discredit." When Ratliff's work took him up to Baggs, Meldrum was ready. One day, he apparently tried to ambush the ranger, but the shot went wide. That evening Ratliff went into Baggs for supplies. As he led his horse to a barn, Meldrum appeared and told him to hand over his gun. Ratliff refused. The two men got ready to shoot it out. Meldrum reached for his gun—"but before he could draw he was looking into the muzzle of a Colts forty-five. . . ." Meldrum was stunned, "completely nonplused . . . his killer instinct vanished. . . ." The forest ranger took Meldrum's gun and strode off. Federal regulation had come to Brown's Park.[3]

The encounter between Ratliff and Meldrum was one of many showdowns over the regulation of big business in the early twentieth century. Of course, these confrontations usually took place in courtrooms and legislative chambers, not in forests and dusty streets. The antagonists were usually attorneys and politicians, not sheriffs and rangers. And the weapons of choice were usually stump speeches, magazine articles, and legal briefs, not

Colt .45s. But the central issues of all these struggles were laid bare in Brown's Park.

Despite the gradual return of prosperity after the depression of the 1890s, business activity posed three great problems in the new century. First, and most obvious, was the continued emergence of large-scale enterprises, not only such transcontinental corporate giants as Standard Oil and United States Steel, but potent local businesses like the Two Bar and the other big ranch operations out West. The consequences of bigness were unsettling: the "rolling juggernauts" of Brown's Park and Wall Street could throw their weight around, could hurt competitors, consumers, and employees. Their threatening power pointed to a second problem, economic interdependence. In an increasingly complex, specialized economy, businesses more and more affected the lives of Americans. For all the talk of individualism, Ann Bassett and other Americans realized that there was no being let alone anymore, even out on the frontier. Finally, Americans had a sense of economic limits, new in the nation's history. For the first time, there was a widespread understanding that forests, land, and other resources were not infinite. In Brown's Park, the ranchers knew that if they overgrazed the range, there would be nothing left in the future. As it was, there might not be enough land to go around in the present.

Bigness, interdependence, limits—these realities compelled Americans to reconsider the right of businesses, large and small, to do as they pleased. Like labor relations, this was a critical issue for the middle class, a battle it had to fight. But progressives and their political allies had an even more difficult time in the struggle to control business. The battlefield was much harder to master. For one thing, there were more combatants than in the fight to stop labor conflict. Given the wide reach of big corporations, every class, including farmers, had vital interests at stake in this confrontation. No group could unilaterally impose its will. Instead, combatants usually had to make alliances, some of them strange and uncomfortable, and win over at least some of the enemy. The clean, seemingly simple drama of Brown's Park, with obvious good guys and bad guys, had few counterparts. In addition, the question of how to control business was more complicated, more technical, and more ambiguous than the labor issue. The fate of a single corporation could be played out in a confusing swirl of legal actions in multiple courts that lasted years and left behind a long trail of paperwork—and no clear outcome.

Further, the progressives disagreed on how to fight. More than any other issue of the early twentieth century, this one relentlessly exposed the limitations of the progressives' common ideological understanding. Progressivism was a deeply rooted orientation toward the basic matters of day-to-day human existence, never a policy blueprint. That was often a great strength. Sharing a fundamental agenda, progressives could usually go their separate ways and still serve a common purpose. In the battle to change other people, temperance advocates, settlement workers, Country Life crusaders, and school reformers did not have to think much of the others' particular specialties; they seldom bumped into one another and came into conflict. The battle to control business required much more unity; to achieve this difficult goal, the progressives had to march together under one policy banner. But there were several banners on this battlefield, and progressive ideology did not tell middle-class men and women which one to choose. Some progressives wanted to break up big businesses; some wanted to regulate them. Some preferred to build up federal power; some preferred to rely on the states.

Finally, the struggle over business was still more difficult for the progressives and other combatants because the conflict had a tendency to spill over the boundaries of the battlefield. In one case after another, corporate behavior and regulation forced new issues—about the rich, about the nature of American politics. Neither Theodore Roosevelt nor any other politician managed to contain the battle over business.

The twentieth century began amid a remarkable structural transformation of the economy. Since the 1870s, a constellation of circumstances—a nationwide railway network, abundant raw materials, emerging technologies, available finance capital, favorable government policies—had produced a new kind of industrial firm. The circumstances varied from business to business: John D. Rockefeller exploited the developing uses of petroleum; James B. Duke suddenly produced millions of cigarettes with the continuous-process Bonsack cigarette machine; "Captain" Frederick Pabst used temperature-controlled tank cars to send beer around the country. But the results were the same. These and other businessmen created vertically integrated firms that engaged in every aspect of an industry, from the extraction of raw materials to the production of finished goods, to marketing, sales, and service.

Pabst had his own saloons, his own barrel plants, even his own timberlands. These vast firms, employing thousands of workers, needed new kinds of accounting techniques and new kinds of management. Worth hundreds of millions of dollars, they also needed new forms of ownership. Too much for one owner or even several partners, the giant firms organized as trusts and, increasingly, as joint-stock corporations. Rockefeller created Standard Oil; Duke founded American Tobacco; Pabst launched what became the Pabst Brewing Company. When Andrew Carnegie sold Carnegie Steel, a privately held partnership, in 1901, J. P. Morgan and his associates had to turn this billion-dollar business into a corporation, United States Steel, whose shares were traded on the New York Stock Exchange.[4]

The creation of United States Steel was part of an unprecedented wave of mergers that gave the issue of bigness new urgency in the Roosevelt years. During the depression of the 1890s, many large firms, particularly newer mass-production industrial companies, had engaged in debilitating competition with one another. Desperate to cover high fixed costs, they had cut their prices to disastrously low levels. Unable to join together in pools and selling agencies to stop competition, the firms had begun to merge. From 1897 until 1904, the "great merger movement" turned 1,800 companies into just 157. The names of the new firms proclaimed their long reach: Continental Cotton and United States Glue; National Biscuit and National Glass; American Bicycle and American Brass. Typically, each of the new corporations controlled more than 40 percent of its industry's market; about a third of them each controlled more than 70 percent of a market. This horizontal integration of firms in the same business, along with their vertical integration, changed the face of the American economy. Giant corporations had not wiped out small business by any means. They did not dominate every part of the economy. But they commanded key sectors, from food products to petroleum to fabricated metals to lumber and paper. And no one knew whether or not the merger movement would stop.[5]

The rise of large-scale corporations was unsettling, even frightening. Big business, as one newspaper warned, could well "lead to one of the greatest social and political upheavals that has been witnessed in modern history." The corporations had some unabashed celebrants and some implacable foes. But most Americans seemed ambivalent. United States Steel, Standard Oil, and the rest were certainly remarkable creations. They offered opportunities for well-to-do investors, white-collar managers, and working-class wage earners; they provided a host of new goods and services, often at lower costs. Yet, corporate leaders, proud members of the upper ten, struck an arrogant pose. As a North Carolina editor angrily observed, "[A]ll sense of shame has been lost by the corporations." They wielded disturbing economic power: more than one industry had become an oligopoly, basically controlled by a handful of large firms. The corporations could hurt consumers by raising the price of goods; they could hurt farmers and businessmen by raising railroad rates and hiking the cost of raw materials; they could hurt workers by cutting wages and demanding more productivity; they could hurt competitors by slashing the price of finished products and raising the price of raw materials; they could hurt towns, cities, whole regions of the country by manipulating freight charges and putting railroads and factories in one locale or another. Further, the corporations, entangled in a web of banks, insurance companies, and brokerage houses, gave enormous power to a handful of financiers—the Morgans, Stillmans, and Harrimans. More broadly, the corporations sustained the upper class and its troubling social, cultural, and political aspirations.[6]

By the 1900s, Americans had developed at least five approaches to the threat of big business. The simplest solution was to do nothing, to leave corporations essentially undisturbed. This laissez-faire approach reflected powerful cultural imperatives: the enduring appeal of individual freedom, the deep commitment to private property rights, the continuing faith in "natural" economic laws. For much of the upper ten, no doubt, laissez-faire was simply the rationalization of their self-interest. For other advocates, it was a pragmatic recognition of economic reality. "Corporations," a Virginia publisher resolved: "The most efficient agents for the promotion of modern progress. If an evil, then a necessary evil. . . ."[7]

Most Americans were less willing to leave evil undisturbed. More and more advocated socialism, the public ownership of the means of production. By the early 1900s, socialist ideas had a widening appeal among workers, farmers, the middle class, and even occasionally the upper ten. Some municipalities already accepted a limited form of socialism—the public ownership of so-called natural monopolies such as water works, gas plants, and other utilities. As the popularity of Bellamy's *Looking Backward* suggested, middle-class Americans could at least fantasize about the communal ownership of industry. But most progressives were not prepared to turn this fantasy into reality.[8]

Despite their obvious differences, laissez-faire and socialism shared ironic similarities. Both policies accepted, even celebrated, large-scale business. Both approaches could lead to the end of competitive capitalism. Clearly, public ownership of corporations would limit competition and constrict the marketplace. So would laissez-faire: unchecked corporations would also limit competition and shrink the marketplace.

In contrast, the three other approaches to big business aimed to preserve competitive capitalism through some form of ongoing government intervention. Antitrust, regulation, and compensation offered different but not always incompatible alternatives. Grounded in a popular tradition of hostility to monopoly stretching back to the colonial era, antitrust would break up businesses that thwarted competition. Since the Gilded Age, a number of states, particularly in the South, had passed antitrust laws and taken corporations to court. Arkansas filed suit against insurance companies; Texas took on oil companies; North Carolina went after the American Tobacco Company. At the national level, Congress endorsed antitrust by passing the Sherman Act in 1890. "Every contract, combination in the form of trust or otherwise, or conspiracy, in restraint of trade or commerce among the several States, or with foreign nations, is," the act announced, "hereby declared to be illegal." In the new century, many Americans strongly supported antitrust. Among them were leading progressive activists and politicians, such as Boston lawyer Louis Brandeis and William Jennings Bryan.[9]

Unlike antitrust, regulation accepted the existence of threatening businesses but tried to control their behavior. Corporations would be allowed to continue only under the watchful eye of government. Like antitrust, regulation originated in the colonial period and became popular again in the Gilded Age. For instance, state governments had established railroad commissions to oversee a range of practices including stock issues and freight charges. At the federal level, the most important expression of the regulatory impulse also focused on railroads. In 1887, Congress created the Interstate Commerce Commission to monitor the railways' charges and trade practices. In the twentieth century, such progressives as Social Gospel leader Lyman Abbott and journalist Herbert Croly ardently advocated an expansion of governments' regulatory control over business.[10]

Compensation, the last approach, also accepted the existence of troubling businesses but would force them to return some of their wealth to the community. Many Americans bitterly resented the minuscule tax burden on corporations. "Why," a Wisconsin resident inquired, "should I have to pay my property tax bill, especially during hard times, when a big outfit . . . dodges [theirs]?" By the 1900s, a number of states and municipalities had imposed taxes on railroads, insurance companies, and other corporations. Americans, especially in the South and West, also resented so-called foreign corporations—businesses chartered and headquartered in other states. "I am fed up," a Texan announced, "with these big eastern life-insurance companies coming in here and taking our money back with them. . . . Texas is not a colony of the State of New York!" Fueled by this anger, some states tried unsuccessfully to pass laws forcing corporations to invest locally. In 1905, Texas did manage to enact an investment incentive measure that reduced taxes on insurance companies investing in the state. Compensation also had its progressive advocates, especially interested in corporate taxation.[11]

All five approaches to corporations were problematic. However grounded in American values, laissez-faire struck many people as inadequate, even dangerous, in an unstable economy and a divided society. Many businessmen, for all their brave talk about competition and the survival of the fittest, had begun to fear unregulated capitalism. Despite Ann Bassett's black-and-white picture, there were even big cattlemen who welcomed federal regulation of the range. Socialism, in contrast, seemed too radical for a society that still celebrated personal freedom and private property and still dreaded strong central government. Compensation was too limited an instrument: it was a way to punish misbehaving businesses and a way to redirect at least some wealth. Taxation, by itself, was a rather blunt instrument for changing specific corporate policies. And Americans were not yet willing to endorse taxes large enough to make a big business small. When Congress adopted the first corporate tax in 1909, the measure claimed only a tiny portion of corporate revenues.[12]

Antitrust and regulation also suffered from their infringement on personal freedom and property rights and their dependence on state action. The practical problems of governmental authority further jeopardized antitrust and regulation. The nation's federal system, with its confusing array of jurisdictions, made the task of economic control difficult. Big businesses seldom acted within a single state; those "foreign" corporations could readily elude state governments. The United States government had a far wider reach, of course. Washington controlled the nation's borders, the territories, and federally owned land like Brown's Park. Moreover, the Constitution granted the federal government authority over commerce between the states. But all these prerogatives added up to rather little at the turn of the century. The Interstate Commerce Commission had proven weak and ineffectual. So had the Sherman Act when the Supreme Court, ruling in the E. C. Knight case in 1895, declared that the American Sugar Refining Company's manufacturing operations only incidentally involved commerce, and were thus beyond the antitrust law. Unable—and apparently unwilling—to control existing corporations, Washington also lacked the authority to impose limits on new ones: the states, not the national government, granted charters to corporations.[13]

Despite all these constraints, the nation had the opportunity to take hold of big business in the progressive era. Too many people, fearing the consequences of unrestrained corporate growth, wanted more public control over corporations. There was a mandate for change—but no agreement on what that change should be.

The outcry over the merger movement guaranteed that antitrust would be given a thorough test. Two cases—Northern Securities and Standard Oil—illustrated the possibilities and limits of antitrust. These successful prosecutions underscored federal authority, broke up big economic combinations, and hurt the interests of some of the nation's most powerful capitalists. Yet, these and other antitrust prosecutions in the 1900s and 1910s hardly restructured American capitalism or toppled the upper ten.

As Theodore Roosevelt settled into the White House, he was an unlikely champion of antitrust prosecutions. In spite of his distaste for business values, the President favored large-scale enterprise. "This is an age of combination . . . ," he observed. "The corporation has come to stay. . . ." Eager to forestall radicalism, Roosevelt worked to calm the public fears about corporations early in his presidency. "Much of the complaint against corporations is entirely unwarranted," he reassured an audience in 1902. But the President believed that big business required regulation. "[These] corporations," he maintained, "should be managed with due regard of the public as a whole." As in the anthracite coal strike, Roosevelt set out to establish the federal government as the representative of that public interest.[14]

With that goal in mind, the President could welcome a popular antitrust suit against a corporate villain, despite his antipathy to the Sherman Act. He had an ideal opportunity, with two villains and an impressive supporting Wall Street cast, when E. H. Harriman, ruler of the Union Pacific Railroad, and James J. Hill, ruler of the Great Northern, let their battle for control of Northwestern railroads get out of hand late in 1901. To succeed, each man needed to take over the vital lines of the Chicago, Burlington, and Quincy Railroad. To win that prize, the two financiers called on powerful allies in Wall Street: James Stillman of National City Bank and Jacob Schiff of Kuhn, Loeb & Company backed Harriman; J. P. Morgan himself supported Hill. When the Hill forces refused to let Harriman share in the CB&Q, Daisy Harriman's uncle went after the Northern Pacific Railroad, a crucial part of Hill and Morgan's plans. The resulting contest for Northern Pacific stock set off a frenzy of fear and speculation well beyond Wall Street. "Cold print," wrote Stillman's biographer, "fails utterly to convey the tension and the terror which such events cause, the helpless indignation of the rest of the world when Pan stamps his hoof in lower Manhattan." The panic and the rising price of Northern Pacific stock brought the combatants to their senses: they decided to merge their interests in a single vast firm, the Northern Securities Company, which would hold shares in the Great Northern, the Northern Pacific, and the CB&Q. But this anticompetitive solution infuriated Northwesterners. Quickly, the governor of Minnesota brought together the governors and attorneys general of nearby states to consider how "to fight the great railway trust." As Minnesota began legal action against this obvious restraint of trade, the Roosevelt administration stepped in. On February 19, 1902, the United States Department of Justice announced plans to file an antitrust suit against the Northern Securities Company.[15]

For Wall Street, the government's action was "a sudden and severe shock," a "bolt from the blue." On February 22, J. P. Morgan went down to Washington to confront the President. According to Roosevelt, Morgan told him, "If we have done anything wrong, send your man to my man and they can fix it up." "That can't be done," Roosevelt snapped back. The financier asked whether the President was "going to attack my other interests, the Steel Trust, and the others?" Roosevelt said no, "unless we find out that in any case they have done something that we regard as wrong." When Morgan left, the President remarked, "That is a most illuminating illustration of the Wall Street point of view. Mr. Morgan could not help regarding me as a big rival operator who either intended to ruin all his interests or else could be induced to come to an agreement to ruin none." No doubt the tale grew in telling; but it surely revealed the Washington "point of view." Roosevelt could accept, and even welcome, the formation of United States Steel; he could not accept the treatment of the President of the United States as a mere "rival operator." The suit went ahead.[16]

In 1904, the Supreme Court ruled five to four that the Northern Securities Company had indeed violated the Sherman Act. The case, the first successful federal prosecution of a single, tightly integrated interstate corporation, was a signal victory for Theodore Roosevelt. So was the administration's successful suit in 1902 to prevent the unpopular meatpacking companies of the "beef trust" from conspiring to fix prices and restrain competition. With these triumphs, Roosevelt won acclaim as the great "trustbuster." But Washington's trustbusting power was uncertain. It was not yet clear whether the Sherman Act applied to all corporations restraining interstate trade. It was not clear either whether the President, despite his trustbusting reputation, had the will or the interest to go after every one of those firms. If there could be what Roosevelt called "good" or "honest" monopolistic corporations, then the scope of antitrust, for all its popularity with Americans, might be very narrow.[17]

Nevertheless, antitrust remained a vital force, especially at the state level. In the Roosevelt years, there was a groundswell of anger at John D. Rockefeller's Standard Oil, with its complex of state-chartered corporations. From 1902 to 1904, Ida M. Tarbell exposed "The History of the Standard Oil Company" in nineteen articles in the pages of *McClure's.* By 1904, the people of Kansas had begun to wonder why Standard paid the state's independent oil producers so little for their crude oil and charged consumers so much for the company's refined oil. Kansans held angry meetings and considered whether the state should build its own refinery. As a newspaper observed, " . . . in every community men of careful business judgment . . . are willing to waive prejudices against state interference in private business . . . for the sake of curbing the power of Standard Oil." The state set up a refinery, passed various regulatory measures, and began an antitrust suit. "After a little," a Kansan promised, "the people of the country will raise up and hang a few Rockefellers and other kinds of buzzards who rob the people, not forgetting to include in the general hangings a squad or two of high court judges." No judges or Rockefellers swung by the neck, but other states joined in the attack on Standard Oil. In well-publicized hearings, the attorney general of Missouri documented the company's arrogance and its restraint of trade. By 1907, Standard Oil faced action by at least eight states. To avoid testifying, Rockefeller hid like a criminal on the run. Once, he had to escape his estate, Pocantico, north of Manhattan, by taking a boat to a hideaway in New Jersey.[18]

Rockefeller also had to deal with the federal government. In August 1906, the government took the Standard Oil Company of Indiana to court over no fewer than 1,462 violations of federal law. The most serious federal threat was an antitrust suit. More than ever, Roosevelt condemned antitrust. "It is generally useless to try to prohibit all restraint on competition . . . ," he argued, "and where it is not useless it is generally hurtful." The President preferred to make private arrangements with large-scale businesses about their competitive practices. But Roosevelt could not ignore grassroots antitrust sentiment. For that matter, he disliked John D. Rockefeller. In 1905, Roosevelt had ordered a federal investigation of Standard Oil. Completed the next year, the inquiry showed that the company "has habitually received from the railroads, and is now receiving, secret rates and other unjust illegal discriminations." Further, Standard Oil exercised "monopolistic control . . . from the well of the producer to the door step of the consumer." In November 1906, Washington filed suit under the Sherman Act to dissolve the Standard Oil Company of New Jersey and its subsidiary corporations. This time Rockefeller made himself available to testify. A federal circuit court ruled against the company in 1909. Two years later, the United States Supreme Court upheld the judgment and ruled that Standard must allow its subsidiary corporations to function freely and independently and must itself go out of business. It would stand as the most famous court-ordered breakup of a corporation until American Telephone and Telegraph, almost eight decades later. Rockefeller was golfing with a Roman Catholic priest at Pocantico when he heard the news. "Father Lennon," he said calmly, "have you some money?" Learning about the verdict on safari in Africa, now former President Roosevelt exulted over "one of the most signal triumphs for decency which has been won in our country."[19]

In delivering this blow to Rockefeller and Standard Oil, however, the Court also delivered a blow to the progressive advocates of antitrust. A majority of the justices enunciated the "rule of reason": the Sherman Act did not prohibit all restraints of interstate trade, only "unreasonable" ones. In other words, a monopoly was illegal only if it was created illegally. The ruling did not spare big-business men altogether; in fact, it left them still uncertain about which business dealings were or were not illegal. Meanwhile, the new President, William Howard Taft, a stickler for the law and the courts, brought more antitrust suits than his predecessor ever had. The Taft administration even went after United States Steel, with a prosecution that named Andrew Carnegie, Morgan, Rockefeller, and Charles Schwab, among others, as defendants.[20]

Despite Taft's vigorous prosecutions, the results were disappointing. The structure of corporate oligarchy shook, but never collapsed. Standard Oil and Rockefeller were a case in point. The newly independent Standard companies flourished in the years after the antitrust case. Despite the breakup, Rockefeller did not need Father Lennon's money after all. The sale of stock in the Standard subsidiaries made the magnate a billionaire, the richest man in the world. Rockefeller's reputation even improved. The testimony of this old, seemingly doddering man in the Standard trial had artfully countered the image of the evil incarnation of monopoly. "Now that Rockefeller has emerged from seclusion and is seen in the fierce light of a public inquiry," a newspaper commented, "he appears no such monster as the public fancy has painted." In the years to come, Rockefeller's massive philanthropy further burnished his reputation. For that matter, Carnegie, Harriman, Morgan, Stillman, and all the rest maintained their fortunes, their power, and their standing. In the meantime, Woodrow Wilson's Democratic administration made an ineffectual attempt to bolster the Sherman Act. Playing to popular sentiment for antitrust during the presidential campaign of 1912, Wilson had promised "a second struggle for emancipation," an economic program that would break the chains of monopoly and restore competition. Yet, in 1914, Congress managed only the Clayton Act, a loophole-ridden measure that tried unsuccessfully to provide more specific definitions of restraint of trade and harsher penalties for breaking the Sherman Act. By the First World

War, the antitrust campaign had boosted the authority of the federal government; but new legislation and lawsuits had not undermined the most powerful and creative leaders of the upper ten.[21]

As the antitrust crusade pushed ahead in the 1900s and 1910s, Americans also vigorously and contentiously explored how to regulate big business. Out of the welter of regulatory struggles, two early episodes—the fight for the regulation of food and drugs, and the battle over conservation—illustrated both the promise and the limits of attempts to control business on an ongoing basis. Successful regulation required not only a powerful sense of urgency but a broad, cross-class coalition. Progressives and their political allies triumphed in the struggle for pure food and drugs by invoking disparate Americans' shared identity as consumers. Even so, this cause also needed to win over some business opponents, or at least force their acquiescence to regulation. In the conservation battle, reformers never managed to produce a self-conscious consumers' coalition. Instead, there was a battle of different groups who acted on their interest as producers. In these circumstances, progressives could easily find themselves on the defensive, their cause described as socialist usurpation and their enemies trumpeting the virtues of individualism.

Americans had worried for years about the purity of their food and drugs. Everyone knew about "embalmed" beef, with "an odor similar to that of a dead human . . . injected with preservatives," that had been served to American soldiers during the Spanish-American War. By the turn of the century, there were concerns about the safety of dyes and preservatives used in food, about the introduction of "artificial" foods such as glucose, and about the adulteration and misrepresentation of food and drugs. The work of Harvey W. Wiley, chief of the Bureau of Chemistry in the U.S. Department of Agriculture, had helped to substantiate some of these concerns. More important, Wiley, a talented publicist, had artfully built support for protective legislation: there was, for example, his well-known "poison squad" of employees and medical students, "young, robust fellows" who supposedly risked their lives by testing food laced with borax and other preservatives. Nevertheless, the campaign for a national law protecting consumers of food and drugs had gotten nowhere by the end of Roosevelt's first term.[22]

Then middle-class journalism, driven by progressive concerns, did the work of exposure. In 1905, the *Ladies' Home Journal* disclosed the fraudulent advertisements used to sell Lydia Pinkham's Vegetable Compound and other home remedies. Later that year, Samuel Hopkins Adams exposed patent medicines as "The Great American Fraud" in the pages of *Collier's.* Well into 1906, Adams revealed the deceptive claims for the powers of Peruna and Liquozone. Documenting the liberal use of narcotics in catarrh powders and other nostrums, he condemned the "shameful trade that stupefies helpless babies and makes criminals of our young men and harlots of our young women."[23]

No sooner had Adams's articles appeared than the public began to learn more about meat. Branded "The Greatest Trust in the World" by *Everybody's Magazine,* the big meatpacking corporations of Chicago were already unpopular for their high prices. In 1905, the Supreme Court had upheld an antitrust injunction against Swift & Company, Armour & Company, and the other big firms. Then a novel by a young socialist writer, Upton Sinclair, revealed how they produced their expensive meat. *The Jungle* was the depressing story of a Lithuanian couple, Jurgis and Ona, struggling to survive in Chicago. Sinclair intended to dramatize the plight of poor workers, but his readers were affected more by the disclosures about the meatpacking plants, like "Durham's," where Jurgis worked. *The Jungle* described careless meat inspectors from the Department of Agriculture; it described canned meats made with fat, suet, dyed tripe, and "hard cartilaginous gullets"; it described "potted chicken" made with no chicken at all; it described the "old and crippled cattle"—"cattle . . . with boils . . . foul-smelling stuff"—used by the packers; it described meat tainted by sawdust, human spit, and rat excrement; and it described "Durham's Pure Leaf Lard," made from the bodies of workers who fell accidentally into the great lard vats. Sinclair gathered these details into a broader indictment of corporate deception. "The great corporations which employed you lied to you, and lied to the whole country—" Jurgis bitterly reflects, "from top to bottom it was nothing but one gigantic lie." The sensational revelations of *The Jungle* appalled the public, infuriated the meatpackers, and cut the sale of meat. By the end of 1906, the book had perhaps a million readers.[24]

One of them was Theodore Roosevelt, who had reason to be sensitive about the meatpacking business. His administration had disappointed the public with a relatively harmless report on the beef trust; that report, in turn, persuaded a judge to dismiss a federal indictment against some packers on the grounds that Washington had forced them to incriminate themselves. After meeting with Sinclair, the President sent his own investigators to Chicago. A late convert to the cause, Roosevvelt endorsed a federal meat-inspection bill proposed by his friend Senator Albert J. Beveridge, a Republican progressive from Indiana.[25] Roosevelt's support for the measure also reflected his increasingly grandiose sense of federal, and especially presidential, power. As the merger movement developed and the upper ten remained controversial, the President had begun to criticize corporations as "subjects without a sovereign." Of course, the "sovereign" he had in mind for them was the federal government; lesser authorities simply would not do. "It is an absurdity to expect to eliminate the abuses in great corporations by State action," he claimed. "The National Government alone can deal adequately with these great corporations."[26]

By the spring of 1906, both meat inspection and pure food and drugs legislation had many supporters. This was not a simple, black-and-white fight between the public on one side and big business on the other. But the pure food and drugs issue encouraged a broad range of Americans to think of their identities as consumers, as people who were imperiled by rotten meat or adulterated drugs. Physicians, federal experts, and women's groups supported legislation. State officials, assiduously courted by Harvey Wiley, agreed that federal supervision was necessary. So did Westerners, angry at the "foreign" corporations from the East and Midwest. So, too, did more than a few of those corporations. Pabst, H. J. Heinz, and other producers, setting individualism aside, recognized the benefits of federal regulation: Washington's supervision could bring order and stability to the business; it could protect the big companies from state supervision; it could make the business too expensive for potential competitors. At the least, regulation could rescue the corporations from their public predicament in 1906. Roosevelt's investigators had largely confirmed the essentials of *The Jungle;* the meatpackers were unable to discredit Sinclair's account. Under the circumstances, a crucial group of food and drug producers accepted the inevitability of regulation and tried to shape the legislation to protect their interests as much as possible.[27]

The packers did manage to weaken Beveridge's meat-inspection bill a bit:

the government, not the packers, would pay for inspection; companies would not have to date their products. But the bill went through both houses of Congress. That success finally opened the way for approval of the Pure Food and Drug Bill. Roosevelt signed the two measures into law on the same day in 1906. In different ways, they represented a significant widening of federal regulatory power. The Pure Food and Drug Act empowered the secretary of agriculture to impose fines and imprisonment on producers caught selling adulterated or misbranded goods in the marketplace; the Meat-Inspection Act, in contrast, empowered inspectors from the Department of Agriculture to go into packinghouses to prevent bad meat from coming to market at all. It was no disaster for the food and drug companies. These measures increased consumer confidence, which ultimately helped business. But the companies had to give away some of their freedom to Washington. With understandable exaggeration, Senator Beveridge concluded that the meat act was "THE MOST PRONOUNCED EXTENSION OF FEDERAL POWER IN EVERY DIRECTION EVER ENACTED."[28]

The fight over pure food and drugs illuminated the conditions for progressive success in regulating business. This was the perfect issue to capitalize on popular worries about economic interdependence. Galvanized by the fear of eating poisoned food or taking adulterated medicine, Americans from different groups felt their common identity as consumers. Like the effort to establish a third, "public" force in labor conflict, progressives had found a useful rhetorical means of uniting and mobilizing a range of Americans. But the pure food and drugs crusade still needed some business support, or at least acquiescence, in order to prevail.[29]

The same conditions held true when Woodrow Wilson's Democratic administration attempted to increase federal regulatory power. In 1913, the President successfully played on Americans' fears of the Money Trust, the network of big banks with interlocking directorates that supposedly controlled the nation's economy. The result was the adoption of the Federal Reserve Act, a compromise measure establishing a centralized banking arrangement to stabilize the nation's rickety, uncoordinated, and dangerously vulnerable currency and banking systems. Some progressives wanted even stronger legislation in order to break the power of the Money Trust, but even so, the Federal Reserve Act extended the federal government's power enough to call down the fury of conservatives. The great men of Wall Street and their conservative journalistic allies railed at this "financial heresy," this "preposterous offering of ignorance and unreason." "We are turning . . . toward practices which history shows have invariably led to decadence, to degradation, and the downfall of nations," warned conservative Republican Senator Elihu Root of New York. "We are setting our steps now in the pathway which through the protection of a paternal government brought the mighty power of Rome to its fall. . . ."[30]

The Wilson administration also risked repeating the fall of Rome by endorsing increased federal control over unfair trade practices. Conservatives predictably and vainly condemned any "socialistic program" giving the government "vast and inquisitorial powers." But a range of Americans, fearful of uncontrolled economic interdependence, readily supported a further expansion of federal power. In 1915, Congress passed legislation creating a five-member Federal Trade Commission empowered to halt businesses' unfair trade practices with cease-and-desist orders enforced by federal courts.[31]

The same conditions did not recur in the battle of conservation policy. By the 1900s, a growing number of people questioned the uncontrolled exploitation of natural resources. The conservation movement had emerged among cultivated Easterners, but its most famous spokesman was a Californian, John Muir. In 1892, Muir had founded the Sierra Club, the first major conservationist organization in the United States. Muir believed passionately that sublime nature could restore enervated modern men and women; forests were, he wrote in 1902, "fountains of life" for "tired, nerve-shaken, over-civilized people." To preserve the beauty of nature, Muir wanted forests and parks permanently withheld from economic development. "[W]ildness is a necessity," he said. Muir's arguments played strongly to the middle-class urge for the "simple life" so evident in the attack on overdecorated Victorian homes and in the rise of the Country Life movement. Conservationists reflected other progressive concerns as well. By preventing the wealthy from monopolizing resources, conservation would ensure opportunity and equality for succeeding generations. "'Better help a poor man make a living for his family than help a rich man get richer still,'" declared Gifford Pinchot, chief of the Bureau of Forestry in the Department of Agriculture. "That was our battle cry and our rule of life."[32]

The conservation movement had a pragmatic side. Rejecting the wanton exhaustion of resources in the present, some conservationists also rejected the preservation of those resources for eternity. Instead, Pinchot and others wanted conservation to promote efficient economic development. Overgrazing the range had to be stopped so that future generations could feed their cattle. Forests should be protected not so much for their therapeutic quality as for their economic value: they provided wood for fuel and construction; less obviously, they prevented floods and promoted a more reliable supply of water for farming. This economic argument certainly widened the appeal of conservationism. But just as certainly, the conservation movement, committed to aesthetics, therapy, democracy, efficiency, and development, would suffer internal divisions.[33]

Whatever their potential differences, conservationists of all stripes converged on a condemnation of individualism that was so typically progressive. "[W]hat we want is the best for the people, not the individual," a conservationist said flatly. Pursuing their personal interests, the despoilers of nature jeopardized the community. A Colorado newspaper, scoring "the robbers of the public domain," argued that "not one of these men cares for the forest or the general good. . . . And their business subverts the general good." Identifying their movement with the public interest, conservationists, like other progressives, logically turned to the state to restrain the individual.[34]

By the turn of the century, the state had not responded very much. Conservationists' most significant achievement was a little-noticed act of Congress in 1891 that gave the President the authority to create forest reserves such as Brown's Park on government-owned land. Beyond that, the conservation movement met strong resistance from so-called insurgents. These anticonservationists refused to believe that unrestricted development was dangerous. Eager for their share of "progress," the insurgents beat back the conservationists.[35]

Theodore Roosevelt's accession to the presidency tipped the balance of the struggle. The President was almost inevitably a conservationist. Characteristically, Roosevelt embodied all the contradictions of the conservation movement. The naturalist who loved birds and the former rancher who loved the West wanted to preserve nature. "When I hear of the destruction of a species," he wrote, "I feel just as if all the works of some great writer had perished." The hunter who had stalked animals and had lived off the land wanted to preserve natural resources for economic development. "Forest protection is not an end of itself," Roosevelt observed in his first message to Congress in 1901; "it is a means to increase and sustain the resources of our country and the industries which depend upon them." The President saw conservation as a matter of parental responsibility. "We must handle the water, the wood, the grasses, so that we will hand them on to our children and our children's children in better and not worse shape than we got them," he insisted. Accordingly, Roosevelt, like the conservation movement, was prepared to limit individual freedom for the good of the nation. "In the past, we have admitted the right of the individual to injure the Republic for his present profit," the President noted in 1901. "The time has come for a change."[36]

To force that change, Roosevelt articulated an ambitious program in his first term. He wanted camping grounds, game preserves, and new forest reserves. He wanted responsibility for those reserves, previously divided between the Interior and the Agriculture Departments, concentrated in Agriculture's Forest Bureau. There they would be run by Gifford Pinchot, who was Roosevelt's kind of man: a Yale graduate, a student of forestry in Europe, the former manager of George Washington Vanderbilt's magnificent Biltmore estate, and a committed public servant. Roosevelt wanted water resource management. He wanted a leasing system to regulate the use of federal grazing lands. And he wanted land, as he told Congress in 1902, "held rigidly for the home-builder, the settler who lives on his land, and for no one else." To make sure the home-builder and the settler got that land, he wanted responsibility for it taken away from the corrupt General Land Office and handed over to Pinchot's bureau. To make the land useful, Roosevelt wanted federal support for Western irrigation projects.[37]

The President accomplished a good deal when the law did not require him to seek congressional action or approval. By executive order, he created the Pelican Island wildlife refuge in Florida, the Crater Lake National Park in Oregon, and more than fifty bird reserves in twenty states and territories. In 1903, he appointed a Public Lands Commission to study federal land policy. Roosevelt could not do much more without Congress, however. In 1902, the House and Senate passed the Newlands Act, a land reclamation measure that allowed federal support for irrigation projects. But Congress went no further because conservation was still too controversial. Not surprisingly,

Roosevelt's emphasis on the use of resources disappointed John Muir and his followers. That emphasis did reassure many large cattle and lumber companies, which, unlike the Two Bar outfit, could accept and even welcome orderly development. But many of their smaller competitors, unlike Ann Bassett, could not support a policy that might cut off access to the land. More broadly, the opponents of conservation understood that this "oppressive" movement threatened individual property rights. "My own idea," Senator Henry Moore Teller, Republican of Colorado, told the Public Land Commission, "is that what is everybody's is nobody's. . . . For any permanent business . . . you have got to have some form of possessory right." The Western insurgents resented the meddling of Easterners and experts—what Republican Representative Herschel Hogg of Telluride, Colorado, called the "goggle-eyed, bandy-legged dudes from the East and sad-eyed, absent-minded professors and bugologists." Suspicious of the federal government, Hogg rejected the idea "that all of honesty and patriotism and virtue is to be found only in the departments at Washington. . . ." Conservation was increasingly popular, but these fears and resentments doomed Roosevelt's plans for leasing and land reform in his first term.[38]

After his reelection in 1904, the President returned energetically to conservation. Bowing to his wishes, Congress gave authority over forest reserves to Gifford Pinchot's Bureau of Forestry in 1905. Encouraged by the increasing popularity of conservation in the West, the President added millions of acres to Pinchot's domain. The chief forester zealously extended his power: he won the right to use revenues from fees and leases and the authority to arrest those who broke "laws and regulations relating to the forest reserves and national parks." The bureau, reflecting his earnest professionalism, became the Forest Service. Meanwhile, Roosevelt, worried about the corrupt disposal of valuable federal land, withdrew from entry 66 million acres of possibly coal-rich government land in 1906. Under authority granted by Congress that year, the President also eventually established eighteen national monuments.[39]

Despite support from large cattle and lumber companies, Roosevelt's policy still encountered strong opposition. To the insurgents, conservation threatened civilization. "We cannot remain barbarians to save timber," fumed Henry Moore Teller. The Westerners believed that conservation would doom economic development. "The genius of growth must not be buried alive . . . by the federal government," declared *The Denver Post.* More than ever, the insurgents objected to the growing power of Gifford Pinchot. They called him a "Russian Czar or a Turkish Sultan," a "rapacious venal, petty aristocrat maliciously bent on destroying everybody." And they assailed the antidemocratic practices of "Pinchotism." "[If] you had breathed the spirit of liberty for thirty years on Colorado mountain tops, you would understand and hate 'Pinchotism' as I do," said one man. "It is diametrically opposed to all true Americanism." To Pinchot's predecessor, conservation seemed "decidedly paternalistic, if not socialistic." To other Westerners, conservation resembled Washington's treatment of Native Americans. "I like self-government," a Western sawmill operator told the President: "[T]o be placed under a bureau and in a reservation is too much like going back to the kind of government you impose upon your Indians."[40]

These attitudes spurred the resistance by the Two Bar outfit and other Westerners in 1906 and 1907. In Colorado and other states, meetings of insurgents objected to the grazing tax and to plans for leasing federal land. The tax had to be paid, but leasing was defeated back East in Washington, D.C. Not only that, Republican Senator Charles Fulton of Oregon added an amendment to an agricultural appropriation bill stipulating that "hereafter no forest reserve shall be created, nor shall any addition be made, to one heretofore created, within the limits of the states of Oregon, Washington, Montana, Colorado, or Wyoming, except by an act of Congress." The issue of executive power, underlying all the struggles over regulation, had finally come to a head in this challenge to the President. Apparently thwarted, Roosevelt managed a last, bold stroke. On March 4, 1907, he established twenty-one more national forests in the West. Then he signed the agriculture bill into law. "Very few of the autocratic monarchs of the world would so dare to set aside the will of the people this way," a western newspaper objected. Nevertheless, the President's conservation policy had reached its limit. Congress went on to restrict Pinchot's use of fees and to defeat Roosevelt's drive to reform the management of water resources. The implications of the president's approach to conservation and other economic issues had become all too obvious. As the *Chicago Tribune* noted, the Roosevelt administration showed "a marked tendency toward the centralization of power in the United States and a corresponding decrease in the old time sovereignty of the states, or of the individual."[41]

The fallout from Roosevelt's aggressive conservation policy lasted for years: it contributed to a deadlock with Congress toward the end of his administration and then it poisoned his successor's administration. Taft, troubled by such bold expansion of federal authority, believed the states should play the more active role in conservation. Soon the followers of Taft and Roosevelt were embroiled in a nasty dispute over the fate of conservation. Before it was over, Taft had fired Pinchot for undermining the secretary of the interior, Richard Achilles Ballinger, an old Pinchot antagonist. The "Ballinger-Pinchot" controversy, in turn, cost Taft progressive support and helped doom his presidency. Woodrow Wilson, in turn, moved still more cautiously. Pleasing conservationists, his administration opened Alaska for careful development. But controversy soon followed. Wilson and his followers supported the Stock-Raising Homestead Act of 1916, which unintentionally made it too easy for big ranchers to exploit Western grazing lands in the public domain. The administration's efforts to regulate the development of hydroelectric power and oil and mineral resources in the public domain foundered amid opposition from conservatives and infighting among conservationists before the First World War.[42]

The travail of conservation was rooted in its limitations as a progressive issue. Pinchot, Roosevelt, Wilson, and others were unable to build a sense of shared public urgency about conservation that would overwhelm opponents; the fate of grazing lands did not alarm most Americans in the way that the fear of eating poisoned beef did. Instead of conjuring up a broad consumer coalition, conservation became largely a battle of different producer interests vying for favor. In these circumstances, Roosevelt's heavy-handed use of authority only activated latent fears about centralized power and threats to property rights. The conservationists' attack on individualism was countered by a reassertion of individual rights and, tellingly, by charges of autocracy. The conservation cause, like other progressive regulatory crusades, certainly did move forward in the 1900s and 1910s. But, without a broad base of popular support, it would be a long struggle.

As the conservation issue suggested, the volatile struggles to control business tended to explode into still broader disputes about politics and power. This tendency especially marked notorious scandals in the insurance industry in the 1900s. At a time of great pride among businessmen, the leaders of the largest insurance companies stood out for their remarkable pretensions. Based in New York City, the Big Three—the Mutual Life Insurance Company, the Equitable Life Assurance Society, and the New York Life Insurance Company—had grown enormously in the Gilded Age. At the turn of the century, they faced challenges from two newer giants, the Metropolitan Life Insurance Company in New York and the Prudential Insurance Company in Boston. With millions of policyholders and billions of dollars in assets, the executives of the five companies liked to describe themselves as "trustees of the most sacred trust . . . on earth." Accordingly, they felt their business demanded special qualities. "Our profession," said George Perkins, an executive of the Equitable and an associate of J. P. Morgan, "requires the same zeal, the same enthusiasm, the same earnest purpose that must be born in a man if he succeeds as a minister of the Gospel." Not surprisingly, then, the insurance business was suffused, in the words of the Prudential's president, with an "all-pervading spirit of beneficence and . . . ingrained love of the golden rule."[43]

Unfortunately, all that beneficence and love had led to many questionable practices. Still more unfortunately, the public learned about those practices from a series of sensational revelations in middle-class magazines during 1904 and 1905. Writing for *Everybody's Magazine,* Thomas Lawson, a supposedly penitent stock speculator, detailed the evils of "Frenzied Finance" on Wall Street. In this series of articles, and in a follow-up devoted to the insurance industry, Lawson excoriated the Big Three for their cavalier treatment of policyholders and their strong ties to the financial "system" of Morgan, Rockefeller, and the other great magnates. As Lawson's articles ended, *Era Magazine* began a new insurance series, titled "The Despotism of Combined Millions." By 1905, the public had a clear picture of abuses among the leading insurance companies: high premiums; low returns on policies; low dividends on company stock; the impotence of policyholders and small shareholders; and the enormous financial power of company executives.[44]

Then, a struggle for control of the Equitable Life Insurance Company, unsparingly reported in the *New York World,* broke the insurance scandal wide open. The president of the Equitable, James W. Alexander, bitterly resented James Hazen Hyde, the son of the company's founder, who would take full charge of a majority interest in the firm on his thirtieth birthday in 1906. In fairness to Alexander, there was much to resent. With his violet boutonniere, his flashy coach-and-four, his red-heeled patent leather pumps, and his indiscreet elitism, Hyde was a caricature of the upper ten. With no obvious talents, he already earned, in his twenties, a salary of $100,000 a year as a vice president of the Equitable. Because the firm owned stock in so many other businesses, no fewer than forty-eight companies had named him to their boards of directors. "I have wealth, beauty, and intellect," this Harvard man supposedly exclaimed; "what more could I wish!" On January 31, 1905, Hyde gave a lavish Louis XV costume ball as a coming-out party for his niece. Enthusiastically exaggerated in the pages of the *World*, the affair at Sherry's restaurant conjured up the Bradley Martin ball. And like the Bradley Martins, Hyde soon paid a heavy price for his indiscretion. Alexander denounced Hyde's "public coaches, special trains, elaborate banquets, costly and ostentatious entertainments, accompanied . . . by continuous notoriety of a flippant, trivial cheap description." The battle for control of the Equitable was on. Thanks to the newspapers, the public received frequent dispatches from the front.[45]

Hyde and the Equitable could not divert attention from themselves. The company tried an in-house investigation; the sympathetic New York State Superintendent of Insurance undertook a generally friendly examination. But the public only got angrier. Shareholders formed committees to insist on the right to vote for company directors. Insurance commissioners in other states began to look into the company. To extricate himself and rescue the Equitable, Hyde decided to sell his stock. James Stillman was purportedly ready to give him $10 million, but Hyde sold his shares to New York speculator Thomas Fortune Ryan for $2.5 million. To stop the public outcry, Ryan promised to transfer the authority to vote the stock to a three-man committee that included former President Grover Cleveland, the epitome of ponderous public rectitude. But the controversy would not stop; instead, it enveloped the whole insurance industry. Finally, the New York State legislature decided to investigate the Equitable and the other leading companies.[46]

Held in New York City Hall from September to December, the legislature's hearings were an unprecedented public inquiry into the affairs of business corporations. Ably conducted by chief investigator Charles Evans Hughes, the dramatic sessions in the aldermen's chambers turned into an unexpected disaster for the insurance companies. Week after week, Hughes, a corporation lawyer, astutely laid bare the questionable practices of "the trustees of the most sacred trust . . . on earth." Those trustees stayed home sick in bed, fled the country, or turned up, embarrassed, on the witness stand. There, Hughes forced them to reveal their iron control of corporation offices, their huge salaries, their costly insurance policies, their miserly dividend payments, their power in the financial markets, and, especially, their secret political activity. What had begun as an economic scandal quickly mushroomed into a political crisis.[47]

Hughes's hearings laid bare the insurance companies' extensive and apparently successful attempts to buy influence in Albany and other state capitals. Most Americans already knew that politicians were corruptible. But the hearings were a revelation about the role of business itself in perverting democratic politics. Through clandestine lobbyists in state capitals and huge surreptitious contributions to Republican presidential campaigns, including the Roosevelt campaign of 1904, the insurance companies had arrogantly tried to bend the political system to their will. Hughes asked E. H. Harriman, a member of the Equitable's board, whether the financier had "political influence" because of his ties to the New York State Republican boss and governor, Benjamin Odell. "Well," Harriman replied, "I should think that Mr. Odell had political influence because of his relations with me." Under astute questioning from Hughes, the aging U.S. Senator Thomas Collier Platt, Odell's predecessor as state Republican boss, acknowledged receiving cash campaign contributions from the insurance companies. In return for that money, Platt felt, in Hughes's words, "a moral obligation . . . to defend them." Platt's fellow senator, Chauncey Depew, a director of the Equitable, admitted receiving a secret $20,000 annual retainer from the company but did not clarify his relationship to the "Depew Improvement Company," a real estate firm that had received an improper loan from the insurance firm. As even a conservative business paper acknowledged, Hughes turned up "so much that is unsavory, so much that offends the moral sense." Thomas Lawson put it less tactfully. Once the insurance companies "loomed before the American people as the greatest, most respected, and most venerable institutions in our broad land," he declared. "To-day they stand for all that is tricky, fraudulent, and oppressive." The companies were, attorney Louis Brandeis concluded, "the greatest economic menace of to-day."[48]

Their reputation destroyed, the insurance companies clearly would be subjected to greater public control. But that control could take a number of forms. And so a new battle began in 1905. Not surprisingly, Theodore Roosevelt dismissed the states' regulation of insurance companies as "inadequate" and favored federal supervision. For their part, the insurance men had reason to prefer federal regulation to what they labeled "the inharmonious, exacting, and often conflicting laws of fifty different States" and "the inconveniences, hardships, impositions and scandals . . . of State Supervision." "Every company would naturally prefer just one set of regulations," the president of the Prudential, John F. Dryden, had declared, "for that would make it so much easier to shape policy." Federal regulation could also save the insurance companies the cost of protecting themselves from state legislators. Moreover, in the present crisis, friendly supervision from Washington could help restore public confidence in the companies.[49]

Despite support from Roosevelt and company executives, the drive for federal regulation foundered. Legal experts doubted that the insurance industry was interstate commerce and thus subject to Washington. State insurance commissioners saw federal regulation as a threat to their power. Given the interest of large insurance companies in regulation, smaller firms suspected some kind of trick. Even executives of the leading companies, like much of the upper ten, rejected federal intervention in their affairs. "The panacea for all imagined evils in this great country seems to be Legislation—more legislation—Restriction—Limitation, Restraint," complained the president of Mutual Life. "Why not trust sometimes to the operation of natural laws?" Some opponents also feared that federal regulation of insurance would lead to still more governmental interference in the economy. "If the door is once opened, it is opened wide to federal supervision of another class of business," warned Massachusetts attorney and reformer Moorfield Storey. "What we want to do is to set our faces against the first step." At the same time, other critics argued that regulation would help Washington and the insurance companies, but not the people. "Federal supervision," Louis Brandeis contended, "would serve only to centralize still further the power of our Government and to increase still further the powers of the corporations."[50]

Federal regulation bills had already failed in 1901, 1903, and 1904; they failed again in 1905 and 1906. A proposal for a National Bureau of Insurance, located in the Department of Commerce and Labor, never got out of committees in the House and Senate. Meanwhile, the states moved aggressively to deal with the insurance problem. In Florida, Governor Napoleon Bonaparte Broward proposed that the state itself provide insurance for its people.

That was too radical an idea. But across the country, states held conferences and staged investigations. In 1906, New York State restricted insurance companies' investments, lobbying activities, selection of directors, and even the total value of their new insurance policies. In 1907 alone, twenty-nine states from New York west to California, and from North Dakota south to Louisiana, imposed new regulations on insurance companies. The wave of legislation reflected the continuing vitality of grassroots solutions to the problem of business; it also reflected a pragmatic reconciliation of government regulation and individualist ideology. This was, as Louisiana's insurance commissioner put it, "a popular movement to invoke the supreme power of the State to check the unequal and constantly increasing advantage of concentrated corporate power over individual effort."[51]

Scandal and legislation substantially changed the insurance companies, particularly the Big Three. The giant firms were out of politics and out of high finance. In the long term, forced to narrow their ambitions, they prospered under the new rules. In the short term, they lost business and they lost face. James Hazen Hyde, like the Bradley Martins before him, decided to leave for what became a thirty-five-year "rest" in Europe. At the pier in New York, he received a lone farewell gift: the loyal restaurateur Louis Sherry gave him a cold ham.[52]

There were consequences for the politicians and politics as well. Even a Republican newspaper in upstate New York conceded, "The wrath of thousands of private citizens whose voices are never heard in public is at white heat over the disclosures." As the hearings ended, the old party structures came under pressure. Particularly in New York City, voters showed new independence from party allegiance. In 1906, Odell lost his place at the head of the state party; Hughes, his political career ignited by scandals, became governor, and eventually a Republican presidential nominee and a justice of the U.S. Supreme Court. In the near run he presided over a revolution in policymaking, as progressive economic measures passed through the state legislature. The insurance scandals, an economic event, had proved the catalyst in the political ascendancy of progressivism in New York State.[53]

The volatile linkage between business and politics was revealed again in the controversy set off by the publication of a series of sensationalist articles about the U.S. Senate. In 1906, the progressive David Graham Phillips, author of *The Reign of Gilt,* published a slashing series of articles in *Cosmopolitan* magazine on "The Treason of the Senate." In angry cadences, Phillips denounced Nelson Aldrich and other U.S. senators of both major parties for serving big business rather than the people. The "stealthy and treacherous" Senate, Phillips argued, had done all it could to obstruct popular control of business. Further, Phillips articulated a notion stirred up by the insurance revelations and other episodes: big business was not the only cause of economic inequality in America; government deserved a share of the blame, too. The Senate, Phillips declared, "is, in fact, *the final arbiter of the sharing of prosperity.* The laws it permits or compels, the laws it refuses to permit, the interpreters of laws it permits to be appointed—these factors determine whether the great forces which modern concentration has produced shall operate to distribute prosperity equally or with shameful inequality and cruel and destructive injustice." The conclusion was plain: the problem of business would not be solved by antitrust, regulation, and compensation alone; the people also had to reform their government. Instead of letting state legislatures continue to elect senators, the voters had to claim that right for themselves. With "The Treason of the Senate," the battle over business had flared again into a battle over democracy.[54]

Theodore Roosevelt feared the consequences. Trying as always to mediate the opposing forces of American society, the President believed that attacks on corporations and government risked going too far. He was particularly upset with Phillips's series of articles, so typical of the journalism of exposure in middle-class magazines. First in off-the-record remarks to the Washington press corps in March and then in a public address in April, the President tried to restrain progressive journalists. He recalled "the Man with the Muck-Rake" in John Bunyan's *Pilgrim's Progress,* "the man who could look no way but downward, with the muck-rake in his hand; who was offered a celestial crown for his muck-rake, but who would neither look up nor regard the crown he was offered, but continued to rake to himself the filth of the floor." Roosevelt agreed that the nation had problems. "There is filth on the floor," he conceded; "and it must be scraped up with the muck-rake. . . ." But the President cautioned "the men with the muckrakes" to remember the positive aspects of American life: "There are beautiful things above and roundabout them; and if they gradually grow to feel that the whole world is nothing but muck, their power of usefulness is gone." Above all, Roosevelt advised them not to create "a morbid and vicious public sentiment." "At this moment we are passing through a period of great unrest—social, political, and industrial unrest," the President observed. "So far as this movement of agitation throughout the country takes the form of a fierce discontent with evil, of a firm determination to punish the authors of evil, whether in industry or politics, the feeling is to be heartily welcomed as a sign of healthy life." But Roosevelt warned against promoting "a line of cleavage . . . which divides those who are well off from those who are less well off" and turning "this movement of agitation" into "a mere crusade of appetite against appetite, . . . a contest between the brutal greed of the 'have-nots' and the brutal greed of the 'haves.' . . ." Instead, the President concluded, people should accept "the inevitable inequality of conditions."[55]

Roosevelt's rebuke to Phillips caused a sensation and created an enduring term—*muckraking*—for investigative journalism. But the President had gone too far in defending the economic and political status quo against progressivism. Rivals like William Jennings Bryan were quick to outflank Roosevelt on the left. Back from a trip around the world at the end of August, the Nebraskan made a well-publicized speech in New York's Madison Square Garden. With the presidential election of 1908 clearly in mind, Bryan denounced the power of big business. "Plutocracy is abhorrent to the republic," he insisted; "it is more despotic than monarchy, more heartless than aristocracy, more selfish than bureaucracy. . . . Conscienceless, compassionless and devoid of wisdom, it enervates its votaries while it impoverishes its victims." Bryan wanted to break up the corporations that supported the upper ten. Rejecting Roosevelt's tolerant policy, the Democrat declared that the Sherman Act "must be enforced, not against a few trusts, as at present, but against all trusts, and the aim must be to imprison the guilty, not merely to recover a fine." Bryan wanted to preserve economic competition, but now he recognized that at least one industry could no longer be made competitive. And so he advocated a state and federal takeover of the railroads. "[P]ublic ownership," Bryan maintained, "is necessary where competition is impossible." Socialism had never been more respectable.[56]

Outflanked on the left, Roosevelt also took fire from the right. As in the anthracite strike, he found himself assailed by the very class he was trying to protect. "Mr. Roosevelt is a bugaboo to Wall Street," the magazine *World's*

"Signs of friction": The upper-class extravagance of the Bradley Martin costume ball, 1897. *Harper's Weekly*, 1897

The costs of class conflict: A fire and a funeral during the great railroad strike of 1877. *Harper's Weekly*, 1877, from the Library of Congress

Victorian father: John H. Addams in middle-age.
SPECIAL COLLECTIONS, UNIVERSITY OF ILLINOIS AT CHICAGO

Progressive daughter: Jane Addams, age eight.
SPECIAL COLLECTIONS, UNIVERSITY OF ILLINOIS AT CHICAGO

The progressive confrontation with prostitution: A prim reformer and prostitutes outside a brothel. CLIFFORD G. ROE, *HORRORS OF THE WHITE SLAVE TRADE: THE MIGHTY CRUSADE TO PROTECT THE PURITY OF OUR HOMES* (LONDON: ROE AND STEADWELL, 1911)

The working-class family economy: A mother and daughters make artificial flowers in a tenement apartment. LIBRARY OF CONGRESS

Leading the progressive charge: Theodore Roosevelt on horseback. LIBRARY OF CONGRESS

The prerogatives of the upper ten: J. P. Morgan lashes out at a photographer.
LIBRARY OF CONGRESS

The "middle-class paradise": Decorous, secluded leisure at Chautauqua.
LIBRARY OF CONGRESS

Crossing the boundaries of progressive America: The classes mingle at Coney Island's Dreamland. LIBRARY OF CONGRESS

"In My Merry Oldsmobile": The booming music business salutes the booming auto industry. RARE BOOK, MANUSCRIPT, AND SPECIAL COLLECTIONS LIBRARY, DUKE UNIVERSITY

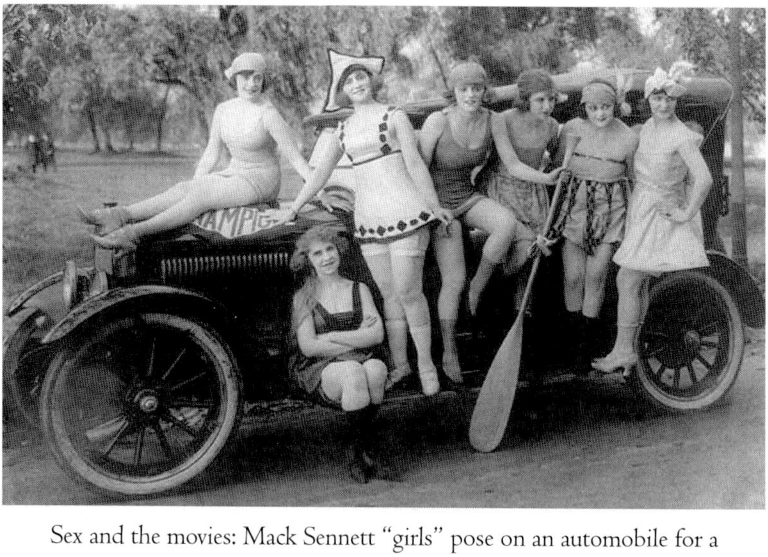

Sex and the movies: Mack Sennett "girls" pose on an automobile for a Mack Sennett film. LIBRARY OF CONGRESS

Rebel at rest: Mabel Dodge Luhan in the lotus position.
BEINECKE LIBRARY, YALE UNIVERSITY

Heavyweight champion Jack Johnson, a smiling threat to the progressive order.
LIBRARY OF CONGRESS

Molding the young during World War I: The Food Administration's progressive propaganda.
LIBRARY OF CONGRESS

The end of the Progressive Era: A haunted Woodrow Wilson at his final cabinet meeting in 1921.
LIBRARY OF CONGRESS

Work observed. "The average trader has an hallucination that the President hates Wall Street and would destroy it if he could."[57]

So Roosevelt moved back toward the left. It was not too hard, given his longstanding distaste for the values of the upper ten. The President could accept big business, but not its control of American culture. "It must not be, it shall not be," he had insisted in 1902, "the civilization of a mere plutocracy, a banking-house, Wall-Street-syndicate civilization. . . ." By the last years of his presidency, he was quite ready to assail big business. Dedicating a memorial to the Pilgrims at Provincetown, Massachusetts, in August 1907, Roosevelt took note of the worldwide financial unease following a federal court's verdict earlier that month levying an unprecedented $29 million fine on Standard Oil for anticompetitive practices: "[I]t may well be that the determination of the government (in which, gentlemen, it will not waver) to punish certain malefactors of great wealth, has been responsible for something of the trouble; at least to the extent of having caused these men to combine to bring about as much financial stress as possible, in order to discredit the policy of the government and thereby secure a reversal of that policy, so that they may enjoy unmolested the fruits of their own evil-doing." Roosevelt pledged "no let up in the effort to secure the honest observance of the law; for I regard this contest as one to determine who shall rule this free country—the people through their governmental agents, or a few ruthless and domineering men whose wealth makes them peculiarly formidable because they hide behind the breastworks of corporate organization." Once again, he had coined an enduring term: *malefactors of great wealth.* But now it was Roosevelt who was dividing the classes. His position had grown cloudy.[58]

It was made still cloudier by his continuing need to reconcile regulation and individualism. The President acknowledged the limitations of the individualist creed. "No small part of the trouble that we have comes from carrying to an extreme the national virtue of self-reliance, of independence in initiative and action," he said in his annual message to Congress in December 1907. Still, Roosevelt could not abandon his belief that the individual mattered most in life. "Much can be done by wise legislation and by resolute enforcement of the law," he observed in 1906. "But still more must be done by steady training of the individual citizen, in conscience and character, until he grows to abhor corruption and greed and tyranny and brutality and to prize justice and fair dealing." Yet, Roosevelt was the one endorsing large-scale business organizations and building an intrusive government. "Some persons speak as if the exercise of such governmental control would do away with the freedom of individual initiative and dwarf individual effort," the President observed dismissively in his Annual Message to Congress in 1906. "This is not a fact." No public figure spoke more vigorously about these issues; none more openly tied himself in knots. The task of reconciling the opposing forces and keeping the battle contained was impossible.[59]

As they struggled to control business, progressives generally enjoyed the advantage of prosperity. From the end of the depression of the 1890s through the First World War, the American economy generally grew. But there were exceptions, moments when progressives and their antagonists alike were reminded that the business cycle endured and that controlling business was not the only economic challenge of the age. One such moment arrived fairly suddenly in the autumn of 1907, when a full-blown crisis enveloped the American financial system. The results embarrassed capitalists, progressives, and Theodore Roosevelt.

In October, a worldwide shortage of credit mercilessly exposed the limitations of the nation's banking and currency systems. A collapse of copper prices raised fears about banks and trust companies heavily involved in the mining industry. On October 22, frightened depositors made a run on the Knickerbocker Trust Company, which had extensive involvement with copper; the company closed the next day. The terror spread: in the streets of Manhattan, there were "men and women dashing about in the manner of ants when their hill is trod on." As the banks and trust companies of New York struggled to meet their obligations, the whole banking system of the country seemed suddenly in peril. Morgan, Stillman, and the rest of the great money men labored to hold things together. John D. Rockefeller publicly pledged half his possessions to the cause. With millions of Rockefeller's dollars on deposit, the National City Bank played a key role in the crisis. "They always come to Uncle John when there is trouble," Rockefeller bragged. Even so, the federal government had to step in. Roosevelt's secretary of the treasury, George Cortelyou, provided the banks with $37 million and then $31 million. Still the run continued; the banks stopped payments to depositors. Stillman's protégé, Frank Vanderlip, remembered long after that "my graying hair became white in that panic year of 1907."[60]

As the Panic entered a second week and the Trust Company of America became the focus of worry, Roosevelt was drawn into a dubious deal. The money to save the company would have to come from the financial markets, but they were supposedly jeopardized by the weakness of Moore and Schley, a firm of underwriters. The fate of Moore and Schley, in turn, depended on the sale of its shares in the Tennessee Coal and Iron Company. With money from those shares, Moore and Schley would survive, the stock market would stay high, and firms could then afford to put up the money to save the Trust Company of America. But who would buy the shares in Tennessee Coal and Iron? United States Steel was willing—if the government would agree not to take the acquisition to court under the Sherman Act. The leaders of the steel corporation, Elbridge Gary and Henry Clay Frick, met with the President on November 4 to explain the firm's noble proposal. They did not dwell on the fact that this bargain-basement acquisition would give United States Steel a powerful hold on the Southern market. Roosevelt indicated he had no objection to the deal, which promptly went forward.[61]

Through November, the government sold bonds to banks on easy terms; thus fortified, the banks rode out the Panic. Confidence returned, the credit shortage diminished, workers kept their jobs—the country seemed fine. Nevertheless, the Panic of 1907 had changed things. "As a matter of fact it marked the end of an era," wrote James Stillman's friendly biographer. "That tidal wave of speculation, which had crashed over in a destructive flood, receded at length, leaving a changed world both for the public and for the financial captains."[62]

At first glance, the Panic was a humiliation for these men. They had been tossed about like yachts in a hurricane off Long Island. Despite all their wealth, they had needed the help of the federal government to save themselves. Yet, the Panic also confirmed their power and influence. The government had had no choice but to help the "financial captains." Roosevelt had accepted the Tennessee Coal and Iron deal. In November, Elbridge Gary began to bring together the leaders of the steel industry to discuss matters of common concern; Washington tolerated these "Gary dinners," an open display of anticompetitive collusion. Further, the great industrial firms showed real strength in the uncertain economic climate. Instead of renewing the price-cutting wars of the 1890s, U.S. Steel and other companies maintained their prices after the Panic.[63]

At the same time, the financial crisis was a blow to Roosevelt and his plans for enhancing national power. The President insisted that the Panic demonstrated the need for more federal regulation. "In the recent business crisis it is noteworthy that the institutions which failed were institutions which were not under the supervision and control of the National Government," Roosevelt maintained. "Those which were under national control stood the test." Ever more critical of both "unrestricted individualism" and "the old doctrine of States' rights," the President called for "a national incorporation act." He wanted the government to be able to inspect corporations' books. He wanted the Interstate Commerce Commission to regulate issues of railroad securities, to determine the physical value of railway lines, and even to set railway rates. Condemning the Sherman Act's prohibition of all combination in restraint of trade as "worse than folly," the President wanted the scope of the law limited by Congress.[64]

"That fellow . . . ," observed "Uncle Joe" Cannon, the Republican Speaker of the House, "wants everything, from the birth of Christ to the death of the devil." Roosevelt got nothing—no Christ, no devil, no legislative program. Instead, he found himself trapped in an argument about responsibility for the Panic. Opponents claimed that the administration's program in general and the judgment against Standard Oil in particular had precipitated the crisis. "The runaway policy of the present Administration can have but one result," John D. Rockefeller told a reporter. "It means disaster to the country, financial depression, and chaos." Even Americans receptive to antitrust and regulation wondered whether too much government interference inhibited economic growth.[65]

The criticism of Roosevelt was an ironic tribute to the impact of progressive attempts to deal with the problem of business: Americans wondered about excessive government only because federal control of business had increased so much. During the administrations of Roosevelt, Taft, and Wilson, laissez-faire was largely discredited; socialism, largely untried. Instead, antitrust and regulation were legitimated and elaborated. To be sure, the progressives, divided between antitrust and regulation, sacrificed much of their potential impact. The fleeting chance to break up monopoly power and return to the golden age of competition was lost. While the federal government broke up some corporations, big businesses became more firmly established. At the same time, the structure of federal regulation was still rudimentary. In all, the upper ten retained remarkable financial power. Yet, they had also ceded to government the right to intervene across an increasing number of areas: competitive practices, stock issues, prices, resources, consumer safety. A regulatory wedge had opened that opponents would exploit and widen in years to come.

Nevertheless, there was a note of caution, sounded most clearly by the Panic of 1907. In the middle of economic crisis, the federal government had turned to capitalists, not progressives. Like the struggle to control work, the Panic intensified questions about the fate of democracy in America. The power of the "financial captains" and the obvious solicitude of President Roosevelt only added to the strain on a political system breaking under the weight of the insurance scandals, the "Treason of the Senate," and so many other struggles. When Roosevelt had denounced the "malefactors of great wealth" at Provincetown, he noted the "contest . . . to determine who shall rule this free country." More and more Americans, realizing the obvious corruption of politics and government, wondered who was winning that contest. In 1908, the Democratic platform demanded, "Shall the People Rule?" Bryan, the Democrats' nominee, put the question more specifically. "Shall the people," he asked, "control their own Government and use that Government for the protection of their rights and for the promotion of their welfare?" It was a deceptively simple question. Who were "the people"? Out in Brown's Park, the answer had seemed obvious to Ann Bassett. But across the nation in the years ahead, it was not obvious at all. Were Bassett and the other small cattle ranchers "the people"? Were the Two Bar outfit and the other insurgents? Were Harry Ratliff and Gifford Pinchot? Were Morgan and Rockefeller, when they bailed out the banking system, part of the people, too? The questions only multiplied.[66]

CHAPTER SIX

The Shield of Segregation

"Ugh!" Theodore Roosevelt exclaimed. "I have got to wash my hands." As so often during his presidency, he had just shaken hands with hundreds, even thousands, of visitors to the White House. Now, on this day early in 1909, he hurried upstairs to find a washbasin. It had been a gilded affair, a full-dress reception for army and navy officers, replete with cabinet members, diplomats, and Supreme Court justices. But Roosevelt felt soiled, even threatened, by his contact with these people. "Ugh!" he exclaimed again. "Shaking hands with a thousand people! What a lot of bugs I have on my hands, and how dirty, filthy I am!" The President washed his hands immediately. "Now I am clean," he said with relief.[1]

In this diverse, industrializing nation, Americans had to put up with people different from themselves. Even presidents had to mingle with constituents. But when and where they could, many Americans pulled back from people who seemed different. Frightened, wary, or, like Roosevelt, repelled by contact with others, people drew boundary lines around themselves. This impulse to separate was fundamental to American society. The early twentieth century became the great age of segregation in the United States, a time of enforced public separations. The word *segregation* itself took on its modern definition in the first years of the new century: *segregation* meant "Jim Crow," the laws and practices that separated white from black in the states of the old Confederacy. Americans have liked to pretend that Jim Crow was a regional aberration, an exception to our history. But segregation was not something that happened only in the South—boundary lines were established everywhere in the early twentieth-century United States. And segregation did not happen only to African-Americans: the boundary lines also set apart Native Americans, immigrants, and workers.[2]

Progressives seldom contested the increasing division of Americans into separate enclaves. In fact, middle-class activists and their political representatives eagerly led some of the campaigns to draw new social boundary lines dividing different groups. The progressives' support for segregation is, at first glance, surprising. Believing in "association," progressives so often tried to bring diverse people together. Believing in their power to manipulate the social and material environment, progressives so often refused to accept difference as a fundamental fact of national life: people could be changed and thus made more alike. But there were limits to the progressives' optimistic faith in transforming other people. Segregation revealed both a sense of realism and an underlying pessimism in the middle class. Even as they labored urgently to end the differences between classes, the progressives felt some social differences would not be erased for many years. And some differences, they believed, could not be erased at all.

Segregation was a complicated social phenomenon, and it served a complicated purpose for the progressives. Superficially a deviation from progressivism, segregation actually drew on basic progressive values and aims. True to their mission to create a safe society for themselves and their children, the progressives turned to segregation as a way to halt dangerous social conflict that could not otherwise be stopped. True to their sense of compassion, the progressives turned to segregation as a way to preserve weaker groups, such as African-Americans and Native Americans, facing brutality and even annihilation. Unlike some other Americans, progressives did not support segregation out of anger, hatred, and a desire to unify whites; but they certainly displayed plenty of condescension and indifference, as well as compassion. Segregation was never the separation of equals; one party always ended up with less—less power, less wealth, less opportunity, less schooling, less health care, less respect. Progressives fairly readily accepted the inequitable arrangement of segregation. They did so because usually there were worse alternatives. Most of the progressives told themselves that separation allowed reform to continue. Protected by the shield of segregation, the fundamental project of transforming people could go on in safety. But the cost was great.[3]

On Monday, July 23, 1900, a steamy day in the city of New Orleans, something gave inside Robert Charles. Thirty-four, unmarried, unemployed, well read, and black, Charles was upset over the violence and discrimination directed against African-Americans in the South; the son of Mississippi slaves, he doubted that blacks had any future in the United States. That night he was waiting on a doorstep with his roommate Lenard Pierce for two black women when a white policeman told the men to move on. As Charles, dark brown, six feet tall, and strong, got up, the policeman struck him with a billy club and pulled a gun. Charles took out his own .38 Colt; both men fired; both were wounded in the leg. Charles ran away to his apartment on Fourth Street, where the police confronted him later that night. Pointing his Winchester rifle, Charles shot police captain John Day through the heart. "You———," Charles yelled, "I will give you all some!" He shot a patrolman through the eye, and escaped again.[4]

The next day policemen and white mobs looked for Robert Charles. These white citizens of New Orleans had their frustrations, too. Black men like Charles seemed to threaten white jobs and white women. Less and less willing to mix with African-Americans at all, many whites had unhappily watched the state legislature defeat a bill that would have segregated the city's streetcars. Now whites noticed that blacks were obviously satisfied with Charles's "war on whites." So the police arrested African-Americans that day, but no one could find Charles, this "monster" and "unreasoning brute," this "ruthless black butcher" and "bloodthirsty champion of African supremacy." On Wednesday, the twenty-fifth, frustrated whites met at the monument to Robert E. Lee and resolved to lynch Robert Charles. Thousands marched to the parish prison and to the Storyville vice district, but in vain: no Charles. That night, whites killed three African-Americans and sent about fifty to the hospital. For good measure, the mobs killed two whites accidentally and, when refused rides on the streetcars, beat three white streetcar workers. On Thursday, whites killed three blacks and hurt at least fifteen more—but still no Charles. Then, on Friday, an African-American revealed Charles's hideout on Saratoga Street. When the police turned up, Charles shot and killed a sergeant and a corporal. As hundreds and then thousands of people surrounded and fired into the building, Charles killed three more whites and wounded nineteen. When the mob accidentally set fire to the building in an attempt to smoke him out, Charles emerged, wounded but with his derby cocked defiantly on his head. Somehow he made it across the street and into a room, where a policeman shot him dead.

That was not the end, however. The mob shot Charles's body over and over; they pulled it into the street, where the son of one of the dead policemen smashed Charles's face. Three more black men died that day, uncounted others were beaten, and a black school was set ablaze. Finally, some weeks later, Lewis Forstall, an African-American, shot and killed the black man who had ratted on Robert Charles.

The Robert Charles riot reminded people of what they knew deep down: of all the social differences at the start of the twentieth century, those between black and white were the most volatile, the most difficult to control. Southerners understood that truth best of all. Seven million, nine hundred twenty-three thousand African-Americans, 90 percent of blacks in America, lived in the South; blacks made up 32 percent of the region's population. After the Civil War, the abolition of slavery and the reconstruction of the South had empowered African-Americans and threatened white Southerners. But in the 1870s and 1880s, blacks had seemingly been contained; the white Redeemers had thrust African-Americans decisively back into their "place." Violence, intimidation, and fraud kept them from political power; the sharecropping system bound them to white landowners and merchants. Yet, as the Charles riot made plain, race relations had not been controlled after all. Old passions and new truths had combined to stir up the South toward the end of the nineteenth century.[5]

For all the hyperbole of its boosters, the "New South" of the late nineteenth and early twentieth centuries was an unsettling place. The uneven, painful processes of urbanization and industrialization were transforming the region and creating a new terrain for race relations. In the growing cities and towns of the New South, in Birmingham, Atlanta, Spartanburg, and Durham, white and black were thrown together in streets, restaurants, schools, and other public places. At the gates of sawmills, iron mills, and cotton mills, the races jostled each other in the search for jobs. On the land, things seemed more stable, even stagnant, but Southern agriculture was going through its own difficult transformation: hard times on the farm and the relative decline of the countryside made the races uncomfortably aware of each other. The New South created new people, too. The younger whites, who had not grown up with the paternalist example of the old antebellum planter class, were less tolerant of blacks. Equally, there were "New Negroes," young black men like Robert Charles, less deferential because they had not grown up in slavery. There was also a new African-American middle class of well-dressed landholders and business owners whose visible success mocked the failures of poorer whites. Upper-class whites had their own, frightening "New Negroes"—the African-Americans of the Farmer's Alliance and the People's Party who made common cause with poor whites against the Democratic Party, the railroads, the merchants, and all the men in power. The New South was unstable, not only because it divided black and white but because it still might unite them.[6]

Under the circumstances, many Southern whites, out of unthinking emotion or cool calculation, had new reason to turn on blacks. The result was a fresh brand of racism, hysterical and harsh, proclaimed in legislatures, country stores, and newspaper columns. The titles of popular books summed up the essential racist message—*The Negro a Beast; The Negro: A Menace to American Civilization.* African-Americans, no longer raised in the stern school of slavery, were said to be headed back into primitive, uncontrolled savagery. Running through all this was an irrational fear of black sexual competition, of the bestial "New Negro" who preyed on white women. That fear, which also testified to the tensions between white men and women in the Victorian South, produced torrents of lurid rhetoric. In the United States Senate in 1907, Democrat Ben Tillman of South Carolina portrayed blacks "pulsating with the desire to sate their passions upon white maidens and wives"; he described the white Southern victim, "her body prostituted, her purity destroyed . . . robbed of the jewel of her womanhood by a black fiend." "Our brains reel under the staggering blow and hot blood surges to the heart . . . ," Tillman railed. "We revert to the original savage."[7]

Some white Southerners did just that. Seemingly determined not to coexist with blacks, these people turned to violence. They went, the Alabama minister and progressive Edgar Gardner Murphy observed, "from the contention that no negro shall vote to the contention that no negro shall learn, that no negro shall labor, and . . . that no negro shall live." In towns and cities across the region, there were fights and race riots. As in New Orleans in 1900, so in Wilmington, North Carolina, in 1898. In rural areas especially, there was the lynching party. Rebecca Latimer Felton of Georgia, a Methodist layleader and journalist, urged white men to do their duty. "[If] it takes lynching to protect woman's dearest possession from drunken, ravening human beasts," Felton exclaimed in 1897, "then I say lynch a thousand a week if it becomes necessary." They never did manage that thousand a week, but mobs of Southern whites answered Felton's call. What had been mainly a way for white Americans to whip and discipline other whites became an increasingly vicious means for Southern whites to exterminate blacks. Nationwide, lynchings escalated in the 1880s and peaked at 230 in 1892. The numbers fell off somewhat because black men took pains to avoid trouble. Even so, there were 115 reported lynchings in America in 1900; 106 of the victims were black. Essentially unchecked by local, state, or national government, white Southerners usually invoked some imaginary assault on a white woman in order to murder a black man. There were hangings, shootings, burnings, castrations. Afterward, interested whites might claim an ear, a toe, or a finger as a keepsake, perhaps a souvenir watch fob. "You don't understand how we feel down here," a Mississippian told a Northern visitor in 1908; "when there is a row, we feel like killing a nigger whether he has done anything or not." A Mississippi African-American summed up the vulnerability of his race. "They had to have a license to kill anything but a nigger," he recalled. "We was always in season."[8]

To more-moderate whites, including progressives and the wealthy, it seemed as if the South had gone out of control. These men and women were disgusted by the lynch mobs. The lyncher, wrote Andrew Sledd, professor of Latin and Greek at Atlanta's Emory College, in 1902, acted "to gratify the brute in his own soul, which the thin veneer of his elemental civilization has not been able effectually to conceal." Whites like Sledd preferred the antebellum slaveholders' paternalist judgment of African-Americans: the black man was a submissive child, not an uncontrollable beast. Moreover, the moderates understood some basic realities: blacks were too numerous, their labor too important, for them to be driven from the South; corrupt elections, extralegal lynching parties, and race riots threatened the social order, damaged the region's reputation, and put economic development at risk. Obviously, there had to be some new means of stabilizing race relations.[9]

The solution, crafted in the 1890s and the 1900s, was a dramatic intensification and codification of segregation. White and black had been divided in many ways since the end of the Civil War, but now separation of the races became the regional creed, a way of life—"the elementary working hypothesis of civilization in our Southern States," as Edgar Gardner Murphy put it. "Ours is a world of inexorable divisions," he explained. "[G]ood fences make good neighbors." Those divisions were achieved through an intricate process of accommodation and challenge that proceeded unevenly but inexorably across the South. Everywhere, what had been de facto in the late nineteenth century became de jure by the twentieth; new segregation laws made the racial boundaries clearer, more rigid. Through differing mixtures of law and custom, every Southern town, city, county, and state tried to achieve two goals: first, to send an unmistakable message of racial inequality that would intimidate blacks and reassure whites; second, to deprive blacks of so much economic and political opportunity that they could never threaten white power.[10]

So whites arranged to put African-Americans in their "place" once again. More than ever before, that "place" was a literal, physical space as well as a matter of psychology and behavior. By statute and unwritten rule, whites denied blacks equal access to public facilities. African-Americans could not get into many hotels, restaurants, theaters, saloons, pool halls, bathhouses, swimming pools, and hospitals at all. They could get into other public places only by accepting segregated, inferior accommodations—back pews in churches, back seats in streetcars, balcony "nigger heavens" in theaters, "nigger cars" on railroad trains. And of course, black children had to attend separate schools—and of course, those schools were grossly underfunded. There was also a trend toward residential segregation in the early twentieth-century South. Traditionally, in towns and cities, blacks had often lived close to whites in servants' quarters or back alleys, in unimposing buildings across a street or a vacant lot. Now, even in such older communities as New Orleans, Charleston, and Savannah, white prejudice and economic forces were increasingly consigning blacks to their own sections of town. No Southern community had a true ghetto sealing off virtually all of the black population, but many towns and cities had one or more predominantly African-American sections, known predictably enough as "darktown" and "niggertown."

Jim Crow reached into the economy as well. In the tobacco business, the skilled jobs went to whites, the unskilled jobs, to blacks. African-Americans could get manual work in the iron mines and foundries of northern Alabama and in the bituminous coal mines of Tennessee and Kentucky. But the cotton mills of the Piedmont were for whites only. In general, blacks were condemned to the dirtiest, least skilled, lowest paying, most demeaning jobs—the "nigger work" of gang labor and domestic service.

Segregation also drew boundary lines through politics. For years since Reconstruction, whites had resorted to violence and fraud to keep down the black vote. Now, powerful whites turned to the law, to legalized disfranchisement, to keep blacks away from the ballot box without violence. Beginning with a constitutional convention in Mississippi in 1890, disfranchisement swept across the states of the old Confederacy in the next two decades. The effect of legal change on black voter turnout was harsh and unambiguous: there was about a 60 percent drop in black voting after suffrage restriction. By the end of the first decade of the twentieth century, Southern African-Americans were almost as far from the levers of power as they had been in slavery.[11]

Although Jim Crow exacted countless costs, it was not the worst possibility for African-Americans, as progressives and other moderate whites rationalized. An ongoing race war or expulsion from the South could have been far worse. Were it not for segregation, wrote one of Mississippi's white newspaper editors in 1910, the state would have had "more race clashes and dead niggers than have been heard of since reconstruction." It was a self-serving remark, but truthful too. The boundaries of Jim Crow seemed to bring a measure of stability to the South: lynchings fell off from 115 nationwide in 1900 to 57 in 1905. For whites, there was no reason to doubt that segregation had indeed become "the elementary working hypothesis of civilization in our Southern States." And there was no reason to doubt that Jim Crow was there to stay.[12]

Certainly the North was unlikely to intervene, in part because the region had its own difficulties with race relations. As the African-American leader W. E. B. Du Bois observed in 1901, "The Negro Problem is not the sole property of the South." At the turn of the century, there were only 911,000 African-Americans outside the Southern states. Living mainly in Northern cities and towns, these blacks made up less than 1 percent of the non-Southern population. But they posed a problem to many whites nonetheless. The passage of civil rights laws after the Civil War had hardly wiped away old antagonisms in the Northern states. Most whites held an enduring stereotype of backward "darkies" and "coons," expressed by such songs as "All Coons Look Alike to Me" and such vaudeville figures as Doolittle Black and Julius Crow. White Northerners also heard and read about the alleged brutality of the African-American; like white Southerners, they could think of the black man as a beast and a competitor. As black Southerners began to flee Jim Crow and rural poverty, the prospect of economic competition loomed. By 1906, an observer could already note the "prevailing dread of an overwhelming influx from the South." And so, Northern race relations had their own volatility. In New York City in August 1900, one month after the Charles riot in New Orleans, a race riot broke out in the Tenderloin, the black section on the West Side of Manhattan. As in New Orleans, it began with an altercation between a black man and a white policeman; as in New Orleans, a policeman died; as in New Orleans, white mobs, aided and abetted by the police, staged a "nigger chase" through the streets.[13]

Accordingly, the North drew its own boundaries between black and white. The Northern version of segregation was generally milder than Southern Jim Crow, not because Northern whites were more virtuous but because blacks were less numerous and therefore less dangerous. Whites in the North did not insist so much on writing Jim Crow into state and local law, and they did not segregate their communities quite as thoroughly. Still, Northern segregation resembled Southern segregation in important respects. As in the South, communities kept African-Americans out of hotels, restaurants, theaters, and parks or condemned them to inferior accommodations. Such cities as Boston and New Haven retained integrated schools, but many other communities made sure black and white children did not learn in the same classrooms. Northern churches became less receptive to black worshipers; the Young Men's Christian Association did not want black members. Occasionally the Northern segregators did their work with almost Southern flair. In Cincinnati, the white members of the YMCA, to make sure that there was no implication of racial equality, even compelled local African-Americans to rename their own organization the "Young Boys' Christian Association."

The trend toward residential segregation was at least as strong in the North as in the South. Northern cities did not yet have the kind of black ghettoes that would develop later in the twentieth century. African-Americans often shared neighborhoods with predominantly working-class white immigrants who could not afford to live elsewhere. But especially as migration from the South increased, Northern communities were quickly developing predominantly black districts. New York had the Tenderloin and San Juan Hill; Cleveland had Central Avenue; other towns and cities had their own "Niggertown," "Buzzard's Alley," "Bronzeville," "Nigger Row," "Chinch Row," or "Black Bottom." Typically, these neighborhoods had poor housing and poor sanitation. The police usually allowed vice districts, with gambling and prostitution, to develop there too. In all, these were dangerous places to live. San Juan Hill got its name because the sharp incline up West Sixtieth Street and the numerous racial battles reminded New Yorkers of Theodore Roosevelt's famous charge up a Cuban hill of the same name during the war with Spain; "Death Avenue," the district's western boundary, got its name because so many black children died on the open railroad tracks of Eleventh Avenue. African-Americans lived in such places, of course, because limited incomes and white prejudice made it difficult to go anywhere else in town. Members of the small black middle class had the wherewithal to move into better white neighborhoods, but these men and women ran into hostile white homeowners and realtors. In some areas, whites were already resorting to restrictive covenants to make sure blacks would stay out.[14]

Economic segregation was a reality in the North as well as in the South. Clustered in low-status occupations, Northern African-Americans had trouble getting manufacturing jobs, joining unions, and keeping positions as waiters and barbers. Blacks' reputations as strikebreakers made relations with white workers even more tense. In politics, at least, Northern blacks did not face disfranchisement in the twentieth century. But their political power was eroding. African-Americans held fewer state and local offices and played a smaller role in political parties. "The plain fact is," progressive journalist Ray Stannard Baker confirmed in 1909, "most of us in the north do not believe in any real democracy as between white and colored men."[15]

Baker was guilty of understatement. Even white progressives, North as well as South, did not believe in any sort of equality between the races at the turn of the century. A time of environmentalist thinking, the Progressive Era was equally a time of race thinking. As the nineteenth century ended, science increasingly endorsed many Americans' belief that some races were better than others and that racial characteristics were hereditary and therefore quite possibly unalterable. Influenced by these ideas, white progressives held a range of opinions about race. Some, like Social Gospel leader Josiah Strong, were equally ardent believers in the superiority of Anglo-Saxons—"all-conquering," "more vigorous, more spiritual, more Christian"—to all other races in the United States and around the globe. "Is there room for doubt," Strong demanded, "that this race . . . is destined to dispossess many weaker races, assimilate others, and mold the remainder, until, in a very true and important sense, it has Anglo-Saxonized mankind?" A few reformers, like the Illinois factory inspector, New York settlement house resident, socialist, and journalist William English Walling, were ardent supporters of black rights. Condemning "race hatred," Walling insisted that "we must come to treat the negro on a plane of absolute political and social equality." The majority of progressives, clinging to a firm belief in African-American inferiority, fit somewhere in between. Most Northern progressives said notably little about their racial views. By and large, it was an awareness of class differences, not racial differences, that animated middle-class reform. Firm believers in white superiority, most progressives were nevertheless more interested in making the world middle-class than in making it Anglo-Saxon.[16]

White progressives in the South did not have the luxury of silence about race. Perhaps the best known Southern reformer, Edgar Gardner Murphy, spoke out frequently on the subject; in the process, he made very clear how well segregation fit with progressive values. Murphy approached the question of African-Americans' status from both the pessimistic perspective of race thinking and the optimistic perspective of environmentalism. "There is a distinct assumption of the negro's inferiority," he said; "but there is also a distinct assumption of the negro's improvability. It is upon the basis of this double assumption that the South finds its obligation." That obligation was to abandon antiblack violence and institute segregation. In addition to halting racial strife, Jim Crow would, Murphy believed, allow the process of reform to continue among African-Americans as it did elsewhere among whites. Safe behind the racial boundary line, Southern blacks were becoming new people. "The segregation of the race has thrown its members upon their own powers and has developed the qualities of resourcefulness . . . the noblest of the gifts of freedom, the power of personal and social self-dependence," Murphy maintained. "The very process which may have seemed to some like a policy of oppression has in fact resulted in a process of development." Furthermore, Jim Crow was swelling the ranks of the black middle class. Murphy rejoiced that "the social and educational separation of these races has created the opportunity and the vocation of the negro teacher, the negro physician, the negro lawyer, the negro leader of whatever sort." Such developments would continue, Murphy knew, if the South responded to his urgent crusade for better education for blacks as well as whites. In typically progressive terms, Murphy concluded that government activism could change the environment of African-Americans and therefore improve the race. "The fact that the negro is a negro, the State may not alter," he acknowledged; "but the fact that the negro—quite as much at the North as at the South—has not been adequately accorded the economic support of the profounder social forces of security, opportunity, and hope, the State may largely alter if it will. Will it do?" Murphy and other progressives believed the answer should be "yes"—as long as the boundary lines of segregation remained firmly drawn.[17]

Those Southern politicians dependent on progressive support repeated Murphy's argument in somewhat cruder form. In 1901, Governor Charles Brantley Aycock of North Carolina put the case for Jim Crow bluntly to a black audience. "No thoughtful, conservative, and upright Southerner has for your race aught but the kindest feelings, and we are willing and anxious to see you grow into the highest citizenship of which you are capable," he explained:

> But to do this it is absolutely necessary that each race should remain distinct, and have a society of its own. Inside of your own race you can grow as large and broad and high as God permits. . . . But all of them in the South will insist that you shall accomplish this high end without social intermingling.

For Aycock and other Southern leaders, there were no alternatives. Segregation's "violation," the governor bluntly warned his black audience, "would be to your destruction. . . ."[18]

As Jim Crow took hold with progressive support or acquiescence, the highest levels of the federal government did virtually nothing to help black Americans. Not surprisingly, the conservative United States Supreme Court gave segregation its imprimatur. In 1896, a majority of the justices ruled in *Plessy v. Ferguson* that segregation was legal on Louisiana trains as long as blacks were provided "separate but equal" accommodations.

The progressive presidents were not going to contest the ascendancy of "separate but equal," no matter how truly unequal the state of affairs for blacks in the South and in the North. Theodore Roosevelt shared the progressives' condescending view of African-Americans. For the President, race was a crucial, though often vague, category. In private, racial epithets came easily to his lips—his was a world of "micks," "dagos," "chinks," and "japs." Race had multiple meanings for him: it referred to the distinctions of color, the differences among white, red, black, and yellow; it conjured up a romantic vision of a superior white Anglo-Saxon and Teutonic heritage; it included a "bio-social" theory that acquired characteristics could be inherited. This was perhaps the most hopeful aspect of the President's thinking about race. A neo-Lamarckian, Roosevelt believed that environment and culture could modify heredity. Although races could go wrong and decline over time, presumably they could also improve. Yet, Roosevelt held out little hope for blacks. The President carefully avoided calling African-Americans "niggers," but he had no doubts about their merits. He confided to a friend in 1906 that "as a race and in the mass they are altogether inferior to the whites." As always with Roosevelt, class made a difference: he approved of more refined, middle-class blacks. But African-Americans could never be assimilated into the national "Race"; there could be no intermarriage with whites.[19]

These ideas pushed Roosevelt toward a position rather similar to that of the progressives. Like them, he had a paternalist view of the black race. Like them, he deplored violence and instability. Like them, he considered Jim Crow preferable to turmoil as a solution for "the terrible problem offered by the presence of the negro on this continent." So, rather than use federal power to mitigate segregation, he preferred to let the South handle its own race problems. "The white man who can be of most use to the colored man is that colored man's neighbor," Roosevelt explained. "It is the southern people themselves who must and can solve the difficulties that exist in the South."[20]

Believing he needed the support of black Southern Republicans, the so-called Black-and-Tans, in order to assure his nomination in 1904, Roosevelt did appoint some "colored men of good repute and standing" to federal jobs. In the process, he consulted Booker T. Washington on patronage matters and invited him to the White House for dinner in October 1901. But that invitation angered Southern whites. The Washington dinner was, according to a Memphis paper, "the most damnable outrage that has ever been perpetrated by a citizen of the United States." Washington never dined at the White House again. Although Roosevelt relished standing his ground on some disputed appointments, he remained the careful politician. Safely nominated and reelected in 1904, Roosevelt leaned away from the Black-and-Tans toward their white Republican rivals, the Southern "Lily Whites." Touring the South in 1905, the President reassured whites by stressing his Southern background and his admiration for the South, the Confederacy, and Robert E. Lee; he even sent roses to Stonewall Jackson's widow. It was, said a black leader, "national treachery to the Negro."[21]

Roosevelt condemned lynching during his second term, but he also revealed his profound reservations about African-Americans.[22] In an infamous episode in 1906, Roosevelt dishonorably discharged 170 black soldiers of the U.S. Army who had declined to tell what they knew, if anything, about a nighttime rampage through streets of the inhospitable town of Brownsville, Texas. Angered that the town's white-owned saloons either refused to serve blacks or forced them to drink in back rooms, ten or twenty of the soldiers had shot and killed a bartender and wounded a police lieutenant. The raid was, Rooosevelt fumed, "unparalleled for infamy in the annals of the United States Army"; the guilty soldiers were "bloody butchers" who should have been hanged. "If the colored men elect to stand by criminals of their own race because they are of their own race," the President warned, "they assuredly lay up for themselves the most dreadful day of reckoning." It was a sorry performance. The administration eventually agreed to let the soldiers appeal to an army panel for the right to reenlist—but only fourteen of them made it back into the service. Roosevelt left the whole matter out of his memoirs, as well he might have.[23]

Roosevelt's successors did not do much more for African-Americans. President William Howard Taft sought the support of white Southern Republicans and made clear he would not interfere with the region's social arrangements. Woodrow Wilson, a son of Virginia elected to the White House in large part by the votes of white Southerners, did more than tolerate segregation. As President, he allowed a number of federal departments to segregate their black employees in Washington and demote or fire black federal workers in the South. In an angry White House encounter with the black leader William Monroe Trotter in 1914, Wilson finally admitted what was obvious: that he believed segregation was the best policy for African-Americans.[24]

A few progressives knew better. More than almost any other reformer, Jane Addams managed to get past racist culture and acknowledge the sham of "separate but equal." Contradicting the cherished creed of Edgar Gardner Murphy and other progressives, Jane Addams wrote in 1911 that segregation made it harder, not easier, to improve the welfare of African-Americans. The creation of "a colony of colored people" in large cities, Addams insisted, broke down the black family and weakened its ability to bring up its children amid urban temptation. The leader of Hull-House worked with national black leaders, but Hull-House did not, as her friend and associate Louise de Koven Bowen conceded, make much of an effort to cross racial boundaries and promote association among different races. Addams raised funds for the Frederick Douglass Center, one of the very few settlements serving both blacks and whites. But African-Americans, Bowen noted, "were not always welcomed warmly" at Hull-House. Years later, Addams herself summed up the progressives' failure—with a persisting, telling note of condescension. Despite the predicament of African-Americans, she admitted in 1930, "we are no longer stirred as the Abolitionists were, to remove fetters, to prevent cruelty, to lead the humblest to the banquet of civilization."[25]

In these circumstances, "the humblest" had only a few, difficult alternatives: accommodate segregation; resist; or leave the country. Some African-Americans were indeed interested in going. Robert Charles belonged to the International Migration Society, which pledged to get African-Americans to Liberia. He was also a follower of Henry M. Turner, bishop of the African Methodist Episcopal Church, who called on blacks to go back to Africa. But Charles did not leave America; instead, he stood his ground and fought. Then and afterward, many blacks, workers in particular, admired his resistance and embroidered his story. "[T]here never has been anything authentic that Robert Charles was captured," the pioneering New Orleans jazz pianist, composer, and bandleader Jelly Roll Morton insisted years later. Blacks even made up a song about Charles. But they also understood what it meant to make his choice, to risk white violence. "I once knew the Robert Charles song," Jelly Roll Morton admitted, "but I found out it was best for me to forget it and that I did in order to go along with the world on the peaceful side. . . . [I]t was a trouble breeder."[26]

In the short run, at least, the choice for most African-Americans was to accommodate segregation, much as earlier generations had accommodated slavery. Like the slaves, twentieth-century blacks had to learn to live a double life. Inwardly, they did not have to believe in white supremacy and black inferiority, but outwardly, they had to offer deference and submissiveness. For safety's sake, this feat of self-control had to be mastered early in life.[27]

Benjamin Mays, born on a farm ten miles outside the town of Ninety Six in Greenwood County, South Carolina, in 1894 or 1895, was the child of former slaves. His first memory was of the mob of white men on horseback who "cursed my father, drew their guns and made him salute, made him take off his hat and bow down to them several times." Young Benjamin saw bloodhounds hunting a black man; he watched a black man, on the run from whites, hide in a swamp. In the process, Benjamin began to understand the arbitrary nature of white power. "Negroes always got the worst of it," Mays remembered. "Guilt and innocence were meaningless words: the Negro was always blamed, always punished." Mays also began to understand the limited scope of black power. "Among themselves, Negroes talked much about these tragedies," he noted. "They were impotent to do anything about them." Benjamin saw what happened to blacks who talked back to whites or, worse, struck back at them. And so, as a child, he learned mutualistic lessons similar to those learned by Hamlin Garland on the farm and Rahel Golub in the tenement and the sweatshop; but he focused more on some very different lessons: not to talk about racial matters, not to get too close to white women, not even to mention the black boxer Jack Johnson, who whipped a white man to win the heavyweight championship in 1908. "In this perilous world," Mays observed, "if a black boy wanted to live a halfway normal life and die a natural death he had to learn early the art of how to get along with white folks. . . . [I]t behooved Negroes to be humble, meek, and subservient in the presence of white folks." Even that might not be enough: "No matter how they acted, it was not always possible for Negroes to 'stay out of trouble'; the many who cringed and kowtowed to white people the most were in just as much danger as the few who did not. How could a Negro avoid trouble when his 'place' was whatever any white man's whim dictated at any given time?" Benjamin recognized the toll that this life took on his people. "It certainly 'put the rabbit' in many Negroes," he wrote. "Negroes lived under constant pressures and tensions all the time in my community. . . . To be at ease, to be relaxed, to be free were luxuries unknown to Negroes in Greenwood County and in most sections of the South." Some frustrated African-Americans fought among themselves. "It was difficult," Mays concluded, "virtually impossible, to combine manhood and blackness under one skin in the days of my youth."[28]

The principles that Benjamin Mays learned as a boy guided some black leaders as well. At the turn of the century, prominent African-Americans, North and South, pursued a strategy of accommodation. The most famous of them was Booker T. Washington, a slave at his birth in Virginia in the 1850s, founder of Alabama's Tuskegee Institute for blacks in the 1880s, and adviser to Republican politicians and Northern philanthropists by the 1890s. In a speech at the Atlanta Cotton States and International Exposition in 1895, Washington offered what became known as the "Atlanta Compromise." With an eye on moderate whites, Washington urged blacks to accept segregation and disfranchisement and concentrate instead on economic progress through self-help, thrift, and hard work. "In the long run it is the race or individual that exercised the most patience, forbearance, and self-control in the midst of trying conditions that wins . . . the respect of the world," he insisted. "An inch of progress is worth more than a yard of complaint." To make that progress, Washington favored the kind of industrial education offered at the Tuskegee Institute rather than higher education in the liberal arts. A politician at heart, Washington knew how to say different things to different people: whites could hear the promise of acquiescence; blacks, the promise of upward mobility and eventual equality. "It is not within the province of human nature," Washington declared, "that the man who is intelligent and virtuous, and owns and cultivates the best farm in his county, shall very long be denied the proper respect and consideration." Washington's optimism—"look always upon the bright side of life," he would say—must have been hard to take sometimes. But he also offered a vision of black solidarity, strength, and separateness: "We are a nation within a nation." And Washington himself lived the double life. Privately, he pushed a more assertive policy. At various times, he worked behind the scenes to limit disfranchisement legislation and Jim Crow practices on the railroads. Yet, outwardly, like young Benjamin Mays, he preached accommodation.[29]

At the beginning of the new century, Booker T. Washington had many willing listeners. The black middle class—African-Americans who had some property and income and hoped for more—generally accepted his strategy. Many working-class blacks, at least in the South, probably did too. But there were already signs that some African-Americans disliked so much accommodation. Beginning in the late 1890s, blacks in many Southern communities refused to ride on segregated streetcars. By shaming the streetcar owners and hurting their profits, these black boycotters hoped to end one element of Jim Crow in the South. The boycott movement peaked from 1900 to 1906, with actions in more than twenty-five Southern cities, but the results were disappointing. The loss of black riders was not enough to make whites give up Jim Crow on the cars.[30]

During these years, Booker T. Washington also began to face direct challenges to his leadership. Prominent African-Americans resented Washington's influence over black educational institutions and newspapers and his ties to white philanthropists and politicians. Some blacks believed that Washington's strategy of accommodation was shameful. William Monroe Trotter, the Harvard-educated editor of the African-American paper the Boston *Guardian,* labeled Washington a "self-seeker" and a "coward." Other blacks questioned Washington's fundamental strategic choice to emphasize economic development and acquiesce in disfranchisement.[31]

The strongest, most comprehensive challenge to Washington came from W. E. B. Du Bois, a professor at Atlanta University. Brought up in western Massachusetts, educated at Fisk, Harvard, and Berlin in the 1890s, Du Bois was already, in his thirties, a powerful intellectual and an accomplished sociologist. Once essentially a follower of Washington, Du Bois had come to question the trade-offs of the "Atlanta Compromise." That became quite clear in 1903 when Du Bois published *The Souls of Black Folk,* complete with an essay criticizing Washington for advocating "submission." Du Bois feared that economic progress would be impossible unless blacks had political rights. Emphasizing the importance of educated blacks, the "talented tenth," for the progress of the race, Du Bois also rejected Washington's focus on industrial rather than higher education. Joining the Socialist Party in 1904, Du Bois seemed willing to range far beyond Washington's conventional Republicanism and individualism.

Du Bois offered more than a rejoinder to Washington. In his work, Du Bois explored the duality of African-American identity: "One ever feels his twoness—an American, a Negro; two souls, two thoughts, two unreconciled strivings; two warring ideals in one dark body, whose dogged strength alone keeps it from being torn asunder." Du Bois envisioned a pluralist America, one in which blacks could be themselves rather than appear as whites wanted them to appear. The nation had to be black as well as white. "He would not bleach his Negro soul in a flood of white Americanism, for he knows that Negro blood has a message for the world," Du Bois wrote. "He simply wishes to make it possible for a man to be both a Negro and an American, without being cursed and spit upon by his fellows, without having the doors of opportunity closed roughly in his face."[32]

To help create a pluralist America, Du Bois arranged for a small meeting on the Canadian side of Niagara Falls in July 1905. What came to be known as the Niagara Movement firmly rejected accommodation of Southern whites, protested disfranchisement, praised collegiate as well as industrial education, and demanded protest as well as economic self-help. "We do not hesitate to complain," the meeting declared, "and to complain loudly and insistently." By 1909, the Niagara Movement had helped give rise to a new organization that became the National Association for the Advancement of Colored People a year later. The association included white supporters and benefactors—Lillian Wald and William English Walling, for instance—as well as African-Americans. Du Bois became its director of publicity and research and began to edit its journal, aptly named *The Crisis*.[33]

There were other African-American protests, including a passionate campaign against lynching. Georgia African-Americans held an Equal Rights Convention at Macon in 1906. "We must encourage Negro businessmen," the convention's president, William Jefferson White, declared. "And at the same time we must agitate, complain, protest, and keep protesting against the invasion of our manhood rights . . . and above all organize these million brothers of ours into one great fist which shall never cease to pound at the gates of opportunity until they shall fly open." Bishop Henry M. Turner was still bolder. "To the Negro in the country the American flag is a dirty and contemptible rag . . . ," he declaimed. "I wish to say that hell is an improvement upon the United States when the Negro is involved." Few African-Americans were ready to go that far. Many may have liked what Du Bois had to say—but they also heeded Washington's message. North and South, the realities of white power tempered black emotion. The streetcar boycotts faded away; the NAACP struggled. A true African-American mass movement against segregation was a long way off.[34]

The differences between Du Bois and Washington are obvious, and often remarked. The ideas they shared, including an uneven relationship to progressivism, are less plain but nonetheless revealing about the prospects for a "middle-class paradise" in America. Du Bois and Washington, along with other black middle-class leaders, shared the often condescending attitude of white progressives toward a working class supposedly in need of improvement. The African-American elite spoke of "uplifting the race." To achieve that goal, they emphasized the same kind of programs, especially educational and recreational reform, that progressivism emphasized. And they employed the same kinds of organization: women's clubs, religious groups, and such settlements as the Robert Gould Shaw House in Boston, the Lincoln House in Manhattan, the Neighborhood Union in Atlanta, Locust Street Settlement in Hampton, Virginia, Flanner House in Indianapolis, and Plymouth Settlement House in Louisville. As in progressivism, women played a prominent role. With black men cut off from the ballot and political participation, black women artfully capitalized on male deference to their roles as mothers and guardians of the home in order to press the African-American cause. It was, for instance, women such as Mary Church Terrell and the outspoken journalist Ida B. Wells-Barnett who led the black protest against lynching.[35]

Still, the necessities of life in Greenwood County and New Orleans, in San Juan Hill and the Tenderloin, also moved African-American activism away from progressivism. Unlike Edward Bellamy and so many other white progressives, black Americans had little reason to place their faith in state power and little to reason to believe they could gain it. Skepticism about the state in turn helps explain African-Americans' rather Victorian emphasis on self-help and self-development. At a time when the white middle class stressed the importance of association, of the individual's adjustment to the group, the black middle class necessarily invoked a more old-fashioned individualism of "patience, forbearance, and self-control." And finally, at a time when white progressives stressed social unity, and worked to make social groups more alike, African-Americans were determined to maintain their sense of difference in the United States. Whether it was Du Bois writing of black "twoness" or Washington talking of "a nation within a nation," African-American activism, for all its similarities to progressivism, also pointed away from white reform and its notion of human identity.

African-Americans had good reason to chart an independent course from progressivism. Segregation, the progressive solution, not only exacted a heavy toll from blacks in lost freedom, power, and opportunity; Jim Crow did not even make the United States a safe place. Across the country, the lynching of blacks actually increased from fifty-seven in 1905 to eighty-nine in 1908. Atlanta saw four days of white mob violence in September 1906, inspired by the usual rumors of black attacks on white women. Black Atlantans fled the city's center in terror; the rioting spread even into the black middle-class section of Brownsville, home of W. E. B. Du Bois. Perhaps twenty-five black people, as well as one white, died. During the Roosevelt administration, racial violence struck the North as well. Evansville, Indiana, was the site of rioting in 1903. In August 1908, there was a riot in Springfield, Illinois, the home of Abraham Lincoln. Two blacks and four whites died; the homes of blacks were burned. "Lincoln freed you," white rioters shouted, "now we'll show you where you belong!" "[The] conditions in Springfield are not peculiar to that city," a reporter wrote. "Almost every community in the country is face to face with the same possibilities. A mob may form in an hour." Despite segregation, it seemed, differences between black and white might not be safely contained after all.[36]

Differences between red and white were much easier to manage. At the start of the twentieth century, Native Americans posed little threat to whites. Far less numerous than African-Americans, the Indians seemed to be declining. Federal census takers enumerated 248,253 Native Americans in 1890; ten years later, even though the Indian Wars had come to an end in 1891, the census counted only 237,196. The Indians were more diverse and more fragmented than the African-American population. At least 170 tribal groups were spread across the country, from the Penobscot and Passamaquody in Maine to the

Seminoles in Florida to the Luisenos and Cahuillas in Southern California to the Makahs and Puyallups in Washington. The largest numbers of Native Americans lived in the states and territories west of the Mississippi River. More than 64,000 lived in Indian Territory and Oklahoma Territory, which would be joined to form the state of Oklahoma in 1907. Given these numbers, Indians did not pose the sort of social, economic, and political challenge that whites felt from blacks. And Native Americans had seemingly been put in their "place" even more decisively than African-Americans had been put in theirs during the Redemption. Defeated in the Indian Wars, largely confined to reservations, and denied citizenship rights, the Indians were effectively excluded from the mainstream of white America.[37]

Nevertheless, Native Americans had become a problem by the turn of the century. Their "place" had become uncertain, not because of their actions but because of the machinations of whites. The Native Americans had one resource that white society did covet—land. Throughout the late nineteenth century, whites wanted further access to the lands controlled by the tribes. At the same time, other whites, mainly the sort of genteel New England Republicans who had once backed Reconstruction, wanted to draw Native Americans into white society. The confluence of these desires was the federal policy of assimilation, which emerged in the 1870s and 1880s, and which received its fullest legislative expression in the Dawes Severalty Act of 1887. The white assimilationists intended to dismantle Native American culture, dissolve the tribes, and educate Native American children in schools—all to turn the Indians into individualistic, hard-working citizens of the United States. The Dawes Act, also known as the General Allotment Act, served this goal by providing for the gradual distribution of collectively held tribal lands to individual Native Americans—and to whites. Given the motives of its white supporters, this was at once a cynical and an optimistic policy: Indians would be exploited, but they would be transformed. It also underscored the exceptional status of Native Americans in the United States. At a time when workers, immigrants, and blacks were suspect, when boundaries were being drawn across America, the line between Indians and whites would be obliterated.

Assimilation had disappointed its advocates by 1900. For land-hungry whites, the implementation of the Dawes Act was too slow; they wanted quicker access to Indian land. For whites sympathetic to Native Americans, assimilation did not seem to be working; it even appeared to be hurting the Indians. Of some three thousand Cheyenne and Arapaho on allotted lands in western Oklahoma, less than 20 percent were raising their own crops in 1900. The rest depended on food rations handed out by the federal Indian agent. Between rations, the agent reported, "gaunt hunger stalks them. . . ." The allotment of land at the Fort Hall Reservation in Idaho, progressive journalist Ray Stannard Baker noted in 1903, had left the Indians there "exactly as before, looking on imperturbably, eating, sleeping, idling, with no more thought of the future than a white man's child."[38]

Whites were also having second thoughts about obliterating Native American culture. With the frontier apparently gone, the Indians now seemed like artifacts of a vanished, romantic past. Perhaps those artifacts should be preserved. Finally, the development of racial thought raised questions about assimilation. Some science suggested that racial differences were substantial and hard to overcome. Even neo-Lamarckians, who believed that environment and culture could affect racial characteristics, doubted that Indians could change very much. Influenced by Darwinism, some observers suggested that Native Americans, although perhaps superior to blacks, faced a bleak future in the struggle for survival. After "a hundred years of vain struggle ending with the pathetic present," predicted William Henry Holmes, head of the Bureau of American Ethnology, early in the new century, the Indians were "fading out to total oblivion in the very near future. All that will remain to the world of the fated race will be a few decaying monuments, the minor relics preserved in museums, and something of what has been written."[39]

All these developments produced a new view of assimilation, especially among whites who cared deeply about Native Americans. If the Indians could not change, if their survival was in doubt, then perhaps full assimilation into the white world was a mistake. It might be better to keep them separate—not wholly excluded, as in the years before the Dawes Act, but still separate. The increasingly urbanized and bourgeois Hamlin Garland, captivated by Native American life, exemplified the new thinking. Between 1895 and 1900, the writer made five trips to visit reservations from Oklahoma and the Dakotas west to Arizona and Washington. Inspired by these trips, Garland wrote romantic short stories, novels, and essays centered on Native Americans and the old West. Saddened and angered by the Indians' condition, Garland also became a vocal critic of the assimilation policy. "The allotment of lands in severalty," he wrote in a magazine article in 1902, "which began in land-lust and is being carried to the bitter end by those who believe a Stone Age man can be developed into a citizen of the United States in a single generation, is in violent antagonism to every wish and innate desire of the red man, and has failed of expected results. . . ." In a telling measure of his conversion to middle-class progressive culture, Garland deplored the attempt to turn the Native American into an individualist making his or her way in the world like a Victorian son out to earn his fortune. Individualism, Garland believed, was antithetical to the Native American's way of life. "All his duties—even his hunting—have always been performed in company with his fellows," Garland noted. "He is a villager, never a solitary. He dreads solitude. . . . Naturally, those who were resolute to make the Indian a solitary took little thought of this deep-seated mental characteristic, being confident that resolute whacking would jar his brain-cells into conformity with those of a white man of the same age."

The "resolute whacking" could not go on. "As a nation, we can't afford to rest under the stigma of inhuman cruelty," Garland insisted. "These red men are on our conscience." Since they were "like children," he reasoned, "We are answerable for them, just as we are answerable for the black man's future." Garland's solution was to keep Indians away from whites. In most cases, he wanted to maintain Native Americans on the reservation, the "isle of safety." Native Americans who had already received allotments should be allowed to pool their lands together to form villages away from white settlements. Of course, there could be no intermarriage of white and red. In this way, Native Americans would be preserved. With his paternal concern for the childlike race, with his fear for the good name of whites, Garland sounded like Edgar Gardner Murphy and the white progressives who advocated Jim Crow. And like many Southerners, he saw the triumph of an enlightened segregation as proof of white supremacy. "[Only] when we give our best to these red brethren of ours," Garland maintained, "do we justify ourselves as the dominant race of the Western continent."[40]

Garland's voice was heard in the White House. He became one of the members of the "Cowboy Cabinet," the progressive white men from the West and Midwest whom Theodore Roosevelt consulted when he made Indian policy for his administration. The President had calmed down since his younger days in the 1880s, when he had declared, "I don't go so far as to think that the only good Indians are dead Indians, but I believe nine out of every ten are, and I shouldn't like to inquire too closely into the case of the tenth." Now, he too was nostalgic about the passing of the frontier and the old Indian cultures. With his racial views, he too was dubious about the prospects for assimilation. To be sure, Roosevelt believed that Indians, like blacks, had some respectable individual representatives. Similarly, some tribes, such as the Cherokee, were better than others. And naturally, the combative Roosevelt admired Indians for being such good fighters. He even believed that Indians, unlike blacks, should be allowed to marry whites. But the great majority of Native Americans had, he knew, only limited prospects. "A few Indians may be able to turn themselves into ordinary citizens in a dozen years," Roosevelt said after leaving the presidency. "Give to these exceptional Indians every chance; but remember that the majority must change gradually, and that it will take generations to make the change complete. . . . Some Indians can hardly be moved forward at all."[41]

Accordingly, Roosevelt wanted to modify the federal government's commitment to assimilation along typically progressive lines. "In dealing with the Indians our aim should be their ultimate absorption into the body of our people," he wrote carefully in his annual message to Congress in 1902. "But in many cases this absorption must and should be very slow." Roosevelt wanted the federal government to become less involved in Indians' lives. As was the case with Jim Crow in the South, he believed local whites should have more of a say in determining relations with the other race. Allotment of Indian lands would continue—but assimilation would be slow indeed.[42]

Roosevelt's Indian policy took its clearest form with his appointment of Francis Leupp as commissioner of Indian Affairs in 1905. A graduate of Williams College, a journalist, and an advocate of civil service reform, Leupp was Roosevelt's kind of man. "The commonest mistake made . . . in dealing with the Indian," Leupp declared, "is the assumption that he is simply a white man with red skin." Whites should not imagine that education, individual landholdings, and citizenship would make Native Americans into whites. The aim of federal Indian policy, therefore, should be "improvement, not transformation." Under Leupp, the Bureau of Indian Affairs changed the education of Native American children. Like blacks in the South, Indian pupils supposedly did not need higher learning so much as practical preparation for low-skilled jobs. Deemphasizing the ambitious boarding schools that took young Indians away from reservations, the bureau instead stressed vocational training on the reservations. Leupp also weakened the bureau's policy of placing Native American children in white public schools. During Leupp's tenure in office, the public schools got away with rejecting Indians or putting them in segregated classrooms.[43]

As to citizenship rights for Native Americans, one of the fundamental aims of the assimilationists, Leupp was blunt. "Citizenship has been a disadvantage to many Indians," he announced. "They are not fitted for its duties or able to take advantage of its benefits." Under the Dawes Act, citizenship went automatically to Native Americans receiving an individual allotment of tribal land. But in 1906 the Roosevelt administration secured passage of the Burke Act, which broke the automatic linkage between allotment and citizenship. Now an Indian receiving allotted lands could not become a citizen of the United States for twenty-five years or until determined competent by the secretary of the interior. Since so few Native Americans were citizens, it was hardly necessary to disfranchise them. Still, a string of court decisions and state laws made Indian voting unlikely. In some places, for instance, Native Americans had to prove they were assimilated in order to cast a ballot. The notable exception would prove to be the state of Oklahoma, where Indians were both numerous and, ironically, willing to join whites in the disfranchisement of blacks. But most Native Americans, like most African-Americans, had no access to political power. At best, the Indians were wards of the federal government, dependent on Leupp, Roosevelt, and Congress.[44]

It was a dangerous dependency. Under pressure from white Westerners, the federal government opened up more tribal lands to white exploitation and made it easier for Indians to sell their allotments to whites. The Supreme Court, with its ruling in *Lone Wolf v. Hitchcock* in 1903, signaled its approval. So the Roosevelt administration allotted the Rosebud Sioux, Uintah, Crow, Flathead, and Wind River Reservations to Native Americans, with the surplus available to whites. Under Leupp, the land cessions continued. Western whites called for this or that reservation to be opened up and Congress would oblige. The Burke Act, by slowing Indian citizenship, made it even easier. In May 1908 alone, 2.9 million acres of the Standing Rock and Cheyenne River Reservations were opened up. All told, many millions of acres passed out of Indian hands during the Roosevelt administration.

There was little that Native Americans could do about federal policy.

Few in number, scattered across the country, the Indians lacked even the limited resources of blacks: a fairly significant middle class, a cadre of educators and officeholders, and metropolitan newspapers. And over the years, the Indians had been far more savagely subdued. Still, Native Americans resisted the authority of the federal agents where they could.

Roosevelt and Leupp would have none of that. If Native Americans would not willingly accept federal policy, if there was a conflict between red and white, then the government would end it by force and coercion. During Roosevelt's administration, there were numerous illegal arrests of Indians. A notable instance involved the Aneth Navajo of southern Utah, who had managed to avoid the reservation and government schooling. But in 1903 the Bureau of Indian Affairs set up a new agency at Shiprock, New Mexico, forty miles from Aneth. The agent, William T. Shelton, wanted Navajo children to attend the government boarding school at Shiprock. The Aneth headman, Bai-a-lil-le, and a group of followers would not send their children to the boarding school; Bai-a-lil-le, an impressive medicine man in his early forties, would not even go to Shiprock for talks in 1907. Furthermore, if Shelton was foolish enough to come to Aneth, the agent had better be "prepared to fight" because Bai-a-lil-le "wanted to fight" and "was not afraid to die." Shelton went to Aneth nevertheless. He got no fight, but no satisfaction either. Bai-a-lil-le, refusing federal authority, threatened witchcraft. By then, Francis Leupp had been drawn into the affair; in October, two troops of the Fifth Cavalry were sent to deal with the Aneth Navajo. In a surprise dawn raid on the hogans of Bai-a-lil-le and his people, the cavalry tried to make arrests and wound up killing two Navajo and wounding one. Bai-a-lil-le and nine of his followers were sent summarily to Arizona for hard labor without term. The Indian Rights Association, a group of white assimilationists, protested this draconian and illegal treatment. In reply, Leupp offered a testy and startling defense of his actions: " . . . there comes a time in the experience of every man who has authority when he has got to make his own laws."

Now Roosevelt had to defend his commissioner. The Navajo were, the President insisted, "a group of notorious outlaws, led by a medicine man . . . an Indian of the type of Geronimo in earlier days." Roosevelt, like Leupp, was impatient with the constraints of the law: "Devoutly as all of us may look forward to the day when the most backward Indian shall have been brought to the point where he can be governed just as the ignorant white man is governed in one of our civilized communities, that day has not yet arrived." Arguing the case in court, the government even maintained that the Navajo were "prisoners of war." As with the Brownsville case, racism had led the Roosevelt government into an excess of arbitrary authority. In March 1909, the Arizona Supreme Court ordered the release of Bai-a-lil-le and his followers. There were limits to federal power, but there was still no doubt about the government's capacity to compel obedience. Bai-a-lil-le had to promise peaceful behavior and an end to witchcraft; the medicine man even went to Shiprock to speak to the Native American pupils at the government school about the importance of education.[45]

As the story of Bai-a-lil-le made plain, Native Americans were not free to reject the United States. But they were not free to become full members of the nation, either. The Taft administration left things as they were; so did the Wilson administration. The Indians were caught between exclusion and integration; like African-Americans, they were segregated.[46]

Far from the emptiness of southern Utah, in crowded cities, other boundary lines were being drawn between Americans. Urban residents, thrown together with strangers on city streets, felt the need for security and privacy. They wanted to know that other pedestrians would not presume to address them or bother them. Already by the late nineteenth century, one could, in effect, be alone in a crowd on the street. "The crowd is the embodiment of isolation," a European visitor to Chicago had noted in the 1870s. The urban planner Frederick Law Olmsted observed the same quality in city people: "Every day of their lives they have seen thousands of their fellow-men, have met them face to face, have brushed against them, and yet have had not experience of anything in common with them." This sense of separation was, one suspects, a particularly middle- and upper-class concern. Certainly it was the middle class that most self-consciously elaborated rules for conduct in public. A well-bred person did not stare at others. A gentleman paid attention to a lady without drawing *too* much attention to her—tipping his hat, speaking only if she spoke first. "All rights, and the essence of true politeness," read the book *Social Etiquette of New York,* "are contained in the homely maxim, 'MIND YOUR OWN BUSINESS'; which means by a pretty evident implication, that you are to let your neighbor's business alone."[47]

These rules of public behavior were not the only urban boundary lines. At the turn of the century, American cities were becoming increasingly segregated by more than race: the different classes and ethnic groups were also pulling away from each other. This residential segregation was a prosaic process, without the sad spectacle of allotment or the brazen drama of disfranchisement; rather, it was the sum of millions of individual decisions, the product of economic inequality and technological change. Well into the nineteenth century, American cities had been "walking cities," in which different social groups mixed together in neighborhoods because workers needed to live within walking distance of their jobs. By 1900, the omnibus, the street railway, the subway, and the elevated train had made it possible for many people to live some distance from work; different groups did not necessarily have to share neighborhoods. The transformation of class relations, the profound sense of difference between groups, made such separation seem desirable. The upper ten, as we have seen, lived apart in urban fortresses, exclusive suburbs, private clubs, and boarding schools. The middle class was also moving away from downtown areas to newer neighborhoods at the city's edges and to developing suburbs. But many workers, native-born and immigrant, could not afford to commute or to pay for better housing. As a result, the poorest city residents, the least skilled, the lowest paid, were becoming concentrated in their own neighborhoods. These people were not as isolated as blacks, but they were segregated nonetheless. The degree of residential segregation varied from one ethnic group to another; in general, the new immigrants from Eastern and Southern Europe were more concentrated in enclaves than, say, the Germans and the Irish. And immigrants from different countries often shared neighborhoods. But by and large, New York, Chicago, Detroit, San Francisco, and other cities were becoming segregated urban worlds in which the different classes and ethnic groups were less likely to bump against one another in streets and stores and schools, and in which Rahel Golub could live for five years without "a glimpse of" America. Like Native Americans and Southern blacks, immigrants paid a political cost. Around the country, state legislatures, usually with support from progressives, deprived aliens of their longtime right to vote.[48]

Even as the different boundary lines were drawn across the United States in the 1900s, Americans explored alternatives. For some people, segregation was not enough; they wanted the complete exclusion of people different from themselves. Not content to let immigrants live apart in urban enclaves, these Americans, including some progressives, advocated immigration restriction, a wall built around the United States. And some Americans, advocates of the "science" of eugenics, advocated another kind of wall—selective breeding, which would make sure the wrong sort of people never got born in the United States in the first place.

Immigration restriction was difficult to achieve, however.[49] The United States had a long history of ambivalence toward immigrants, but it had an equally long history of their acceptance. Naturally, immigrants and their children wanted immigration to continue. So did businessmen eager for cheap and plentiful labor. Many native-born Americans had long been confident that immigrants could be assimilated into the national life. Progressive activists, excited by the power of environmental reform, tended to maintain that confidence. In 1902, Jacob Riis wondered whether the immigrants streaming through Ellis Island, the successor to Castle Garden, would become good Americans. "While the flag flies over the public school, keep it aloft over Ellis Island and have no misgivings," he told his readers. "The school has the answer to your riddle." He might have added the settlement house, the playground, the model tenement, the institutional church, and a host of other progressive devices. But many Americans' confidence in assimilation was breaking down amid the myriad social divisions of the early twentieth century. McKinley's assassin, Leon Czolgosz, was a native-born American, but his Eastern European name and anarchist views stirred fears of the new immigration. The New England patricians of the old Immigration Restriction League, among them Roosevelt's close friend Senator Henry Cabot Lodge of Massachusetts, were active again. So were the members of the American Federation of Labor, mostly men of English, Irish, and German stock, who feared that new immigrants would break strikes and accept low wages. There was clearly no national consensus in favor of immigration restriction.[50]

As a result, presidents were caught in a political tangle. Sensitive to businessmen's need for workers, Theodore Roosevelt was also concerned about social conflict in a polyglot America. Although the President had favored some sort of immigration restriction before, he clearly had to be careful now in the White House. In his first annual message to Congress at the end of

1901, Roosevelt called for new legislation. "Our present immigration laws are unsatisfactory," he wrote. "We need every honest and efficient immigrant fitted to become an American citizen, every immigrant who comes here to stay, who brings here a strong body, a stout heart, a good head, and a resolute purpose to do his duty well in every way and to bring up his children as law-abiding and God-fearing members of the community." But Roosevelt wanted "to exclude absolutely not only all persons who are known to be believers in anarchistic principles or members of anarchistic societies, but also all persons who are of a low moral tendency or of unsavory reputation." He did not endorse the favored device of the Immigration Restriction League, a literacy test for immigrants. But he did ask for "a careful and not merely perfunctory educational test" in order "to decrease the sum of ignorance, so potent in producing the envy, suspicion, malignant passion, and hatred of order, out of which anarchistic sentiment inevitably springs." Finally, bowing to organized labor, Roosevelt demanded the exclusion of "all persons . . . who are below a certain standard of economic fitness." Such a step, the President concluded, "would stop the influx of cheap labor, and the resulting competition which gives rise to so much of bitterness in American industrial life; and . . . would dry up the springs of the pestilential social conditions in our great cities. . . ."[51]

Despite Roosevelt's support, comprehensive immigration restriction did not come quickly or easily. The Immigration Act of 1903 gave the government the power to keep out alleged anarchists but omitted a literacy or educational test. Restrictionists made more progress when they concentrated on nonwhite immigrants. Relatively few in number, Asian immigrants were clearly vulnerable in the land of Jim Crow. In 1902, the Chinese Exclusion Act of 1882, which made Chinese immigration and citizenship difficult, was up for renewal in Congress. White Westerners had long resented the Chinese and discriminated against them. Roosevelt, looking ahead to the presidential campaign in 1904, favored the continued exclusion of Chinese of the wrong sort. The House and Senate obliged. "Congress has done its work so well," Secretary of State John Hay told Roosevelt, "that even Confucius could not become an American."[52]

Even as Washington dealt with the Chinese, immigration from Japan became an issue. One or two thousand Japanese a year had entered the country in the 1890s. But in 1900, 12,635 migrated to the United States; by 1903, the number jumped to 19,968. Most of the Japanese lived in California, where whites discriminated against them. Soon the state legislature was demanding Japanese exclusion. Had it been a matter only of white public opinion, the federal government would have readily obliged. But Roosevelt also had to take into account diplomatic relations with the Japanese government. Events in California soon forced his hand. In October 1906, the San Francisco School Board ordered segregation of Asian students. Responding to protests from Japan, Roosevelt sent an emissary to California to reason with San Francisco officials. When the emissary was rebuffed, Roosevelt called the action of the school board "a wicked absurdity . . . a confession of inferiority in our civilization." The President made clear his intention to protect Japanese immigrants, but that angered white Westerners and even worried white Southerners about the fate of Jim Crow. So Roosevelt shifted ground and worked out what was called the Gentlemen's Agreement with Japan. To placate the Japanese government, Roosevelt induced the San Francisco School Board to give up segregation and the California legislature to back away from anti-Japanese legislation; the price was a provision in the Immigration Act of 1907 authorizing the President to stop any immigration "to the detriment of labor conditions." Then, in 1908, after much delay, Roosevelt secured Japan's agreement to restrict migration to the United States.[53]

During the Japanese controversy, sentiment to restrict white immigration made slow but discernible progress. One reason was the gradual spread of the newer scientific racism, which drew distinctions not only between people of different colors but between different white ethnic groups. In *The Races of Europe,* published in 1899, economist William Z. Ripley had divided whites into three groups: the tall, blond, northern Teutonics; the shorter and heavier central Alpines; and the darker southern Mediterraneans. This kind of thinking made it easier for some Americans to see Southern and Eastern European immigrants as representatives of a different and inferior race—"beaten members of beaten breeds," sociologist E. A. Ross called them. As the rise of Jim Crow, the demise of Indian assimilation, and the exclusion of the Japanese suggested, a perception of racial difference could justify all sorts of action. In 1906 and 1907, there was renewed agitation for a literacy test. The Immigration Restriction League and the American Federation of Labor favored it; so, too, did white Southerners and Westerners mindful of their own racial arrangements. Senator Furnifold M. Simmons of North Carolina brought

Southern oratory to the cause. The new immigration, he thundered, was "nothing more than the degenerate progeny of the Asiatic hordes which, long centuries ago, overran the shores of the Mediterranean . . . the spawn of the Phoenician curse." But the literacy test still had too many opponents. Roosevelt did not risk endorsing it publicly. In the end, the Immigration Act of 1907 doubled the entrance fee for immigrants from two to four dollars and set up an investigative commission on immigration. Agitation for the literacy test continued after Roosevelt left office. Still, the measure remained too controversial for any president. Taft vetoed a version of the literacy test in 1913. Wilson did the same in 1915. But the drive for immigration restriction, through the literacy test and other devices, would continue.[54]

Meanwhile, some Americans advocated another kind of exclusion. In the 1900s, the nation was learning about eugenics, a so-called science born in Great Britain and inspired by new discoveries in genetics. The advocates of eugenics started with the Darwinian principle that the acquired traits of one generation were not inherited by the next. The only way, then, to improve the genetic stock of the human race was by encouraging the reproduction of people with desirable traits and discouraging the reproduction of people with undesirable traits. In urging the well-to-do to reproduce and avoid "race suicide," Theodore Roosevelt drew on a crude form of eugenics. By 1910, the former president was offering the new movement his support. But American eugenists, led by Charles Benedict Davenport, the director of the pioneering Eugenics Record Office at Cold Spring Harbor, Long Island, focused less on encouraging the right sort of people to become parents and much more on stopping the wrong people from reproducing. In a sense, the eugenists, with their focus on the unborn, were the ultimate exclusionists. The eugenics movement was obsessed with the danger to the American population apparently posed by the "feebleminded" and the insane. Eugenists campaigned particularly for state laws allowing the involuntary sterilization of the inmates of mental institutions. Indiana enacted such a law in 1907, and a number of states followed this "Indiana idea." Nationwide, some two hundred sterilizations occurred in the Progressive Era, mainly in Indiana and California.[55]

By and large, the progressives did not support exclusion; it was too controversial for them to insist on the literacy test, too disturbing to contemplate involuntary sterilization. In any event, they much preferred segregation, which proved to be easier to implement and more compatible with their faith in transforming people. Yet, the progressive support for the different forms of Jim Crow was a critical moral blunder. Segregation certainly reflected the power of progressives and other privileged whites, but it also revealed their weakness. The boundary lines of early twentieth-century America were a confession of frailty, an admission that the powerful could not create a harmonious, let alone homogeneous, nation anytime soon. Segregation was also a failure of imagination and nerve. The rise of progressivism represented a remarkable reworking of middle-class ideology, a creative deployment of a host of devices for reform, and a bold determination to take on some of the most basic and intractable issues of human existence. Willing to believe that a kind of "paradise" might really be attainable some day, progressives showed little fear in dealing with problems of gender, family, class, and economy—but not of race.

By agreeing to segregation, the progressives contradicted their own basic wisdom, their belief in the necessity of association. "It is precisely in the sundering of our society into classes, that have little in common, *that are no longer neighbors*, that our peril lives," Jacob Riis typically observed. "A people cannot work together for the good of the state if they are not on speaking terms." Instead of making African-Americans, Native Americans, and immigrants the literal and figurative neighbors of other Americans, the progressives too often worked to keep these groups apart. In the process, progressivism ensured that a greater sense of social distance would grow over time. This was true not only for Native Americans, African-American sharecroppers, and immigrant workers, who obviously began the age of segregation already some distance from middle-class culture. It was true even for the African-American elite that otherwise shared so much with the white middle class. Segregation ensured that the "talented tenth" would never feel fully comfortable with progressivism and the forms of New Deal and Great Society liberalism that succeeded it. Progressives did much to ameliorate class conflict over the course of the twentieth century; in exchange for the short-term stabilization of racial conflict in the 1900s and 1910s, they may well have made race relations worse over the long term.[56]

The progressives paid a further price for segregation. In its battles with the upper ten and entrenched political power, the middle class obviously needed allies. At their most successful, the progressives managed to promote inclusive notions, such as consumers and "the people," that could unify and mobilize diverse Americans. The crusades for segregation revealed just how pinched, narrow, and self-defeating the progressives' definition of "the people" could be. At times, progressivism seemed to be, as one historian put it, "for whites only." The progressives were all too willing to segregate the ballot box, to keep blacks, Indians, and Asians away from political opportunity. Moreover, segregation was never solely about race, important as racial identity so clearly was for progressives and other Americans. Reformers considered so many people of other races inferior because of their class status as well as their skin color: the vast majority of African-Americans in the South were problematic because they were poor, uneducated, and working-class as well as black. In fact, there was a certain racial even-handedness about some progressives' view of the lower orders. Reformers such as Edgar Gardner Murphy may not have thought much of blacks, but they did not think much of poor whites either. Murphy certainly considered African-Americans inferior to whites—but not all that inferior. "What is true . . . of the negro masses," he wrote, "is largely true of the white masses."[57]

This outlook helps explain the fundamental paradox of progressive politics. To battle the rich and their political satellites, progressives rallied "the people" and supported a clutch of reforms intended to open up political participation. The initiative, referendum, and recall, the direct election of United States senators, and direct primaries were supposed to make it easier for Americans to get into politics and attack privilege. But a narrow definition of "the people" dictated antiparticipatory reforms as well. So progressives supported disfranchisement for African-Americans in the South, Native Americans in the West, and immigrants all across the country. By requiring potential voters to enroll days or even weeks before election day and to prove their identity, voter registration laws made it more time-consuming to vote. The progressives' political strength was their ability to project the "people" against the powerful; their political weakness was their willingness to segregate the ballot box and thereby keep so many Americans out of the battle against privilege.[58]

More than this, the progressives' condescension toward other groups, so clearly highlighted by segregation, frittered away much of the middle-class advantage in the struggle for power in America. At a time when the upper ten were culturally isolated, in part because of progressive attacks, the middle class made its reservations about the mass of American people all too clear. Progressives often spoke of their commitment to democracy. But many reformers, so critical of individualism and individual rights, were not very democratic at all. "The idea of the liberty of the individual is not a sound basis for a democratic government," Washington Gladden insisted. The emphasis on individual rights, such as suffrage, was "a radical defect in the habitual thinking of the average American." For the Social Gospel leader, suffrage was a "duty" rather than a "right," and so presumably it could be taken away. Workers and farmers, suspicious of upper-class individualism, had good reason to wonder about the attitudes and intentions that lay behind segregation, disfranchisement, and other progressive reforms. Segregation in all its forms was convenient, but costly, for the progressives.[59]

It might have been different. However convenient, segregation and disfranchisement were not foreordained. The progressives themselves advanced an alternative. Progressivism emerged in part from the desire to release middle-class women from a form of segregation. Even as the middle class accepted and urged the segregation of other races and ethnic groups in the late nineteenth and early twentieth centuries, it was increasingly willing to break down the segregation of the sexes by allowing women to cross social boundary lines into public spaces. In the cities, department stores became a legitimate place for women. Some streets became respectable female public space, too. There was, for instance, New York City's famous Ladies' Mile, up Broadway from Fourteenth to Twenty-third Streets, where women could stroll and window-shop with no question about their morals.

At the start of the twentieth century, women also intensified their quest to cross the boundary line that separated them from the ballot box. With the vote won only in Colorado, Idaho, Utah, and Wyoming, suffragists began to reconsider their traditional tactic of quietly lobbying male politicians. By 1909, the National American Woman Suffrage Association and other suffragist groups were holding public rallies. And some women, influenced by the English suffragettes, were taking to the streets to demand the vote. In October 1908, Anna Howard Shaw, president of the National American Woman Suffrage Association, led a parade of the Iowa Equal Suffrage Association at Boone, Iowa. "After much urging from her and the president, and with great trepidation and many misgivings on the part of the members, a procession was formed and marched through the principal streets," the suffrage movement's official history noted. "[It] required much courage to take part in it." Unfortunately for the country and for the progressives themselves, they did not have much more courage to spare in the age of segregation.[60]

PART THREE

Disturbance and Defeat

CHAPTER SEVEN

The Promise of Liberation

Sherwood Anderson was born in Camden, Ohio, in 1876, the centennial year of a nation dedicated to freedom. For all its inequality, the United States remained a land of liberation in the late nineteenth century. As Anderson grew up in the 1880s and 1890s, Americans could still set themselves free from many of their predicaments. Movement—geographical mobility—epitomized the promise of liberation: Richard Garland moved to the Dakota Territory; Hamlin Garland and Jane Addams moved to Chicago. The Golubs left Europe for New York; the Bradley Martins and James Hazen Hyde left New York for Europe. Sherwood Anderson moved, too. In 1884, his family went to Clyde, Ohio. In 1895, Anderson left behind this confining town and his depressing home for a geographical and occupational odyssey. He went to Erie, Ohio, to Cuba, and, like Hamlin Garland and Jane Addams before him, to Chicago. He became "a laborer, a farm hand, a soldier, a factory hand." After a year at Wittenburg College in Springfield, Ohio, Anderson went back to Chicago in 1900. He became an advertising man, married an industrialist's daughter, and eventually had three children. In 1907, the Andersons moved on to Elyria, Ohio, where Sherwood set up his paint business, the Anderson Manufacturing Company.[1]

Wealthy and independent, Anderson had thrown off the constraints of Clyde, moved freely across the land, and made himself a success. But somehow he no longer felt free. Instead, Anderson was trapped—in his job, his marriage, and his identity. By the 1910s, he was unhappy with his "nasty," "unclean" work. He was unhappy with his family. "The woman I had got as wife and the children I had got by her simply did not exist for me," Anderson later recalled. And he was unhappy with himself. "I was in business for a long time, and the fact is," he admitted, "I was a smooth son of a bitch." He tried to escape through golf, alcohol, and adultery. "[P]resently I was unfaithful to my wife," Anderson remembered. "Most of the bright young business men I knew were. Why not?" Yet, fashionable adultery did not set him free. Anderson tried writing: his work was full of yearning for rural life, for the vanishing preindustrial world. But part-time writing did not set him free either.[2]

Unable to liberate himself, Anderson tried to hide. Like those other unhappy men, Charles Spencer and Julian West, Anderson retreated deep into his home. Rather than a basement or an underground crypt, he chose a room "in a wing of the house, upstairs, a room to which the noises of the house did not penetrate . . . often." Anderson kept everyone out of this room: he cleaned it himself and kept it locked. Up there at night, away from his family, he read, played with toy soldiers, and slept. In this room the totality of Anderson's confinement became clear: he was trapped not only in marriage, business, and bourgeois living; he was trapped in himself. Anderson found he could not hide from "the thing," from "eternal questioning of self." It was all, he confessed, "self-absorption, ambition, self, self, self."[3]

Sherwood Anderson's entrapment was not unusual by the 1900s. Across America, the liberating possibilities of the nineteenth century seemed to give way to the confining realities of the twentieth. Americans found themselves enmeshed in new institutions—segregation, big business, and the activist, regulatory state. Space and time seemed to close in on people. As many Americans now knew, there were limits to the nation's land and resources. In 1893, historian Frederick Jackson Turner had pointed out that the American frontier, the zone of land available for expansion and new settlement, had disappeared. Even the vastness of the world was becoming known and finite. When Robert Peary got to the North Pole in 1909 and Roald Amundsen reached the South Pole in 1911, there seemed to be no unexplored territory left around the globe. Time had become more confining, too. Frederick Winslow Taylor and his disciples used stopwatches to regiment work. An interconnected world, spanned by empires, could no longer tolerate the many local variations of time: in 1912, the International Conference on Time called for a uniform system of time zones around the world. By that year, Americans could clearly see the outlines of modern existence—binding, confining, constraining, limiting.[4]

In that year, too, Sherwood Anderson's incarceration became unendurable. "It came with a rush, the feeling that I must quit buying and selling, the overwhelming feeling of uncleanliness," he would write later. "I was in my whole nature a tale teller." In his office on November 28, he was dictating a letter to his secretary. "The goods about which you have inquired," Anderson began, "are the best of their kind made in the—." He stopped suddenly and stood up. "What's the matter?" the secretary asked. Pale, Anderson only laughed "the American laugh." Finally he stepped toward her. "I have been wading in a long river," he said, "and my feet are wet." And then he went out the door—"out of a long and tangled phase of my life, out of the door of buying and selling, out of the door of affairs." Leaving the building, Anderson followed a railroad track across a bridge and set out toward the nearby city of Cleveland. Apparently suffering from amnesia, he slept in ditches and trudged on. Four days later, "bedraggled" and "unkempt," dazed and unable to give his name or address, Anderson turned up in Cleveland. A druggist had him taken to a hospital.[5]

It was liberation, of a sort. Anderson did go back home and his memory did return, but in reality he had left his old identity behind. He had begun to set himself free. There was nothing romantic, immediate, or neat about the process. Anderson was ill for some time. When he moved away from Elyria in 1913, at first he returned to the ad business in Chicago. It would be a while before Anderson had the courage to end his marriage and his career in advertising and to devote himself wholly to writing. The novel that made his name as a "tale teller"—*Winesburg, Ohio*—did not appear until 1919. But Anderson had liberated himself. He had broken out of the prison of society and self and moved on to a new identity.[6]

Sherwood Anderson was only one of many Americans who suddenly and unexpectedly broke free from the constraints of a society built by industrialization, ordered by Victorianism, and reformed by progressivism. The progressives were sure that there was no individual escape in this confined society; Americans had to face one another, live with industrial capitalism, and embrace reform. "We believe," a Social Gospel organization announced confidently in 1914, "that the age of sheer individualism is past and the age of social responsibility has arrived." "So now we realize that Americans are not free to release themselves," Woodrow Wilson told an audience in 1912. "We have got to live together and be happy in the family. . . . Now there is no divorce for us in our American life. We have got to put up with one another, and we have got to see to it that we so regulate and assuage one another that we will not be intolerable to each other." In fact, as Sherwood Anderson learned that year, divorce and release were possible. The confining structures of progressive America confronted a host of disruptive forces—cultural, intellectual, political, technological, and economic. By the time *Winesburg, Ohio* appeared, it was clear that the twentieth century would not be quite so regulated and orderly, so progressive, after all.[7]

In a variety of ways, Americans instinctively tried to recover a lost sense of freedom in the 1900s. Yearning to break out of enclosures into open space, they chafed at the confinement of houses and rooms, the prison of Sherwood Anderson. This impulse for space was especially evident in the popular architecture of the Midwestern "Prairie School," and above all, in the work of Frank Lloyd Wright, its most famous practitioner.[8]

Wright, a friend of Jane Addams and a participant in the arts and crafts movement, was in some ways a progressive. An advocate of simplicity in architecture, he had helped lead the attack on cluttered, ornate Victorian homes in the 1890s. Wright assailed those "bedeviled" and "senseless" houses, those "self-inflicted insults," all "mixed to puzzle-pieces." In their place, he offered simpler dwellings with cleaner lines, more in keeping with the stripped-down, leaner culture of the progressive middle class.[9]

Wright's life took him well beyond progressive values, however. Ten years older than Sherwood Anderson, Wright, too, had known free movement and then frustrating confinement. In 1887, he had left rural Wisconsin for a new life as an architect in Chicago. By the 1900s, Wright, too, was a success: prosperous and prominent, he was the proprietor of his firm and the patriarch of his family in the suburb of Oak Park. But Wright was somehow uninvolved in the lives of his wife and children. Like Anderson, he was an adulterer. Nearing forty, Wright felt he was on a "closed road," "up against a dead end." "I could see no way out," he would recall. "When family-life in Oak Park . . . conspired against the freedom to which I had come to feel every soul was entitled, I had no choice, would I keep my self-respect, but go out a voluntary exile into the uncharted and unknown." In the spring of 1909, he left his family and Oak Park for his mistress and Florence, Italy. "I went out into the unknown," Wright said, "to test faith in freedom." Despite the scandal, he soon began building a new house and a new life with his mistress in Wisconsin.[10]

Not surprisingly, Wright had a powerful sense of personal prerogative. Unlike the progressives, he staunchly defended individualism. In 1910, he titled an essay "The Sovereignty of the Individual." As a democracy, the United States must, he insisted, put "a life-premium upon Individuality," which was "a great, strong national Ideal." Wright abhorred the progressive attempt to inhibit individual impulse and appetite. "The passions have all contributed to the progress of life," he would insist. "Legislation can be no friend to moral growth except by the 'Hands off!' or the 'Stand back, please,' that allows the individual in the purely private and deeply personal concerns of his own life, to do or die *on his own.*" Accordingly, Wright rejected the progressive project to reshape human beings from without. Society, he declared, "must consist of individual units, great and strong in themselves, not units yoked from outside in bondage but united by spirit from inside with the right to freely move. . . ."[11]

Many influences shaped Wright's architecture, but prominent among them were his celebration of individualism and his desire for space. Wright wanted "this new sense of space-within . . . the poetic principle of freedom itself as a new revelation in architecture." For him, the problem with Victorian architecture was not just clutter and excess; it was also the denial of space and freedom. The "typical American dwelling," he later wrote, did not have "any such sense of space as should belong to a free man among a free people in a free country." Instead, the house was a collection of segregated boxes, a "cellular sequestration that implied ancestors familiar with the cells of penal institutions. . . ."[12]

So Wright aimed for "The Destruction of the Box." His breakthrough came in 1904, with the design and construction of the Larkin Soap Building in Buffalo, New York. "I found a natural opening to the liberation I sought," he recalled, "when (after great struggle) I finally pushed the staircase towers out from the corners of the main building, made them into freestanding, individual features." In the residential dwellings he designed, Wright tried to do away with doors and partitions in order to make "the whole lower floor as one room. . . ." He tried to turn walls into "humanized screens." "They do define and differentiate," he noted, "but never confine or obliterate space." Wright also got rid of the hiding places for men like Julian West, Charles Spencer, and Sherwood Anderson. The architect did not like storage areas, especially the "unwholesome basement." Since he wanted rooms to rise to cathedral ceilings, he also dispensed with the attic. With all these devices, Wright hammered away at the segregation and confinement of modernity. "The house became more free as 'space' and more livable, too," he concluded triumphantly. "Interior spaciousness began to dawn."[13]

At the same time, Wright created a sense of exterior spaciousness as well. He wanted dwellings to merge with the landscape, to maintain continuity with nature. While providing privacy for their occupants, Wright's houses opened to the world. Instead of traditional double-hung windows, swinging casement windows "associated the house with out-of-doors—gave free openings, outward." Wright did not want his houses to stick up too far out of the flat sweep of the Midwestern prairie. Without basements and attics, they kept close to the earth. Their low roofs emphasized the horizontal plane. This "natural" communion with the landscape ultimately gave the "prairie style" of architecture its name. For Wright, the "[m]ore intimate relation with outdoor environment and far-reaching vista" restored a sense of open space to modern life. With the "outside coming in; and the space within . . . going out," Wright's houses seemed to break through physical constraints. The prairie style set life in motion again.[14]

That feeling of movement across space, so basic to Frank Lloyd Wright's architecture, began to pervade American culture once more in the 1910s. New technologies freed people who were stuck in place. A revolution in transportation literally moved Americans across the landscape; a revolution in communication figuratively allowed them to transcend the here and now.

The most dramatic new form of transportation was the airplane. After centuries of dreaming and experimentation, powered flight became a reality on the beach at Kitty Hawk, North Carolina, on December 17, 1903. That morning, Wilbur and Orville Wright, brothers and bicycle mechanics from Dayton, Ohio, set up their "Flyer" alongside the Atlantic. At about 10:35, with Orville lying at the controls, the fragile twin-engined biplane lifted several feet off the sand and flew 120 feet in twelve seconds. It was several years before Americans quite realized what the Wright brothers had accomplished. In 1908, the Wrights held the first public demonstration of the airplane at Fort Myers, Florida. The next year, Wilbur flew around the Statue of Liberty. In 1910, Glenn Curtis made news with a flight from Albany to New York City. In 1911, Calbraith P. Rodgers enthralled the public with his arduous forty-nine-day cross-country flight from New York to California.

By then, Americans understood that the airplane represented a great advance beyond all the balloons, dirigibles, and gliders that had come before. Soaring, turning, swooping, the plane signaled liberation and promised new life. As an observer noted, planes reached "the realm of absolute liberty." They would break down barriers and bring people together. In 1909, a poet wrote, "Hearts leaped to meet a future wherein unfenced realms of air have mingled all earth's peoples into one and banished war forever from the world." Flying would even create a new kind of person. Charlotte Perkins Gilman envisioned "aerial" man, who would be, she said, "butterfly, psyche, risen soul."[15]

Of course, there were not yet very many risen souls in the 1910s: the airplane was hardly a part of everyday life. Around the country, visitors to state fairgrounds might pay an exhibition flier for a quick ride in his plane. It was not until 1914 that the first scheduled commercial flights took place. Aerial liberation was a privileged sensation.[16]

Meanwhile, a more widespread transportation revolution was taking place on the ground. Since the late nineteenth-century, a host of innovations had begun to change a foot-powered, horse-drawn society. By 1900, people could ride the electric-powered Otis elevator instead of trudging up the stairs; they could take electric-powered street railways instead of the old horse-cars. Thanks to the introduction of pneumatic tires and other improvements, Americans had peddled off on a bicycling craze in the 1890s. With more than four million bicycles on the road by 1896, "wheelmen" seemed to be everywhere.[17]

By the 1910s, the most significant new form of transportation—the one most clearly reshaping American life and culture—was the automobile.

Improved roads, mainly in Northern cities, made cars more practical than before. Municipalities had built fine parkways, such as the Harlem River Speedway in New York and the Charles River Speedway in Boston. Urban streets, so often simply dirt or rough cobblestones, were increasingly paved with smooth macadam or asphalt. The automobile had improved, too. Steam and electric cars were giving way to autos powered by the internal combustion engine. But even the gas-driven automobile, first sold in the 1890s, remained a primitive contraption in the 1910s. Drivers needed a good deal of skill and brute strength to steer and brake, and to fix frequent flat tires and mechanical breakdowns. Although the electric starter was introduced in 1912, most autos still had to be cranked to life by hand.[18]

Despite its limitations, the early automobile aroused great expectations. The novelist Edith Wharton called the car "an immense enlargement of life." Automobility stimulated a sense of individual power and freedom. Unlike a train on tracks, a magazine noted, the "motor vehicle . . . is individualistic and independent, hence its charm." To *Harper's Weekly,* the car represented "the feeling of independence—the freedom from timetables, from fixed and inflexible routes, from the proximity of other human beings . . .; the ability to go where and when one wills . . .; and the satisfaction that comes from a knowledge that one need ask favors or accommodation from no one nor trespass on anybody's property or privacy."[19]

Like the airplane, the auto promised liberation, integration, and harmony. According to some observers, cars would free the middle class and even the poor from cities. A nation of drivers would find that the auto "broke down class distinctions." It would also, as the mayor of Atlanta, Georgia, promised in 1909, "weld together . . . the most distant parts of our beloved country." Sometimes the automobile seemed therapeutic: car rides would preserve the elderly and soothe all ages. "Trade your doctor bills for an automobile," urged an advertisement. But more often the car had a powerful, unsettling impact. "The motor car brought a disturbance of all values, subtle or obvious," Frank Lloyd Wright reported, "and it brought disturbance to me." The architect loved to tear through Oak Park at up to sixty miles an hour in his custom-made yellow Stoddard Dayton sports car. Wright's infatuation with speed was common. Manufacturers named their cars the Jackrabbit, the Rocket, the Bullet, the Arrow, the Flyer. Formal auto races were well under way: the first Indianapolis 500 took place in 1911. By 1915, motorists had already begun to stage their own informal drag races.[20]

That very unsettling, disruptive quality fostered resistance to the automobile. Critics condemned the "insane desire" and the "mania for speed." Worried about safety, editorial writers decried "The Murderous Automobile," "The Deadly Auto," and "The Auto Menace." "Of all the menaces of today, the worst," thundered Woodrow Wilson, then the president of Princeton University, in 1906, "is the reckless driving of automobiles."[21]

Instead of uniting classes and regions, the car threatened to divide them even more. At first, only the upper ten could afford to buy such an expensive plaything and hire a chauffeur to drive and maintain it. Vanderbilts and Belmonts paraded their autos through Newport, motored down Fifth Avenue, and sped—sometimes wildly—across Long Island. The spectacle offended many onlookers. For years, *The New York Times* condemned "devil wagons" as "an evil extravagance," a dangerous enticement to the middle class. The car portended social upheaval. "It's a terror and a juggernaut," *The Times* warned, "like that which led the nobility and the privileged classes into the excesses which precipitated the French Revolution." "[N]othing has spread socialistic feeling in this country more than the automobile," Woodrow Wilson complained. "To the countryman they are a picture of the arrogance of wealth, with all its independence and carelessness."[22]

For many a "countryman," the automobile represented the arrogance of the city as well. Rural residents resented the urban folk who drove their cars into farm country. In Pennsylvania and West Virginia, counties banned cars from country roads. Outside Sacramento, California, farmers blocked traffic by digging ditches across roads. Elsewhere, rural Americans tried to stop drivers and automobiles with broken glass, tacks, logs, chains, cables, barbed wire, horsewhips, and gunfire. Up in Minnetonka, Minnesota, a farmer shot a chauffeur in the back. The rural resistance to luxury and innovation that Hamlin Garland had encountered on the farm lived on in the 1910s.[23]

Nevertheless, the car had a seductive appeal. Manufacturers sold only 4,000 motor vehicles in 1900. By 1907, when the carmakers sold 43,000 vehicles, the United States had surpassed Europe as the world's leading manufacturer of automobiles. In 1908, Henry Ford introduced his Model T, a functional, relatively low-priced car. That year, William C. Durant and his associates formed General Motors. In 1910, Ford opened the first, modern mass-production plant in Highland Park, Michigan, to meet the extraordinary demand for his "Tin Lizzie." As the cost of a new Model T dropped from $850 in 1908 to $600 in 1912 and then to $360 in 1916, sales of the Ford jumped from 5,896 to 78,611 and then 377,036. Nationwide, manufacturers sold 1,525,500 motor vehicles in 1916. With only some exaggeration, the *Los Angeles Examiner* could declare in 1914, "The day is here when the smallest tradesman, builder, [or] skilled mechanic can own an automobile economically."[24]

By then, farmers could own an automobile, too. Despite their initial resistance, rural Americans began to recognize the liberating possibilities of the car. There were already about 85,000 autos on farms in 1911; by 1920, there would be more than two million. Farmers typically bought the Model T and other automobiles for sober, practical reasons—to help out around the farm, to carry goods to market. But then these men and their families found that the car could break through the constraints of rural life. As an official of the New Jersey Grange predicted in 1908, the auto "will be an important feature in making farm life more attractive." So long isolated, country people could now visit one another or go to town much more easily. They also could experience the "disturbance of all values" that Frank Lloyd Wright had discovered. Automobiles helped change the rural perception of pleasure. The car exposed country people to the amusements in towns and cities; it took them on trips to such far-off attractions as the Grand Canyon and Yellowstone; it introduced them to the simple joy of touring or speeding through the countryside. "One of the values of the automobile," an observer would note in 1922, "is that by its use many a farmer has been given a new realization of the value of recreation."[25]

By providing new mobility and freedom to women and children, the car could weaken male-dominated, family-centered rural culture. At the same time, the car also promised to halt the flight of sons and daughters from the farm. In lifting so many of the constraints of rural life, automobiles could help persuade young people to stay on the land. Under the picture of a rural family driving in a car, an agricultural magazine asked, "Would any boy or girl wish to leave a farm like this?" In all, in ways both "subtle and obvious," the auto fostered a sense of liberation on the farm. "Never before," concluded an official of the U.S. Department of Agriculture, "had any such proportions of the nationals of any land known the lifting spirit that free exercise of power and independence can bring."[26]

The automobile also offered liberation to another confined group, American women. Many of them wanted very much to take the wheel. "There is a wonderful difference between sitting calmly by while another is driving and actually handling a car herself," wrote Mrs. A. Sherman Hitchcock in 1904. "There is a feeling of power, of exhilaration, and fascination that nothing else gives in equal measure." That "feeling of power" could have a forbidden, erotic quality. In a short story published in 1905, Lady Dorothy Beeston experiences a powerful passion for her automobile, her "Wonderful Monster": "She wanted to feel the throb of its quickening pulses; to lay her hand on lever and handle and thrill with the sense of mastery; to claim its power as her own—and feel its sullen-yielded obedience answer her will." Intoxicated by speed, this married woman lets herself become attracted to her chauffeur. The car had another special appeal for American women: it promised to break down the gender segregation of modern life. Driving took women out of the home and let them move around, safely and respectably, in public. As Jennie Davis of East Orange, New Jersey, pointed out in 1914, "[O]ften the driving of an automobile is a woman's first responsible experience with the streets."[27]

All this was troubling for many Americans. Some women condemned female drivers as "mannish." Men, particularly middle-class men, were even more bothered. As one man put it, "[T]he automobile has given women too much confidence." Another man insisted that "auto riding has a sad effect on motherhood." Many males wanted the car for themselves; they wanted to make it an instrument of masculinity—the means for a man to speed, smoke, and swear by himself or to impress a lady with his prowess as a driver and mechanic.[28]

Not surprisingly, then, men tried to keep women out of the driver's seat. The female race driver Joan Newton Cuneo was banned from racing in 1909 after defeating a well-known male driver, Ralph DePalma. The year before, Cincinnati, Ohio, had considered outlawing women drivers. "The only proper machine for a woman to run is a sewing machine," declared the mayor. But the city, confronted with the opposition of auto manufacturers, never imposed the ban. Men would have to use personal and cultural pressure to deny women the liberation of driving. There were already sneering remarks about "women drivers," who were supposedly "unfitted mentally and physically to operate motor cars safely under varying conditions of traffic." Naturally, the story of the "Wonderful Monster" had to have a suitably instructive ending. Lady Dorothy goes on a fateful drive with her chauffeur one Christmas night: he is killed; she is thrown safely but ignominiously into the cold dampness of a snowbank. Forgiven by her husband, she learns her lesson about "the madness of a passion untamed, the infidelity of her secret pleasure."[29]

Faced with "the unpleasant attitude of men," most women never got the chance to drive. In 1909, women made up only 9 percent of car owners in Maryland and 15 percent of owners in Washington, D.C. Five years later, there were still relatively few female drivers. In 1914, women were no more than 5 percent of the car owners in Tucson, Arizona, and 15 percent of the registered new-car owners in Los Angeles.[30]

Nevertheless, the logic of capitalism would make the car increasingly available to women. Eager to sell automobiles, manufacturers wanted female buyers and drivers. For a time, several companies offered electric cars designed especially for women. Cleaner, quieter, slower, and shorter-ranged than gas-powered cars, these vehicles were clearly less liberating. They did not sell. Ultimately, automobile manufacturers needed to put women behind the wheel of the real thing. Appealing to the woman who "reaches for an ever wider sphere of action," a Ford ad celebrated the automobile's revolutionary impact: "It has broadened her horizon—increased her pleasures—given new vigor to her body—made neighbors of faraway friends—and multiplied tremendously her range of activity. It is a real weapon in the changing order." This was all, the ad declared, a "happy change."[31]

The automobile brought confinement, not liberation, for some Americans. To accommodate middle- and upper-class drivers, working-class adults and children in the cities had to give up an old freedom. For generations, urban streets had been more than thoroughfares: they had been playgrounds and communal gathering places. But car drivers demanded the roads for themselves. Like progressive reformers, they wanted children off the streets. It was a sometimes bloody battle. In Manhattan, autos killed over a thousand children by the First World War. Working-class neighborhoods retaliated with firecrackers, stones, and guns. But gradually the motorists won the war: the streets would be for traffic, not games and sociability.[32]

Inevitably, the automobile prompted attempts at regulation from a society obsessed with social control. By 1906, most states had imposed speed limits ranging from eight miles per hour to twenty-five miles per hour. By

1915, every state had passed a law requiring the registration of motor vehicles. But automotive regulation encountered remarkable resistance. Car owners did not want to register their vehicles or obtain driver's licenses. For that matter, they did not even want to honor municipal parking restrictions, one-way streets, or left-turn bans. And, like Frank Lloyd Wright, they certainly did not want to observe speed limits. Police had a hard time enforcing the laws. In some cases, courts even denied governments the right to limit speeds or to license drivers.[33]

Ironically, many motorists escaped regulation only to feel confined anyway. With the booming sale of automobiles, there was more and more traffic on the roads. By 1910, Americans found they needed a new term—*traffic jam.* By 1914, some cities had a crisis in their streets. At rush hour on New York's Fifth Avenue, pedestrians were already moving along faster than the cars. That year, the city of Cleveland had to install the nation's first modern traffic light on fashionable Euclid Avenue. Liberation was a fitful thing.[34]

A revolution in communication paralleled the revolution in transportation. While the plane and the automobile literally carried Americans across space, newer media of communication let them figuratively transcend the here and now. By the 1900s, two improved technologies of the nineteenth century quickened the pace and immediacy of communication. The wireless telegraph, realized by the Italian Guglielmo Marconi in the 1890s, became commonplace in the new century. In 1903, Theodore Roosevelt and King Edward VII of Great Britain traded ceremonial messages by wireless. The next year, the Marconi Company set up a transatlantic news service. By then, ships at sea used the wireless for distress signals. By then, too, Alexander Graham Bell's telephone, introduced in the 1870s, had become a widespread fact of life. The number of telephones jumped from a million in 1899 to 10 million in 1914. In that year, there was one phone for every ten Americans. The telephone and the wireless made it possible for people to hear about events around town and around the world almost immediately. In 1914, Americans were already making more than a million long-distance phone calls a year. When the great British passenger liner *Titanic* hit an iceberg on its maiden voyage and sank in the Atlantic on the night of April 14, 1912, wireless transmissions broadcast the news of the tragedy early the next morning.[35]

Americans also found it easier than ever to get a sense of distant people, places, and events. By the 1910s, improved technologies allowed newspapers and magazines to publish numerous photographs. The photo supplement of the Sunday paper showered Americans with images of automobiles, millionaires, and politicians. By then, people could also hear sounds they might never hear in person. First patented by Thomas Edison in the 1870s, the phonograph, in various forms, was spreading across the country. In 1914 alone, American manufacturers shipped over half a million phonographs. The machines and recordings were primitive. Edison's phonograph played metal cylinders; the competing gramophone played flat, lacquered 78-RPM disks. To make the cylinders and disks, performers had to talk, sing, or play into a large horn. The recordings were often poor, but they had a powerful impact. At home or at phonograph parlors and touring demonstrations, Americans could hear the oratory of Theodore Roosevelt and William Jennings Bryan, the singing of Enrico Caruso and Marie Michailowa, the concert band of John Philip Sousa, and the sounds of "Pulling in the Gang Plank, Steamboat Bells, Whistle, and Dance on Board with Negro Shouts" supposedly *Down on the Suwanee River.*[36]

The most dramatic new technology that brought distant or unknown sensations to Americans was the motion picture. By 1888, Edison was working on "an instrument which does for the Eye what the phonograph does for the Ear, which is the recording and reproduction of things in motion. . . . This apparatus I call a Kinetoscope 'Moving View.'" Starting in 1893, the public could peer into the peephole of the kinetoscope to see short silent films of blacksmiths hammering an anvil, a man sneezing, or a gymnast performing a backward somersault. In 1894, kinetoscope "parlors" opened up around the country. Beginning in 1895, the Latham eidoloscope, the Edison company's vitascope, the American Mutoscope Company's biograph, and a host of other new devices could project moving pictures on a screen. By 1897, audiences in theaters, lecture halls, and movie parlors around the country could watch short visions of a wider world in motion: *Rough Sea at Dover; The German Emperor Reviewing His Troops; Central Park; McKinley at Home; Automobile Parade; The Horitz Passion Play; Roosevelt Rough Riders; Mitchell Day at Wilkes-Barre, Pa.*; and *Mrs. Nation and Her Hatchet Brigade.* "You see what it means to them," wrote an observer of movie audiences; "it means Opportunity—a chance to glimpse the beautiful and strange things in the world that you haven't in your life; . . . opportunity which, except for the big moving picture book, would be forever closed to you."[37]

In a sense, many Americans had no choice but to get out and look at the "beautiful and strange things in the world." The basic categories of human life, the patterns of thought and belief that structured existence, seemed to be collapsing in the 1910s. While Frank Lloyd Wright set about "The Destruction of the Box" that was the Victorian house, a host of other cultural boxes were tumbling down too. Standing in the ruins, people were free to move and look around as they never had before.

The collapse of categories was an international phenomenon. Europeans, as much as Americans, led the assault on the conceptual certainties that structured and contained human life. On the Continent, scientists' astonishing discoveries were making life more puzzling, more uncertain. Meanwhile, European artists and intellectuals, simultaneously attracted and repelled by bourgeois, industrial society, were smashing established ideas and practices to create a new, modernist culture. Broad and capacious, "modernism" is difficult to pin down even now—which seems appropriate for such a powerful, liberating force. However difficult to define, modernism radiated outward from the salons of Paris and Vienna, Berlin and London, to offer the promise of life without fixed codes and categories.[38]

The combination of modernist culture and scientific revolution had an especially powerful impact on the basic categories of space, time, matter, and self. The old Euclidean certainties about the geometry of three-dimensional space had begun to fall in the nineteenth century. In 1905, the German theoretical physicist Albert Einstein offered his special theory of relativity, which redefined space as an artifact of measurement rather than an inherent property. "We entirely shun the vague word 'space,' of which, we must honestly acknowledge, we cannot form the slightest conception," Einstein declared in 1916, "and we replace it by 'motion relative to a practically rigid body of reference.'" Accordingly, there could be many spaces, even, as he later announced, "an infinite number of spaces, which are in motion with respect to each other." By then, natural scientists could argue that the sense of space was a physiological product varying from animal to animal. And social scientists could maintain that the sense of space was a social construct varying from society to society.[39]

Modernism also contributed to the breakdown of homogeneous space. Beginning in the late nineteenth century, artists had reconceived perspective. Quitting the studio, the impressionists painted from new points of view. More dramatically, Cézanne broke up space by offering more than one point of view on a single canvas and by dragging the background into the foreground of a landscape. Then, in the 1900s, Pablo Picasso, Georges Braque, and other Cubist painters rejected the conventional representation of homogeneous, three-dimensional space. Cubist painting offered many spaces, many perspectives; it even exposed the interior of objects. As a critic noted in 1912, the Cubists had left behind "pure visual space or . . . Euclidean space" for "a different kind of space."[40]

Even as a uniform, public time was established around the world, the concept of time itself became endangered. In Europe, such writers as Oscar Wilde, Franz Kafka, and Marcel Proust portrayed time as heterogeneous: the private time of the individual was different from the public time of society. Meanwhile, the sociologist Emile Durkheim argued that time was a social construct, rather than an absolute. But it was Einstein's work that most damaged the old unitary notion of time. In 1905, his special theory of relativity accounted for the slowing down of time in separate systems. In 1916, his general theory of relativity posited that "every reference body has its own particular time." People live in a universe with, as he would later put it, not one clock but many.[41]

As fixed notions of space and time collapsed, the concept of matter shattered, too. In 1896, the French philosopher Henri Bergson speculated that the division of matter into separate, defined objects was "artificial." During the 1890s, the French scientists A. H. Becquerel and Marie and Pierre Curie discovered and explored radioactivity, the disintegration of the nucleus of an atom: matter, it appeared, could break down. In the 1900s, Einstein further undermined the solidity of matter: it could all be reduced to energy.[42]

With the dramatic reconception of space, time, and matter, human beings almost inevitably began to seem different. The self, the prison of Sherwood Anderson, opened up. The Cubists penetrated and bared the human interior. So did the new X-ray machine. Psychologists, most notably

Sigmund Freud, revealed the frontier of the mind, a vast stage for dreams and desires, for the dramas of repression and sublimation.

The reconceptualization of self and space, time and matter, was accompanied by a broad assault on the notion of form itself. Did life require categories—those boxes—at all? "At present, we are experiencing . . . a struggle of life against form *as such,* against the principle of form," the German sociologist Georg Simmel noted in 1914. "Moralists, reactionaries, and people with strict feeling for style are perfectly correct when they complain about the increasing 'lack of form' in modern life."[43]

By the 1910s, that "struggle of life against form" was apparent in the United States as well as Europe. The struggle had been developing for a long time. Since the late nineteenth century, some Americans had quietly battled against the notion of fixed boundaries and beliefs, the established segregations and certainties of society. In his psychological work, William James tried to break down the distinctions between mind and instinct, between the "higher" and "lower." Such segregation made James—the man who hated the closed "middle-class paradise" of Chautauqua—impatient. "Consciousness . . . does not appear to itself chopped in bits," he wrote in *The Principles of Psychology* in 1890. *"In talking of it hereafter, let us call it the stream of thought, of consciousness, or of subjective life."* In his later, philosophical work, James subverted the idea of certainty. Influenced by the pragmatist thinking of Charles Sander Peirce, James presented truth as relative, not absolute. Ideas had to be continuously tested against experience.[44]

John Dewey further developed the pragmatist philosophy of Peirce and James. And Dewey also battled against the segregation of fixed categories. "We want to bring all things educational together," he wrote in *The School and Society* in 1900; "to break down the barriers that divide the education of the little child from the instruction of the maturing youth; to identify the lower and the higher education, so that it shall be demonstrated to the eye that there is no lower and higher, but simply education." Frank Lloyd Wright revealed that same modernist sensibility in his fight to reform American architecture. "We must," he insisted, "repulse every stupid attempt to imitate and fasten ancient forms . . . upon a life that must outgrow them however great they may seem."[45]

In the 1910s, of course, most Americans never saw one of Wright's buildings or read one of Dewey's books. But the implications of the scientific revolution and modernist culture spread across the country nevertheless. They flowed from colleges and universities, from Harvard, Columbia, and the University of Chicago; they poured from urban salons, from the drawing rooms of Boston, New York, and Chicago. Americans were being exposed to new scientific and artistic discoveries. By 1906, an article in *Popular Science Monthly* could already ask, "Are the Elements Transmutable, the Atoms Divisible, and forms of Matter but Modes of Motion?" Most Americans might not know about Einstein's special theory of relativity, but they did know how new technologies scrambled time. On city streets, electric lights broke down the separation of day and night. In theaters, the movies sped up time by turning caterpillars into butterflies almost instantly. By running film in reverse, movies made time go backward: scrambled eggs became whole again, a diver leaped out of the water back onto his diving board. In *The Life of an American Fireman* in 1902, Edwin S. Porter moved his story back and forth in time. Seven years later, D. W. Griffith made time stop by having his actors stand still at one point during *A Corner on Wheat.*[46]

The disintegration of categories offered new opportunities for personal liberation. No American explored the possibilities more passionately and more purposefully than Mabel Dodge. She had been born Mabel Ganson, the daughter of a wealthy family in Buffalo, New York, in 1879. Her parents, distant and uninvolved, had hardly constrained her. "As a child I had felt no one in front of me . . . ," she recalled. "[M]y parents had seemed like dim, dull figures far, far behind." But she had still felt confined, not free, in her isolated childhood: "[A]n unopened space with no paths in it encircled me," she would remember; "I had to set off alone by myself and I was always alone."[47]

The journey was rough: she left Buffalo, married, had an affair, had a child, and became a widow, all by the age of twenty-four. In 1904, she set out for Europe, where she soon married architectural student Edwin Dodge and went off to live at the Villa Curonia, a fifteenth-century Medici palace in Florence. Dodge collected art objects and people. She met artists, actors, and writers. In 1911, she got to know Gertrude and Leo Stein, who helped introduce her to modernism. Gertrude Stein painted the *Portrait of Mabel Dodge at the Villa Curonia,* which made both artist and model well known in certain circles. But Dodge found no liberation in Europe. Her marriage failed, but she was not free. In November 1912, for the sake of her son's education, she reluctantly boarded a ship to return to America.[48]

To her surprise, Dodge found a changing country. "Something was breaking up and passing slowly away out of the world—," she would observe, "a civilization was going to pieces. . . ." Setting up her household in a brownstone at the corner of Ninth Street and Fifth Avenue, she was close to Greenwich Village, a hotbed of the new and modern. "Looking back upon it now," she wrote in the 1930s, "it seems as though everywhere, in that year of 1913, barriers went down and people reached each other who had never been in touch before; there were all sorts of new ways to communicate, as well as new communications. The new spirit was abroad and swept us all together."[49]

Dodge immediately tried to foster communication across social, cultural, and political boundaries. As in Florence, her home became a gathering place for all sorts of people. These meetings reflected the modernist urge to break out of boxes and conventions. The meetings also reflected the dilemma that would plague modernism for the rest of the century: new ideas and new interactions had a way of hardening into new organizations and new forms. "Why not organize all this accidental, unplanned activity around you, this coming and going of visitors, and see these people at certain hours," a friend suggested. "Have Evenings!" "But I thought we don't believe in 'organization,'" Dodge reproached him. Hadn't she been told "that organizations and institutions are only the crystals of living ideas—and 'as soon as an idea is crystallized, it is dead.'" Her friend offered a rather weak distinction. "Oh, I don't mean that you should *organize* the *Evenings*," he replied. "I mean, get people here at certain times and let them feel absolutely free to be themselves, and see what happens."[50]

At any rate, in January 1913, Dodge began to set people in motion in her apartment. "Imagine, then, a stream of human beings passing in and out of those rooms; one stream where many currents mingled together for a little while," she wrote proudly. "Socialists, Trade-Unionists, Anarchists, Suffragists, Poets, Relations, Lawyers, Murderers, 'Old Friends,' Psychoanalysts, I.W.W.'s, . . . Birth Controlists, Newspapermen, Artists, Modern-Artists, Clubwomen, Woman's-place-is-in-the-home Women, Clergymen, and just plain men all met there and, stammering in an unaccustomed freedom a kind of speech called Free, exchanged a variousness in vocabulary called, in euphemistic optimism, Opinions!" Variegated, unordered, and unpredictable, Dodge's "stream of human beings" was rather like William James's stream of consciousness.[51]

The gatherings at Dodge's apartment helped push her toward a number of modernist projects. She was eager to join the effort to introduce postimpressionist art to the United States. Thanks to the opposition of the conservative National Academy of Design, very little modern work had been exhibited in American galleries. Alfred Stieglitz's Photo-Secession Gallery at 291 Fifth Avenue presented some of the new art, but, as Dodge put it, "the public, the great, blind, dumb New York Public, had never seen anything, had never had any chance to see anything Modern. . . ."[52]

That would soon change. In 1911, Arthur Bowen Davies, Walt Kuhn, and other artists founded the Association of American Painters and Sculptors as an alternative to the National Academy of Design. The AAPS embodied the modernist rebellion against organization. "How to exhibit and protect the producer against the indefinable tyranny every institution sooner or later exerts is our great problem," the association's statement of purpose announced. The AAPS also embodied the celebration of individualism and rejection of convention that was the essence of modernist culture. "We have no canons," the AAPS proclaimed, "except honesty and the ability to express one's self." "Individual independence . . . ," noted Alfred Stieglitz, "—that is the first principle of those who are trying to inject some life into the decaying corpse of art."[53]

Kuhn and Davies thought a major show of the new art was just the kind of injection that the corpse needed. With the help of painter Walter Pach, they began to organize the International Exhibition of Art at the 69th Regiment Armory on Lexington Avenue, between Twenty-fifth and Twenty-sixth Streets. What became known as the Armory Show would be massive and well publicized—just the sort of thing to attract Mabel Dodge. Although she exaggerated her role in the exhibition, Dodge did contribute money, arrange for the loan of paintings, and work "like a dog." *"I am all for it,"* she wrote. "I think it is splendid. . . . There will be a riot & a revolution & things will never be quite the same afterwards."[54]

There was no riot, but Dodge was right—things were not the same after the show. Four thousand people flocked to the opening on February 17, 1913. Over the next month, the press wrote story after story about the show. For Manhattan's high society, the armory became the place to be. There were more than a thousand works of art on display. American artists—Davies, Kuhn, Alfred Maurer, Marsden Hartley, Joseph Stella, and many others—

made up the majority of the exhibit. But the greatest attention focused on the work of such European artists as Cézanne, Braque, Picasso, Marcel Duchamp, Francis Picabia, and Odilon Redon.[55]

The organizers had gotten what they wanted: much of the "great, blind, dumb" public had either glimpsed or read about modern art. To some observers, the Armory Show was a revelation—"sensational," "magnificent," "a bomb shell." The banker James Stillman took a good look at the work of these modern artists. "Something is wrong with the world," he announced. "These men know." Other visitors were not so charitable. To some, the exhibit seemed laughably inexplicable. One after another, people tried to describe the most notorious painting of the show, Duchamp's *Nude Descending a Staircase.* It was "a lot of disused golf clubs and bags," "an assortment of half-made leather saddles," an "elevated railroad stairway in ruins after an earthquake," a "dynamited suit of Japanese armor," and "an explosion in a shingle factory." Some patrons thought they saw insanity at the armory: the show was "a pathological museum" and a "temporary lunatic asylum." "To paint a real, genuine cubist painting," one artist told a reporter, "you have to be genuinely and unquestionably mad."[56]

A number of critics realized that the Armory Show was about liberation. "The AAPS has triumphed over all formal restrictions . . . academic prejudices and conventional cowardice," wrote the reviewer for the New York *Evening Mail.* "It was a privilege to get out of the artistic strait jacket." Some observers did not care for that kind of freedom. "There is," artist Kenyon Cox charged, "only one word for this denial of all law, this insurrection against all custom and tradition, this assertion of individual license without discipline and without restraint; and that word is 'anarchy.'" For people like Cox, modern art encouraged the individualism that progressives wanted to contain and control. The Armory Show, complained art historian Frank Jewett Mather, "accentuates an already exaggerated cult of the individual. . . ." "In a well organized civilization, overt individualism is held in check by law—the profligate is debarred from society, the bomb thrower is imprisoned, the defamer and lunatic is confined, not for the good of the individual, but for the protection of the many who might be harmed," *Art and Progress* commented. "Why, then, we may ask ourselves do we so blithely tolerate these same crimes in art."[57]

Characteristically, Theodore Roosevelt tried to intercede. As always, the former president wanted to accommodate and manage change. After visiting the show, he published "A Layman's View of an Art Exhibition." "The exhibitors are quite right as to the need of showing to our people in this manner the art forces in Europe, forces which can not be ignored," Roosevelt allowed. He liked the absence of "simpering, self-satisfied conventionality" at the show. But Roosevelt, with his "Greek horror of extremes," could not bring himself to endorse "the European extremists whose pictures are here exhibited." Not for the first time, Roosevelt failed to reconcile the oppositions within himself and within American culture. He tentatively praised the cubists and others who "have helped to break fetters." Yet, he could not accept the freedom that resulted; he had to consign these artists to "the lunatic fringe." In the end, Roosevelt—and the progressive values he so often upheld—could not accommodate modernism.[58]

On March 15, the last day of the show, the streets outside the Armory were jammed with cars and carriages. Ten to twelve thousand visitors managed to get into the building, but thousands more had to be turned away. When the exhibits finally closed at ten that night, the organizers, with a band at their head, danced triumphantly through the armory. Much of the exhibition soon went off to Chicago and Boston; Mabel Dodge went off to psychoanalysis.[59]

In the 1910s, psychology and psychotherapy were just becoming fashionable. Of course, such figures as William James, G. Stanley Hall, James Mark Baldwin, Morton Prince, and James Jackson Putnam had been intensely exploring psychology since the late nineteenth century. By the 1900s, many American psychologists had recognized that nervous or mental problems such as Jane Addams's neurasthenia did not have a purely material or physiological basis. By then, too, a small but growing number of Americans believed these problems could be treated with psychotherapy. But it was not until 1909 that the implications of the new psychology really began to reach the public. In September, Sigmund Freud made his first and only visit to the United States. G. Stanley Hall, who was president of Clark University in Worcester, Massachusetts, had invited the Austrian psychoanalyst to help commemorate the school's twentieth anniversary. In a series of well-publicized lectures at Clark, Freud offered a summary of his pioneering work on the mind.[60]

For years after the Clark lectures, Americans wrongly tended to equate psychology with Freud. And they tended to simplify and garble Freud's ideas.

But whatever their misunderstanding of repression, sublimation, dreams, or infantile attachments, Americans recognized that psychology undermined the Victorian concept of the self. Inside the human being was a vast, uncharted, and powerful inner world. In 1915, in two magazine articles on Freud and psychoanalysis, Mabel Dodge's friend Max Eastman articulated the exciting possibilities of a boundless self. "The mind is like a deep mine, or a mysterious well of water, whose conscious surface is not large, but which spreads out to great distances and great depths below," Eastman reported. "And the things that are in these unconscious depths—wishes, images, ideas, loves, hates, fears that we know nothing about—are often much more important than what is on the surface." Unconscious desires produced "countless numbers of diseases that we call nervous, or mental . . . ," Eastman warned. But he ended with a message of hope: psychoanalysis, the exploration of these inner desires, could make *"their morbid effects . . . disappear."*[61]

In Eastman's optimistic account, psychotherapy seemed very much a part of the Progressive Era. Here was the characteristic progressive belief that human beings were malleable, that people's problems could be exposed and put right. But Freudian psychology, like modern art, also tended to subvert progressive values. Freud and Eastman stressed the importance of liberation and individuality. At Clark, Freud lectured against social repression. He rejected the "most extreme" sexual repression in favor of an "incomparably freer sexual life." In the name of psychic health, Eastman insisted that educators and parents let children develop into free individuals. "Education must be thought of as a kind of *emancipation;* and then we shall not meet so many neurotic and semi-neurotic people," he maintained. "And parents who realize that truth, who take care to let their children grow away from them, independent and individual, are doing their real service both to their children and to their race."[62]

Mabel Dodge desperately needed the liberation that psychotherapy apparently had to offer. Dogged by "some black and hideous disorder that was hidden from others and most of all from myself," she was withdrawing from her very public life into herself by late 1914. Once more she felt that sense of confinement so pervasive in modern America: "Still like a bird within a glass-walled room, the spirit was desperately beating its wings against the impediments between it and freedom." Dodge looked for some way to break free. She moved to the country, to Finney Farm north of New

York City. She spent time in Provincetown, Massachusetts, out on the tip of Cape Cod. There, she mixed with the artistic community that would nurture the modernist theater of Eugene O'Neill and the Provincetown Players. There, too, she developed her romantic relationship with painter Maurice Sterne. But nothing seemed to set her free. So she became one of the first Americans to undergo analysis.[63]

First she tried Dr. Smith Ely Jelliffe in New York. Three times a week, this follower of Carl Jung would help Dodge try to deal with herself and with Maurice Sterne. "It became an absorbing game to play with oneself, reading one's motives, and trying to understand the symbols by which the soul expressed itself." At first she found satisfaction. Psychoanalysis helped explain life: it was a "new world where . . . things fitted into a set of definitions and terms. . . . It simplified all problems to name them. There was the Electra complex, and the Oedipus complex and there was the Libido with its manifold activities, seeking every chance for outlet, and then all that thing about Power and Money!" Jelliffe also seemed to be setting her free. "I grew calm and self-sufficient, and felt superior to [Maurice] in the evening. . . ." But Dodge was not sure she wanted or needed to be free from Sterne. And eventually all the hours of symbols and simplification grew tiresome: " . . . the amusing speculations ceased to amuse . . . the old fatigue and depression came back." Dodge stopped her sessions with Jelliffe in the spring of 1916.[64]

For a while, Dodge pursued the "New Thought," the popular form of mind cure practiced by Emma Curtis Hopkins. But in the fall of 1916, Dodge returned to psychotherapy. This time, she tried Dr. A. A. Brill, perhaps the leading American analyst. An Austrian immigrant who had once lived on Rahel Golub's Lower East Side, Brill was an ardent disciple of Freud. Dodge's new therapist would have none of the Jungian speculations of Dr. Jelliffe. When Dodge started in on her "very bad Oedipus complex," Brill interrupted. "Never mind about that," he snapped. "I want your dreams. . . . I want you to bring me in at least one dream every time you come." He also wanted her to get busy. Goaded by Brill, Dodge became a successful newspaper columnist in New York. She was not really free, however: Dodge had rearranged her life, she realized, in order to "pacify" her therapist. The sessions with Brill came to an end.[65]

Dodge continued to wrestle with her troubles. Despite her ambivalence about Maurice Sterne, she married the artist in August 1917. Yet, she soon sent him away to paint in New Mexico. In the end, in good Freudian fashion, it was a dream that set Mabel Dodge in motion again. Awakening one night in November 1917, she had a vision. "I passed from unconsciousness into a state of super-consciousness without transition," she remembered. "I lay staring into the darkness, when before my eyes I saw a large image of Maurice's head." Scared, she kept looking. Sterne's face gave way to another, "with green leaves twinkling and glistening all around it—a dark face with wide-apart eyes that stared at me with a strong look, intense and calm." Dodge realized what it was. "This was an Indian face and it affected me like a medicine after the one that had been before it," she explained. "I sighed and let it take me and cleanse me. . . ." Soon she had a letter from Maurice in Santa Fe. "Dearest Girl—," he wrote. "Do you want an object in life? Save the Indians, their art-culture—reveal it to the world!" And so Mabel Dodge set out for New Mexico to save Native Americans and to save herself. In motion, she was liberated again.[66]

It was fitting that Dodge went off to help people of another race. Of all the categories under assault in the 1910s, race was the most resistant, the most unyielding. By then, a few whites could join people of color in hacking at the racist foundations of segregation. In 1911, anthropologist Franz Boas published *The Mind of Primitive Man,* a book that undermined distinctions between supposedly civilized and uncivilized peoples. Boas's work ultimately proved influential, but it did not change popular thinking very much in the 1910s.[67]

Other Americans, meanwhile, labored just as hard to shore up the structures of racism. In 1916, Madison Grant published *The Passing of the Great Race,* a stern reaffirmation of inherent, unalterable racial inequality. Grant derided the "widespread and fatuous belief in the power of environment, as well as of education and opportunity to alter heredity. . . . [S]peaking english, wearing good clothes, and going to school and to church, does not transform a negro into a white man." But Grant worried that racial mixing would reduce the white race to the level of Indians and blacks. "We Americans must realize," Grant concluded, "that the altruistic ideas which have controlled our social development during the past century, and the maudlin sentimentalism that has made America 'an asylum for the oppressed,' are sweeping the nation toward a racial abyss."[68]

There was not much danger of falling in. America remained segregated. The new technology of movies, however liberating otherwise, reinforced racial stereotypes: early movies included such titles as *Watermelon Contest; The Pickaninnies; Nigger in the Woodpile; Dancing Nig;* and *How Rastus Got His Pork Chops.*[69]

Yet, African-Americans also broke out of their close confinement. A small but growing stream of blacks had been leaving the segregation and oppression of the South behind. In the first decade of the new century, Texas suffered a net loss of 10,000 African-Americans to migration; Mississippi lost 31,000; and South Carolina lost 72,000. Most of these outmigrants headed toward the industrial centers of the North. Unsure just what they would find there, black men, women, and children certainly expected to enjoy more freedom than in the South. Like Hamlin Garland, Jane Addams, and Sherwood Anderson before him, Richard Robert Wright of Augusta, Georgia, set out hopefully for Chicago. Crossing the Ohio River on a train, this young African-American dared to sit down next to a white man and even put a question to him. "How far is it," Wright asked, "to Chicago?"[70]

It would be wrong to romanticize the new century's means of liberation: each had its limitations and its dangers. After their "Flight Out of Egypt," African-Americans would hardly find the Promised Land in Chicago or any other Northern city. Modernist culture would eventually harden into convention. As Mabel Dodge discovered, "Evenings" could turn into organization and psychotherapy could create new kinds of dependence. For Frank Lloyd Wright and Sherwood Anderson, liberation required the betrayal of a wife and the abandonment of children.

The forces of liberation certainly flouted Victorian convention, but Victorianism was already under assault from every side, including the middle class itself. Modernist culture and the other forms of early twentieth-century liberation were much more important for their attack on the newly powerful ideology and practice of progressivism. Worrying about big business and other old foes, the progressives were suddenly outflanked by new forces and new enemies—and even by apparent traitors in their own ranks such as Frank Lloyd Wright and John Dewey. The forces of liberation challenged the segregation and confinement so essential to the progressive social order. They upheld "The Sovereignty of the Individual" that had been denied by progressive thought. Less obviously, they subverted the whole notion of a verifiable, objective reality—one of the hardest-won prizes of the progressive struggle. Twentieth-century American reform depended on a confrontation with facts: cold statistics of child labor or corporate oligopoly; Jacob Riis's hard-edged photographs of urban poverty; muckraking revelations from Samuel Hopkins Adams and David Graham Phillips; realist fictions by Hamlin Garland and Upton Sinclair. Instead of clear facts and certain reality, modernism offered the slippery stream of consciousness, the uncertain depths of unconsciousness, the multiple perspectives of cubism, and the intensely subjective individualist perspectives of Sherwood Anderson and Mabel Dodge.

Most of all, modernism, movies, and migration promoted uncertainty. The outcome of all those liberations, like the African-American journey northward, was unknown; the destination, like Chicago, was unclear. For that matter, there was no certainty that Americans even wanted to arrive at a final destination. Chicago or any other place could turn into a new box, a new prison. Eventually, Sherwood Anderson and at least some of his generation realized that the promise of liberation might be more a matter of movement than anything else. "The American is still a wanderer, a migrating bird not yet ready to build a nest," Anderson maintained. Gertrude Stein saw it too. "[T]the American thing is the vitality of movement . . . ," she would note. "[T]his generation does not connect itself with anything, . . . that is why it is American. . . ." Her friend Mabel Dodge would see the situation more wistfully. "The world is full of lost souls, creatures who have lost their moorings, who have broken out of the pattern of established life and are whisked about with no sense of either past or future," she would observe in her memoirs. "They don't know whether they're going or coming, or what it is all about." No one could be quite so sure about the course of American life. "We are on the way—towards what?" Sherwood Anderson wondered. "How many Americans want to go—but where do they want to go?"[71]

CHAPTER EIGHT

The Pursuit of Pleasure

Just after two o'clock in the afternoon on Saturday, October 14, 1911, Christy Mathewson stood on the low pitcher's mound of the Polo Grounds. It was a crisp, slightly hazy fall day—"real hard cider weather with just the right tang to it," a newspaperman noted. Mathewson's New York Giants were about to face the visiting Philadelphia Athletics in the first game of the World Series. Forty thousand fans—"a mighty outpouring of humanity," a "sport-maddened multitude"—filled the ballpark on Coogan's Bluff, up above New York's Harlem River. "[N]ever have we seen a baseball crowd like that . . . ," the reporter exclaimed. "It was tremendous, it was inspiring, it was majestic." Crazed by "Dementia baseballibus," the crowd roared in the stands. Photographers ringed the field. But Mathewson, alone on the mound, stood calm and quiet in the forbidding black uniform of the National League champion Giants. The pitcher's "head was held high and his eye, with slow, lordly contempt, swept the Athletics." "Play ball!" shouted umpire Bill Klem. Looking in at his catcher, Mathewson prepared to throw his first pitch.[1]

Christy Mathewson was something new in America: a professional athlete who inspired hero worship. For decades, Americans had condemned ballplayers as "bums . . . too lazy to work for a living." Professional athletes seemed to devote their lives to pleasure instead of production, to dissipation instead of self-control. In the eyes of critical Victorians, baseball players were all too likely to be uneducated German- or Irish-Americans from suspect backgrounds. But the man known affectionately as "Matty" and "Big Six" came from a respectable Pennsylvania farm family whose Scots forebears had arrived in America nearly three centuries before. Mathewson's parents lived the Victorian code: they opposed alcohol and tobacco; they believed in hard work and education; they taught "the Golden Rule"; they sent their son to college at Bucknell.

Instead of following his parents' plans and becoming a preacher, Mathewson signed a contract to play ball. "I suppose it was just not to be," his mother sighed. "And yet sometimes I find consolation in the thought that perhaps he *is* a preacher. His work has brought him before the multitude in a kindly manner; his example is a cleanly one. He reaches the masses of the people in his own way and he must give them something through his character." By 1900, Mathewson was a member of the New York Giants. By 1911, he was indisputably the greatest right-handed pitcher of his day, master of the tricky "fadeaway" screwball, winner of as many as thirty-five games in a single season. Through it all, Matty remained true to his parents' values. He was a "Christian gentleman" who refused to pitch on Sundays. For an admiring nation, he was the personification of virtue. Mathewson, a writer noted, "talks like a Harvard graduate, looks like an actor, acts like a businessman and impresses you as an all-around gentleman."[2]

"Big Six" was superb on that October day. After scoring a run off Mathewson in the second inning, the Athletics could not touch him the rest of the game. He was, *The New York Times* exulted, "the big Shaman, the Wizard, the Warlock." The Giants tied up the game in the fourth, went ahead in the eighth, and won 2 to 1. "It was," *The Times* concluded, "a great game, a great crowd, and a great day. . . ."

After this auspicious beginning, the Series turned into a bitter disappointment for Mathewson and the rest of the Giants. Big Six lost the third game three days later; he lost the fourth game in front of a jeering crowd in Philadelphia on the twenty-fourth. Two days after that, the Giants lost the series. "Matty . . . ," admitted *The Times,* had "failed."[3]

Still, there were compensations. The Series set a record for attendance and receipts, which meant that Mathewson received a loser's share of $2,346—more money than most Americans made in a year. His regular annual salary was $10,000. Moreover, he had a newspaper column during the

Series. As soon as the games ended, he went with the Giants on an exhibition tour of Cuba. Then he helped prepare a book on the art of baseball, *Pitching in a Pinch,* which would sell briskly under his name. Before the season, he had already launched "The Matty Books," a series of fictional baseball stories for boys. He had also appeared in a vaudeville sketch, *Curves 1910,* at New York's Hammerstein Theatre, for $1,000 a week. Matty had decided that he did not care for vaudeville routines. But in 1912, he would help write a play, *The Girl and the Pennant,* for the New York stage and star in a motion picture, *Breaking into the Big Leagues.*[4]

With his vaudeville routine, his play, his movie, his books, and his ball games, Christy Mathewson was deeply involved in an emerging complex of commercialized pleasure in early twentieth-century America. He was both the product and the instrument of a powerful liberating force—the yearning for leisure and enjoyment. Raised within Victorian culture, Mathewson had nevertheless allowed baseball, the pastime of his youth, to shape his life; he had left his hometown for a career devoted to a game. In the process, Matty had become a symbol for millions. By his example, he showed Americans that they could reconcile old values with new enjoyments. His mother was right: Mathewson *was* a kind of preacher, an evangelist for a new religion of pleasure. He made people believe that it was all right to spend money on amusements, flock to the Polo Grounds, and succumb to "Dementia baseballibus."

Of course, Christy Mathewson was exceptional—not only for his pitching talent but also for the ease and grace with which he accommodated middle-class morality and commercialized pleasure. Many Americans could not make that accommodation so readily. Like other liberating forces, pleasure was profoundly disruptive. The increasing popular fascination with leisure and amusements unsettled the nascent order of progressive America. The spread of enjoyment broke down segregating barriers, reshaped personal identity, and exalted individualism. In the 1910s, the drive for pleasure was as hard to handle as a Mathewson fadeaway.

Changing economic conditions underlay the new world of pleasures. Thanks to increasing productivity and the demand for a shorter workweek, American workers spent notably fewer hours on the job by the 1910s. Average working hours in the unionized building trades dropped from 48.3 a week in 1900 to 44.8 in 1915. Hours in manufacturing decreased from 59 to 55 during these years. Where they could, women workers exchanged the long hours of domestic service that Rahel Golub had hated for briefer stints in factories, stores, and offices. "The shorter work day brought me my first idea of there being such a thing as pleasure," said one young female worker. "Before this time it was just sleep and eat and hurry off to work." Workers also received more vacation time. The growing ranks of clerks and sales workers enjoyed paid or unpaid breaks from work. For salaried, middle-class workers, the annual vacation had become a tradition by the 1910s.[5]

Along with more free time, Americans had more money to spend on pleasure. Workers still lived constrained lives, but their economic circumstances gradually improved. Average manufacturing wages rose from $435 a year in 1900 to $568 in 1915. Anthracite coal miners' average pay nearly doubled from $340 in 1900 to $671 during these years. Even domestics saw their average wage grow from $240 to $342.[6]

The national increase of free time and disposable income put pressure on the progressives and their cultural values. In the late-nineteenth-century transition from Victorianism to progressivism, the middle class had abandoned its glorification of work and begun to applaud the responsible use of leisure. But the emergent progressive middle class was rather ambivalent about the role of pleasure in human life. On one hand, the middle class was looking, as a magazine put it in the 1890s, for "a middle ground between the idler and the man who works himself to death." On the other hand, the rigorous control of enjoyments—antiprostitution, prohibition—helped define the public agenda of progressivism; the effort to end the double standard for men and discipline the material excesses of the Victorian house helped define its domestic life. The progressives departed the farthest from Victorianism in their reconsideration of individualism and domesticity; they remained closest to home in their view of pleasure. But something was changing again in the 1900s and the 1910s. By 1908, *Success* magazine could announce "Fun Is a Necessity." "He who can enjoy and does not enjoy," the Yiddish paper *Tageblatt* declared the year before, "commits a sin." Middle-class advocates of restraint were appalled. "Prior to 1880 the . . . main business of life was living," complained vice crusaders in Syracuse, New York. "The main business of life now is pleasure."[7]

New attitudes, more leisure time, and more disposable income helped spur a revolution in commercial amusements. A new complex of entertainments had begun to take shape in the late nineteenth century. First came the World's Fair, which began in Philadelphia in 1876 and continued in Chicago in 1893, Atlanta in 1895, Nashville in 1897, Omaha in 1898, Buffalo in 1901, and St. Louis in 1904. These lavish events deftly mixed culture and excitement, uplift and entertainment. The St. Louis fair, with its amusement park and eleven-acre re-creation of Jerusalem, drew millions of mostly middle-class visitors who took the rides, trooped through haunted houses, and stared at the wonders of the specially constructed "Ivory City."[8]

By the 1890s, amusement parks offered the excitement of the World's Fair on a regular, more convenient basis. These popular attractions had taken over the country, from Paragon Park and Revere Beach in Boston, south to Atlantic City and Palisades Park in New Jersey and Ponce de Leon Park in Atlanta, west to Cheltenham Beach, Riverview, and White City in Chicago, Forest Park Highlands in St. Louis, Carnival Park in Kansas City, and Manhattan Beach in Denver, and all the way out to The Chutes in San Francisco. Not only a metropolitan phenomenon, the parks took root in smaller cities, too. There was the White City in Syracuse, New York, Idora Park in Youngstown, Cedar Point Park in Sandusky, and Electric Park in Galveston. The most famous amusement center was Coney Island, two miles of beachfront along the southwestern end of Long Island, nine miles from Manhattan. Visitors to the different parks at Coney Island, that "seat of a delirium of raw pleasure," found vaudeville, circuses, dancing, bathing, exotic novelty attractions, and mechanical rides.[9]

In cities and towns, vaudeville theaters also offered a kind of pleasure on a regular basis. Beginning in the late nineteenth century, such impresarios as Benjamin Franklin Keith, Edward Franklin Albee, Tony Pastor, and Sylvester Poli charged only a dime for variety shows with "something for everybody"—acrobats, dancers, balladeers, magicians, mind readers, opera singers, comics, celebrities, and sports heroes such as Christy Mathewson. Vaudeville managers stressed the respectability of their productions: the owner of the Hippodrome in Lexington, Kentucky, promised "a moral show, by moral people, for moral people." This strategy succeeded. Vaudeville drew mixed audiences, including many women and white-collar workers. More-traditional theater also flourished by the turn of the century. Instead of demanding two dollars for admission, the new "ten-twenty-thirty" theaters staged melodramas, musical comedies, and revues at prices ranging from thirty cents a seat down front to just ten cents a seat in the upper balcony. From the Casino Theater on Broadway and Thirty-ninth Street in New York City, to the Burt Theater in Toledo, Ohio, and on to the Grand Opera House in San Francisco, audiences flocked to see such productions as *A Fool and His Money, My Wife's Husbands, Are You My Father?, The Wizard of Oz,* and Mathewson's *The Girl and the Pennant.*[10]

Americans also went out to dance. The 1900s witnessed a full-blown dance craze. New York City, announced a journalist in 1909, "is dance mad." The upper ten did the cakewalk at society parties. President Roosevelt "led the cakewalk . . . executing fancy, buck and wing steps," at a White House Christmas party in 1901. Americans of all classes did the grizzly bear, the turkey trot, and the bunny hug. Dancing in public was suddenly more acceptable than before. In New York, the wealthy stepped out at such exclusive cabarets as Maxim's, the Sans Souci, the Jardin de Dance, and the Folies Bergère. The less wealthy, especially young working-class women, filled the dance halls and dance "palaces" that opened in cities and towns across the country. In the 1910s, New York had more than a hundred dancing schools and five hundred dance halls.[11]

The dance craze was driven, in part, by changes in music. New commercial possibilities became clear when Americans unexpectedly bought five million copies of the sheet music for "After the Ball," a wistful waltz of dashed romantic hopes, published by Charles K. Harris in 1892. By the 1910s, the music publishing business in New York had expanded into a cluster of companies along West Twenty-eighth Street between Broadway and Sixth Avenue, known as Tin Pan Alley. The publishers' song pluggers and sheet music supplied Americans with a stream of melodies. So did the World's Fairs, vaudeville theaters, cabarets, restaurants, and dance halls. Piano production nearly doubled from 1899 to 1909; shipments of new phonographs more than doubled over the same period.[12]

The music business introduced the nation to new sounds in the 1900s. While Americans still enjoyed sentimental ballads and operatic arias, fresh and exotic kinds of music enthralled large audiences. Ragtime, with its stunning, syncopated two-beat rhythm, exuded a sense of musical freedom that captivated listeners. Although the new music emerged in various places around the country in the 1890s, ragtime was most associated with African-American composers and instrumentalists from Missouri, such as Tom Turpin, Louis Chauvin, and, above all, Scott Joplin. By the time Joplin published his famous "Maple Leaf Rag" in 1899, ragtime had become a craze. The black band leader James Reese Europe played rags for sophisticated New Yorkers and began making records in 1913. Two years earlier, the white Tin Pan Alley composer Irving Berlin—a product of Rahel Golub's Lower East Side—scored a huge hit with his tune "Alexander's Ragtime Band."[13]

Soon after, Americans developed a fascination with Hawaiian music. In 1912, the successful Broadway play *Bird of Paradise* introduced the "weirdly sensuous music of the island," complete with steel guitar, ukulele, and other traditional Hawaiian instruments. Tin Pan Alley obligingly began to churn out Hawaiian-inspired tunes, such as "Yacka Hula Hickey Dula." For a while, Hawaiian music apparently even outsold other musical genres on record.[14]

At the same time, another sound began to evolve out of African-American blues, ragtime, marches, and other kinds of popular music. As early as 1913, the new music was being called "jass," "jaz," or "jazz." Created by African-Americans, jazz was an exciting form of musical liberation that featured improvised and blues-inflected passages played over a hot, increasingly swinging four-beat rhythm. Even its name conjured up liberation and pleasure—"jazz" referred, possibly, to speed, or, more likely, to sexual intercourse. Jazz was, not surprisingly, a music of dives and dance halls; but it could soon be heard at Vanderbilt parties, where black entertainers demonstrated "jungle rhythms." While the music emerged in various places around the country, most of the first great musicians began their careers in and around New Orleans: the cornet-playing band leaders Buddy Bolden and Freddie Keppard came from the Crescent City; so did the flamboyant Creole pianist and composer, Ferdinand "Jelly Roll" Morton. Their music quickly appealed to young whites. By 1917, the all-white Original Dixieland Jazz Band, whose five members came from New Orleans, was pulling in crowds at Reisenweber's Restaurant in New York and making the first jazz records for the Victor company.[15]

Like public dancing, professional sports became more popular and respectable in the new century. The old sport of horse racing and the new sport of auto racing drew crowds. But baseball was clearly the national game. Minor league teams sprang up around the country: there were no fewer than forty-four separate minor leagues by 1910. Christy Mathewson's fame was rooted in quick expansion at the major league level. The American League had only been formed in 1901; the first World Series had been played just two years later. Soon, confident clubowners, emphasizing the game's respectability, began to replace their rickety wooden ballparks with grand downtown stadia built of concrete and steel: Philadelphia's Shibe Park led off in 1909; Boston's Fenway Park opened in 1912; Brooklyn's Ebbets Field followed the next year. Although the games were still played in the daytime and the seats were still relatively expensive, the major leagues attracted a growing audience—mostly male, but increasingly female as well. Attendance, less than 1 million in 1890, grew to 1.8 million in 1900. With the formation of the American League, turnout at big league games reached a peak of 7.2 million by 1909.[16]

For all the popularity of baseball, ragtime, and vaudeville, none of these amusements rivaled the impact of the motion picture. "With the possible exception of the automobile," *Munsey's* magazine contended, "no other product of human invention has advanced with such amazing swiftness from a toy to a necessity." In 1904, Harry Davis turned a store on Pittsburgh's Diamond Street into a movie house: audiences filled his storefront theater to watch films for the low price of a nickel. The next year, he opened another theater, which he called "Nickelodeon." His "Pittsburgh Idea" spread quickly to Cincinnati, Philadelphia, Rochester, Dallas, Chicago, and Baltimore. There were roughly twenty-five hundred nickelodeons nationwide at the start of 1907; three years later, there were about ten thousand. Perhaps twenty-six million people went to the nickelodeons every week. It was, reported observers, a "frenzy," a "fever," a "craze," a "madness."[17]

All these people—tourists and shoppers, clerks and domestics—crowded into dark, stuffy rooms to watch one-reel, fifteen-minute films. Along with actualities, the nickelodeons showed more and more "story" films. Audiences watched comedies, westerns, and melodramas; they watched *Oh! That Limburger: The Story of a Piece of Cheese, Cowboys and Indians, Uncle Tom's Cabin,* and Mathewson's *Breaking into the Big Leagues.* The films were still silent: nickelodeons usually added live musical accompaniment and sometimes even spoken words and sound effects from behind the screen.[18]

As the novelty of the nickelodeons wore off, they gave way to more spacious, comfortable, elegant, and expensive movie houses in the 1910s. The new places, often located in suburbs, were meant to look like theaters and even exotic "palaces." Milwaukee's new Princess Theater boasted a pipe organ, electric fountains, and mahogany doors. Charging up to twenty-five cents for admission, the movie palaces emphasized their suitability for middle-class and family audiences. Theater owners pushed for "better" movies, appropriate for "the better class of people." In 1913, the huge audiences for two multireel films about the horrors of prostitution—*Traffic in Souls* and *The Inside of the White Slave Traffic*—signaled the potential for longer "features." Two years later, D. W. Griffith's epic about the supposed horrors of Reconstruction, *The Birth of a Nation,* marked a new level of sophistication for the "photoplay." By then, movies had become a respectable entertainment. "People who never before dreamed of entering the portals of a motion picture theater," declared a trade journal, "are gazing with surprise upon the miracles unfolding before them and going away astonished at their own narrow-mindedness in the past."[19]

Like other forms of liberation, the pursuit of pleasure challenged the emerging values and practices of progressivism. The complex of entertainments offered new freedoms and opportunities for groups restricted and confined in early twentieth-century America. It broke down different forms of segregation. It promoted individualism and a more open sexuality. And it contributed to a new, freer identity for women.

To some lucky men, the new entertainments became a ticket out of the working or middle classes. In communities across the country, handfuls of immigrants and other men of modest means quickly grasped the possibilities of vaudeville, baseball, dance halls, and movies. Eager to make their fortunes, these entrepreneurs did not worry too much about the uncertain respectability of new entertainments; they had little social position to maintain. The principal owners of major league baseball teams came from outside the upper ten. John T. Brush, the owner of the Giants, had been an Indianapolis clothier; Charles Ebbets, owner of the Dodgers, started out as a printer. The major owner of vaudeville theaters in New England, Sylvester Poli, was an Italian from Tuscany who started out as a sculptor in a New

York waxworks. Immigrants, especially East European Jews, loomed large in the film business. William Fox, theater owner and then movie mogul, was a peddler from Tuchva, Hungary, who worked as a garment cutter on the Lower East Side of Manhattan. The four Warner brothers, who created a string of nickelodeons and ultimately a giant film studio, were the sons of a peddlar from Kroznashiltz, Poland. Their fellow movie mogul Sam Goldwyn began life as Schmuel Gelbfisz, a glovemaker from Warsaw.[20]

The new world of commercialized pleasures offered opportunities for African-Americans as well. A black man, Jack Johnson, became boxing's heavyweight champion in 1908. Despite frustrations and setbacks, Scott Joplin, James Reese Europe, Jelly Roll Morton, and other African-Americans found at least a decent living and a measure of fame in the music business. "[T]here is no prejudice against the Negro in music . . . ," the *Chicago Tribune* maintained in 1906. "He need not fear that race prejudice will antagonize him." Music seemed to be a way to win respect and equality from whites. An African-American paper, *The Chicago Defender,* happily reported that Europe's successful orchestra was "Jazzing Away Prejudice."[21]

Women had little chance to become entrepreneurs in the entertainment world. Some, like the singer Sophie Tucker and the actress Theda Bara, did make careers as performers. Millions more, especially young, unmarried workers, achieved a new sense of liberation as patrons of commercial amusements. Vaudeville, dance halls, and picture shows, unlike the old saloons, were safe, respectable places for women. "[T]he one place I was allowed to go by myself was the movies," recalled Filomena Ognibene, an Italian garment worker. "My parents wouldn't let me go anywhere else, even when I was twenty-four."[22]

Children also found liberation at the movies. As automobiles pushed them off the streets and progressive reformers herded them into schools, American children lived more regimented lives. But they could escape parents, reformers, and other adults at the nickelodeons and movie palaces. "When the lights went down," Jane Addams reported, "they were free—as they were free nowhere else indoors—to behave like children: to shout, scream, howl, laugh aloud and jump up and down in their seats." No wonder children saved their pennies to go to the movies as often as possible. In one drab Connecticut mill town, nine out of ten children between the ages of ten and fourteen went to the photoplay.[23]

In part by attracting children and women, commercial entertainments fostered social mixing in public. The amusement parks, World's Fairs, movie palaces, ball parks, theaters, and dance halls countered the segregating impulse of progressive America. Earlier entertainments had maintained a kind of exclusivity. The high price of admission at some theaters had effectively kept out workers and the lower middle class. Other theaters confined different classes to different-priced tiers of seats. The reputation of saloons and bawdy houses kept out "respectable" women. But now entertainments mixed ages, classes, and genders.

The World's Fairs established the precedent. With only some exaggeration, the guidebook for the St. Louis fair claimed that "for a period caste and class distinction was eliminated, and common ground was occupied for a trifle." Visitors to amusement parks found a release not only from hard work but from urban segregation. "Coney Island has a code of conduct which is all her own," an observer noted. People from different backgrounds, white-collar workers and immigrants, mixed together curiously, eagerly, on rides and boardwalks. One visitor took note of Coney Island's "frank assumption of equality" in 1906: "Bare human nature, naive and unashamed, stands up at Coney and cries out 'Brother' and the unanimity with which human nature responds is hopeful though disconcerting." Dance halls, declared a journalist in 1913, also produced "a social mixture such as was never before dreamed of in this country—a hodge-podge of people in which respectable young married and unmarried women, and even debutantes, dance, not only under the same roof, but in the same room with women of the town. Liberté—Egalité—Fraternité." Baseball, as Jane Addams recognized, brought men of different classes together in much the same way. "The enormous crowd of cheering men and boys . . . are lifted out of their individual affairs and so fused together that a man cannot tell whether it is his own shout or another's that fills his ears; whether it is his own coat or another's that he is wildly waving to celebrate a victory," Addams wrote. "Does not this contain a suggestion of the undoubted power of public recreation to bring together all classes of a community in the modern city unhappily so full of devices for keeping men apart?"[24]

By the 1910s, the movies offered the leading example of democratic mingling. At first, they had threatened to divide rather than unify Americans. While the automobile was a rich man's toy, the nickelodeon seemed to be a distinctly working-class diversion. But the movie theaters and palaces soon drew in all classes. Film, pronounced *The Nation* in 1913, was the "first democratic art." The movie theater, declared a critic that year, was a place for "the people without distinction of class." William Fox made the claim more extravagantly. "Movies breathe the spirit in which the country was founded, freedom and equality," he announced. "In the motion picture theaters there are no separations of classes . . . the rich rub elbows with the poor and that's the way it should be."[25]

Commercial amusements also brought the sexes together. Amusement parks allowed men and women to mingle, to dance, and to court and even kiss in the "Tunnel of Love." Dance halls and movies encouraged the same kind of socializing. "Note how the semi-darkness permits a 'steady's' arm to encircle a 'lady friend's' waist," a theatergoer observed.[26]

There were limits to social mixing. In their quest for respectability, movie theater owners kept out "the undesirable element," the "mugs," and the "roughs." Squads of ushers carefully policed theaters and baseball stadia. The dance halls made sure men and women did not become too intimate with each other. Nevertheless, commercial amusements raised a disturbing possibility for progressive America: perhaps social segregation was unnecessary and undesirable.[27]

As the world of commercial leisure and entertainment challenged segregation, it also promoted individualism. Dance halls, vaudeville theaters, movie palaces, and ballparks obviously emphasized the importance of personal gratification: the whole point of going out to these attractions was to have a good time for one's self.

The movies, especially, came to celebrate individualism. The film industry began, for obscure reasons, with the denial of individual identity. The first movie actors and actresses were unnamed and unpublicized: they were not even identified in credits at the beginning or end of a film. Like other corporations, motion picture companies such as Biograph tried to promote themselves as brand names, rather than publicize their actors and actresses. But the attempt failed. Motion picture fans demanded to know about their favorite players. As a result, Biograph and the other companies gradually drew attention to individual actors and actresses. At first, popular players were simply an extension of the companies: Florence Lawrence was known only as "The Biograph Girl"; Florence Turner was "The Vitagraph Girl." Other actors and actresses were identified by a distinctive physical feature: Mary Pickford was "the girl with the curls"; Maurice Costello, "the man with the dimples."

Beginning in 1909, films began to include cast lists: the players finally had names. Then the companies started to publicize these newly identified employees. Biograph and the others distributed photographs of actors and actresses and sent them on personal appearance tours. By 1913 or 1914, the "star" had begun to emerge. Movie magazines focused on "personality," on the houses, automobiles, and loves of such "picture personalities" as Mary Pickford, Charlie Chaplin, and Rudolph Valentino. "The future of the moving picture," predicted a newspaper in 1913, "lies with the player."[28]

The films themselves intensified the focus on the individual. By 1915, movie makers had created the close-up shot. Bringing their cameras closer to catch facial expressions, directors could make an actor or actress larger than life. As early as 1909, *Moving Picture World* grasped the players' triumph. Close-ups, like the whole star system, were turning actors and actresses into "a race of giants and giantesses."[29]

This race exalted the individual's power to remake him- or herself. The stars had, in fact, transformed themselves into new people. The dashing Douglas Fairbanks began life as Charles Ulman; his wife and co-star, Mary Pickford, started out as Gladys Smith. Exotic Theda Bara—the supposed child of French aristocracy and Algerian royalty—grew up in Cincinnati as Theodosia Goodman. "We are," declared Mary Pickford, "our own sculptors." That was a subversive claim: progressive reform was all about sculpting other people, not claiming the right and the power to make one's self.[30]

Commercial amusements also struck at progressivism with their relentless emphasis on sex and sexuality. At a time when reformers tried to restrain sexual behavior in general and prostitution in particular, vaudeville, amusement parks, dances, songs, and movies offered a more relaxed and open approach to sex. Vaudeville theaters featured well-known women swimmers posing in their bathing suits. Amusement parks featured exotic dancers: at Coney Island, "Little Egypt" became famous for her provocative "hootchi-kootchi." Elsewhere in the parks, blasts of air lifted women's skirts and couples flocked to the "Tunnel of Love." Drawing couples close together, the new popular dances exuded sexuality. "The 'nigger' dance seems to find its main origin in the crude and heathen sexual customs of middle Africa," fretted a journalist, "afterward passing through the centers of prostitutes in large cities, where the contributions of city savages, from Paris to San Francisco, have been added to it." Even the polite cakewalk struck observers as a "sex dance . . . a milder edition of African orgies."[31]

Tin Pan Alley contributed to the preoccupation with sex. Inspired by the automobile, songwriters turned out such numbers as "Fifteen Kisses on a Gallon of Gas" and "On an Automobile Honeymoon." In the popular song of 1905, "In My Merry Oldsmobile," Johnny Steele cries out: "You can go as far as you like with me, Lucille, in my merry Oldsmobile." Lucille is quite willing: "She says she knows why the motor goes; the sparker's awfully strong." As the song ends, "They spoon to the engine's tune; their honeymoon will happen soon." The movies also highlighted sexual topics. One of the earliest and most popular films revealed *The Anatomy of a Kiss.* Mack Sennett filled his comedies with "the most curvaceous girls I could get." Titles from 1915 and 1916 included *He Did and He Didn't, Wife and Auto Trouble, Temptation,* and *A Bedroom Blunder.*[32]

By 1913, the magazine *Current Opinion* could declare that it was "Sex O'Clock" in the United States. The public control of sexuality, so basic to progressivism, seemed to be slipping away. Movies and other entertainments were not the only cause. Progressive reform itself, through the public discussion of prostitution and venereal disease, contributed to the more open treatment of sex.[33]

So did the development of sexual theory. By the 1910s, many Americans had been exposed to a crude popularization of the ideas of Sigmund Freud. In his lectures at Clark University in 1909, Freud had, most shockingly for his audience, discussed the sexual impulses of the child and their role in adult neuroses. Freud had also condemned the "most extreme" sexual repression and praised an "incomparably freer sexual life." As his work was interpreted for the mass audience, Americans learned that sexual drives could not be denied. "The urge is there," Freud's American disciple, A. A. Brill, explained, "and whether the individual desires or no, it always manifests itself." Even the sedate women's magazine *Good Housekeeping* announced that the sexual instinct "will never be stopped except with satisfactions." Americans also learned some of the ideas of the English sexologist Havelock Ellis, who portrayed sex as "the chief and central function of life . . . ever wonderful, ever lovely." "Why," asked Ellis, "should people be afraid of rousing passions which, after all, are the great driving forces of human life?"[34]

One reason, of course, was the fear of unwanted pregnancy. Although many Americans practiced birth control, contraception remained controversial and contraceptives largely illegal and unavailable. But a grassroots birth control movement challenged this situation in the 1910s.[35] In towns and cities across the country, socialists, Wobblies, and other radicals took the lead in promoting sex education and access to contraceptives. The crusade's best-known figure was the fiery radical Margaret Sanger. A former nurse and socialist organizer, Sanger published a candid series of articles, "What Every Girl Should Know," in a New York newspaper in 1912. Three years later, she coined the term—*birth control*—that would define the movement for years to come.[36]

Sanger justified birth control with a revealing combination of old and new arguments. At first, she offered contraception as a new form of voluntary motherhood, one more way for women to take control of their bodies. Working-class women in particular would be spared the hardships of unwanted pregnancies and large families. Influenced by her friendship with Havelock Ellis, Sanger also used a new argument—that contraception was a means to pleasure. No longer worried about unwanted pregnancies, couples could freely enjoy sexual intercourse. Mabel Dodge, always alert to new forms of liberation, understood the significance of Sanger's argument. "She was the first person I ever knew who was openly an ardent propagandist for the joys of the flesh," Dodge recalled. "This, in those days, was radical indeed, when the sense of sin was still so indubitably mixed with the sense of pleasure." To Dodge, Sanger's campaign, which meant the "sexualizing of the whole body," was "like another attempt to release the energy in the atom . . . something new and releasing and basic."[37]

The birth control movement, like other forms of liberation, undermined progressive values. Sanger echoed Frank Lloyd Wright in condemning the external controls that were so basic to progressivism. "Restraint and constraint of individual expression, suppression of individual freedom 'for the good of society' has been practised from time immemorial; and its failure is all too evident," she said flatly. Like Wright, Sanger defended individualism. "There is no antagonism between the good of the individual and the good of society," she wrote. In fact, individual freedom would promote "the good of society" far more than progressive controls ever had or ever would. "The moment civilization is wise enough to remove the constraints and prohibitions which now hinder the release of inner energies, most of the larger evils of society will perish of inanition and malnutrition," Sanger insisted. She believed passionately that birth control helped release those "inner energies." Through birth control, individuals could take control of their lives. It was, she explained, "a scientific means by which and through which each human life may be self-directed and self-controlled." And so birth control promoted individual freedom. "Primarily," Sanger concluded, "it is the instrument of liberation and of human development."[38]

The birth control movement, along with the popularization of Freud and Ellis and the erotic focus of commercial amusements, signaled a transformation of sexual values and practices in the United States in the 1910s and after. The immediate extent of that transformation should not be exaggerated. Mabel Dodge, for example, tried to carry out Sanger's philosophy of "sex-expression." Still married to Edwin Dodge, Mabel welcomed a male friend "within the curtains of my white bed one night." Expecting "to melt into the joys of the flesh and the lilies and languors of love," she found herself "completely cold to him, completely unresponsive, my blood and nerves not interested." Her partner had the same reaction. So they went to a hotel, but the result was the same. "Never again did we try to find sex-expression," Dodge confessed; "instead we talked and talked and talked about it."[39]

Many other Americans probably did a lot of talking, too. Havelock Ellis could describe marriage as a "tragic condition rather than a happy condition" and could oppose the condemnation of homosexuality. But the vast majority of Americans were not going to stray beyond the limits of monogamy and heterosexuality. Nevertheless, there were signs of change. As Americans demanded more satisfaction from marriage, the divorce rate climbed and the antidivorce movement lagged in the 1910s. Within very strict limits, some communities tolerated homosexuality. Gay men and women apparently created their own public social spaces without crippling interference in at least a few cities and towns. In New York, the homosexual community—the world of "queers" and "fairies"—expanded from the Bowery into Greenwich Village in the 1910s. Meanwhile, the open discussion of heterosexual love continued in songs and on movie screens. The opportunities for heterosocial mixing expanded in amusement parks and dance halls. And the notion that sexual pleasure was a basic, acceptable part of life took firmer hold in American culture.[40]

The public emphasis on sex and sexuality involved more than a new attitude toward pleasure; it signaled a new view of women. Publicly at least, many nineteenth-century Americans had been reluctant to suggest that women were sexual beings, creatures of appetite and desire. But by the 1910s, the Victorian stereotype of the asexual, self-denying woman had almost completely disappeared. The new sexual theory insisted that women and men alike were sensual beings who deserved gratification. "Passion," wrote the best-selling author Dr. Alice Stockham, in 1903, "belongs to the . . . healthy woman as much as to the healthy man."[41]

The new commercial amusements certainly shared that belief. Not surprisingly, they presented women as objects of male desire. Little Egypt's dances and Mack Sennett's movies put women on display. More strikingly, commercial amusements offered men as objects of female desire. Women flocked to gaze at and even touch the "Great Sandow" and other strongmen at World's Fairs and amusement parks. The acknowledgment of female sexuality, implicit in these displays, was explicit in the movies. Beginning in 1915, Theda Bara won enormous popularity as the "vamp," a female sexual vampire with "enough sex attraction to supply a town full of normally pleasing women." In one film after another, Bara captivated and destroyed helpless men. "Kiss me, my fool," she demanded in *A Fool There Was.* Bara's aggressive sexuality, deployed "with prodigal freedom" in such films as *The Serpent, The Vixen, Cleopatra, Salome,* and *When Men Desire,* inspired a host of exotic imitators, including Vilma Banky, Nita Naldi, and Lya de Putti.[42]

The sexual nature of women was also central to a new movement, known as feminism, that emerged in the 1910s. The feminists, like earlier female reformers, were generally white, well educated, Protestant, urban women. Concentrated in New York's Greenwich Village, the feminists included such writers and activists as Crystal Eastman, Henrietta Rodman, Ida Rauh, Neith Boyce, and Susan Glaspell. Youthful, energetic, and aggressive, the feminists quickly organized themselves and publicized their ideas. In 1912, twenty-five women founded Heterodoxy, an organization dedicated to the discussion of a broad range of women's topics. In 1914, Rodman formed a group called the Feminist Alliance. That year, too, Marie Jenney Howe, one of the leaders of Heterodoxy, staged two mass meetings at New York's

Cooper Union devoted to the topic "What Is Feminism?" Answers to that question emerged in the pages of the radical journal *The Masses,* edited by Crystal Eastman's brother, Max. And they appeared onstage in the productions of the Provincetown Players, a summer theatrical group on Cape Cod, Massachusetts. The company, which put on plays by Eugene O'Neill, also staged plays by Boyce and Glaspell.[43]

The feminists broke with earlier female reformers in their conception of women's sexual nature and, accordingly, in much else. "[M]y own generation of feminists . . . ," recalled writer Lillian Symes, "had . . . little in common with the flat-heeled, unpowdered, pioneer suffragette generation which preceded it by a decade or two. . . ." Insisting on women's capacity for pleasure, the feminists of the 1910s demanded what one of them called "sex rights on the part of women." Like earlier female activists, they wanted a single sexual standard for men and women—but one based on mutual sexual gratification, not renunciation and regulation. In short, the feminists sought the same opportunities and satisfactions as men had presumably long enjoyed.[44]

For some feminists, "sex rights on the part of women" meant, at least privately, the acceptance of homosexuality. There were a number of lesbians in Heterodoxy. Most feminists assumed, however, that "sex rights" meant primarily the freedom to pursue heterosexual pleasure. Birth control was inevitably a central feminist cause. It was "an elementary essential in all aspects of feminism," declared Crystal Eastman. "[W]e must all be followers of Margaret Sanger." A few feminists practiced "free love." Henrietta Rodman, for instance, lived openly with a series of men before she finally married in 1913. But the vast majority of feminists, like Rodman herself, did not reject marriage. Rather, they wanted to remake married life on a more exciting, satisfying basis. "I am trying for nothing so hard in my own personal life," said activist Mary Heaton Vorse, "as how not to be respectable when married."[45]

The feminists' insistence on sexual satisfaction put them at odds with older female activists. Those pioneers tended to emphasize women's spiritual, rather than sexual, nature. As early as 1913, feminist Winifred Harper Cooley reported "a violent altercation going on continually . . . regarding this question." Younger and older women alike condemned "the injustices of the man-made world, which has for centuries branded the scarlet letter on the woman's breast, and let the man go scot-free." But that was the extent of the agreement. "[T]he conservative women reformers think the solution is in hauling men up to the standard of virginal purity that has always been set for women," Cooley observed. "The other branch, claiming to have a broader knowledge of human nature, asserts that it is impossible and perhaps undesirable to expect asceticism from all men and women." Cooley thought that she and other feminists were simply "willing to face facts as they are." But older women activists, such as the suffragist Carrie Chapman Catt, believed the feminists were guilty of the "oversexualizing of women." And Charlotte Perkins Gilman warned that sexual freedom was an "indulgence" that could become the basis for women's further oppression in the future.[46]

The feminists also broke with the women's movement and with progressivism because they saw the world in individualist terms. Winifred Harper Cooley described women's plight as the denial of their individuality. Women are "seldom allowed self-expression as individuals," she lamented. "They are never referred to except in their relation to men. It is always 'the wife and mother,' 'the sweetheart and sister,' not simply 'the woman.'"[47]

The feminists insisted on their individuality. The members of Heterodoxy described themselves as "free-willed, self-willed women . . . the most unruly and individualistic females you ever fell among." And the feminists insisted that women should have all the rights of individuals. "Feminism," the Feminist Alliance declared at its first meeting in 1914, "is a movement, which demands the removal of all social, political, economic, and other discriminations which are based upon sex, and the award of all rights and duties in all fields on the basis of individual capacity alone." The novelist Rose Young, a member of Heterodoxy and a speaker at the first Cooper Union meeting, put it more simply. "To me," she said, "feminism means that woman . . . wants to be an individual."[48]

The pursuit of individualism had many consequences, some small and symbolic, some far more sweeping. To emphasize their individuality and independence, a number of married feminists used their maiden names, rather than take their husbands' surnames. More fundamentally, feminists rejected the implicit sexual settlement at the core of the women's movement and progressivism. Unlike Jane Addams and many other activist women of her generation, the feminists were unwilling to give up marriage and children in order to have careers outside the home. Neighbors and observers of the Hull-House neighborhood had often thought of the childless, unmarried Addams as a self-denying saint or a nun. "Feminists are not nuns," Crystal Eastman maintained. "We want to love and to be loved, and most of us want children, one or two at least." But Eastman and the feminists still wanted careers as well. "[A] braver, grimmer, and more fanatical generation . . . behind us . . . had to make the famous choice between 'marriage and a career,'" Lillian Symes explained. "We were determined to have both, to try for everything life would offer of love, happiness, and freedom—just like men."[49]

That determination—to be "just like men," to have it all—considerably raised the stakes in the struggle between men and women. It was nothing new for middle-class women to demand a role outside the home. The feminists added little to the women's movement's call for access to the workplace and the voting booth. But they broke fresh ground by insisting on women's right to pleasure and satisfaction in all phases of life, from the most public to the most intimate. Symes, Eastman, Cooley, and the rest wanted nothing less than to recast the whole relationship between men and women. As a reporter concluded, the feminists required "a complete social revolution."[50]

Like Margaret Sanger's philosophy of "sex-expression," the related feminist vision of a new relationship between men and women was difficult to achieve. The vast majority of women did not have the money necessary for independence and equality. The new world of commercial amusements, however liberating otherwise, did not change that fact. In the 1910s, young working-class women could get away from home and parents at dance halls, vaudeville, and picture shows, but they still depended on men to pay for these pleasures. Unlike the male saloon patrons who treated one another, most of these women could not reciprocate financially with male dates. Instead, they found themselves pressed for sexual favors. In the sexualized realm of commercial amusements, a young woman had to be "game" and "lively"—just the sort of new exploitation that Charlotte Perkins Gilman feared.[51]

Even feminists, with the protection of middle-class codes of conduct and often with the security of their own income, found it difficult to recast their relations with men. Marriage inevitably raised the suspicion that a woman had given up her independence. When Mabel Dodge at last married Maurice Sterne, she bitterly disappointed a woman friend. "[Y]ou had the nerve to live your own life openly and frankly—to take a lover if you wished, without hiding under the law," the friend said accusingly. "You have shown women they had the *right* to live as they chose to live and that they do not lose respect by assuming that right. But *now!* When I think of the *disappointment* in the whole woman's world today!"[52]

If other women's expectations were not enough of a burden, heterosexual feminists also had to deal with men. The feminists attracted a circle of male supporters—writers and activists eager to join in the redefinition of gender relations. Max Eastman, along with fellow writers Hutchins Hapgood and Floyd Dell, enthusiastically subscribed to feminist ideas and even produced some of the key feminist texts of the day. These male feminists saw women's liberation and equality not only as a matter of justice but also as a means of emancipating men themselves. When women no longer depended on them, Dell observed in 1914, men would be truly free. Along with such sympathetic writers as Sherwood Anderson and David Graham Phillips, Dell, Eastman, and Hapgood yearned for the "new woman," independent and exciting, who would galvanize their lives.[53]

Nevertheless, it was hard for these men, however willing, to abandon the acquired habits of masculine privilege. They were not eager to share cooking, cleaning, and the other chores of homemaking. To their surprise, they were not always so eager for the assertive feminist woman, successful at work and demanding in bed. "Most women simply frighten me," Anderson admitted privately in 1916. "I feel hunger within them. It is as though they wished to feed upon me." And male feminists found themselves jealous of women's freedom. Hutchins Hapgood, chronically unfaithful to his wife Neith Boyce, could not handle the prospect of her infidelity or, worse, her creation of a life apart from him. "[W]hether egotistically or not, I *want* all *essentially* that there is of Neith," he confided to a friend in 1909. Phillips wrote longingly about the ideal new woman in his best-selling novels, but he never married one. Instead, he lived in a Manhattan apartment with his sister, who patiently took care of his dress and diet. As Floyd Dell presciently observed in 1914, "Men want the sense of power more than they want the sense of freedom."[54]

Feminists were troubled to discover how much the new feminist man was like the old Victorian man. The celebration of sex and pleasure did not make Hutchins Hapgood's repeated affairs any less hurtful for Neith Boyce.

"[I]n a way I hate your interest in sex, because I suffered from it," she wrote him after first discovering his infidelities. "I assure you that I can never think of your physical passion for other women without pain—even though my reason doesn't find fault with you. . . . The whole thing is sad and terrible. . . ." Years later, Hapgood still insisted on the "healthy vigor and moral idealism" in the attempt to remake the relations between men and women. But, rather worn out by it all, he allowed, too, that feminism had become "a perverse philosophy."[55]

This "perverse philosophy" had a wide impact in the 1910s. "[I]t is no longer possible to ignore [feminism]," announced *Century* magazine in 1914. "I am in effect a feministe," declared Theda Bara (or her press agent). Embodying the feminist ideal, the new stereotype of the flapper girl—slim, fashionable, and fun-loving in her flapping galoshes—displaced the Gibson Girl as the middle-class standard of feminine beauty. Actually, there were few avowed feminists. But feminism commanded a great deal of attention, partly because it was shocking and different, and partly because it was so familiar, too. Radical as it was, feminism had deep roots in the broad cultural reconsideration of women. "The germ is in the blood of our women," *Century* observed. "The doctrine and its corollaries are on every tongue." The feminists had essentially elaborated the antiprogressive logic that was implicit in the changing view of women's nature. They had articulated the movie theaters' and amusement parks' tacit acknowledgment of female individuality and pleasure. *Century* understood that the handful of feminist activists were not the whole story. "Let us study the Revolt of the Women," the magazine suggested, "not in the souls of the volatile few, but of the earnest millions of wives and mothers and workers who are thinking silently in their homes." And, *Century* might have added, who were flocking happily to dance halls, amusement parks, and movie theaters.[56]

The emerging culture of pleasure inevitably provoked hostility. Its expressions—commercial amusements, birth control, feminism—challenged too many cherished values and assumptions. Like other forms of liberation, the open pursuit of pleasure flouted both Victorianism and progressivism. It celebrated the individual, redefined women, and broke through confining barriers. The reaction was immediate. "Commercialized recreation means dissipation," warned John Collier, a social reformer and leader of the People's Institute in New York City.[57]

Many people agreed with him. Sports, dance halls, amusement parks, and birth control all came in for their share of condemnation by an assortment of reformers, politicians, clergymen, clubwomen, and authors. Movies, given their huge popular impact, faced particularly searching criticism. Observers described the "pernicious 'moving picture' abomination" as a "disease" striking "the very life blood of the city." Movie theaters, the suffragist leader Anna Howard Shaw charged, "are the recruiting stations of vice." As another critic explained, the theaters stirred up "primitive passion" and "an overwhelming drive for something that stirs and thrills." They inspired weak-minded patrons to commit crimes. They encouraged poor workers to waste precious pennies. They exposed children to vile ideas. They allowed "too much familiarity between boys and girls." And they led "[g]irls from good homes all in a mad pursuit of pleasure having their moral sense blunted, reaching headlong into danger."[58]

Denunciations such as these spurred the ongoing crusade against vice in early twentieth-century America. In addition to the continuing campaigns against drink, divorce, and prostitution, there were new crusades directed against dancing, movies, and sexual freedom.

The battle to tame public dancing centered on New York City. There, the reformer Belle Moskowitz focused on the danger that unchaperoned girls and young women would be led astray in dance halls, particularly if liquor was available on the premises or nearby. Moskowitz and her allies did not attempt to wipe out public dancing. Instead, the reformer launched a three-pronged effort to clean up the halls. First, Moskowitz helped to secure a state law, which took effect in 1911, banning the sale of liquor in dancing schools and making it more difficult for saloons to feature dancing. Second, she encouraged "substitution"—the opening of alternative dance halls in Manhattan, Brooklyn, and Newark, New Jersey, where dancers were closely chaperoned. Third, she supported attempts to make popular dances less overtly sexual and more sedate. Moskowitz's efforts won nationwide attention during the 1910s. Cities around the country adopted ordinances requiring dance halls to obtain licenses and maintain health and safety standards.[59]

Moving pictures, like dancing, were too popular and too pervasive to try to wipe out. Instead, clergy and other reformers sought to regulate movie theaters and censor the movies. The nation's largest cities witnessed particularly aggressive and revealing battles over theaters and films. In 1906, Chicago gave its police force the authority to close down films depicting "crime, criminals and immoral scenes which appeal to small boys and weak-minded adults." The next year the city enacted the nation's first film censorship ordinance, which banned "immoral or obscene" movies and required a permit to exhibit any film. In 1909, the city established a film censorship commission to carry out the law. Among the films banned in Chicago was the popular white-slavery epic, *Traffic in Souls.*[60]

Meanwhile in New York, church leaders urged the city government to apply Sunday-closing laws to the movie theaters. Under pressure from reformers, the mayor, George McClellan, temporarily closed down the theaters on Christmas Eve in 1908. Thereafter, theater owners would have to apply for licenses. In 1909, the city and New York State barred unaccompanied children from theaters. Across the country, other cities and towns took up measures like those instituted in the great metropolises.[61]

As many Americans anxiously confronted changing sexual mores, the birth control movement came under fire. When Margaret Sanger began to publish a procontraception magazine, *Woman Rebel,* in 1914, postal authorities declared the publication unmailable under the terms of the Comstock Act, the 1873 statute successfully demanded by vice crusader Anthony Comstock and the Society for the Suppression of Vice. Sanger herself was indicted in August 1914 for violating the act's ban on the mailing of "obscene, lewd, or lascivious" materials. Released on her own recognizance, she failed to turn up in court, left her husband and children, and fled to Canada and then to Europe. In her absence, her husband, William, was convicted for distributing her pamphlet on contraception, "Family Limitation," in 1915.[62]

Uneasiness about changing sexual values and practices also led to new federal attempts to control sexual behavior. In 1910, Congress enacted a measure allowing the deportation of any immigrant employed in a "music or dance hall or other place of amusement or resort habitually frequented by prostitutes. . . ." The same year, Congress also passed the White Slave Traffic Act, sponsored by Representative James R. Mann of Chicago. Known as the Mann Act, this measure allowed the federal government to prosecute anyone who transported a woman across state lines for purposes of "prostitution or debauchery, or for any other immoral purpose." Intended to combat coerced prostitution, the Mann Act would be interpreted quite broadly and used against cases of willing prostitution and even noncommercial sex, such as unmarried couples' crossing state lines with the intention of having sexual intercourse. The newly created Bureau of Investigation was charged with enforcing the law.[63]

Despite the efforts of reformers and activists, the campaign against the culture of pleasure produced mixed and generally disappointing results. Dance hall owners blunted opposition by posting rules on the admission of unescorted women, the mixing of strangers, and the character of dance steps. "Do not shake the hips. Do not twist the body," read one set of rules. "Avoid low, fantastic and acrobatic dips." Vernon and Irene Castle, the most famous professional dancers of the day, "spiritualized the dances thought to be hopelessly fleshy" by altering the steps and insisting on their propriety. Meanwhile, local dance hall ordinances proved difficult to enforce when thousands of people went out to dance each night in the cities. Gradually, reformers lost heart and the crusade to regulate the halls petered out.[64]

The crusade against movies and movie theaters was a bit more successful. Anxious to avoid outright government censorship, theater owners and movie producers struck a deal in 1909 with the People's Institute, a settlement house on New York's Lower East Side that had investigated the nickelodeons. The movie companies agreed to submit new films to a National Board of Censorship of Programs of Motion Picture Shows, administered by the People's Institute. The board's impressive advisory group included Andrew Carnegie, Samuel Gompers, university presidents, reformers, and such vice crusaders as Anthony Comstock. Although the board insisted that movie producers take great care in the depiction of crime and sex, the regulators proved remarkably tolerant. They allowed filmmakers to deal with a broad range of controversial topics, including changing sexual mores, as long as movies came to an "appropriate" ending that did not reward wrongdoing. As the board declared in 1911, "the motion picture . . . must be allowed a certain liberty in depicting moral problems." The board's rejection of outright censorship became clear when it changed its name to the National Board of Review in 1915.[65]

Widely influential, the Board of Review frustrated reformers who wanted official censorship. They pushed hard and effectively for mandatory censorship on the local and state levels in some areas of the country. Between

1911 and 1916, Pennsylvania, Kansas, Ohio, and Maryland adopted movie censorship legislation. The resulting Kansas State Board of Review dealt with the explosive Theda Bara's films by cutting or shortening depictions of smoking and drinking, eliminating suggestive intertitles, and striking close-ups of "exposed limbs." In 1915, the United States Supreme Court upheld the Ohio law and, more broadly, the right of government to regulate motion pictures. The movies, insisted the justices, were "a business, pure and simple, . . . capable of evil," rather than examples of protected free speech like the press. Despite the ominous implications of that ruling, the silent movies of the 1910s suffered relatively little at the hands of reformers and the state.[66]

The campaign to regulate sexual behavior also proved frustrating. The federal government obtained more than three hundred convictions under the Mann Act by 1914 but there was little noticeable change in Americans' sexual attitudes and practices. The birth control movement continued to grow. Mary Ware Dennett organized the National Birth Control League in 1915. Meanwhile, the federal government dropped its charges against Margaret Sanger in 1916. The next year, she was convicted and sent to jail for selling contraceptive devices from her clinic in Brooklyn in violation of the New York State penal code. But the prosecution backfired as public sympathy sided with Sanger and support for birth control continued to grow.[67]

One of the main reasons for the mixed results of the campaign against pleasure was the ambivalence of reformers themselves. Too many of them were not convinced that society should wipe out the new amusements. Even such determined progressives as Belle Moskowitz conceded that human beings, especially in a modern society, needed to play. Moreover, the reformers, along with other observers, understood that amusements could serve a conservative, stabilizing role for America. Baseball, for instance, was a "Wholesome Madness" that preserved social equality by bringing together men from different classes. "A tonic, an exercise, a safety-valve, baseball is second only to Death as a leveler," a journalist claimed. "So long as it remains our national game, America will abide no monarchy. . . ."[68]

Reformers had especially great hopes for the power of movies. "Motion pictures are going to save our civilization from the destruction which has successively overwhelmed every civilization of the past," promised Mary Gray Peck of the General Federation of Women's Clubs in 1916. The cinema would be a "grand social worker" who would encourage people to "sleep the sleep of the just." Reformers realized that male workers stayed out of saloons in order to take their families to the movies. The "motion picture house" was, the poet and critic Vachel Lindsay wrote in 1915, "the first enemy of King Alcohol with real power where that King has deepest hold."[69]

Reformers coveted the movies' apparent power to mold public opinion. Determined to remake Americans, the progressives shared the belief of many observers that film now constituted "the greatest single force in shaping the American character." In particular, the motion picture could teach "many moral lessons." As so often, Jane Addams summed up reformers' thinking: "[T]he good in it is too splendid at rock bottom to allow the little evil to control and destroy it." Most Americans agreed.[70]

Meanwhile, the progressives were paying a heavy price for their campaigns to control the movies and other pleasures. For the first time, reformers seemed out of step with the middle class, whose needs and values had given rise to progressivism. "The word 'reformer' in the public mind has come to be associated with . . . persons who interfere with the personal habits of others—bigots!" exclaimed muckraking journalist and progressive reformer George Creel. "In the public mind reformers are persons . . . who peep through keyholes and peep over transoms. A reformer, in fact, is a man who steals up to smell another man's breath!"[71]

Despite the indifferent results of the campaigns against dance halls, movies, and sexual freedom, the new acceptance of pleasure had its limits. Many Americans were unwilling to let commercial amusements obliterate too much of the racial status quo.

Jazz and other new entertainments did create white audiences for African-American creativity and did sometimes allow white and black artists to mix together. Nevertheless, segregation and prejudice pervaded the world of commercial amusements in the 1910s. Vaudeville theaters banned African-Americans or forced them to go in the back door. If blacks were lucky enough to gain admission, they were kept off the main floor and consigned to the cheapest seats up in the balcony. Nickelodeons and storefront movie houses, which had no balconies, refused to admit African-Americans at all. Major league baseball refused to sign black players and sent black patrons to the worst seats in the Polo Grounds and other ballparks. Blacks were generally kept out of amusement parks, except on special days. They were kept out of whites-only dance halls, cabarets, and night clubs altogether.[72]

When they did manage to get into amusement attractions, African-Americans had to watch and hear blatant racism. At World's Fairs, they saw portrayals of "Darkest Africa" or the "Old Plantation Village," complete with "jolly, rollicking niggers." At Coney Island, visitors could "Hit the Nigger" with softballs. At Chicago's Riverview Park, patrons of the "African Dip" could plunge black men into a tank of water. While movies and vaudeville toned down their derisive treatment of immigrant whites, blacks remained open targets. They were mocked as lazy or vicious "coons" by white performers in black face. African-American theatrical artists such as the popular Ernest Hogan had to reinforce the stereotypes by eating watermelon and singing "All Coons Look Alike to Me."[73]

As in other areas of life, African-Americans both adapted and fought back. Kept out of white-dominated entertainments, blacks created their own commercial amusements. Despite frequent white opposition, they built their own theaters, such as Robert Mott's Pekin Theatre on the South Side of Chicago and the American Theatre in Jackson, Mississippi. African-Americans also began to make their own films.

Even as they built their world of commercial amusements, black Americans also fought back against discrimination. In Chicago and other places, African-Americans went to court to challenge segregation in the theaters and movie houses. They protested coon songs and stereotypes. "Certain slang and nicknames should be abolished," declared *The Freeman,* a black paper in Indianapolis, in 1909, "even if it costs bloodshed—the same as it did to abolish slavery." African-Americans demonstrated across the North against *The Birth of a Nation* and its "foul and loathsome misrepresentations of colored people and the glorification of the hideous and murderous band of the Ku Klux Klan." With support from Jane Addams and other pillars of white progressive respectability, these protests persuaded censors to make some cuts in Griffith's movie.[74]

Nevertheless, the new world of commercial pleasure imposed strict limits on African-Americans. The fate of the most successful black performer of all, the great boxing champion Jack Johnson, underscored the limits of liberation in the 1910s. Johnson's story was far different from the saga of Christy Mathewson, who had been born the same year. While Big Six helped make pleasure legitimate, Johnson stirred white America's fears about the dangers of pleasure.

Jack Johnson's life was a testimonial to the liberating power of commercial amusements. Born into poverty in Galveston, Texas, in 1878, Johnson developed into an immensely skilled boxer. His superb defensive style struck many whites as stereotypically lazy. But Johnson—lean, powerful, and shaven-headed—fought with calculated savagery. The boxer held back from knocking out opponents quickly so that he could go on hurting them, cutting and pounding them round after round. Whites criticized Johnson's supposed laziness but they were also afraid of what this "wild beast" might do if he ever faced a white opponent.[75]

Their fears were confirmed when Johnson knocked out the reigning heavyweight champion, the white Canadian Tommy Burns, in a bout halfway around the world, in Sydney, Australia, on Christmas night in 1908. Outraged white opinion then compelled the former American heavyweight champion Jim Jeffries to come out of retirement and challenge Johnson. The racial stakes were obvious when the two fighters entered the ring in Reno, Nevada, a wide-open town best known for its easy divorces, on the Fourth of July in 1910. The fight, declared its promoter, pitted the "Negroes' Deliverer" against the "Hope of the White Race" with much more than the record purse of $101,000 at stake. "If the black man wins," worried *The New York Times,* "thousands and thousands of his ignorant brothers will misinterpret his victory as justifying claims to much more than mere physical equality with their white neighbors." The band played "All Coons Look Alike to Me," and then Johnson, wearing an American flag for a belt and looking "like a black panther," began to beat Jeffries while movie cameras recorded the scene. Bruised, bleeding, his nose broken, the white champion was knocked down for the first time in his career. When the bout finally ended in the fifteenth round, the "dazed" crowd "could hardly believe that he was beaten. . . ."[76]

Across the nation, the white reaction was intense and distraught. "JEFFRIES MASTERED BY GRINNING, JEERING NEGRO," announced the *San Francisco Examiner.* Years later, Benjamin Mays, an African-American, recalled the reaction in Greenwood, South Carolina. "White men in my county could not take it," he remembered. "Negroes dared not discuss the outcome of this match in the presence of whites." But other African-Americans could not contain their joy. "We blacks put one over on you whites," yelled a black man in New York City, "and we're going to do more." In Pittsburgh, African-Americans forced whites off streetcars and took their seats. Four blacks shot up the town of Mounds, Illinois, and killed the black constable who tried to stop them. Around the country, outraged whites attacked and murdered black men.[77]

In the aftermath, festering white rage focused on the new heavyweight champion. It was not just that Johnson had beaten a white man and become a hero to African-Americans. It was not just that boxing struck many people—black as well as white—as savage and barbaric. Whites also reacted so strongly because Johnson epitomized the subversive possibilities of the culture of pleasure. Made rich by a commercial amusement, the champion ostentatiously crossed social boundaries and reveled in sex, speed, and other enjoyments.

For one thing, Johnson ignored the racial divides of progressive America. He carried on relationships with white women and bought a house in the "exclusive," all-white "summer colony" of Lake Geneva, Wisconsin. This bastion of millionaire bankers and corporate directors had been "invaded," *The New York Times* reported. "Its sanctity has sustained the severest blow possible. . . ." While whites feared a full-scale "NEGRO INVASION" of Lake Geneva, Johnson indulged himself. "I always take a chance on my pleasures," he said. He drank hard, danced the grizzly bear, appeared in vaudeville, and opened a café in Chicago. Like Frank Lloyd Wright, another confined man eager to break loose, Johnson was obsessed with speed. Jailed for speeding in one of his expensive cars, Johnson dreamed of driving 200 miles per hour. He challenged the white auto racer Barney Oldfield and, to the relief of whites, lost. Johnson also boldly flaunted his sexuality. While training, he put gauze bandages around his penis to make it appear larger to onlookers. He surrounded himself with prostitutes. After 1906, all the women in his entourage were white.[78]

As soon as he won the championship, Johnson's accomplishments and his defiant life-style earned him the hostile attention of white authorities across the country. In an effort to limit the impact of his victory over a white man, mayors and governors banned showings of the film of the Jeffries fight. For its part, Congress outlawed the interstate transportation of boxing films in 1912. The federal government charged Johnson with smuggling a jeweled necklace into the country. He was arrested and jailed for speeding in San Francisco; he was arrested in New York on the pretext of driving with a

Chicago license plate. Then, in October 1912, Johnson was arrested and charged with the abduction of Lucille Cameron, one of the white women who traveled with him. Federal authorities moved to convict him for violating the Mann Act. In all, Johnson faced charges on eleven counts ranging from prostitution and debauchery to crimes against nature. When he was released on bail, crowds of whites hanged Johnson in effigy and pursued him with cries of "Lynch the nigger!"[79]

Booker T. Washington and other African-Americans also turned on Johnson for crossing racial boundaries. A black writer insisted that any "race-loving Negro, irrespective of his intellectual development, must indefatigably denounce Johnson's debased allegiance with the other race's women. . . ." "JACK JOHNSON, DANGEROUSLY ILL," announced a black paper. "VICTIM OF WHITE FEVER."[80]

Johnson had not violated the Mann Act. He had not trafficked in women or tried to profit from their interstate movement. But the government was determined to get the champion. It had no case, but a white jury readily convicted Johnson for transporting Lucille Cameron from Pittsburgh to Chicago "for the purpose of prostitution and sexual intercourse." "The circumstances in this case have been aggravating," said Judge Carpenter, as he sentenced Johnson to a year and a day in jail, plus a fine of ten thousand dollars. "The life of the defendant by his own admission has not been a moral one." Jack Johnson, lamented *The Freeman* of Indianapolis, had received "a terrible punishment for daring to exceed what is considered a Negro's circle of activities."[81]

After his sentence, Johnson apparently bribed federal authorities in order to slip out of the country. Like Margaret Sanger, he traveled through Canada and then on to Europe. There, the champion fancied he was free in paradise. But in reality, Johnson lived a miserable life in Europe. Paris and London did not welcome this black hero. He found no worthy opponents to fight in the ring. Aging and out of practice, he finally lost his crown to a white man, Jess Willard, in Juarez, Mexico, in 1915. In defeat, Johnson remained a hero for many African-Americans. For years to come, a black man who stood up to whites would be known as a "Jack Johnson." But the real Jack Johnson, like the Bradley Martins before him, was an unhappy fugitive. Trapped in exile, he served as living proof that Americans would not accept all the explosive possibilities of the culture of pleasure.[82]

CHAPTER NINE

The Price of Victory

On the evening of April 2, 1917, a somber and nervous Woodrow Wilson took the rostrum in the House chamber of the Capitol to summon Congress and the nation to war. It was a war that he and most of his countrymen had long wanted to avoid. Begun in Europe in August 1914, World War I pitted France, Great Britain, Russia, and the rest of the Allies against Austria-Hungary, Germany, and the other "Central Powers" in a conflict of unparalleled size, cost, and casualties. To Americans reading newspapers and watching flickering movies, this "Great War" had become a ghastly stalemate, fought by old-fashioned monarchies, using frightening new weapons such as airplanes, submarines, machine guns, and poison gas, all because of colonial aspirations, national and ethnic enmities, and other, often murky reasons. Almost inexplicably, the United States had been drawn closer and closer to the conflict. Despite its officially neutral status, the nation had shipped food and supplies to Great Britain and provided loans to the Allies. Now, in the spring of 1917, Germany's declaration of unrestricted submarine warfare against American shipping and the revelation of Germany's plan to foment a Mexican war against the United States tipped the scales for Wilson. Standing before Congress, he insisted that "the world must be made safe for democracy." So the United States would go into battle on the side of the Allies. "It is a fearful thing," the President told Congress, "to lead this great peaceful people into war, into the most terrible and disastrous of all wars, civilization itself seeming to be in the balance."[1]

Progressivism hung in the balance, too. Wilson's war message came at an awkward moment for the progressive movement. American intervention in Europe threatened to interrupt a satisfying period of public success for reformers. One progressive cause after another had taken shape in new laws and regulatory bodies. The term *progressive* itself had emerged into common political usage in 1909 and 1910. Progressive ideas found mature, eloquent expression in such tracts as *The Promise of American Life*, by Herbert Croly, *Drift and Mastery*, by Walter Lippmann, and *The New Democracy*, by Walter Weyl. More than ever, politicians eagerly wrapped themselves in the progressive mantle. Challenging his hapless successor, William Howard Taft, for the presidency in 1912, Theodore Roosevelt ran under the banner of the new National Progressive Party. Roosevelt lost the election, but the victor, Woodrow Wilson, trumpeted his own progressivism. "[I]f you are not a progressive," he warned, "you better look out. . . ." Wilson's legislative program, the New Freedom, substantially advanced the progressive agenda. "The middle class . . . is the dominant power expressing itself through the Progressives, and through the Wilson administration," Walter Lippmann happily observed. "The middle class has put the 'Money Power' on the defensive. Big business is losing its control of the government." Wilson's triumphant reelection in 1916 seemed to bring the ultimate victory closer still. The decade, as Jane Addams said of the Progressive Party's platform, was bringing reformers "nearer our heart's desire."[2]

Wilson's war message also came just as the cultural ground was shifting dangerously under the progressives' feet. The disturbing forces of liberation were unsettling the tentative structures of the ordered, segregated middle-class paradise. Resurgent individualism, nascent feminism, and new pleasures signaled an underlying change in American culture. Progressive activists, their ideas and careers rooted in the late-nineteenth-century transformation of the Victorian middle class, faced a critical challenge. But before they could even recognize their new circumstances, the onset of the war threatened to divert them, along with the rest of American society.

Instead of interruption, World War I brought the extraordinary culmination of the progressive movement. U.S. participation in the Great War gave progressives their "heart's desire"—the best opportunity they ever had to remake the nation along progressive lines. To manage the war effort, the Wilson government relied on veteran reformers eager to work from progressive blueprints. In the short span of America's nineteen months of war, the Wilsonians and other progressives erected a model of the middle-class utopia on a far greater scale than Hull-House or Chautauqua. The federal government intervened in American life more boldly than ever before with sweeping measures to control all aspects of the economy, halt class conflict, and reshape personal identity. By November 1918, Wilson's progressive design for war had brought victory in Europe. But, as Theodore Roosevelt used to warn friends and loved ones, "God save you from the werewolf and from your heart's desire." Bringing peace to Europe, the progressives created only chaos and conflict at home. Rather than an advertisement for a progressive future, the Wilsonian war effort became the death knell for the progressive movement.[3]

Progressivism did not dictate American entry into the war. Rooted in domestic concerns, in thinking about human nature, gender, class, and pleasure, progressive ideology produced no particular vision of the nation's international interests. Since 1914, progressives themselves had taken positions across the whole spectrum of views on the war. There were ardent supporters of American intervention such as the old Social Gospel leader Lyman Abbott and the young editors of *The New Republic;* there were equally ardent opponents of intervention such as Robert M. La Follette and the pacifist settlement leaders Jane Addams and Lillian Wald.[4]

Whether they embraced the war or dreaded it, progressives and their political champions sensed that the future of their movement was at stake. Some were pessimistic. "This will set back progress for a generation," Jane Addams declared. Even Woodrow Wilson shared this pessimism. "Every reform we have won," the President observed privately, "will be lost if we go into this war." To some activists, bloodshed abroad would most likely distract Americans from reform causes at home. Leading progressive politicians such as La Follette and George Norris feared the war would only line the pockets of the rich.[5]

Many progressive activists were not pessimistic at all. Others, initially opposed to war, gradually found reason for optimism. These progressives saw the conflict as a special opportunity for reform, a chance to promote their agenda at point after point. Fighting the evils of German "autocracy" abroad, the nation would confront, not ignore, social problems at home. "We shall turn with fresh interest to our own tyrannies—to our Colorado mines, our autocratic steel industries, our sweatshops and our slums," Walter Lippmann prophesied. The war effort, Wilson's secretary of war, Newton D. Baker, enthusiastically predicted, would foster a "great remedial process" for the nation. The Great War, maintained the influential progressive journal *The New Republic*, would be "a pretext to foist innovations upon the country."[6]

In particular, the need to raise an army, stimulate the production of food and war materials, and ensure loyalty would require an activist state. "Laissez-faire is dead," declared a reformer. "Long live social control. . . ." The activist state would surely cripple the progressives' old enemy, individualism. "War necessitates organization, system, routine, and discipline," observed the journalist Frederick Lewis Allen. "We shall have to give up much of our economic freedom. . . . We shall have to lay by our good-natured individualism and march in step. . . ." Full of "social possibilities," the war, John Dewey suggested, would constrain "the individualistic tradition" and teach "the supremacy of public need over private possessions."[7]

To the muckraking journalist Ray Stannard Baker, the war offered a fresh chance to fight the popular pursuit of liberation and pleasure that so troubled the progressives. On a visit to Minneapolis in June 1917, he witnessed "a whole common people rolling carelessly and extravagantly up and down these streets in automobiles, crowding insipid 'movie' shows by the tens of thousands—there are seventy-six such houses in this one city—or else drinking unutterable hogsheads of sickly sweet drinks or eating decorated ice cream at candy shops and drugstores! All overdressed! All overeating! All overspending!" Revolted, Baker welcomed the impact of the war on his countrymen. "We need trouble and stress!" he insisted. "I thought once it could be done by some voluntary revolt from comfort and property. . . . But it was not enough. The whirlwind had to come."[8]

Progressives eagerly anticipated a variety of other gains. The suffragist Harriott Stanton Blatch, daughter of Elizabeth Cady Stanton, awaited the increased employment of women outside the home as "the usual, and happy, accompaniment of war." Even Jane Addams resolved to make the best of the war. "[C]ertainly," she recalled, "we were all eager to accept whatever progressive social changes came from the quick reorganization demanded by the war."[9]

The progressives' speedy reconciliation with intervention shocked the young radical critic Randolph Bourne. Writing in the months after Wilson's war message, Bourne especially condemned Dewey and younger progressive thinkers for ignoring the awful realities of the conflict and identifying themselves with "the least democratic forces in American life." "There seems to have been a peculiar congeniality between the war and these men," Bourne charged. "It is as if the war and they had been waiting for each other."[10]

Bourne was right: the progressives needed the war effort, and the war effort needed them. Mobilization posed a gargantuan logistical and economic problem. The United States Army, only the seventeenth-largest in the world and armed with old weapons and a mere day-and-a-half of ammunition, had to be rapidly enlarged, trained, reequipped, and sent across the Atlantic to fight seasoned German troops in Europe. While meeting this daunting demand, the Wilson administration had to maintain the output of food and industrial products to make up for shortfalls by the war-ravaged economies of the Allies. Complicating matters still further, the federal government remained small and fairly weak at the outset of the war despite the years of progressive reform. "The United States was collectively—meaning the State—inefficient and unready . . . ," a progressive observed. "The best minds . . . were not in the State." The result was a halting, chaotic, and ineffective start to the mobilization that would have been comical but for the millions of homeless, hungry, or dying overseas. For instance, the military's bureau chiefs, blithely independent, scrambled to protect their turf and grab all the scarce supplies they could. Busy stockpiling twelve thousand typewriters in the basement, the adjutant general of the army crowed, "There is going to be the greatest competition for typewriters around here, and I have them all." By the winter, the mobilization was in crisis.[11]

To rescue the situation, Woodrow Wilson relied on a group of loyal, progressive associates. Secretary of War Newton D. Baker—the man on whose behalf those twelve thousand typewriters were squirreled away—was a diminutive, boyish, pipe-smoking reformer, deeply committed to purifying dance halls and taming greedy streetcar companies, who had served as the mayor of Cleveland. Secretary of the Navy Josephus Daniels was a plump, abstemious Virginia newspaper editor who favored women's suffrage as well as prohibition. Wilson's key economic policymaker was his tall, ambitious son-in-law—the "crown prince"—William Gibbs McAdoo, a Southerner who made his money as a promoter in New York. He made his reputation there as well by denouncing the city, in good progressive terms, as "the citadel of privilege . . . reactionary, sinister, unscrupulous, mercenary, and sordid."[12]

It was obvious to these men that the government had to become more unified and efficient—no more fighting over typewriters; as important, the government also had to control the economy, the source of typewriters. Wilson's war managers were ready to make use of existing government institutions, including McAdoo's Treasury Department. But the effort to control the economy required a sweeping expansion of federal bureaucracy. By 1918, a government handbook listed almost three thousand mostly new agencies engaged in the mobilization, including the Alimentary Paste War Service Committee and the Chalks and Crayons War Service Committee. In practice, a small core of critical organizations directed the economic war effort.[13]

At the very heart of the mobilization was the War Industries Board (WIB), charged with consolidating all procurement for the army, navy, and the Allies. The WIB emerged in July 1917 out of the Council for National Defense, one of the few federal agencies created to plan for mobilization before the war began. The new organization attempted to regulate the production of key war materials by making agreements with businessmen through nearly five hundred War Service Committees, established to represent particular industries from steel to corsets. With fuel supplies short, the railroads clogged, and the mobilization under fierce attack in March 1918, Wilson named Wall Street financier Bernard Baruch, a forceful, charismatic Jewish Democrat, to head the WIB. A loyal Wilsonsian, the nervous, good-natured Baruch seemed independent of the overwhelmingly Protestant and largely Republican upper ten of New York. "He made his money in Wall Street," explained his WIB colleague Grosvenor Clarkson, "but he took neither his politics nor his economics from it."[14]

Undeterred by the board's earlier struggles, Baruch advanced an ambitious vision for the agency: he and his colleagues identified essential priorities, promoted conservation of scarce resources, influenced prices on key commodities through participation in a Price Fixing Committee, and acted as purchasing agent for the Allies. "It was an industrial dictatorship without parallel—a dictatorship by force of necessity and common consent which step by step at last encompassed the Nation and united it into a coordinated and mobile whole . . . ," wrote Clarkson. "Individualistic American industrialists were aghast when they realized that industry had been drafted. . . ." To Clarkson, the "dictatorship" was a success that both proved the capability of government and reformed the economy. The WIB established that "the whole productive and distributive machinery of America could be directed successfully from Washington. . . ." Thanks to the board's work, "the huge, unwieldy, easy-going individualistic, careless Colossus of the North became an army from its coasts to its placid farms, and learned to put into its blow the whole weight of its incomparable strength."[15]

As the War Industries Board grappled with procurement issues across a wide range of economic activity, other new federal agencies focused on specific problems of the mobilization. Like the WIB, the Food Administration set priorities, promoted production, urged conservation, and attempted to set prices. Its director, the wealthy mining engineer Herbert Hoover, had become an international hero as chairman of the Commission for Relief in Belgium, the great humanitarian endeavor that shipped desperately needed food to the millions of Belgians and French caught in the onset of the Great War. Triumphantly returned to the United States in 1917, Hoover espoused the characteristic progressive critique of the nation's individualist heritage. "We have gone for a hundred years of unbridled private initiative in this country," he said, "and it has bred its own evils and one of these evils is the lack of responsibility in the American individual to the people as a whole. . . ." Hoover's new organization, first established on a voluntary basis in May 1917 and then authorized by Congress in August, functioned through a cadre of experts in Washington, a network of local agents around the country, and two corporations, the United States Grain Corporation and the Sugar Equalization Board, that stabilized prices for cereals, sugar, and coffee.[16]

In similar fashion, the Fuel Administration, created in August 1917, worked to maintain the availability of coal and other fuels. The Fuel Administrator was Harry A. Garfield, the son of the martyred president James A. Garfield and, most recently, the president of Williams College. A progressive, Garfield brought to the mobilization the typical belief in the necessity for association. "We have come to the parting of the ways, we have come to the time when the old individualistic principle must be set aside," he declared in 1917, "and we must boldly embark upon the new principle of cooperation and combination."[17]

Control of agriculture and industry meant little if products could not be transported. Even before the war, the Wilson administration secured the creation of the United States Shipping Board, which could build, commandeer, and operate ships. After American intervention, the government also created the Emergency Fleet Corporation to support the manufacture of badly needed vessels. The nation's railroads, unable to cope with the increased volume of traffic in wartime, provoked even more dramatic federal intervention. Late in 1917, Wilson created the U.S. Railroad Administration with the trusted McAdoo as director general and nationalized the roads as of January 1, 1918.[18]

The Wilson administration's economic agenda necessarily included labor, in some ways the most vital and volatile resource of all. The government had to have a reliable supply of soldiers without taking too many male workers out of critical war industries. An army filled with volunteers seemed much too haphazard. Accordingly, Washington resorted to conscription for the first time since the Civil War. Next to the death penalty, the military draft represents the state's most powerful denial of the autonomy of the individual. The administration was acutely aware that the imposition of the draft for the Union Army had produced bloody rioting in New York City in 1863. Nevertheless, Congress authorized what was tactfully labeled "Selective Service." "It has been an uphill fight to overcome the tradition of voluntaryism," the *New York Tribune* noted. "The idea that one may serve the State or not, as he pleases, had taken deep root in our easy going American individualism." Beginning in the summer of 1917, conscription provided the bulk of the 4.8 million men who served in the military during the war. Thanks to the careful use of draft deferments for workers, the Selective Service Administration managed to minimize the disruption of the most essential industries.[19]

To ensure a smooth mobilization, the Wilson government also needed to halt the class conflict of strikes and lockouts, the labor disruption that had long troubled progressives. Building on the example of special labor boards in some defense industries, the Wilson administration established the National War Labor Board, a typically progressive blending of representatives from organized labor, business, and the public under the direction of the secretary of labor, William Wilson. The NWLB attempted to mediate disputes on the basis of a labor code recognizing workers' rights to fair wages and hours and to collective bargaining. The administration also created a War Labor Policies Board, chaired by the progressive and future Supreme Court justice Felix Frankfurter, to set standards for federal agencies' employment of workers.[20]

The federal government's sway over the war economy did not end there. Partly through the War Trade Board and a host of subordinate bureaus, the Wilson administration closely controlled commerce. To ensure that business could borrow money for war production, the government established the War Finance Corporation, which made needed funds available through the Federal Reserve banks. To make sure that inessential industries did not compete for scarce funds, the government gained authority over private capital issues.[21]

Vastly increasing its own spending, the federal government also needed to take money out of the economy. Congress responded by raising funds through the sale of bond issues, the Liberty Loans, to the public. As progressives advocated, the government also increased taxes on corporations and the wealthy. The Revenue Act of 1917 imposed a top tax rate of 63 percent on the largest individual incomes and levied an excess profits tax on businesses.[22]

Even though the Wilson administration greatly expanded and employed the coercive power of the federal government, the war managers, in typical progressive fashion, preferred to manipulate or cajole, rather than strong-arm, the American people. Characterizing the War Industries Board as a "dictatorship," Grosvenor Clarkson nevertheless recognized that economic mobilization in the United States worked more often by manipulation and persuasion than by fiat. "What civilians did resentfully under compulsion elsewhere," he explained, "they here did cheerfully as a high privilege." Watching the WIB at work, the popular journalist Mark Sullivan grasped how progressives induced that sense of "privilege" in the nation's businessmen. "It was Baruch's pride, and the pride of the men he drew round him, to make a 'stunt' of getting the results without using the power," Sullivan reported. "[I]t was [a] confession of ineptness to be obliged to exert arbitrary authority, to say 'you must,'—they would be a little ashamed if any one knew of their doing anything that way." The men of the WIB certainly relished their authority: they called it "the big stick behind the closet door" and "the pistol in the hip pocket." Yet, as Sullivan concluded, "their zest was to keep the pistol concealed, the closet door locked. If ever tension approached the need of threat, the threat took the form not of reaching for the statutory stick, not of an arbitrary 'got to,' but rather of a gentle insinuation that the Board might bring the recalcitrant to the attention of public opinion, particularly the public opinion of his home community."[23]

The manipulative approach was well in evidence as Wilson's war managers resorted to another progressive device, the complex process of remaking individuals. The American war effort depended on the creation of a loyal patriotic populace, ready to endorse the war and do voluntarily the things necessary to win it. "It was a fight for the *minds* of men, for the 'conquest of their convictions,' and the battle-line ran through every home in every country," recalled the progressive journalist George Creel, who became the most important commander in the struggle. "What we had to have was no mere surface unity, but a passionate belief in the justice of America's cause that should weld the people of the United States into one white-hot mass instinct with fraternity, devotion, courage, and deathless determination."[24]

Creel and his colleagues, veterans of the many progressive campaigns to remake Americans, knew exactly what to do. "You can't make people good by law," Creel maintained. "You've got to change their environment. . . ." Drawing on all they had learned about changing people, the war managers set out to manipulate the physical and intellectual environment in order to produce a new, united citizenry. Not surprisingly, the loyal population the Wilson administration wanted to create was just the one the progressives had long envisioned: an essentially middle-class people who banished individualism, disciplined pleasure, eliminated class differences, and elevated women. "[I]n no sense is patriotism an instinct," Creel explained. "It cannot live side by side with a stark individualism that preaches the doctrine of every man for himself and devil take the hindmost."[25]

Although the war managers knew what to do, theirs was not a simple challenge. American intervention in the Great War had further split a people already deeply divided along social lines. Many Americans, particularly in the Midwest, doubted that the United States had fundamental interests at stake in the European conflict. Many so-called hyphenated Americans—first- and second-generation German-Americans and other ethnics with ties to the Central Powers—felt a natural uneasiness about joining the war against their homelands. The nation's socialists, largely working-class, typically condemned American intervention outright. It would take a good deal of work to create a uniformly loyal population.

The first step was to insulate Americans from antiwar ideas and people. Faced with so much popular hesitation about intervention, the Wilson administration had an obsessive fear of anything even approaching disloyalty—and a blunt determination to root it out. "Woe be to the man or group of men that seeks to stand in our way . . . ," Wilson warned in June 1917. Congress backed up the President's threat with a battery of legislation—the Alien Act, the Alien Enemies Act, the Espionage Act, the Sedition Act, the Selective Service Act, and the Trading with the Enemy Act—that gave the federal government sweeping powers to fine and jail anyone obstructing the war effort in any way. The Sedition Act, for instance, made illegal "uttering, printing, writing, or publishing any disloyal, profane, scurrilous, or abusive language about the United States government or the military." Government officials, such as the pompous, intolerant postmaster general Albert Burleson vigorously implemented the law. Dubbed the "Cardinal" by Wilson, Burleson zealously kept socialist publications out of the mails and effectively threatened the mailing privileges of any journal that even seemed to "impugn the motives of the government and thus encourage insubordination."[26]

Meanwhile, the government used its new authority to go after ostensibly radical individuals and organizations. A federal court sentenced the socialist leader and editor Victor Berger of Milwaukee to twenty years in jail. Another court condemned the labor leader and socialist presidential candidate Eugene V. Debs of Terre Haute, Indiana, to ten years in jail. Federal proceedings in Chicago, Kansas City, and Sacramento sent nearly two hundred members of the radical labor union, the International Workers of the World, to jail.

The government's efforts in turn encouraged local officials and private citizens to join in purging disloyalty. Around the country, a quarter of a million members of the American Protective League opened mail and bugged telephones to spy on suspected traitors and reported the results to Washington. Sometimes the APL took matters into its own hands. In the summer of 1917, members of the league, along with the sheriff of Bisbee, Arizona, detained over a thousand members of the IWW, transported them out of town, and left them in the desert without food or water. Around the country, zealous citizens forced those of suspect loyalty to kiss the flag and sometimes to buy Liberty Bonds as well. Other suspicious people were tarred and feathered, or painted yellow, and hauled out of town. Some were simply beaten. One German-American, Robert Prager, was lynched by a mob in Collinsville, Illinois, near St. Louis. "In spite of excesses such as lynching," editorialized *The Washington Post,* "it is a healthful and wholesome awakening in the interior of the country."[27]

As the Wilson administration made sure Americans would not be exposed to dangerous views, the government also tried to determine just what information and ideas the people would encounter. Soon after his war message, the President issued an executive order establishing the Committee on Public Information to publicize the war effort. George Creel became civilian chair of the new CPI. A passionate advocate of women's suffrage, an ardent supporter of Judge Ben Lindsey and the juvenile court movement, and a combative muckraker, Creel was a quintessential progressive. Like so many other activists, he yearned for an America as harmonious as the small towns where he had grown up in Gilded Age Missouri: "No dividing line between the rich and poor, and no class distinctions to breed mean envies." Creel saw the war as a critical opportunity to advance the progressive agenda, especially the battle against social differences. "When I think of the many voices that were heard before the war . . . interpreting America from a class or sectional or selfish standpoint, I am not sure that, if the war had to come, it did not come at the right time for the preservation and reinterpretation of American ideals," Creel maintained. "A decade or two later it might have found us unconsciously stratified in our own social organization and thinking, the prison-walks of class consciousness shutting out the visions of our nation's youth. . . ." In turn, Creel believed that progressivism, especially in the form of muckraking journalists' earnest exposure of truth, offered the best means of creating a loyal citizenry. Blatant propaganda and official lies would not work, Creel knew. "A free people cannot be told what to think," he declared. "They must be given the facts and permitted to do their own thinking."[28]

Calling on such fellow muckrakers as Ray Stannard Baker and Ida Tarbell, Creel turned the CPI into a relentless publicity machine for Wilson and the war effort. The agency churned out 75 million pamphlets, along with press releases and other publications. Creel employed 75,000 "Four-Minute Men," volunteer speakers ready to tell audiences in theaters and other places the facts about the war. Arthur Bestor, president of that cradle of progressive culture, Chautauqua, managed the Speaking Bureau. Charles Dana Gibson, creator of the Gibson Girl, oversaw the artists who produced posters and the rest of the "pictorial appeals" of the CPI.[29]

In the process, the CPI offered something different from "the simple, straightforward presentation of facts" that Creel promised. The Four-Minute Men, eager to enlist their audiences' emotion, soon began offering lurid tales of alleged German atrocities. Despite the "faith in fact," the CPI resorted to magazine advertisements. Despite the progressives' uneasiness about the medium of film, the CPI produced such sensationalist movie titles as *The Kaiser, the Beast of Berlin* and *The Prussian Cur.* Self-righteously renouncing "European" state censorship, Creel knew very well that other sections of the Wilson government were silencing antiwar sentiment. And he knew, too, that voluntary self-censorship worked quite well and risked less condemnation than did legalized muzzling. "[T]he desired results could be obtained without paying the price that a formal law would have demanded," he wrote candidly after the war. "Better far to have the desired compulsions proceed from within than to apply them from without."[30]

The Wilsonians devoted special attention to promoting loyalty among hyphenated Americans. "There is a wonderful chance in this country to weld the twenty-five or thirty races which compose our population into a strong, virile and intelligent people. . . . [A] splendid race of new Americans," enthused Alexander Whiteside, a leader of the Liberty Loan drive in New England. Various wartime campaigns to "Americanize" European ethnics naturally drew on the prewar efforts of settlement house workers and other progressives to reshape the lives of immigrants. Led by New York social worker Frances Kellor, the Committee for Immigrants in America joined with the Federal Bureau of Education to launch a "War Americanization Plan," including courses in English and citizenship. The CPI established a Division of Work with the Foreign-Born, which produced pamphlets and also monitored foreign-language newspapers and magazines for disloyalty.

For the war managers, almost any part of the war effort provided what Whiteside termed an "educational opportunity" to Americanize ethnics. "Liberty bonds are an excellent method of approach," he explained. "So is food conservation; . . . so is every other form of war activity."[31]

Like the broader campaign to purge disloyalty from the environment, the Americanization campaign had its more coercive and divisive side. Some of the conservative participants in Americanization, such as the Daughters of the American Revolution, were less interested in assimilating immigrants and, especially in the case of German Americans, more interested in obliterating their culture and guaranteeing their submission. Around the country, there were drives to stop the teaching of German in the schools, burn German books, ban German music, and, ludicrously, change German words and names. So, hamburger became liberty steak, and sauerkraut, liberty cabbage. In such an environment, German-Americans offered outward loyalty. The Germania Männerchor of Chicago renamed itself the Lincoln Club; the Deutsches Haus of Indianapolis became the Athenaeum of Indiana. Whether such outward conformity signaled the inner transformation that Creel and other progressives wanted was another matter.[32]

Drawing again on the progressive experience, Wilson's war managers focused on children in the effort to promote properly loyal thinking. To push learning in the right direction, the federal commissioner of education produced biased "war study courses" for the public schools. The federal government had plenty of help. State legislatures, local boards of education, and a host of civic groups joined in to make sure that pro-German materials did not find their way into the hands of children. Meanwhile, colleges and universities were drawn into the pro-war indoctrination, as well. At many campuses, administrators and faculty readily offered special "War Issues" courses that were little more than propaganda.[33]

In addition to promoting the cardinal virtue of loyalty, the progressive war managers worked hard to control the popular appetite for pleasure. Here, too, their progressive inclinations meshed smoothly with wartime necessity. The economic mobilization depended on Americans' willingness to limit their spending on products needed for the war and to use their funds instead to buy Liberty Bonds. Accordingly, the government and its supporters preached the virtues of conservation, thrift, and simplicity. The Conservation Division of the War Industries Board urged "the simple life" for a nation enjoying "the superfluity of luxury and taste" and displaying the "huge folds of fat of a luxurious civilization." One of those folds, interestingly enough, was the automobile, such a disruptive force in progressive America: the WIB needed the auto manufacturers to make trucks and other necessary military equipment instead. But the Conservation Division discovered indulgence everywhere, including the relative plainness of rural America. "Even so rugged and commonplace a thing as a farm wagon is frescoed with the differentiations of taste, custom, section, and makers' pride," the division found. "The farmer has wasted as much on a manure cart as a rich man on a limousine."[34]

Herbert Hoover's Food Administration similarly urged Americans to restrict their appetite for pleasure. Hoover himself passionately deplored the apparent waste and indulgence of the nation's eating habits. He decried the duplication of dining facilities—"the machinery of feeding"—between homes and restaurants; the evening "supper," he said, "is one of the worst pieces of extravagance that we have in this country." Rejecting the rationing of food, Hoover instead planned to pressure Americans to limit themselves voluntarily. "Above all," he later noted, "we knew that, although Americans can be led to make great sacrifices, they do not like to be driven." "We propose," Hoover explained, "to mobilize the spirit of self-denial and self-sacrifice in this country."[35]

So the Food Administration's Education Division exhorted the people to choose "meatless" and "wheatless" days. An avalanche of advertising drove home the message "FOOD WILL WIN THE WAR—DON'T WASTE IT." Half a million volunteers went door to door asking every man, woman, and child to sign pledge cards vowing support of the Food Administration and conservation. A special pledge card for children, "A Little American's Promise," vowed:

At table I'll not leave a scrap
Of food upon my plate.
And I'll not eat between meals but
For supper time I'll wait.
I make the promise that I'll do
My honest, earnest part
In helping my America
With all my loyal heart.

Toddlers who could not sign a pledge card had their own rewritten nursery rhymes:

Little Boy Blue, come blow your horn!
The cook's using wheat where she ought to use corn
And terrible famine our country will sweep,
If the cooks and the housewives remain fast asleep!
Go wake them! Go wake them! It's now up to you!
Be a loyal American, Little Boy Blue!

Before long, *Hooverize* became a verb meaning "to save or economize." And Hoover himself was aptly described as "the benevolent bogey of the nation." In all, the Food Administration effectively mobilized what it called the "compelling force of patriotic sentiment" in the name of thrift.[36]

For all the emphasis on voluntary conservation, the progressives were always willing to achieve their objectives at least in part through compulsion. The mobilization was a golden opportunity for advocates of prohibition, long the foremost progressive weapon in the war on pleasure. Prohibition was now a matter of conservation, since brewing and distilling used up precious grains. Prohibition was still more patriotic because brewers such as Busch, Pabst, and Schlitz so clearly had German roots. After approving a temporary ban on brewing and distilling in the summer of 1917, Congress passed the Eighteenth Amendment, which forbade the sale of alcoholic beverages, the following year. Eventually ratified by the states, prohibition became the law of the land in 1920.[37]

The Great War was a golden opportunity to press other longtime progressive projects for the remaking of Americans. To many progressives, the urgency of war made it all the more important to continue the transformation of social classes by restraining the wealthy and helping workers. For progressives, the wartime tax increases were an intensification of the effort to discipline the upper ten by shrinking and threatening their fortunes. The war effort offered other opportunities to rein in the rich. Seeking compliance from big-business men, the War Industries Board taught these men lessons in cooperative progressive values. Grosvenor Clarkson recounted with satisfaction how a particularly independent, defiant automaker, who had dared to insult WIB chairman Bernard Baruch, was brought to heel.

"No retort was made, but when his coal pile was ordered to be commandeered and the Railroad Administration refused him cars for any purpose, even for his Government business, and it came to his ears that he would soon be taking orders from a smooth-faced lieutenant, if permitted to remain in his own plant at all, he saw a great light," Clarkson reported. "He saw not only his folly, but also his selfishness. His submission was characteristically picturesque, and not wholly printable, but it was submission."[38]

Meanwhile, reformers used the war to push for better conditions for workers. "We cannot afford, when we are losing boys in France, to lose children in the United States at the same time . . . ," Newton D. Baker argued. "[W]e cannot afford, when this nation is having a drain upon the life of its young manhood . . . , to have the life of women workers of the United States depressed." Reformers and the War Labor Policies Board worked to ensure that protection for women workers did not decrease in wartime. When the Supreme Court overturned the Child Labor Act of 1916, reformers successfully pressed for a new law imposing a 10 percent tax on the products of child labor. Housing reform—one of the first progressive campaigns to manipulate workers' environment—also took a major step forward when the federal government used standards drafted by the pioneering tenement crusader Lawrence Veiller to organize numerous housing projects for war workers. In all, the war effort seemed to be advancing the progressives' mission to reduce class differences. "It is a quite thrilling aspect of the situation that just when in many different ways—including a cumulative tax on incomes—the principle is being established . . . that those who have much must reduce their scale of living, it is at the same time considered axiomatic that those whose standard is below normal must rise in the scale for the general good," concluded Robert Woods, the veteran social reformer and president of the National Conference of Social Workers. "We are like those that dream as we see the valleys begin to be exalted, the hills begin to be brought low. . . ."[39]

The war also advanced the status of women, a fundamental progressive goal. Although the number of employed women grew only modestly during the 1910s, the wartime departure of men for military service opened up jobs traditionally denied to women in offices, transportation, and industry. Leaving jobs as domestic servants, seamstresses, and laundresses, women became clerks, telephone operators, streetcar conductors, drill press operators, and munitions makers. Women's new prominence in the workforce led in turn to the creation of a Women's Bureau in the Department of Labor. "This is the woman's age!" exulted Margaret Dreier Robins, president of the Women's Trade Union League. "At last after centuries of disabilities and discriminations, women are coming into the labor and festival of life on equal terms with men."[40]

Women were coming into the polling place as men's equal, too. After struggling with weak leadership in the 1900s, the suffrage movement surged ahead in the 1910s. By 1913, women had full voting rights in nine states and partial rights in twenty-nine more. But defeats in a number of intensely fought state suffrage campaigns had led some suffragists to change strategies. Under the leadership of Quaker activist Alice Paul, the newly formed National Woman's Party focused on winning an amendment to the United States Constitution that would grant suffrage rights to women without the need for a grueling, frustrating state-by-state struggle. Paul and the Woman's Party also advocated more radical tactics for the suffrage movement. To put pressure on Woodrow Wilson, members of the Woman's Party began picketing the White House in January 1917. The declaration of war made the Wilson administration touchier about the pickets holding embarrassing signs that questioned democracy in America. More than two hundred pickets were arrested; some, declining to eat, were painfully force-fed. Meanwhile, women played a visible, important role in the war effort and staged vast suffrage parades. Seven more states granted women the vote in 1917 alone. Succumbing to the obvious trend, Wilson finally endorsed women's suffrage as "vital to winning the war" in September 1918. Congress adopted the Nineteenth Amendment, which was ratified in 1920.[41]

The war inevitably focused progressives' attention on one group they had previously ignored: soldiers. To some observers, military service promised to help erase the social differences that so troubled middle-class reformers. An enthusiastic congressman called the military "a melting pot which will . . . break down distinctions of race and class and mold us into a new nation and bring forth the new Americans." But military service also posed a threat. Reformers, including the progressive at the head of the War Department, feared that American boys would be corrupted at the nation's military bases even before they faced temptation "over there" in a decadent Europe. "[H]omesick soldiers" would be, Newton D. Baker warned, "easily led aside into unwholesome diversions and recreations, patronizing cheap picture shows, saloons, dance halls and houses of prostitution." It was imperative, then, to remake the values and beliefs of these men. In Baker's famous phrase, the soldiers needed to don "invisible armor" against temptation. "I want them," the earnest, fast-talking secretary of war explained, "to have an armor made up of a set of social habits replacing those of their homes and communities, a set of social habits and a state of social mind born in the training camps, a new soldier state of mind, so that when they get overseas and are removed from the reach of our comforting and restraining and helpful hand, they will have gotten such a set of habits as will constitute a moral and intellectual armor for their protection overseas."[42]

In response to Baker's call, progressive activists brought all their transformative powers to bear on the new recruits in the vast army cantonments set up around the country. A new Commission on Training Camp Activities, led by former settlement house worker Raymond Fosdick, worked with a host of civilian organizations, including the Red Cross, the YMCA, and the National Playground Association of America, to create a new environment in and around the cantonments. As in the broader loyalty campaign, the reformers labored to eliminate dangerous ideas and practices and then to establish wholesome environmental influences in their place—all so that the soldier would be, in Fosdick's slogan, "Fit to Fight." "No more bunny hugs or moonlight waltzes at public dance halls in Des Moines," reported the soldiers' newspaper at Camp Dodge, twelve miles away. "Jazz music must be toned down. Chaperones chosen from the federation of women's clubs will be appointed to serve each week." Aided by provisions of the Selective Service Act that authorized the President to ban alcohol and to arrest women around bases, the military closed down saloons and brothels near the cantonments.[43]

To replace the temptations of vice, social workers set up classes, sports, and group singing for soldiers. The *Official Army Song Book* included such approved songs as "All Hail the Power of Jesus' Name," "America, the Beautiful," "In an Old-Fashioned Town," and "Yaaka Hula Hickey Dula." As one historian put it, the Commission on Training Camp Activities "tried to create a massive settlement house around each army camp." In the process, Baker and the commission believed they would reform not only the soldiers but much of urban America as well. "[T]his work," the secretary of war prophesied, "is going to contribute not only to the strength of the army, making it vigorous and sound physically, mentally and morally, but it is going to advance the solution of that vexing and perplexing and troublesome city question which has for so many years hung heavy on the conscience of our country."[44]

Navy Secretary Josephus Daniels had already begun to impose his staunchly progressive views on naval life before Wilson's war message. A teetotaler, Daniels had ended officers' wine privileges aboard ship, and in the process had taught the navy's upper class a lesson. To uplift less fortunate working-class sailors, he had established off-duty schools for the illiterate and less educated. An advocate of women's rights, the secretary now oversaw the enrollment of more than eleven thousand female sailors and Marines—"yeomanettes" and "marinettes." Daniels welcomed the creation of a navy version of the Commission on Training Camp Activities, also headed by Raymond Fosdick. Doing its part to forge "invisible armor" in the port city of New Orleans, the navy forced the closing of the famed Storyville vice district, where so many pioneering jazz musicians played.[45]

Supplementing the efforts of the Commission on Training Camp Activities, other reformers used soldiers and sailors as a model of how government should protect workers and how men should meet their domestic obligations to women and children. Partly shaped by former Hull-House resident Julia Lathrop of the Children's Bureau, the Military and Naval Insurance Act of 1917 provided reeducation to disabled servicemen and compensation to them, as well as to the families of soldiers and sailors killed in the war. The measure also compelled each serviceman to deduct an allotment from his pay, enhanced by the government, for the support of his family back home.[46]

As the Military and Naval Insurance Act and other innovations took hold, progressive activists eagerly declared the war effort a success for themselves and for their broader project of transforming the nation. Staffing one new agency after another, they felt needed. "We scurry back and forth to the national capital; we stock offices with typewriters and new letterheads; we telephone feverishly, regardless of expense," a social worker happily reported. "It is all very exhilarating, stimulating, intoxicating." Social workers and social welfare organizations, declared Robert Woods, "have . . . in no slight degree provided the framework and motive power by which the civilian life of the nation has been brought together into a great system wholly unexampled in the history of the country."[47]

The progressives were sure, too, that this "great system" had changed American society. "Political shibboleths that men heeded in 1916 are as dead as the mummies of Egypt," insisted Josephus Daniels, "and public men who try to galvanize them will be interred in the catacombs that overlook Salt River." The deadest shibboleth of all was individualism. "[T]he great European war . . . is striking down individualism and building up collectivism," exulted George Perkins, the J. P. Morgan partner and ardent supporter of Theodore Roosevelt. "It is leveling class distinctions and recognizing in every direction that the rights of one must give way to the rights of many." The mobilization effort, Grosvenor Clarkson agreed, "is a story of the conversion of a hundred million combatively individualistic people into a vast cooperative effort in which the good of the unit was sacrificed to the good of the whole. . . ."[48]

In the process, so many other critical progressive causes had apparently succeeded as well. "[A]ll these things are now so possible, so well-nigh achieved," Robert Woods exclaimed, "—the regularization of employment, the establishment of a minimum status of well-being, the reduction of the favored classes to simplicity of life, the exercise of industrial conflict and the allaying of the hatreds of class, race and sect, the concentration of all minds and all interests upon the increase of the national product, the elimination of leisure except as a respite from labor. . . ." The fundamental progressive project of remaking human beings seemed that much more possible as well. The war effort, social worker Felix Adler believed, had brought the nation closer to the creation of "the perfect man," a "fairer and more beautiful and more righteous type than any . . . that has yet existed." Assessing the benefits of the war, Grosvenor Clarkson voiced the thought of many progressives. "[I]t almost," he concluded, "makes war appear a blessing instead of a curse."[49]

So eager to claim success, progressive activists tended to overlook serious shortcomings in their design for victory. Certainly the mobilization achieved its original purpose: the Allies won the war, which came to an end in

November 1918. But the war effort had not achieved a dramatic remaking of the population. Basically loyal, soldiers and civilians were not quite the new people the progressive war managers had envisioned.

Despite the efforts of the Commission on Training Camp Activities, many doughboys refused to put on their "invisible armor." Responding to a questionnaire about soldiers' off-duty activities, one doughboy simply wrote, "Wine, women and song." Another answered, "Some gambled, some drank, some women." Some soldiers angrily resented the attempt to reform them. "You ask us to give our lives for our beloved country, which we are only too willing to do—but you deprive us of the privilege of a glass of wine or beer even at our meals—and—most of all you deny us the freedom of our God-given rights of manhood!" an artillery officer wrote angrily to Newton D. Baker. "I have spoken with hundreds of men on these subjects and while they are willing to forgo all liquor simply because you request it, they feel that in being denied their sex instincts they are virtually held as slaves—not as freemen."[50]

A vigorous campaign to prevent venereal disease among the troops in France had only mixed results. "Those splendid fellows who fought their country's enemies so valiantly and successfully, failed utterly, in tremendous majority, when it came to fighting those other enemies that are constantly waiting to gain the mastery," admitted George Walker, one of the leaders of the campaign. "These are those natural enemies, the impulses that hide in the innermost reaches of the human soul, urging it to indulgence, with all sorts of hopes and promises of that fleeting thing, happiness, and binding it to the enduring consequences. . . . [O]f all the intangible elements of the human mechanism, the erotic impulse is the most to be dreaded, the most to be suspected, just as it is the hardest to control and the most exacting in the terrible payment it almost invariably exacts, once it gets the upper hand." In Bordeaux, Paris, Tours, and other French communities, U.S. military leaders had a hard time keeping prostitutes away from doughboys and a hard time, too, making bemused French military men understand why abstinence was important. It was not just that American soldiers indulged in vaginal intercourse with prostitutes. Worse, from Walker's perspective, the doughboys discovered "abnormal or perverted relations," by which he apparently meant anal intercourse. "It is the old, inescapable story of vice that is at first shunned, then condoned, then embraced," Walker lamented. "[T]he Americans in a very short time were indulging in perversions almost as willingly and as frequently as the French."[51]

Back home, the progressives had difficulty controlling civilians' impulses as well. There was a sense that the American people, flush with money, had succumbed to their appetites and had gratified their desires—not so much with prostitutes as with legal pleasures. The problem in the United States was not venereal disease but rather the spread of what one writer called the "infectious disease" of *"aristocratitis,"* especially among the middle class. This malady, he explained, manifested itself in a preoccupation with automobiles, oriental rugs, and fur coats. "[T]here are too many of us upon whom it has never dawned that middle class is precisely what we are," the commentator admitted. "Numerous very common folks are ludicrously trying to keep up the appearance of being aristocrats."[52]

The progressives themselves had contributed to "aristocratitis." Sharing the progressive ambivalence about pleasure, Wilson's war managers could not quite bring themselves to crack down fully on leisure and consumption. The War Industries Board, as Grosvenor Clarkson apologetically explained, had not halted or seriously limited many "inessential" industries because their products inspired Americans to work and fight hard. "Ice-cream and candy look like dispensable luxuries when men are dying for lack of shell steel," Clarkson noted, "but the driven worker in the roaring bays of factories is but human, and even in war-time he cannot be a Jack-of-all-work-and-no-play." Rahel Golub, tempted years before by the forbidden pleasure of penny candy, would probably have agreed. The same was true for soldiers. "The doughboys would not have gone very cheerfully to the front if they had thought that they were to return to an impoverished and disorganized homeland," Clarkson wrote. "Certainly there was no occasion for a dramatic sacrificial gesture . . . as was urged by the extreme 'forgodsakers,' to whom every soda fountain, ice-cream parlor, jewelry shop, candy store, automobile pleasure car agency, theater, movie-house, pie bakery, etc., was an offense."[53]

Overall, optimistic hopes for the creation of the "perfect man" went unrealized. "[W]e must dissipate the erroneous notion that the war has radically changed the average person's ideals and mode of life," one observer cautioned. "He merely lives the life he has lived. In spite of much shouting and of many programs there are no signs of the creation of a new social order or of an effective quickened sense of humanity."[54]

While the progressive design failed in some ways, it seemed all too successful in others. For some Americans, the enormous expansion of federal authority—conscription, economic controls, prohibition, the loyalty campaign—constituted an unwarranted invasion of individual and state's rights. Conservatives angrily labeled the wartime government dictatorial and autocratic. "With the entry into the war our government was practically turned into a dictatorship," a Harvard instructor complained. "Executive agencies which were responsible only to the chief magistrate and which exercised the most pervasive and inquisitorial authority over citizens were suddenly brought into being." He insisted that "our war experience should shake us out of the fetish worship of governmental machinery into which some of us seem to have slipped."[55]

Journalist Mark Sullivan sweepingly summed up the conservative case against the progressive mobilization. "Of the effects of the war on America, by far the most fundamental was our submission to autocracy in government," Sullivan maintained. "Every male between 18 and 45 had been deprived of freedom of his body. . . . Every person had been deprived of freedom of his tongue, not one could utter dissent from the purpose or the method of war. . . . Every business man was shorn of dominion over his factory or store, every housewife surrendered control of her table, every farmer was forbidden to sell his wheat except at the price the government fixed. . . . The prohibition of individual liberty in the interest of the state could hardly be more complete." To Sullivan, the war had reversed the course of history. "It was the greatest submission by the individual to the state that had occurred in any country at any time. It was an abrupt reversal of the evolution that had been under way for centuries. . . . Now in six months, in America the state took back, the individual gave up, what had taken centuries of contest to win."[56]

Many Americans in 1918 may not have cared much whether the work of centuries had been undone. But they did resent particular burdens and sacrifices that the wartime government imposed on them. Businessmen were predictably angry at Washington's incursion into every phase of their affairs. The wealthy fulminated against the income tax. Some consumers disliked the pressure to cut back on meat and wheat. Many rural Americans, with their strong culture of independence, detested conscription, especially for such a dubious cause.[57]

Many Americans seemed willing to put up with both American intervention and government-imposed restrictions and sacrifices. But people were less willing to accept the unanticipated economic consequences of the Wilsonian mobilization. Ordinary Americans had generally viewed the income tax as a levy intended for the rich. The cost of the war, however, forced the Wilson administration to draw the middle class into the tax structure. The Revenue Act of 1917 imposed taxes on incomes as low as a thousand dollars a year. Moreover, the war set off the worst inflation in many years. Businesses could not keep up with consumer demand, in part because the excess-profits tax made it harder for them to invest in new productive capacity. Treasury Secretary McAdoo, the Crown Prince, made things worse with policies that vastly increased the money supply. The result was a 102 percent rise in the cost of living from 1914 to 1920—and a great deal of complaining about HCL, the "High Cost of Living." Wheat and pork producers particularly resented inflation because Hoover's Food Administration had worked to hold down the prices of their products. But all groups, including the progressives' middle-class constituency, resented HCL. "It is unquestionably the middle class that were the chief victims of the war-time high cost of living," a writer claimed. "Ministers perhaps suffered as badly as anybody. Thousands of capable middle-aged men left the teaching profession, discouraged and in many cases embittered. . . . Civil service employees had cause to worry, too; in fact, all salaried employees."[58]

To many middle-class Americans, the Wilson government's labor policy had made HCL still worse. As in the past, when employers and unions managed to settle their differences as the progressives wanted them to do, the middle class nevertheless complained about the resulting price increases of consumer goods and services. Senator Hiram Johnson of California, a staunch supporter of the government takeover of the railroads, was appalled by how much it cost in higher wages and higher freight rates. The federal government's largesse was "outrageously generous to the railroads and shamefully unjust to the people." While big business and labor flourished, the progressive ranted, "God pity the forgotten middle class who foot the bill!" Johnson was calm enough to assess the consequences of middle-class unhappiness for the progressive agenda: the prospect of government ownership, he admitted, "has been postponed for a couple of generations."[59]

HCL was not the only unintended consequence of the mobilization. At point after point, the war managers' policies appeared to unleash the very forces that progressives had long sought to control. After the armistice, America seemed to be a society in chaos.

For all the Wilsonians' attempts to mediate labor differences during the war, the conflict contributed to an extraordinary surge in labor militancy. Thanks to the strong demand for workers in the war economy, unions flourished. The American Federation of Labor saw its membership soar from 2.6 million in 1916 to 5 million in 1920. After patriotically holding its demands in check during the war, the labor movement wanted to push its agenda in the postwar—the more so because HCL was eating into the income of its membership. In 1919, there were 2,600 strikes nationwide—the most in a single year in American history to that point. In Seattle, a shipyard strike in January escalated into a citywide general strike by 60,000 that tied up the community in February. In April, 8,000 New England telephone operators, mostly women, struck for higher wages and recognition of their union. In August, members of the fledgling Actors Equity walked out on audiences in several New York City theaters. As Broadway stars Eddie Cantor, Marie Dressler, and Ethel, Lionel, and John Barrymore walked the picket lines of the union and George M. Cohan helped bankroll the employers' opposition, the strike spread to other cities before producers caved in, accepted collective bargaining, and granted the eight-performance week. In September, about 250,000 steel workers started a nationwide strike for recognition of their union and better working conditions. Bituminous coal workers walked out in November, but the steel strike collapsed in January with twenty men killed, more than $100 million in wages lost, and no concessions from the steel magnates.[60]

As class conflict seemed to surge out of control, another progressive mainstay—the system of racial segregation—appeared to crack as well. The Wilson administration, built on the support of white Southern Democrats, had no inclination to tinker with the racial status quo. The nation's 367,000 black troops faced persistent discrimination and denigration. But the fact that some of those troops were armed and fought well was upsetting for Southern whites. Thanks to the availability of jobs in booming war industries, the black migration to the North continued to swell. The African-American population of Chicago, Milwaukee, and other cities increased dramatically. That was troubling for white Southern employers who lost cheap black labor; it was also troubling for white Northern workers who feared African-American competition. The result was a chain of race riots, largely instigated by the white working class. In East St. Louis, Illinois, in July 1917, thirty-nine blacks and nine whites died in rioting mainly fomented by white labor leaders eager to rid the city of African-American workers. The next year there were deadly riots in Chicago, Houston, and other cities; in 1919, the number of urban race riots reached twenty-five. Ominously, the Ku Klux Klan, reborn on Stone Mountain, Georgia, in 1915, began to grow rapidly.[61]

The Klan surged in part because it now condemned white immigrants as well as blacks. One of the largely unintended consequences of the fervent wartime campaigns to Americanize foreigners and promote "one hundred percent Americanism" was an increase in nativism. Rather than push to segregate immigrants, the Klan and many Americans now supported outright immigration restriction. Just before U.S. entry into the war in 1917, Congress finally passed the controversial literacy test for immigrants. By 1921, Congress was ready to pass a restriction bill that capped immigration and set especially low quotas on migration from Eastern and Southern Europe.[62]

Finally, the Wilson administration failed to contain its loyalty campaign. With the ascendancy of the Bolsheviks in Russia's November Revolution of 1917, Americans faced a new regime that condemned capitalism, opposed private property, and had abandoned the Allies to pursue a separate peace with Germany. Their imaginations fired by lurid stories of communist barbarism in Russia, many Americans equated "Bolshevism" with radicalism and treason. The Bolshevik revolution became yet one more reason to denounce domestic troublemakers such as the socialists and IWW. So, communist rule was described as a "compound of slaughter, confiscation, anarchy and universal disorder . . . the paradise of IWW's and the superlative heaven of anarchists and direct-action Socialists." The fear of Bolshevism only intensified with the formation of the Communist Labor and the American Communist parties in 1919.[63]

By then, the whole superheated postwar atmosphere—the pressures of HCL, race riots, strikes, and intolerance—had produced a frenzied, largely irrational search for Bolsheviks in America. "Not within the memory of living Americans, nor scarcely within the entire history of the nation, has such a wave of fear swept over the public mind as occurred during the twelve or fifteen months following the armistice," an observer noted. The wave gained strength just before May Day 1919, when unknown individuals or groups mailed bombs to the staunchly antilabor mayor of Seattle, Ole Hanson, and other public figures, including Supreme Court Justice Oliver Wendell Holmes, Jr.; Postmaster General Burleson; John D. Rockefeller; and J. P. Morgan, Jr. In Boston, New York, Cleveland, and elsewhere, angry soldiers and civilians broke up socialist parades and meetings in retaliation. A month later, there were bombings at various places around the country, including the Washington home of U.S. Attorney General A. Mitchell Palmer.[64]

In response, the "Red scare" became still more intense. Passions were fanned by probusiness organizations, including the elite and increasingly conservative and antiradical National Civic Federation, the American Defense Society, and the National Security League, which was supported by Rockefeller and Morgan. Business organizations such as the National Association of Manufacturers used the scare as an excuse to attack labor as Reds and Bolsheviks and to call for the open shop. The newly formed American Legion, already 650,000 strong by the fall, eagerly supported the anti-Bolshevik campaign and fed the popular hysteria; so did the Ku Klux Klan.

Government played a key role in the antiradical frenzy. State Senator Clayton Lusk of New York held well-publicized hearings on Bolshevism and equally well-publicized raids on supposed nests of radicals. Spurred by fear of Bolshevism and hope for the Democratic presidential nomination in 1920, A. Mitchell Palmer began a federal counterattack. On August 1, he created the General Intelligence Division, led by the zealous young J. Edgar Hoover, to ferret out dangerous radicalism. In November, Palmer staged raids nationwide on the Union of Russian Workers. Several hundred members of this anarchist organization were arrested in twelve cities. Around the country, state and local officials were inspired to stage similar raids. Basking in adulation, Palmer shipped 249 deportees, mostly members of the URW, to the Soviet Union on an army transport ship, the *Buford,* in December. There was no legal basis for deporting most of the passengers on the vessel dubbed the "Soviet Ark." In January, Palmer ordered further raids, which scooped up more than 4,000 supposed radicals in thirty-three cities across twenty-three states. The attorney general promised more Soviet arks would sail soon. That same month, the New York State legislature refused to seat five duly elected socialists.

The chaos of the Red scare, race riots, strikes, and inflation became the menacing backdrop for a struggle to determine the direction of postwar America. With a nod to the nation's experience after the Civil War, Americans debated the coming "Reconstruction" of their nation after this new and terrible Great War. Many progressive activists, confident despite the tribulations around them, wanted to continue to use their blueprint for the country. Pointing to the accomplishments of the wartime regime, Robert Woods asked naively, "[W]hy should it not always be so? Why not continue on into the years of peace this close, vast, wholesome organism of service, of fellowship, of creative power?"[65]

The progressives were in a bad position to win the debate. Already weakened by all the complaining about the war effort, reformers found themselves badly damaged by the Red scare. Businessmen and conservatives quickly learned to denounce progressive academics, churchmen, and journalists as "parlor Bolsheviks." As a bit of ironic verse emphasized, progressives became prime targets of hysteria:

. . . So when I disagree with you I'll call
you Bol-she-vik! veek! veek!
It's a scream and it's a shriek;
It's a rapid-fire response to any
heresy you squeak.

You believe in votes for women? Yah!
the Bolsheviki do.
And shorter hours? And land reforms?
They're Bolshevistic too. . . .

Bolshevik! veek! veek!
A reformer is a freak!
But here's a name to stop him, for it's
like a lightning streak. . . .[66]

Peace advocates such as Jane Addams found themselves particular targets of the Red scare. Addams's wartime speeches on behalf of the Food Administration, the CPI, and Liberty Bonds made no difference: she was branded a radical and a Bolshevik. In January 1919, Addams was first on a list of sixty-two individuals supposedly holding "dangerous, destructive and anarchistic sentiments" that an employee of the Military Intelligence Division of the War Department provided to a subcommittee of the U.S. Senate. Newspaper headlines turned her into a radical caricature: "Jane Addams in Movement to Uphold Lenine [sic]"; "Reds Upheld by Jane Addams as Good Americans." Her income from writing and lecturing fell. "My dear Miss Addams, believe me," a letter writer told her, "you are an awful ass, truly awful."[67]

It was a stunning fall from grace for the woman so long seen as the incarnation of saintly goodness. "In America in 1912 it was unsafe to mention Jane Addams' name in a public speech unless you were prepared for an interruption, because the mere reference to her provoked such a storm of applause," a British visitor noted. "[A]fter the war . . . I realized with a shock how complete was the eclipse of her fame . . . her popularity had swiftly and completely vanished. . . . How well I remember . . . the silence that greeted the name of Jane Addams!"[68]

Many of her progressive colleagues and friends were part of that silence. If so revered a figure as Addams was vulnerable, other progressives felt vulnerable too, and kept quiet: that was how the Red scare, like McCarthyism years later, worked. Even before the Red scare, reformers had shied away from defending the pacifist activists and politicians who opposed the war. "Many of us," wrote Chicago lawyer and reformer Donald Richberg, "now can look back upon the heroic efforts of men like La Follette and Norris in the Senate . . . , of women like Jane Addams, and feel a little small and ashamed that, even if we did not join with those who scowled and spat upon them . . . yet we watched them through troubled, puzzled eyes." Their silence, Richberg realized, hastened the end of progressivism as a vital force in American life. "Thus we prepared for the final dissolution of the progressive movement," he admitted. "To doubt, to question the wisdom of the powers that be, to advance new and disturbing ideas, had ceased to be an act of virtue, the proof of an aspiring spirit. Such attitudes were 'radical' and 'destructive.'" With the Red scare, things only got worse. "Progressivism," Richberg noted, "was losing its supreme asset—respectability."[69]

Partly as a result, the progressives found themselves without powerful political champions. Woodrow Wilson, preoccupied with the organization of the postwar world, did little to shape reconstruction policy before the armistice. Increasingly eager to win Senate approval for the Versailles treaty, with its provision for a League of Nations, Wilson needed the votes of conservatives who deplored the progressive agenda. The President, meanwhile, felt the full force of the popular backlash against the progressive war effort. In the elections just days before the end of the war, his party lost control of both houses of Congress. The Republicans, a Democratic congressman from Nebraska told the White House, benefited "from the disgruntled, namely, the man peeved because he was short of help, the man opposed to the draft, the man forced to buy bonds and contribute to war activities against his will, and the man pinched by the income tax. . . ."[70]

The political logic was plain: in his annual message to Congress at the beginning of December 1918, the President repudiated the progressive approach to reconstruction. "Our people . . . do not wait to be coached and led," Wilson asserted. "They know their own business, are quick and resourceful at every readjustment, definite in purpose, and self-reliant in action." Given the nature of the American people, an aggressive reconstruction policy would have been ineffective and divisive. "Any leading strings we might seek to put them in would speedily become hopelessly tangled because they would pay no attention to them and go their own way," the President predicted. "[F]rom no quarter have I seen any general scheme of 'reconstruction' emerge which I thought it likely we could force our spirited business men and self-reliant labourers to accept with due pliancy and obedience."[71]

Before long, Wilson was utterly consumed by his quixotic quest for the League of Nations, his health shattered by a stroke, his political fortunes destroyed. But he had already abandoned the progressive movement in the eventful month of November 1918. The government quickly dismantled almost all of the wartime agencies and boards. "Can anyone," Walter Lippmann inquired bitterly, "name a single piece of constructive legislation and administration carried through since the armistice?"[72]

With Wilson useless, the progressive activists had nowhere to turn. The charismatic Robert La Follette still suffered from his opposition to the war. The progressives' old hero, Theodore Roosevelt, was gone. An ardent advocate of American intervention in the war, he had gotten his "heart's desire" only to have his beloved son Quentin shot down in the sky over France in July 1918. Six months later, prematurely aged, Theodore Roosevelt was dead at sixty. "I could only press my face into the pillow and cry like a child," Donald Richberg confessed. "There were many others who wept that day."[73]

As early as September 1917, Randolph Bourne had anticipated the outcome. In one of his essays, he suggested a fundamental irony of the war for the United States. In Europe, the conflict was sweeping away old regimes, those doddering monarchies of another age, and would lead to a collectivist future. But in America, the war would undermine the new regime, progressivism, and point the nation back toward its individualist, conservative past. "[A]lthough it becomes more and more evident that, whatever the outcome of the war, all the opposing countries will be forced to adopt German organization, German collectivism, and have indeed shattered already most of the threads of their old easy individualism, we," Bourne despaired, "have taken the occasion rather to repudiate that modest collectivism which was raising its head here in the shape of the progressive movement in national politics." What was canny intuition in 1917 became obvious reality by 1919 and 1920. "We have come to the conclusion that there isn't going to be any radical, quick reconstruction in America," admitted the progressive Henry Bruère. "The tendency is toward reaction back to pre-war conditions."[74]

The presidential election of 1920 made the nature of that reaction clear. What should have been a progressive triumph—the first national contest under women's suffrage—marked instead the reemergence of political conservatism after years of defeat and demoralization. Saddled with Wilson's record and his insistence on the unpopular League of Nations, the Democrats had little chance of victory. The party nominated a weak ticket led by Governor James Cox of Ohio, a newspaper publisher with a modest progressive reputation and equally modest political skills. His running mate was Assistant Secretary of War Franklin Roosevelt, a handsome, genial cousin of Theodore Roosevelt with apparently little substance.[75]

The Republican ticket was hardly more imposing. Like Cox, the Republican presidential nominee, Senator Warren G. Harding, was an Ohio newspaper publisher. Like Roosevelt, the tanned Harding was handsome and seemingly insubstantial. The Republican vice presidential nominee, Governor Calvin Coolidge of Massachusetts, had gladdened the hearts of businessmen and other conservatives the year before by calling in troops to stop a strike by police in Boston. But the Republicans did not need much of a ticket to win in 1920. With astute management by party chairman Will Hays and pioneering ad man Albert Lasker, the Grand Old Party made the most of the Wilsonians' debacle.

Predictably, Republican orators portrayed the horrors of a society in chaos, disordered by war and Wilsonianism. "In the shock of war, through long years of bitter conflict, moral restraints were loosened and all the habits, all the conventions, all the customs of life, which more even than law hold society together, were swept aside," Senator Henry Cabot Lodge insisted. "In the name of democracy we established autocracy," Harding said flatly. The war administration, contended the Republican nominee, indulged in "extravagance" and introduced "the withering hand of government operation" into the economy. A speaker at the Republican convention summed up the results. "Under the weak hands of a timorous government the social disorders and class-minded isms caught from the world-struggle have grown to alarming proportions," this Kansas Republican lamented. He offered a catalog of the resulting evils: "The unchecked encroachment of sinister greed, the appalling waste of public money, the immoral pandering to class interest and class prejudice. . . ."[76]

It was easier for the Republicans to attack the progressive war effort than to detail an alternative vision. In a famous phrase, Harding vaguely promised the nation "not nostrums, but normalcy." What normalcy meant was not yet clear. But the Republicans definitely wanted a return to a more individualistic society. Gradually during the war and its aftermath, Republican leaders had begun to rehabilitate that progressive anathema, "individualism." "What is the source of American power?" asked the conservative Elihu Root. "I undertake to say it is not American wealth or American laws. It is the individual character of each unit of the hundred millions of the American people." For Root, victory in World War I was the result of individuals, not of organizations and the state: "Our part of this war was won by the American private in arms and by the American private, man and woman, creating the material supplies and furnishing the moral power behind the American private in arms." These "privates" were successful, in Root's view, not because of the Commission on Training Camp Activities or other progressive programs. "It was the individual soldier, because the practice of liberty and the individual character created by independent manhood, that knew no superior, made the strongest manhood in the world for the winning of this War." In the 1920 campaign, Harding and Coolidge confidently celebrated individualism. "The group must not endanger the individual . . . ," Harding lectured. The government's "abiding purpose has been the recognition of the rights and the development of the individual," Coolidge added. "To the individual has been left power and responsibility, the foundation for the rule of the people."[77]

Despite these bold claims for individualism, the Republicans were cautious as they confronted the progressivism that had held sway for a generation. Harding, Coolidge, and the rest sensed what despairing progressives did not—that the nation would not abandon progressivism and its ideas completely. There would be no return to 1914, Calvin Coolidge promised. "That day is gone." Harding even called himself a "rational progressive," a neat term suggesting at once how much the reputation of progressivism had suffered and how much progressivism still counted. In the same way, Republicans carefully qualified their individualism. They called themselves "new individualists." Herbert Hoover, one of the chief interpreters of that new individualism, took to describing himself as "an American individualist" and his creed as "progressive individualism."[78]

Like "normalcy," the "new individualism" was an uncertain commodity. But it was enough. Harding and Coolidge won in a landslide that made the progressives' predicament unambiguously clear. "We're in about the rottenest period of reaction that we have had in many years," Hiram Johnson sadly confided to a friend. "What a God damned world!" swore the progressive Republican newspaper editor William Allen White.[79]

Republican conservatives were just as sure that God had in fact blessed the world—or at least America—once again. "The radicalism which had tinged our whole political and economic life from soon after 1900 to the World War period was passed," Calvin Coolidge contentedly observed. "There were still echoes of it, and some of its votaries remained, but its power was gone." Looking back years later, Coolidge explained that "the demobilization of the country was practically complete, people had found themselves again, and were ready to undertake the grand work of reconstruction in which they have since been so successfully engaged." Caught up in the joy of that moment, Coolidge—taciturn in public, acerbic in private—allowed himself to talk like a progressive. "In that work we have seen the people of America create a new heaven and a new earth," Coolidge rhapsodized. "The old things have passed away, giving place to a glory never before experienced by any people of our world." For many years, it was the progressives who had imagined utopia—"a new heaven and a new earth"—

and summoned the nation to build it. Now Coolidge and the conservatives claimed the right to dream and lead. The "old things" had indeed "passed away": progressive ideas would linger, occasional progressive legislation would still pass; but the Progressive Era was over.[80]

Conclusion

The 1920s were, Jane Addams sadly concluded, "a period of political and social sag." Progressive activists achieved a few victories such as the Sheppard-Towner Act of 1921, which provided modest federal funds to support instruction in hygiene for expectant and new mothers. But reformers by and large had to sit back and watch the Republican administrations of Warren G. Harding, Calvin Coolidge, and Herbert Hoover pursue a politics of individualism and laissez-faire. Influenced by his experiences in the Wilson government, Hoover tried to promote collaborative "association" between government and businessmen. Yet, essentially the Republicans gutted the economic accomplishments of the Progressive Era by cutting the hated income tax, ignoring organized labor and the poor, and allowing big business to dominate federal regulatory agencies. The 1920s made clear that the progressives had seriously overestimated the power and the will of the state to limit corporations.[1]

Reformers also found themselves increasingly alienated from middle-class culture. The emphasis on individual freedom and the pursuit of pleasure, especially among the young, left aging progressives disappointed and even aghast. Charlotte Perkins Gilman bemoaned "the lowering of standards in sex relations, approaching some of the worst periods in ancient history. . . . [N]ow the very word 'chastity' seems to have become ridiculous." George Creel fumed at "the fustian that children must be permitted to 'express' themselves without a hint of parental interference." "Children *have* to be trained, just as gardens have to be weeded," said the master manipulator of the Committee on Public Information. Jane Addams, too, was deeply disturbed by the younger generation's "astounding emphasis upon sex" and "their sense of release and their new confidence in self-expression." Youth, she charged, had "gone back to liberty for the individual." As a result, they lacked "reforming energy."[2]

It was all immensely dispiriting. "Few indeed are the progressives of my generation who have survived the bludgeoning of these years," sighed Donald Richberg in 1930. "Death and defeat and discouragement have taken most of them out of the public service."[3]

Then the progressives got a reprieve. The shocking stock market crash of 1929 and the ensuing Great Depression destroyed the Republican regime and its laissez-faire political economy. Franklin Roosevelt's triumphant New Deal, intent on regulating big business and helping the weak, seemed to be working from the old progressive blueprints. A veteran of the Wilson era, Franklin Roosevelt clearly cherished his progressive roots. His administration summoned many an old progressive: George Creel, Josephus Daniels, Cordell Hull, Harold Ickes, Donald Richberg. From seats in Congress, William Gibbs McAdoo, George Norris, and others voted for New Deal measures. "Once again, as in the days of Theodore Roosevelt and Woodrow Wilson, the progressive forces of the nation were massed in phalanx formation," Creel initially exulted, "and everywhere people had thrown off apathy and were aflame with enthusiasm for the New Deal and its drive against every evil that menaced the democratic process."[4]

Yet, surprisingly, many of the surviving progressive activists supported Roosevelt and the New Deal only reluctantly. The majority, in fact, opposed the Democratic regime of the 1930s and 1940s. Casting her last presidential ballot in 1932, Jane Addams voted for Herbert Hoover. After a look at the inside of the Roosevelt administration, George Creel became perhaps the most fevered progressive opponent of the President, the New Deal, and the liberal creed generally. "'Liberalism!' he spat. "Not in all history has a word been so wrenched away from its true meaning and dragged through every gutter of defilement."[5]

Today, it is hard to believe that a majority of progressives actively opposed FDR—but they did. Their critique gives us a glimpse as to why liberal politics—indeed, *all* politics—has been disappointing ever since the Progressive Era. Creel and other progressives criticized Roosevelt and his followers for going too far in increasing the size of the federal government, intruding in the economy, and catering to organized labor.[6]

At the same time, old progressives disliked New Deal liberalism for not going far enough. They rightly sensed what historians have too often ignored—the degree to which Roosevelt abandoned key elements of progressivism. Brilliant politician that he was, FDR learned from the debacles of the Wilsonian war government and the 1920 presidential election. In particular, he recognized that the progressives paid a heavy price for their bold attempts to reshape personal identity. As President, Roosevelt largely avoided the rhetoric of personal transformation. He sensed that most Americans wanted the federal government to limit the individualism of the big businessmen whom his cousin Theodore had once called "malefactors of great wealth" and whom he branded "economic royalists." And FDR knew, better than the old progressives, how much the people were eager for Washington to help ensure their prosperity. But, like the Republicans of the 1920s, he realized that most Americans wanted to be left free to pursue pleasure, to indulge in the individual gratification of consumerism. The task of government was to make sure Americans could afford pleasure, and then get out of the way.[7]

Tellingly, one of Roosevelt's first acts as President in 1933 was to support the repeal of prohibition, the ultimate symbol of the progressives' attempts to constrain individualism and pleasure. Explaining his position the year before, Roosevelt termed prohibition a "complete and tragic failure" caused by "this very good reason: we have depended too largely upon the power of governmental action. . . ." Unlike many committed progressive activists, Roosevelt understood that liberalism needed to strike a new balance between the individual and the state. "We know," he declared, "that the old 'rights of personal competency,' the right to read, to think, to speak, to choose and live a mode of life, must be respected at all hazards." For all the growth of federal regulatory power during the 1930s and 1940s, Roosevelt's New Deal was less ambitious than the progressives' bold bid to create the middle-class paradise. The reformers of the late nineteenth and early twentieth centuries were prepared to use a host of coercive and manipulative practices in order to transform diverse Americans into middle-class people. Abandoning much of the coercion and manipulation, the New Deal focused on making it possible for people to share the pleasures of consumption. Roosevelt himself underscored the difference in ambition when he mentioned his old boss, Woodrow Wilson, during a campaign speech in 1932. "It is interesting, now, to read his speeches," Roosevelt observed. "What is called 'radical' today (and I have reason to know whereof I speak) is mild compared to the campaign of Mr. Wilson."[8]

The future was less radical still. In the late 1940s and early 1950s, the start of the Cold War built up the power of the federal government and set off a new Red scare that rivaled the original as a means of enforcing conformity. But the determination to fight the Cold War was not accompanied by any consuming desire to reform America. In the 1960s, Lyndon Johnson did want to reform the nation and make it a "Great Society." Like the progressive movement, the liberal Great Society increased federal regulatory power over the economy for the protection of consumers and the environment, moved to ameliorate poverty, promoted and influenced the education of children, and expanded social welfare programs. Following the grudging efforts of John F. Kennedy, Johnson moved dramatically to end the segregation and disfranchisement of blacks that progressives had helped to put in place. But the leaders of the Great Society had no progressive illusions about dismantling corporations, transforming Americans' identity, and making a middle-class paradise. Seeking an end to the culture and practice of segregation and to lift the very poor out of poverty, the Johnson administration did not otherwise try to convert the whole range of Americans into new, middle-class people or to discipline leisure and pleasure in any fundamental way. Johnson and his followers sought a Great Society, not a utopia.[9]

Johnson's Great Society resembled the progressive movement in another way: the reform movement of the 1960s also produced social chaos. The race riots and antiwar demonstrations, the failure of the "war on poverty," and the high inflation and deindustrialization of the 1960s and 1970s all reinforced the basic lesson of the Progressive Era that reformers should not try too much. And like the travails of the progressive movement at the end of World War I, the Great Society's crisis helped rehabilitate conservatism. The New Right, built on the celebration of individual freedom and the condemnation of government activism, rose swiftly from Barry Goldwater's landslide loss in the 1964 presidential election to Ronald Reagan's first presidential victory in 1980. But the ensuing "Reagan Revolution" attempted comparatively little and achieved less: big government remained intact, the right to abortion remained in place. Like the apostles of both Red scares, the conservatives of the 1980s attacked the things they did not like: the supposed values of the 1960s, homosexuality, secular humanism, and so on. But the Reaganites never undertook an elaborate campaign to re-create Americans' identity along conservative lines. The Reagan era was a revolution only in name.[10]

As the "war on terrorism" continues to take shape, we wonder how much this unconventional battle will transform the nature of American society. But it seems unlikely that the exigencies of the struggle will encourage American leaders to undertake anything as ambitious as the progressives' "great work of reconstruction." That prospect is at once a disappointment and a relief.

Notes

Preface

1. Progressivism, long at the center of historians' interest in the American past, has had many different and distinguished interpreters. Among the most significant studies of progressivism are Daniel Aron, *Men of Good Hope: A Story of American Progressives* (New York, 1951); Eric Goldman, *Rendezvous with Destiny: A History of Modern American Reform* (New York, 1952); Richard Hofstadter, *The Age of Reform: From Bryan to F.D.R.* (New York, 1955); Gabriel Kolko, *The Triumph of Conservatism: A Reinterpretation of American History, 1900–1916* (New York, 1963); James Weinstein, *The Corporate Ideal in the Liberal State* (Boston, 1968); Robert H. Wiebe, *The Search for Order, 1877–1920* (New York, 1967); David P. Thelen, *The New Citizenship: Origins of Progressivism in Wisconsin, 1885–1900* (Columbia, MO, 1972); John D. Buenker, *Urban Liberalism and Progressive Reform* (New York, 1973); John Morton Blum, *The Republican Roosevelt*, 2nd ed. (Cambridge, MA, 1977); Richard L. McCormick, *The Party Period and Public Policy: American Politics from the Age of Jackson to the Progressive Era* (New York, 1986); Nell Irvin Painter, *Standing at Armageddon: The United States, 1877–1919* (New York, 1989); John Milton Cooper, Jr., *Pivotal Decades: The United States, 1900–1920* (New York, 1992); Alan Dawley, *Struggles for Justice: Social Responsibility and the Liberal State* (Cambridge, MA, 1993); Elizabeth Sanders, *Roots of Reform: Farmers, Workers, and the American State, 1877–1917* (Chicago, 1999). Several important essays usefully assess the vast literature on progressivism: Peter G. Filene, "An Obituary for 'The Progressive Movement,'" *American Quarterly*, 22 (1970); John D. Buenker, "The Progressive Era: A Search for a Synthesis," *Mid-America*, 51 (1969), 175–93; Daniel T. Rodgers, "In Search of Progressivism," *Reviews in American History*, 10 (1982), 113–32; Richard L. McCormick, "Public Life in Industrial America, 1877–1917," in Eric Foner, ed., *The New American History*, rev. ed. (Philadelphia, 1997), 107–32.

Chapter One

1. H. H. Kohlsaat, *From McKinley to Harding: Personal Recollections of Our Presidents* (New York, 1923), 53.
2. Stanley L. Jones, *The Presidential Election of 1896* (Madison, WI, 1964); Robert D. Marcus, *Grand Old Party: Political Structure in the Gilded Age, 1880–1896* (New York, 1971), 195–250; Walter Dean Burnham, *Critical Elections and the Mainsprings of American Politics* (New York, 1970), 71–90.
3. Frederick Townsend Martin, *Things I Remember* (New York, 1913), 29–30, 49–50, 197; *New York Times*, Feb. 7, 1897.
4. Martin, *Things I Remember*, 280–81; *New York Times*, Jan. 23 and Feb. 2, 1897; "Dr. Rainsford's Warning to the Rich," *Literary Digest*, 14 (Feb. 6, 1897), 417–18.
5. Frederic Cople Jaher, "The Gilded Elite: American Multimillionaires, 1865 to the Present," in W. D. Rubinstein, ed., *Wealth and the Wealthy in the Modern World* (New York, 1980), 199; Martin, *Things I Remember*, 280–84; *New York Times*, Feb. 3, 7, 9–11, 1897.
6. *Chicago Tribune*, Feb. 11–12, 1897; Martin, *Things I Remember*, 227, 231–34, 281, 284–85; Lucius Beebe, *The Big Spenders* (Garden City, NY, 1965), 71–72.
7. Robert E. Gallman, "Trends in the Size Distribution of Wealth in the 19th Century: Some Speculations," in Lee Soltow, ed., *Six Papers on the Size Distribution of Wealth and Income* (New York, 1969), 12–15; Jaher, "Gilded Elite," 195–97, 222–23, 237; Jocelyn Maynard Ghent and Frederic Cople Jaher, "The Chicago Business Elite: 1830–1930. A Collective Biography," *Business History Review*, 50 (Autumn 1976), 305; F. W. Taussig and C. S. Joslyn, *American Business Leaders: A Study in Social Origins and Social Stratification* (New York, 1932), 271–77. Drawing on the United States Census, Taussig concludes that in 1900 only 1.8 percent of employed males were executives or owners of large businesses; only 3.3 percent were professionals. Many of those professionals did not possess much wealth.
8. Pitrim Sorokin, "American Millionaires and Multi-Millionaires: A Comparative Statistical Study," *Journal of Social Forces*, 3 (May 1925), 627–40; Jaher, "Gilded Elite"; Frederic Cople Jaher, *The Urban Establishment: Upper Strata in Boston, New York, Charleston, Chicago, and Los Angeles* (Chicago, 1982); Sven Beckert, *The Monied Metropolis: New York City and the Consolidation of the American Bourgeoisíe, 1850–1896* (Cambridge, 2001); John N. Ingham, *The Iron Barons: A Social Analysis of an American Urban Elite, 1874–1965* (Westport, CT, 1978), esp. 15, 18, 19; Richard Jensen, "Metropolitan Elites in the Midwest, 1907–1929: A Study in Multivariate Collective Biography," in Frederic Cople Jaher, ed., *The Rich, the Well Born, and the Powerful* (Urbana, IL, 1973), 285–303; Maynard and Jaher, "Chicago Business Elite"; T. B. Priest, "Elite and Upper Class in Philadelphia, 1914," *Sociological Quarterly*, 25 (Summer 1984), 319–31; E. Digby Baltzell, *Philadelphia Gentlemen: The Making of a*

National Upper Class (New York, 1962); Eleanor Bruchey, "The Business Elite in Baltimore, 1880–1914" (Ph.D. diss., Johns Hopkins University, 1967); Frances W. Gregory and Irene D. Neu, "The American Industrial Elite in the 1870's: Their Social Origins," in William Miller, ed., *Men in Business: Essays on the Historical Role of the Entrepreneur,* Torchbook ed. (New York, 1962), 193–211; Herbert G. Gutman, *Work, Culture, and Society in Industrializing America: Essays in American Working-Class and Social History* (New York, 1976), 211–33; three articles by William Miller—"The Business Elite in Business Bureaucracies: Careers of Top Executives in the Early Twentieth Century," "American Historians and the Business Elite," and "The Recruitment of the American Business Elite"—in Miller, ed., *Men in Business,* 286–337.

9. Andrew Carnegie, *The Gospel of Wealth and Other Timely Essays,* ed. Edward C. Kirkland (1900; Cambridge, MA, 1962), 18; Andrew Carnegie, *Problems of To-day: Wealth, Labor, Socialism* (Garden City, NY, 1908).
10. John D. Rockefeller, *Random Reminiscences of Men and Events* (Garden City, NY, 1933), 152–54; Yehoshua Arieli, *Individualism and Nationalism in American Ideology* (Cambridge, MA, 1964), 335.
11. Ibid., 336; Stuart M. Blumin, "The Hypothesis of Middle-Class Formation in Nineteenth-Century America: A Critique and Some Proposals," *American Historical Review,* 90 (April 1985), 305; Mary P. Ryan, *Cradle of the Middle Class: The Family in Oneida County, New York, 1790–1865* (Cambridge, 1981), 145–85; Gillian Brown, *Domestic Individualism: Imagining Self in Nineteenth-Century America* (Berkeley, CA, 1992).
12. Herbert N. Casson, *The Romance of Steel: The Story of a Thousand Millionaires* (New York, 1907), 158–160.
13. Bruchey, "Business Elite in Baltimore," 6, 139; Miller, "Business Elite in Business Bureaucracies," 286–305; Stuart Morris, "Stalled Professionalism: The Recruitment of Railway Officials in the United States, 1885–1940," *Business History Review,* 47 (Autumn 1973), 318; Anna Robeson Burr, *The Portrait of a Banker: James Stillman, 1850–1918* (New York, 1927), 43, 65, 96; Frank A. Vanderlip, *From Farm Boy to Financier* (New York, 1935), 232.
14. Ibid., 203; Mrs. J. Borden Harriman, *From Pinafores to Politics* (New York, 1923), 62.
15. Vanderlip, *From Farm Boy to Financier,* 196; Herbert L. Satterlee, *J. Pierpont Morgan: An Intimate Portrait* (New York, 1939), 126–27, 181, 188, 264, 272, 333.
16. Ingham, *Iron Barons,* 101–2.
17. Daniel Walker Howe, "Victorian Culture in America," in Howe, ed., *Victorian America* (Philadelphia, 1976), 3–28; Barbara Welter, "The Cult of True Womanhood: 1820–1860," *American Quarterly,* 18 (Summer 1966), 151–74; Nancy F. Cott, *The Bonds of Womanhood: "Woman's Sphere" in New England, 1780–1835* (New Haven, CT, 1977); Elaine Tyler May, *Great Expectations: Marriage and Divorce in Post-Victorian*

America (Chicago, 1980), 15–22; Karen Halttunen, *Confidence Men and Painted Women: A Study of Middle-Class Culture in America, 1830–1870* (New Haven, CT, 1982); Kathryn Kish Sklar, *Catharine Beecher: A Study in American Domesticity* (New Haven, CT, 1973).

18. Frederic Cople Jaher, "Style and Status: High Society in Late Nineteenth-Century New York," in Jaher, ed., *The Rich, the Well Born, and the Powerful*, 274–76; Jaher, "Gilded Elite," 229; Ralph Pulitzer, *New York Society on Parade* (New York, 1910), which discusses the role of the "Great Hostess" throughout; Steven B. Levine, "The Rise of American Boarding Schools and the Development of a National Upper Class," *Social Problems*, 28 (Oct. 1980), 63–94; James McLachlan, *American Boarding Schools* (New York, 1970); Ingham, *Iron Barons*, 92–93.
19. May King Van Rensselaer, *The Social Ladder* (New York, 1924), 48–50, 239–40; Sorokin, "American Millionaires," 630–31; Jaher, "Gilded Elite," 250–52.
20. Daniel T. Rodgers, *The Work Ethic in Industrializing America, 1850–1920* (Chicago, 1978), 1–29; Harrimann, *From Pinafores to Politics*, 35–36.
21. Burr, *Portrait of a Banker*, esp. 40–41, 98, 180–86, 194, 197, 198–99, 336; Vanderlip, *From Farm Boy to Financier*, esp. 108, 121, 125–26, 128, 132–35, 221–23; Edward C. Kirkland, *Dream and Thought in the Business Community, 1860–1900* (Ithaca, NY, 1956), 160; Matthew Josephson, *The Robber Barons: The Great American Capitalists, 1861–1901* (New York, 1934), 32–33.
22. Satterlee, *J. Pierpont Morgan*, 171–72; Harold C. Livesay, *Andrew Carnegie and the Rise of Big Business* (Boston, 1975), 45; Thorstein Veblen, *The Theory of the Leisure Class* (New York, 1899).
23. For the houses, see Merrill Folsom, *Great American Mansions and Their Stories* (New York, 1963), 55–62, 107–14, 197–206, 251–63; John Tebbel, *The Inheritors: A Study of America's Great Fortunes and What Happened to Them* (New York, 1962), 108–34; John Foreman and Robbe Pierce Stimson, *The Vanderbilts and the Gilded Age: Architectural Aspirations, 1879–1901* (New York, 1991); Jaher, "Gilded Elite," 199; Kirkland, *Dream and Thought*, 29–49; Jan Cohn, *The Palace or the Poorhouse: The American House as a Cultural Symbol* (East Lansing, MI, 1979), 115–42. For other pleasures, see Beebe, *Big Spenders;* Dixon Wecter, *The Saga of American Society, 1607–1937* (New York, 1937); Jaher, "Gilded Elite," 198–200.
24. Harrimann, *From Pinafores to Politics*, 51–52; Jaher, "Style and Status," 258–84; Van Rensselaer, *Social Ladder*, 211–12; Eric Homberger, *Mrs. Astor's New York: Money and Social Power in a Gilded Age* (New Haven, CT, 2002).
25. Rose Cohen, *Out of the Shadow* (New York, 1918), 9–81. For issues of memory about Rahel Golub's Cherry Street and the Lower East Side of which it was a part, see Hasia R. Diner, *Lower East Side Memories: A Jewish Place in America* (Princeton, NJ, 2000); Hasia R. Diner, et al., eds., *Remembering the Lower East Side: American Jewish Reflections* (Bloomington, IN, 2000).

26. Cohen, *Out of the Shadow*, 93–95.
27. Ibid., 108.
28. Ibid., 110–11.
29. Ibid., 123–27.
30. Ibid., 138–40, 144–45, 199–207.
31. U.S. Bureau of the Census, *Historical Statistics of the United States*, Bicentennial ed., 2 vols. (Washington, D.C., 1975), I, 139–45, 468. Richard Jules Oestreicher neatly underscores the commonalities of waged labor in *Solidarity and Fragmentation: Working People and Class Consciousness in Detroit, 1875–1900* (Urbana, IL, 1986), 13–25. The inclusion of farm laborers deserves comment. Whatever the differences between rural and urban America, unskilled labor was much the same in the two settings. Moreover, many of the unskilled moved back and forth between town and country. In summer, laborers who worked in streets and steel mills would leave to work on farms and orchards. Semiskilled textile workers also journeyed between farm and factory. See Virginia Yans-McLaughlin, *Family and Community: Italian Immigrants in Buffalo, 1880–1930* (Ithaca, NY, 1977), 40–41; David Montgomery, *The Fall of the House of Labor: The Workplace, the State, and American Labor Activism, 1865–1925* (Cambridge, 1987), 58–111, esp. 59; Jacquelyn Dowd Hall, James Leloudis, Robert Korstad, Mary Murphy, Lu Ann Jones, and Christopher B. Daly, *Like a Family: The Making of a Southern Cotton Mill World* (Chapel Hill, NC, 1987); Lawanda Cox, "The American Agricultural Wage Earner, 1865–1900: The Emergence of a Modern Labor Problem," *Agricultural History*, 22 (Jan. 1948), 95–114; Fred A. Shannon, *The Farmer's Last Frontier: Agriculture, 1860–1897* (New York, 1945), 359–67; Toby Higbie, "Indispensable Outcasts: Harvest Laborers in the Wheat Belt of the Middle West, 1890–1925," *Labor History*, 38 (Fall 1997), 393–412; I. A. Newby, *Plain Folk in the New South: Social Change and Cultural Persistence, 1880–1915* (Baton Rouge, 1989), 6, 61, 82–95.
32. U.S. Bureau of the Census, *Historical Statistics of the United States*, I, 164–67, 468. See also Peter R. Shergold, *Working-Class Life: The "American Standard" in Comparative Perspective, 1899–1913* (Pittsburgh, 1982), 46, 62; Hall et al., *Like a Family*, 77–81.
33. Leslie Woodcock Tentler, *Wage-Earning Women: Industrial Work and Family Life in the United States, 1900–1930* (New York, 1979); John Bodnar, *The Transplanted: A History of Immigrants in Urban America* (Bloomington, IN, 1985), 76; David Nasaw, *Children of the City at Work and at Play* (New York, 1985), 39–41; James R. Barrett, *Work and Community in the Jungle: Chicago's Packinghouse Workers, 1894–1922* (Urbana, IL, 1987), 90–91; Newby, *Plain Folk in the New South*, 240; Yans-McLaughlin, *Family and Community*, 161–64; Shergold, *Working-Class Life*, 77–85, 89.
34. Alexander Keyssar, *Out of Work: The First Century of Unemployment in Massachusetts* (New York, 1986); Oestreicher, *Solidarity and Fragmentation*, 14; Barrett, *Work and Community*, 28–31; Newby, *Plain Folk in the New South*, 145–61; Donna R. Gabaccia,

From Sicily to Elizabeth Street: Housing and Social Change Among Italian Immigrants, 1890–1930 (Albany, NY, 1984), 93–94; John Modell, "Changing Risks, Changing Adaptations: American Families in the Nineteenth and Twentieth Centuries," in Allan J. Lichtman and Joan R. Challinor, eds., *Kin and Communities: Families in America* (Washington, D.C., 1979), 120–28.

35. Ronald C. Brown, *Hard-Rock Miners: The Intermountain West, 1880–1920* (College Station, TX, 1979), 74–98; Higbie, "Indispensable Outcasts," 398–99; Richard Steven Street, "Tattered Shirts and Ragged Pants: Accommodation, Protest, and the Coarse Culture of California Wheat Harvesters and Threshers, 1866–1900," *Pacific Historical Review*, 67 (Nov. 1998), 581, 583; Hall et al., *Like a Family*, 81–86; Newby, *Plain Folk in the New South*, 125, 187–89, 193–96; Barrett, *Work and Community*, 69–71; Patricia A. Cooper, *Once a Cigar Maker: Men, Women, and Work Culture in American Cigar Factories, 1900–1919* (Urbana, IL, 1987), 44–48; Sorokin, "American Millionaires," 628–29; Jaher, "Gilded Elite," 229–30, 248–49; Shergold, *Working-Class Life*, 191; Montgomery, *Fall of the House of Labor*, 15–16; Olivier Zunz, *The Changing Face of Inequality: Urbanization, Industrial Development, and Immigrants in Detroit, 1880–1920* (Chicago, 1982), 251–54; U.S. Bureau of the Census, *Historical Statistics of the United States*, I, 55.

36. Stephan Thernstrom, *The Other Bostonians: Poverty and Progress in the American Metropolis, 1880–1970* (Cambridge, MA, 1973), esp. 220–61; Thomas Kessner, *The Golden Door: Italian and Jewish Mobility in New York City, 1880–1915* (New York, 1977); John Mitchell, "An Exposition and Interpretation of the Trade Union Movement," in Charles S. MacFarland, ed., *The Christian Ministry and the Social Order* (New Haven, CT, 1913), 90.

37. Alice Kessler Harris, *Out to Work: A History of Wage-Earning Women in the United States* (New York, 1982), 75–180; Tentler, *Wage-Earning Women;* Jacqueline Jones, *Labor of Love, Labor of Sorrow: Black Women, Work, and the Family, from Slavery to the Present* (New York, 1985), 110–42; Bodnar, *Transplanted*, 78–80; Shergold, *Working-Class Life*, 64–77, 84–89; Hall et al., *Like a Family*, 15, 43, 64–70, 74–78; Newby, *Plain Folk in the New South*, 220, 236–44; Tamara K. Hareven, *Family Time and Industrial Time: The Relationship Between Family and Work in a New England Industrial Community* (New York, 1982), 85–119, 190–217; Judith E. Smith, *Family Connections: A History of Italian and Jewish Immigrant Lives in Providence, Rhode Island, 1900–1940* (New York, 1985), 47–52, 61; Sydney Stahl Weinberg, *The World of Our Mothers: The Lives of Jewish Immigrant Women* (Chapel Hill, NC, 1988), 130–37; Yans-McLaughlin, *Family and Community;* David M. Katzman, *Seven Days a Week: Women and Domestic Service in Industrializing America* (New York, 1978), 82–85, 184–222; Barrett, *Work and Community in the Jungle*, 51–54, 72–73, 96–99; John Modell and Tamara K. Hareven, "Urbanization and the Malleable Household: An Examination of Boarding and Lodging in American Families," in Hareven, ed., *Family and Kin in Urban Communities, 1700–1930*

(New York, 1977), 164–86; David M. Katzman, *Before the Ghetto: Black Detroit in the Nineteenth Century* (Urbana, IL, 1973), 75; Brown, *Hard-Rock Miners*, 32.

38. Newby, *Plain Folk in the New South*, 123–24, 219, 240, 420; Hall et al., *Like a Family*, 56–65; Mark J. Stern, *Society and Family Strategy: Erie County, New York, 1850–1920* (Albany, NY, 1987), esp. 53 and 240; Timothy L. Smith, "Immigrant Social Aspirations and American Education," *American Quarterly*, 21 (Autumn 1969), 523–43; John Bodnar, "Materialism and Morality: Slavic American Immigrants and Education, 1890–1940," *Journal of Ethnic Studies*, 3 (Winter 1976), 1–20; Weinberg, *World of Our Mothers*, 167–83; Hareven, *Family Time and Industrial Time*, 73–74, 190–93; Tamara K. Hareven and John Modell, "Family Patterns," in Stephan Thernstrom, ed., *Harvard Encyclopedia of American Ethnic Groups* (Cambridge, MA, 1980), 348–49; Bodnar, *Transplanted*, 72–78; Zunz, *Changing Face of Inequality*, 72–78, 250–54; Nasaw, *Children of the City;* Smith, *Family Connections*, 52–61; Barrett, *Work and Community*, 93–95.

39. Nasaw, *Children of the City*, 112–14; Elizabeth Ewen, *Immigrant Women in the Land of Dollars: Life and Culture on the Lower East Side, 1890–1925* (New York, 1985), 99–101; Brown, *Hard-Rock Miners*, 32–33.

40. Nasaw, *Children of the City*, 130–31; Ewen, *Immigrant Women*, 104–5; Bodnar, *Transplanted*, 72–73; Smith, *Family Connections*, 60; Newby, *Plain Folk in the New South*, 236; Hareven, *Family Time and Industrial Time*, 108–10, 166–73, 180, 187.

41. Montgomery, *Fall of the House of Labor*, 15; S. J. Kleinberg, *The Shadow of the Mills: Working-Class Families in Pittsburgh, 1870–1907* (Pittsburgh, 1989), 219–20; Linda Gordon, *Heroes of Their Own Lives: The Politics and History of Family Violence* (New York, 1988); Ewen, *Immigrant Women*, 101; Weinberg, *World of Our Mothers*, 109–10; Newby, *Plain Folk in the New South*, 129–32, 236; Hall et al., *Like a Family*, 95.

42. Smith, *Family Connections*, 23–35, 61–62, 94–95; Bodnar, *Transplanted*, 57–84; Ewen, *Immigrant Women*, 30–47, 71; Yans-McLaughlin, *Family and Community;* Gabaccia, *From Sicily to Elizabeth Street*, 57–61; Hareven, *Family Time and Industrial Time*, 85–119, 154–217.

43. Cohen, *Out of the Shadow*, 74; Shergold, *Working-Class Life*, 58–59, 251–52; Hall et al, *Like a Family*, 77; Newby, *Plain Folk in the New South*, 142–44; Cooper, *Once a Cigar Maker*, 41–42; Brown, *Hard-Rock Miners*, 63–64; Katzman, *Seven Days a Week*, 111–15; U.S. Bureau of the Census, *Historical Statistics of the United States*, I, 168–73.

44. Oestreicher, *Solidarity and Fragmentation*, 3; Smith, *Family Connections*, 23; Shergold, *Working-Class Life;* John Modell, "Patterns of Consumption, Acculturation, and Family Income Strategy in Late-Nineteenth-Century America," in Tamara K. Hareven and Maris A. Vinovskis, eds., *Family and Population in Nineteenth-Century America* (Princeton, NJ, 1978), 212–14; Ewen, *Immigrant Women*, 47, 55; Roy Rosenzweig, *Eight Hours for What We Will: Workers and Leisure in an Industrial City, 1870–1920* (Cambridge, 1983), 61; Newby, *Plain Folk in the New South*, 7, 208–10;

Cox, "American Agricultural Wage Earner," 104; Melvyn Dubofsky, "Hold the Fort: The Dynamics of Twentieth-Century American Working Class History," *Reviews in American History*, 9 (June 1981), 250–51.

45. Nasaw, *Children of the City*, 133–35; Ewen, *Immigrant Women*, 26–27; Shergold, *Working-Class Life*, 204–6; Kathy Peiss, *Cheap Amusements: Working Women and Leisure in Turn-of-the-Century New York* (Philadelphia, 1986); Nan Enstad, *Ladies of Labor, Girls of Adventure: Working Women, Popular Culture, and Labor Politics at the Turn of the Twentieth Century* (New York, 1999), 17–83.

46. E. C. Moore, "The Social Value of the Saloon," *American Journal of Sociology*, 3 (July 1897), 1–12; Rosenzweig, *Eight Hours for What We Will*, 35–90; John M. Kingsdale, "The 'Poor Man's Club': Social Functions of the Urban Working-Class Saloon," *American Quarterly*, 25 (Oct. 1973), 472–89; Thomas J. Noel, *The City and the Saloon: Denver, 1858–1916* (Niwot, CO, 1996); Perry R. Duis, *The Saloon: Public Drinking in Chicago and Boston, 1880–1920* (Urbana, IL, 1983); Lawrence W. Levine, *Highbrow, Lowbrow: The Emergence of Cultural Hierarchy in America* (Cambridge, MA, 1988), 178–98; Francis G. Couvares, *The Remaking of Pittsburgh: Class and Culture in an Industrializing City, 1877–1919* (Albany, NY, 1984), 31–50; Madelon Powers, *Faces Along the Bar: Lore and Order in the Workingman's Saloon, 1870–1920* (Chicago, 1998); Nasaw, *Children of the City*, 124.

47. John D'Emilio and Estelle B. Freedman, *Intimate Matters: A History of Sexuality in America* (New York, 1988), 194–201; Ruth Rosen, *The Lost Sisterhood: Prostitution in America, 1900–1918* (Baltimore, 1982); Peiss, *Cheap Amusements*, 45.

48. Rosenzweig, *Eight Hours for What We Will*, 58–62, 78–79, 103–17; Moore, "Value of the Saloon," 4; Kingsdale, "'Poor Man's Club,'" 480, 485–86; Powers, *Faces Along the Bar*, 93–118; Mark Peel, "On the Margins: Lodgers and Boarders in Boston, 1860–1900," *Journal of American History*, 72 (March 1986), 813–34; Joanne J. Meyerowitz, *Women Adrift: Independent Wage Earners in Chicago, 1880–1930* (Chicago, 1988); Street, "Tattered Shirts and Ragged Pants," 589–98; Couvares, *Remaking of Pittsburgh*, 20–22; Cooper, *Once a Cigar Maker*, 85–86, 94–122; Oestreicher, *Solidarity and Fragmentation*, 16, 64–65; Montgomery, *Fall of the House of Labor*, 3–4, 17–19; Herbert Croly, *The Promise of American Life* (1909; Boston, 1989), 127.

49. Hamlin Garland, *A Son of the Middle Border* (New York, 1917), 6–7, 45–46; Jean Holloway, *Hamlin Garland: A Biography* (Austin, TX, 1960); Joseph B. McCullough, *Hamlin Garland* (Boston, 1978); Eric Foner, *Free Soil, Free Labor, Free Men: The Ideology of the Republican Party Before the Civil War* (New York, 1970), 11–72.

50. Garland, *Son of the Middle Border*, 31, 85–86, 100, 139, 155.

51. Ibid., 158, 177–78.

52. Ibid., 70.

53. Gilbert C. Fite, *American Farmers: The New Minority* (Bloomington, IN, 1981), 20–29; Gilbert C. Fite, *Cotton Fields No More: Southern Agriculture, 1865–1900* (Lex-

ington, KY, 1984), 1–29, 34–39; Fred A. Shannon, "The Status of the Midwestern Farmer in 1900," *Mississippi Valley Historical Review,* 37 (Dec. 1950), 491–510; Shannon, *Farmer's Last Frontier,* 125–47, 351–56; Donald L. Winters, *Farmers Without Farms: Agricultural Tenancy in Nineteenth-Century Iowa* (Westport, CT, 1978); Jeremy Atack, "Tenants and Yeomen in the Nineteenth Century," *Agricultural History,* 62 (Summer 1988), 6–32; Allan G. Bogue, "Farm Tenants in the Nineteenth-Century Middle West," in Trudy Huskamp Peterson, ed., *Farmers, Bureaucrats, and Middlemen: Historical Perspectives on American Agriculture* (Washington, D.C., 1980), 103–19; Gilbert C. Fite, "The Agricultural Trap in the South," *Agricultural History,* 60 (Fall 1986), 38–50; J. Wayne Flynt, *Poor but Proud: Alabama's Poor Whites* (Tuscaloosa, AL, 1989), 59–91; Neil R. McMillen, *Dark Journey: Black Mississippians in the Age of Jim Crow* (Urbana, IL, 1989), 111–53; U.S. Bureau of the Census. *Historical Statistics of the United States,* I, 139, 458, 461, 463, 465–66.

54. Ibid., I, 483; David B. Danbom, *The Resisted Revolution: Urban America and the Industrialization of Agriculture, 1900–1930* (Ames, IA, 1979) 7; Shannon, "Status of the Midwestern Farmer," 498, 501; Thomas J. Morain, *Prairie Grass Roots: An Iowa Small Town in the Early Twentieth Century* (Ames, IA, 1988), 58–62; Sally McMurry, *Families and Farmhouses in Nineteenth-Century America: Vernacular Design and Social Change* (New York, 1988), 3–4, 10–49; Fite, *Cotton Fields No More,* 33–34; Anne Patton Malone, "Piney Woods Farmers of South Georgia, 1850–1900: Jeffersonian Yeomen in an Age of Expanding Commercialism," *Agricultural History,* 60 (Fall 1986), 63–69.

55. Kenyon L. Butterfield, "Rural Life and the Family," in *Papers and Proceedings, Third Annual Meeting, American Sociological Society* (Chicago, 1909), 107; Theodore Saloutos and John D. Hicks, *Twentieth-Century Populism: Agricultural Discontent in the Middle West 1900–1939* (Lincoln, NE, 1951), 12–13; McMurry, *Families and Farmhouses in Nineteenth-Century America,* 56–86; Stewart E. Tolnay, "Family Economy and the Black American Fertility Transition," *Journal of Family History,* 11 (July 1986), 267–83; Robert L. Griswold, "Anglo Women and Domestic Ideology in the American West in the Nineteenth and Early Twentieth Centuries," in Lillian Schlissel, Vicki L. Ruiz, and Janice Monk, eds., *Western Women: Their Land, Their Lives* (Albuquerque, 1988), 15–33; Katherine Harris, "Homesteading in Northeastern Colorado, 1873–1920: Sex Roles and Women's Experience," in Susan Armitage and Elizabeth Jameson, eds., *The Women's West* (Norman, OK, 1987), 167, 171–72, 186–87; Jacqueline S. Reinier, "Concepts of Domesticity on the Southern Plains Agricultural Frontier, 1870–1920," in John Wunder, ed., *At Home on the Range: Essays on the History of Western Social and Domestic Life* (Westport, CT, 1985), 57–70; Flynt, *Poor but Proud,* 202–3; McMillen, *Dark Journey,* 129–30; Newby, *Plain Folk in the New South,* 49–51; Hall et al., *Like a Family,* 14–15; Melissa Walker, *All We Knew Was To Farm: Rural Women in the Upcountry South, 1919–1941*

(Baltimore, 2000), 69–97; Dorothy Schwieder, "Labor and Economic Roles of Iowa Farm Wives, 1840–1880," in Peterson, ed., *Farmers, Bureaucrats, and Middlemen,* 153, 161–64; Mary Neth, "Gender and the Family Labor System: Defining Work in the Rural Midwest," *Journal of Social History,* 27 (Spring 1994), 563–77; Norton Juster, *So Sweet to Labor: Rural Women in America, 1865–1895* (New York, 1979).

56. Danbom, *Resisted Revolution,* 6, 13–15, and 147, n. 9; Glenda Riley, "Farm Women's Roles in the Agricultural Development of South Dakota," *South Dakota History,* 13 (Spring/Summer 1983), 99; McMillen, *Dark Journey,* 128–29; Jack Temple Kirby, *Rural Worlds Lost: The American South, 1920–1960* (Baton Rouge, 1987), 163–67; Flynt, *Poor but Proud,* 81–82, 197–200; Elizabeth Hampsten, *Read This Only to Yourself: The Private Writings of Midwestern Women, 1880–1910* (Bloomington, IN, 1982), 102–10; Deborah Fink and Alicia Carriquiry, "Having Babies or Not: Household Composition and Fertility in Rural Iowa and Nebraska, 1900–1910," *Great Plains Quarterly,* 12 (Summer 1992), 157–68; Stewart E. Tolnay, "Fertility of Southern Black Farmers in 1900: Evidence and Speculation," *Journal of Family History,* 8 (Winter 1983), 315–17; Tolnay, "Family Economy and the Black American Fertility Transition," 268, 272–75; Harris, "Homesteading in Northeastern Colorado," 170–71; Newby, *Plain Folk in the New South,* 50–52; Hall et al., *Like a Family,* 15–18; Benjamin E. Mays, *Born to Rebel: An Autobiography,* ed. Orville Vernon Burton (1971; Athens, GA, 1987), 6, 8–9; Wayne E. Fuller, *The Old Country School: The Story of Rural Education in the Middle West* (Chicago, 1982), 47–48, 122; Shannon, *Farmer's Last Frontier,* 372–76; Rae McGrady Booth, "Memoirs of an Iowa Farm Girl," *Annals of Iowa,* 38 (Fall 1966), 468; Fite, *Cotton Fields No More,* 41–42; C. Vann Woodward, *Origins of the New South, 1877–1913* (Baton Rouge, 1951), 398–400; Garland, *Son of the Middle Border,* 161, 209–10.

57. Danbom, *Resisted Revolution,* 12–13; Jane Marie Pederson, "Country Visitor: Patterns of Hospitality in Rural Wisconsin, 1880–1925," *Agricultural History,* 58 (July 1984), 359; J. Sanford Rikoon, *Threshing in the Midwest, 1820–1940: A Study in Traditional Culture and Technological Change* (Bloomington, IN, 1988); Theodore Saloutos, "The Immigrant Contribution to American Agriculture," *Agricultural History,* 50 (Jan. 1976), 59; Fite, *Cotton Fields No More,* 50–52; Shannon, *Farmer's Last Frontier,* 329–48; Garland, *Son of the Middle Border,* 165, 173, 204.

58. Amos G. Warner, "Three Phases of Coöperation in the West," *Publications of the American Economic Association,* 2 (Mar. 1887), 10–11, 39–46; Garland, *Son of the Middle Border,* 191; Hal S. Barron, *Mixed Harvest: The Second Great Transformation in the Rural North, 1870–1930* (Chapel Hill, NC, 1997), 110–12.

59. J. R. Elliott, *American Farms: Their Condition and Future* (New York, 1890), 126; Paul H. Johnstone, "Old Ideals Versus New Ideas in Farm Life" in *The Yearbook of Agriculture 1940: Farmers in a Changing World* (Washington, D.C., 1940), 117, 138, 148, 158; Barron, *Mixed Harvest,* 13–16; Saloutos and Hicks, *Twentieth-Century Populism,*

111; Shannon, *Farmer's Last Frontier,* 3–4; Danbom, *Resisted Revolution,* 9–10; Fite, *Cotton Fields No More,* 30–31; Garland, *Son of the Middle Border,* 238–39.

60. McMurry, *Families and Farmhouses in Nineteenth-Century America,* 7, 177–208.

61. Kirby, *Rural Worlds Lost,* 173–74; McMurry, *Families and Farmhouses in Nineteenth-Century America,* 147; Harris, "Homesteading in Northeastern Colorado," 167–71; Donald B. Marti, "Sisters of the Grange: Rural Feminism in the Late Nineteenth Century," *Agricultural History,* 58 (July 1984), 247–61; Julie Roy Jeffrey, "Women in the Southern Farmers' Alliance: A Reconsideration of the Role and Status of Women in the Late Nineteenth-Century South," in Edward Magdol and Jon L. Wakelyn, eds., *The Southern Common People: Studies in Nineteenth-Century Social History* (Westport, CT, 1980), 267–88; Griswold, "Anglo Women and Domestic Ideology in the American West," 18; Newby, *Plain Folk in the New South,* 52.

62. Fite, *American Farmers,* 10–11; Danbom, *Resisted Revolution,* 4–7; Joann Vanek, "Work, Leisure, and Family Roles: Farm Households in the United States, 1920–1955," *Journal of Family History,* 5 (Winter 1980), 424–25; Newby, *Plain Folk in the New South,* 43–48; McMillen, *Dark Journey,* 121, 137–40; Neth, "Gender and the Family Labor System," 568–69; Garland, *Son of the Middle Border,* 117–19, 129.

63. Gavin Wright, "American Agriculture and the Labor Market: What Happened to Proletarianization?," *Agricultural History,* 62 (Summer 1988), 183–85; Michael Merrill, "Cash Is Good to Eat: Self-Sufficiency and Exchange in the Rural Economy of the United States," *Radical History Review,* 4 (Winter 1977), 42–72; Michael Merrill, "Putting 'Capitalism' in Its Place: A Review of Recent Literature," *William and Mary Quarterly,* 3d ser., 52 (Apr. 1995), 315–26; Steven Hahn, *The Roots of Southern Populism: Yeoman Farmers and the Transformation of the Georgia Upcountry, 1850–1890* (New York, 1983); Malone, "Piney Woods Farmers of South Georgia," 51–84; Danbom, *Resisted Revolution,* 4–5; Fite, "Agricultural Trap in the South," 41–42; William Bernard Graber, "Farm Family Enters the Modern World," *Palimpsest,* 68 (Summer 1987), 88–89; Saloutos, "Immigrant Contribution to American Agriculture," 58; Mark Friedberger, "The Farm Family and the Inheritance Process: Evidence from the Corn Belt, 1870–1950," *Agricultural History,* 57 (Jan. 1983), 1–13.

64. Garland, *Son of the Middle Border,* 123, 152; Vanek, "Work, Leisure, and Family Roles," 424; Ted Ownby, *Subduing Satan: Religion, Recreation, and Manhood in the Rural South, 1865–1920* (Chapel Hill, NC, 1990); Flynt, *Poor but Proud,* 45, 190, 207, 211–12; Kirby, *Rural Worlds Lost,* 162.

65. Wright, "American Agriculture and the Labor Market," 196; Cox, "American Agricultural Wage Earner," 106, 109; Higbie, "Indispensable Outcasts," 400–402; Morain, *Prairie Grass Roots,* 60–61; Garland, *Son of the Middle Border,* 174–75.

66. Gilbert C. Fite, "The Pioneer Farmer: A View Over Three Centuries," *Agricultural History,* 50 (Jan. 1976), 283–84; Shannon, *Farmer's Last Frontier,* 368–72; Fite,

Cotton Fields No More, 35–37; Flynt, *Poor but Proud,* 88; Danbom, *Resisted Revolution,* 8; Garland, *Son of the Middle Border,* 30–31, 92–93, 105–6, 145, 155; Hamlin Garland, *A Daughter of the Middle Border* (New York, 1921), x; McMurry, *Families and Farmhouses in Nineteenth-Century America,* 6, 135–76.

67. Fite, *Cotton Fields No More,* 48–67; Morton Rothstein, "Farmer Movements and Organizations: Numbers, Gains, Losses," *Agricultural History,* 62 (Summer 1988), 161–81; Congressional Quarterly, *Guide to U.S. Elections* (Washington, D.C., 1975), 279, 300; Woodward, *Origins of the New South,* 321–49; J. Morgan Kousser, *The Shaping of Southern Politics: Suffrage Restriction and the Establishment of the One-Party South, 1880–1910* (New Haven, CT, 1974).
68. Don F. Hadwiger, "Farmers in Politics," *Agricultural History,* 50 (Jan. 1976), 157–58, 161–65; John Higham, *Strangers in the Land: Patterns of American Nativism 1860–1925* (1955; New York, 1973), 68–105; Donald Kinzer, *An Episode in Anti-Catholicism: The American Protective Association* (Seattle, 1964); Saloutos, "Immigrant Contribution to American Agriculture," 45–67; Shannon, *Farmer's Last Frontier,* 45–50; Kathleen Neils Conzen, "Historical Approaches to the Study of Rural Ethnic Communities," in Frederick C. Luebke, ed., *Ethnicity on the Great Plains* (Lincoln, NE, 1980), 1–18; Bradley H. Baltensperger, "Agricultural Change among Nebraska Immigrants, 1880–1900," in Luebke, ed., *Ethnicity on the Great Plains,* 170–89; Robert C. Ostergren, "European Settlement and Ethnicity Patterns on the Agricultural Frontiers of South Dakota," *South Dakota History,* 13 (Spring/Summer 1983), 49–82.
69. U.S. Bureau of the Census, *Historical Statistics of the United States,* I, 465–66; Saloutos, "Immigrant Contribution to American Agriculture," 48; Flynt, *Poor but Proud,* 212–17; McMillen, *Dark Journey,* 11–53, 120; Woodward, *Origins of the New South;* C. Vann Woodward, *Tom Watson, Agrarian Rebel* (New York, 1938).
70. Garland, *Son of the Middle Border,* 170–71, 215, 228–29, 398, 403–4, 414.
71. U.S. Bureau of the Census, *Historical Statistics of the United States,* I, 134, 457, 482–83; Fite, *American Farmers,* 7–9, 15; Shannon, *Farmer's Last Frontier,* 349–56; Danbom, *Resisted Revolution,* 18–19; Elliott, *American Farms,* 36–44.
72. Garland, *Son of the Middle Border,* 138–39, 155–56, 170–71.
73. Ibid., 173, 205.
74. Ibid., 205.
75. Holloway, *Hamlin Garland;* McCullough, *Hamlin Garland.*
76. Barron, *Mixed Harvest,* 155–91.
77. Fite, *American Farmers,* 12–15; Wright, "American Agriculture and the Labor Market," 200–202; Hal S. Barron, *Those Who Stayed Behind: Rural Society in Nineteenth-Century New England* (Cambridge, 1984); Danbom, *Resisted Revolution,* 19; Garland, *Son of the Middle Border,* 440.
78. U.S. Bureau of the Census, *Historical Statistics of the United States,* I, 177–78; Leon

Fink, *Workingmen's Democracy: The Knights of Labor and American Politics* (Urbana, IL, 1983); Oestreicher, *Solidarity and Fragmentation,* 76–221; Philip Taft, *The A.F. of L. in the Time of Gompers* (1957; New York, 1970). For a different view of craft unionists' openness to organizing less-skilled workers, see Richard Schneirov, "Rethinking the Relation of Labor to the Politics of Urban Social Reform in Late Nineteenth-Century America: The Case of Chicago," *International Labor and Working-Class History,* 46 (Fall 1994), 93–108.

79. Oestreicher, *Solidarity and Fragmentation,* 119–28, 180–87; Nick Salvatore, *Eugene V. Debs: Citizen and Socialist* (Urbana, IL, 1983), 147–219; Congressional Quarterly, *Guide to U.S. Elections,* 281.
80. U.S. Bureau of the Census, *Historical Statistics of the United States,* I, 12, 105–9, 117, 392.
81. Nasaw, *Children of the City,* 34; Montgomery, *Fall of the House of Labor,* 23–25, 174; Gwendolyn Mink, *Old Labor and New Immigrants in American Political Development: Union, Party, and State, 1875–1920* (Ithaca, NY, 1986); Andrew Dawson, "The Parameters of Craft Consciousness: The Social Outlook of the Skilled Workers, 1890–1920," in Dirk Hoerder, ed., *American Labor and Immigration History, 1877–1920s: Recent European Research* (Urbana, IL, 1983), 135–55; Couvares, *Remaking of Pittsburgh,* 9–30; Oestreicher, *Solidarity and Fragmentation,* 13–25, 36–38, 52–57; Cooper, *Once a Cigar Maker,* 24–25; Shergold, *Working-Class Life,* 227–29.
82. Frank Capra, *The Name Above the Title: An Autobiography* (New York, 1971), xi, 6–7, 9.
83. Cohen, *Out of the Shadow,* 187–90.
84. Ibid., 225–29; Gabaccia, *From Sicily to Elizabeth Street,* 100–102.
85. Jaher, "Gilded Elite," 265; Satterlee, *J. Pierpont Morgan,* 185; Josephson, *Robber Barons,* 336–37; Casson, *Romance of Steel,* 203; Cornelius Vanderbilt, Jr., *Farewell to Fifth Avenue* (New York, 1935), 17–18.
86. John Tebbel, *The Inheritors: A Study of America's Great Fortunes and What Happened to Them* (New York, 1962), where Vanderbilt is quoted on 133; Jaher, "Gilded Elite," 190–94, 256–63; *New York Times,* Dec. 23, 1894.
87. Jaher, "Style and Status," 266, 269–70, 276; Van Rensselaer, *Social Ladder,* esp. 172–73; Satterlee, *J. Pierpont Morgan,* 265.
88. Jaher, "Gilded Elite," 206–8; Rockefeller, *Random Reminiscences,* vi; Kirkland, *Dream and Thought,* 38; Josephson, *Robber Barons,* 47–48; Casson, *Romance of Steel,* 159.
89. Rockefeller, *Random Reminiscences,* 20–21, 24–26, 140–41; Ron Chernow, *Titan: The Life of John D. Rockefeller, Sr.* (New York, 1998), 50, 237–42.
90. John Ensor Harr and Peter J. Johnson, *The Rockefeller Century* (New York, 1988), 3–57; Rockefeller, *Random Reminiscences,* 139.
91. Andrew Carnegie, *Autobiography of Andrew Carnegie* (Boston, 1920), 6, 31, 88–89; Carnegie, *Gospel of Wealth,* 14, 16, 26, 63; Joseph Frazier Wall, *Andrew Carnegie,* 2nd ed. (Pittsburgh, 1989), 795–884.
92. Carnegie, *Gospel of Wealth,* 20, 25, 56.

93. Ibid., 21–22, 57–58, 64.
94. Ibid., 23; Jaher, "Gilded Elite," 205–6, 208.
95. Vanderbilt, *Farewell to Fifth Avenue,* 3–5.

Chapter Two

1. Jane Addams, *Twenty Years at Hull-House* (New York, 1910), 12; Jean Bethke Elshtain, *Jane Addams and the Dream of American Democracy: A Life* (New York, 2002), 33–37; Allen F. Davis, *American Heroine: The Life and Legend of Jane Addams* (New York, 1973), 3–5.
2. Addams, *Twenty Years at Hull-House,* 23, 31; Davis, *American Heroine,* 5.
3. Addams, *Twenty Years at Hull-House,* 1, 6, 9, 11–13; Davis, *American Heroine,* 5–6.
4. Addams, *Twenty Years at Hull-House,* 32, 52, 64, 66; Davis, *American Heroine,* 10–32; Christopher Lasch, *The New Radicalism in America, 1889–1963: The Intellectual as a Social Type* (New York, 1965), 3–18.
5. Addams, *Twenty Years at Hull-House,* 71; Davis, *American Heroine,* 32–43; Lasch, *New Radicalism in America,* 18–23.
6. Figures are drawn from U.S. Bureau of the Census, *Historical Statistics of the United States. Colonial Times to 1970,* Bicentennial ed., 2 vols. (Washington, D.C., 1975), I, 139–42, with modifications suggested by F. W. Taussig and C. S. Joslyn, *American Business Leaders: A Study in Social Origins and Social Stratification* (New York, 1932), 273.
7. Burton J. Bledstein, "Introduction," in Burton J. Bledstein and Robert D. Johnston, eds., *The Middling Sorts: Explorations in the History of the American Middle Class* (New York, 2001), 1–25, helpfully summarizes the problem of defining the middle class.
8. Cindy Sondik Aron, *Ladies and Gentlemen of the Civil Service: Middle-Class Workers in Victorian America* (New York, 1987), 22–25; Stuart M. Blumin, *The Emergence of the Middle Class: Social Experience in the American City, 1760–1900* (Cambridge, 1989), 108–21, 146–63; Ethel Spencer, *The Spencers of Amberson Avenue: A Turn-of-the-Century Memoir,* eds. Michael P. Weber and Peter N. Stearns (Pittsburgh, 1983), 10, 126–27, 74, 79, 39, 40, 28.
9. Mary P. Ryan, *Cradle of the Middle Class: The Family in Oneida County, New York, 1790–1865* (Cambridge, 1981); Stephen Mintz and Susan Kellogg, *Domestic Revolutions: A Social History of American Family Life* (New York, 1988), 43–65; Stuart M. Blumin, "The Hypothesis of Middle-Class Formation in Nineteenth-Century America: A Critique and Some Proposals," *American Historical Review,* 90 (April 1985), 299–338; Blumin, *Emergence of the Middle Class;* Karen Lystra, *Searching the Heart: Women, Men, and Romantic Love in Nineteenth-Century America* (New York, 1989); Harvey Green, *The Light of the Home: An Intimate View of the Lives of Women in Victorian America* (New York, 1983), 3–58; Richard Sennett, *Families Against the City: Middle Class Homes of Industrial Chicago, 1872–1890* (Cambridge, MA, 1970); John

D'Emilio and Estelle B. Freedman, *Intimate Matters: A History of Sexuality in America* (New York, 1988), 174; Mark J. Stern, *Society and Family Strategy: Erie County, New York, 1850–1920* (Albany, NY, 1987), esp. 51–53 and 64–69; James Reed, *The Birth Control Movement and American Society: From Private Vice to Public Virtue* (1978; Princeton, NJ, 1983), 3–18, 21–22, 32–33; Linda Gordon, *Woman's Body, Woman's Right: A Social History of Birth Control in America* (1976; New York, 1977), 16–21; David I. Macleod, *Building Character in the American Boy: The Boy Scouts, YMCA, and Their Forerunners, 1870–1920* (Madison, WI, 1983), 6–8; John S. Gilkeson, Jr., *Middle-Class Providence, 1820–1940* (Princeton, NJ, 1986), 54; Joseph Kett, *Rites of Passage: Adolescence in America 1790 to the Present* (New York, 1977), 151–88; U.S. Bureau of the Census, *Historical Statistics of the United States*, I, 378.

10. Gwendolyn Wright, *Moralism and the Model Home: Domestic Architecture and Cultural Conflict in Chicago, 1877–1913* (Chicago, 1980); Gwendolyn Wright, *Building the Dream: A Social History of Housing in America* (Cambridge, MA, 1981), 96–113; Clifford Edward Clark, Jr., *The American Family Home, 1800–1960* (Chapel Hill, NC, 1986), 3–102; Spencer, *Spencers of Amberson Avenue*, 73; Kenneth T. Jackson, *Crabgrass Frontier: The Suburbanization of the United States* (New York, 1985), 103–37; Matthew Edel, Elliott D. Sclar, and Daniel Luria, *Shaky Palaces: Homeownership and Social Mobility in Boston's Suburbanization* (New York, 1984); Blumin, *Emergence of the Middle Class*, 275–85.
11. Ellen K. Rothman, *Hands and Hearts: A History of Courtship in America* (New York, 1984) 242–43; Mintz and Kellogg, *Domestic Revolutions*, 108–11; Elaine Tyler May, *Great Expectations: Marriage and Divorce in Post-Victorian America* (Chicago, 1980), esp. 167; William O'Neill, *Divorce in the Progressive Era* (New Haven, CT, 1967); Christopher Lasch, *The World of Nations: Reflections on American History, Politics, and Culture* (New York, 1973), 35–43; D'Emilio and Freedman, *Intimate Matters*, 174, 180–83; Ruth Rosen, *The Lost Sisterhood: Prostitution in America, 1900–1918* (Baltimore, 1982); Reed, *Birth Control Movement and American Society*, 42–43, 56–57, 107; Howard P. Chudacoff, *The Age of the Bachelor: Creating an American Subculture* (Princeton, NJ, 1999), 45–74.
12. Spencer, *Spencers of Amberson Avenue*, 38, 121–35.
13. Charlotte Perkins Gilman, *The Living of Charlotte Perkins Gilman: An Autobiography* (New York, 1935), 82–106; O'Neill, *Divorce in the Progressive Era*, 127–36; Mary Armfield Hill, *Charlotte Perkins Gilman: The Making of a Radical Feminist, 1860–1896* (Philadelphia, 1980); Tom Lutz, *American Nervousness, 1903: An Anecdotal History* (Ithaca, NY, 1991); Francis G. Gosling, *Before Freud: Neurasthenia and the American Medical Community, 1870–1910* (Urbana, IL, 1987); Marijke Gijswijt-Hofstra and Roy Porter, eds., *Cultures of Neurasthenia from Beard to the First World War* (Amsterdam and New York, 2001).
14. Ruth Schwartz Cowen, *More Work for Mother: The Ironies of Household Technology from*

the Open Hearth to the Microwave (New York, 1983), 69–101, 154–60; Green, *Light of the Home,* 59–92; Susan Strasser, *Never Done: A History of American Housework* (New York, 1982); Kate Gannett Wells, "Why More Girls Do Not Marry," *North American Review,* 152 (Feb. 1891), 179.

15. Barbara Miller Solomon, *In the Company of Educated Women: A History of Women and Higher Education in America* (New Haven, CT, 1985), 43–140; Helen Lefkowitz Horowitz, *Alma Mater: Design and Experience in the Women's Colleges from Their Nineteenth-Century Beginnings to the 1930s* (New York, 1984); Rosalind Rosenberg, *Beyond Separate Spheres: Intellectual Roots of Modern Feminism* (New Haven, CT, 1982), 1–27; Spencer, *Spencers of Amberson Avenue,* 81–84.
16. Rothman, *Hands and Hearts,* 184–85; Gilkeson, *Middle-Class Providence,* 167; Wells, "Why More Girls Do Not Marry," 175–81; Mark C. Carnes, "Middle-Class Men and the Solace of Fraternal Ritual," in Carnes and Clyde Griffen, eds., *Meanings for Manhood: Constructions of Masculinity in Victorian America* (Chicago, 1990), 37–66.
17. Peter G. Filene, *Him/her/self: Sex Roles in Modern America,* 2nd ed. (Baltimore, 1986), 69–93; Blumin, *Emergence of the Middle Class,* 184; Rothman, *Hands and Hearts,* 95–96, 99; Aron, *Ladies and Gentlemen of the Civil Service,* 20–21; E. Anthony Rotundo, *American Manhood: Transformations in Masculinity from the Revolution to the Modern Era* (New York, 1993), 251–55; E. Anthony Rotundo, "Body and Soul: Changing Ideals of American Middle-Class Manhood, 1770–1920," *Journal of Social History,* 16 (Summer 1983), 23–38; D'Emilio and Freedman, *Intimate Matters,* 178–83; Robert L. Griswold, "Divorce and the Legal Redefinition of Victorian Manhood," in Carnes and Griffen, eds., *Meanings for Manhood,* 96–110; Angel Kwolek-Folland, *Engendering Business: Men and Women in the Corporate Office, 1870–1930* (Baltimore, 1994), 41–69; Gail Bederman, *Manliness and Civilization: A Cultural History of Gender and Race in the United States, 1880–1917* (Chicago, 1995), 10–20.
18. Spencer, *Spencers of Amberson Avenue,* 26–27, 121–22.
19. Edward Bellamy, *Looking Backward, 2000–1887,* ed. Robert C. Elliott (1888; Boston, 1966), 15.
20. Ibid., 156–159.
21. Ibid., 26, 156–57, 159–60.
22. Gordon, *Woman's Body, Woman's Right,* 95–115; Reed, *Birth Control Movement and American Society,* 34–45; Paul Boyer, *Urban Masses and Moral Order, 1820–1920* (Cambridge, MA, 1978); David J. Pivar, *Purity Crusade: Sexual Morality and Social Control, 1868–1900* (Westport, CT, 1973); D'Emilio and Freedman, *Intimate Matters,* 130–61; Alison M. Parker, *Purifying America: Women, Cultural Reform, and Pro-Censorship Activism, 1873–1933* (Urbana, IL, 1997), 9–128; Margaret Marsh, "Suburban Men and Masculine Domesticity, 1870–1915," in Carnes and Griffen, eds., *Meanings for Manhood,* 111–27; Clyde Griffen, "Reconstructing Masculinity from

the Evangelical Revival to the Waning of Progressivism: A Speculative Hypothesis," in ibid., 183–204.

23. Lake Placid Conference on Home Economics, *Proceedings of the Sixth Annual Conference,* September 19–24 1904 (Lake Placid, NY, 1904), 31; Lake Placid Conference on Home Economics, *Proceedings of the Fourth Annual Conference, September 16–20, 1902* (Lake Placid, NY, 1902), 22; Wright, *Moralism and the Model Home,* 150–70; Clark, *American Family Home,* 157–62; Dolores Hayden, *The Grand Domestic Revolution: A History of Feminist Designs for American Homes, Neighborhoods, and Cities* (Cambridge, MA, 1981); Rosenberg, *Beyond Separate Spheres,* 1–53; Sarah Stage, "Ellen Richards and the Social Significance of the Home Economics Movement," in Stage and Virginia B. Vincenti, eds., *Rethinking Home Economics: Women and the History of a Profession* (Ithaca, NY, 1997), 17–33.
24. Lake Placid Conference on Home Economics, *Proceedings of the Fourth Annual Conference,* 22; Lake Placid Conference on Home Economics. *Proceedings of the First, Second and Third Conferences. Sept. 19–23 1899. July 3–7 1900. June 28–July 5 1901* (Lake Placid, NY, 1901), 5.
25. Karen J. Blair, *The Clubwoman as Feminist: True Womanhood Redefined, 1868–1914* (New York, 1980); Elizabeth Hayes Turner, *Women, Culture, and Community: Religion and Reform in Galveston, 1880–1920* (New York, 1997), 151–84; Eleanor Flexner and Ellen Fitzpatrick, *Century of Struggle: The Woman's Rights Movement in the United States,* enlarged ed. (Cambridge, MA, 1996), 171–72; Andrew Chamberlin Rieser, "Secularization Reconsidered: Chautauqua and the De-Christianization of Middle-Class Authority, 1880–1920," in Bledstein and Johnston, eds., *Middling Sorts,* 136–50.
26. Flexner and Fitzpatrick, *Century of Struggle,* 136–70, 195–217.
27. Aron, *Ladies and Gentlemen of the Civil Service,* 48–54, 60; U.S. Bureau of the Census, *Historical Statistics of the United States,* I, 140.
28. Caroline L. Hunt, *The Life of Ellen H. Richards* (Boston, 1912); Wright, *Moralism and the Model Home,* 123; Ruth Bordin, *Frances Willard: A Biography* (Chapel Hill, NC, 1986).
29. Addams *Twenty Years at Hull-House,* 85, 92; Davis, *American Heroine,* 43–66; Lasch, *New Radicalism,* 23–27.
30. Wright, *Moralism and the Model Home,* 105–49. The middle class's public use of domestic rhetoric is discussed further in chapter 3 below.
31. Richard T. Ely, "Industrial Liberty," *Publications of the American Economic Association,* 3rd Series, 3 (Feb. 1902), 66, 77–78; Addams, *Twenty Years at Hull-House,* 41–42. See also Walter Rauschenbusch, *Christianity and the Social Crisis,* ed. Robert D. Cross (1907; New York, 1964), 250.
32. Gilkeson, *Middle-Class Providence,* 129–30; Aron, *Ladies and Gentlemen of the Civil Service,* 5, 23–39, 79–86, 93; Rotundo, *American Manhood,* 248–51; Olivier Zunz, *Making America Corporate: 1870–1920* (Chicago, 1990); Andrew Wender Cohen, "Obsta-

cles to History?: Modernization and the Lower Middle Class in Chicago, 1900–1940," in Bledstein and Johnston, eds., *Middling Sorts,* 189–200.

33. Bellamy, *Looking Backward,* 136; W. S. Rainsford, *The Story of a Varied Life: An Autobiography* (New York, 1922), 328; David E. Shi, *The Simple Life: Plain Living and High Thinking in American Culture* (New York, 1985), 183; Gilkeson, *Middle-Class Providence,* 93–135; Lois W. Banner, *American Beauty* (1983; Chicago, 1984) 106–53.
34. Washington Gladden, *Recollections* (Boston, 1909), 294–95; James Weir, Jr., M.D., "The Methods of the Rioting Striker and Evidence of Degeneration," *Century,* 48 (Oct. 1894), 952–54; T. J. Jackson Lears, *No Place of Grace: Antimodernism and the Transformation of American Culture, 1880–1920* (New York, 1981), 30–31; Daniel T. Rodgers, *The Work Ethic in Industrial America, 1850–1920* (Chicago, 1978), 34, 69–70; Sidney Fine, *Laissez-Faire and the General-Welfare State: A Study of Conflict in American Thought, 1865–1901* (Ann Arbor, MI, 1956), 173.
35. Herbert Gutman, "The Workers' Search for Power," in H. Wayne Morgan, ed., *The Gilded Age,* rev. ed. (Syracuse, 1970), 31–53; David O. Stowell, "Small Property Holders and the Great Strike of 1877: Railroads, City Streets, and the Middle Classes," *Journal of Urban History,* 21 (Sept. 1995), 741–63; Walter Rauschenbusch, "The Stake of the Church in the Social Movement," *American Journal of Sociology,* 3 (July 1897), 21–24, 29–30.
36. Addams, *Twenty Years at Hull-House,* 110, 158, 214; Stanley Buder, *Pullman: An Experiment in Industrial Order and Community Planning, 1880–1930* (New York, 1967); Carl Smith, *Urban Disorder and the Shape of Belief: The Great Chicago Fire, the Haymarket Bomb, and the Model Town of Pullman* (Chicago, 1995), 177–270; Almont Lindsey, *The Pullman Strike: The Story of a Unique Experiment and of a Great Labor Upheaval* (Chicago, 1942).
37. Addams, *Twenty Years at Hull-House,* 214–17; Victoria Brown, "Advocate for Democracy: Jane Addams and the Pullman Strike," in Richard Schneirov, Shelton Stromquist, and Nick Salvatore, eds., *The Pullman Strike and the Crisis of the 1890s* (Urbana, IL, and Chicago, 1999), 130–58; Elshtain, *Jane Addams,* 101–3.
38. Addams, *Twenty Years at Hull-House,* 32; Jane Addams, "A Modern Lear," *The Survey,* 24 (Nov. 2, 1912), 131–32.
39. Ibid., 132–33, 135.
40. Ibid., 132, 136; Jane Addams, *Democracy and Social Ethics,* ed. Anne Firor Scott, (1902; Cambridge, MA, 1964) 137, 165–66, 275.
41. Brown, "Advocate for Democracy," 142–45; Janice L. Reiff, "A Modern Lear and His Daughters: Gender in the Model Town of Pullman," in Schneirov, Stromquist, and Salvatore, eds., *Pullman Strike and the Crisis of the 1890s,* 65–86; Elshtain, *Jane Addams,* 111–13; Addams, "A Modern Lear," 134–35.
42. Walter Rauschenbusch, "The Ideals of Social Reformers," *American Journal of*

Sociology, 2 (Sept. 1896), 211; Washington Gladden, *The New Idolatry: and Other Discussions* (New York, 1905), 130; Washington Gladden, *Social Salvation* (Boston, 1902), 11–15; Nicholas P. Gilman, "The Reaction Against Individualism," *Unitarian Review,* 25 (March 1886), 218–34; Fine, *Laissez-Faire and the General-Welfare State,* 174–75; Donald K. Gorrell, *The Age of Social Responsibility: The Social Gospel in the Progressive Era, 1900–1920* (Macon, GA, 1988), 9–114; Susan Curtis, "The Son of Man and God the Father: The Social Gospel and Victorian Masculinity," in Carnes and Griffen, eds., *Meanings for Manhood,* 68–71; Susan Curtis, *A Consuming Faith: The Social Gospel and Modern American Culture* (Baltimore, 1991), 1–88.

43. Bellamy, *Looking Backward,* 26, 161–62; Edward Alsworth Ross, *Social Control: A Survey of the Foundations of Order* (1901; Cleveland, 1969), 87; Fine, *Laissez-Faire and the General-Welfare State,* 198–251; Richard T. Ely, *Ground Under Our Feet: An Autobiography* (New York, 1938), 121–64; O'Neill, *Divorce in the Progressive Era,* 44–47, also 63, 72–74, 170–71, 174; Wright, *Moralism and the Model Home,* 106–7, 116, 166–69.
44. Bellamy, *Looking Backward,* 54, 79, 118.
45. Rodgers, *Work Ethic in Industrial America,* esp. xiii; Aron, *Ladies and Gentlemen of the Civil Service,* 94; Gilkeson, *Middle-Class Providence,* 165–67, 173; Jerome Bjelopera, "The Lower Middle Class in Philadelphia, 1870–1920: A History" (Ph.D. diss., Temple University, 1999), 232–36.
46. Cindy S. Aron, *Working at Play: A History of Vacations in the United States* (New York, 1999), 1–177; Gilkeson, *Middle-Class Providence,* 168–73; Theodore Morrison, *Chautauqua: A Center for Education, Religion, and the Arts in America* (Chicago, 1974), 119–28, 149–59, 330–33; May, *Great Expectations;* Richard Wightman Fox, "The Discipline of Amusement," in William R. Taylor, ed., *Inventing Times Square: Commerce and Culture at the Crossroads of the World* (New York, 1991), 83–98.
47. Gilman, *Living of Charlotte Perkins Gilman,* 323; Gordon, *Woman's Body, Woman's Right,* 95–115; D'Emilio and Freedman, *Intimate Matters,* 171–221; William G. Shade, "'A Mental Passion': Female Sexuality in Victorian America," *International Journal of Women's Studies,* 1 (Jan./Feb. 1978), 19–24; Beryl Satter, *Each Mind a Kingdom: American Women, Sexual Purity, and the New Thought Movement, 1875–1920* (Berkeley, CA, 1999), 1–149.
48. Blumin, *Emergence of the Middle Class,* 185–88; Aron, *Ladies and Gentlemen of the Civil Service,* 24; Rothman, *Hands and Hearts;* 166–68; Mark A. Swiencicki, "Consuming Brotherhood: Men's Culture, Style and Recreation as Consumer Culture, 1880–1930," *Journal of Social History,* 31 (Summer 1998), 782–85 788–91. Colin Campbell, *The Romantic Ethic and the Spirit of Modern Consumerism* (Oxford, 1987) has particularly influenced the view of consumption here.
49. Clark, *American Family Home,* 103–32; Wright, *Moralism and the Model Home,* 19–21, 34–35, 73–114; Green, *Light of the Home,* 93–111; Katherine C. Grier, *Culture and*

Comfort: Parlor Making and Middle-Class Identity, 1850–1930 (Washington, D.C., 1988), 64–210.

50. Gladden, *New Idolatry,* 5–6, 9, 92; Richard T. Ely, *The Social Law of Service* (Cincinnati and New York, 1896), 235–36.
51. Bellamy, *Looking Backward,* 54, 60, 62, 66, 96, 120; Wright, *Moralism and the Model Home,* 118–49; Clark, *American Family Home,* 131–70; Sally McMurry, *Families and Farmhouses in Nineteenth-Century America: Vernacular Design and Social Change* (New York, 1988), 168–69; Shi, *Simple Life,* 175–89; Cheryl Robertson, "Male and Female Agendas for Domestic Reform: The Middle-Class Bungalow in Gendered Perspective," *Winterthur Portfolio,* 26 (Summer/Autumn, 1992), 123–41; Bridget A. May, "Progressivism and the Colonial Revival: The Modern Colonial House, 1900–1920," *Winterthur Portfolio,* 26 (Summer/Autumn, 1992), 107–22.
52. John Higham, *Writing American History: Essays on Modern Scholarship* (Bloomington, IN, 1970), 77–88; Bjelopera, "Lower Middle Class in Philadelphia," 204–14; Steven Hardy, *How Boston Played: Sport, Recreation, and Community, 1865–1915* (Boston, 1982), 147–67; Richard Hammond, "Progress and Flight: An Interpretation of the American Cycle Craze of the 1890s," *Journal of Social History,* 5 (Winter 1971–72), 235–57; Rotundo, *American Manhood,* 223–27, 239–44; Green, *Light of the Home,* 144–64; Harvey Green, *Fit for America: Health, Fitness, Sport, and American Society* (New York, 1986).
53. John F. Kasson, *Houdini, Tarzan, and the Perfect Man: The White Male Body and the Challenge of Modernity in America* (New York, 2001), 21–76; Banner, *American Beauty,* 45–65, 154–74; Martha Banta, *Imaging American Women: Idea and Ideals in Cultural History* (New York, 1987), 211–18; Lynn D. Gordon, "The Gibson Girl Goes to College: Popular Culture and Women's Higher Education in the Progressive Era," 1890–1920," *American Quarterly,* 39 (Summer 1987), 211–30; Charlotte Perkins Gilman, *Women and Economics: A Study of the Economic Relation Between Men and Women as a Factor in Social Evolution,* ed. Carl N. Degler (New York, 1966), 148–49.
54. Addams, *Twenty Years at Hull-House,* 187.
55. George H. Mead, "The Working Hypothesis in Social Reform," *American Journal of Sociology,* 5 (Nov. 1899), 367; Dmitri Shalin, "G. H. Mead, Socialism, and the Progressive Agenda," *American Journal of Sociology,* 93 (Jan. 1988), 913–51; Yehoshua Arieli, *Individualism and Nationalism in American Ideology* (Cambridge, MA, 1964), 339; Addams, *Twenty Years at Hull-House,* 180–82; Fine, *Laissez-Faire and the General-Welfare State,* 185–96, 210–11; John L. Thomas, *Alternative America: Henry George, Edward Bellamy, Henry Demarest Lloyd and the Adversary Tradition* (Cambridge, MA, 1983); Robert M. La Follette, *La Follette's Autobiography: A Personal Narrative of Political Experiences* (Madison, WI, 1913), 19; Gilman, *Living of Charlotte Perkins Gilman,* 131, 198; Rauschenbusch, "Ideals of Social Reformers," 211–14; Richard T. Ely, *Socialism: An Examination of Its Nature, Its Strength and Its Weakness, with Sugges-*

tions for Social Reform (New York, 1894); John R. Commons, "Progressive Individualism," *American Magazine of Civics*, 6 (June 1895), 561–74; Mari Jo Buhle, *Women and American Socialism, 1870–1920* (Urbana, IL, 1981), 49–103. My interest here is in the social origins of middle-class ideas about socialism, as well as individualism. James Kloppenberg, *Uncertain Victory: Social Democracy and Progressivism in European and American Thought, 1870–1920* (New York, 1986), especially 199–246, explores in much more detail the intellectual history of the international search for what he terms the "via media" between socialism and laissez-faire. I believe that individualism, while clearly linked to laissez-faire, played a more catalytic role in the transformation of middle-class ideology.

56. Addams, *Twenty Years at Hull-House*, 109, 186; Davis, *American Heroine*, 67–134.
57. Addams, *Democracy and Social Ethics*, 137, 165–66, 275; Addams, "A Modern Lear," 137.
58. Rauschenbusch, "Ideals of Social Reformers," 208–10; Gladden, *New Idolatry*, 131, 187, 191; Josiah Strong, *Religious Movements for Social Betterment* (New York, 1900), 12–15, 21–22.
59. Ely, *Social Law of Service*, 127–28.
60. Addams, *Twenty Years at Hull-House*, 285, 315.
61. Ibid., 209, 229; Kathryn Kish Sklar, *Florence Kelley and the Nation's Work: The Rise of Women's Political Culture, 1830–1900* (New Haven, CT, 1995), 206–85; Kathryn Kish Sklar, Anja Schüler, and Susan Strasser, eds., *Social Justice Feminists in the United States and Germany: A Dialogue in Documents, 1885–1933* (Ithaca, NY, 1998), 90–114.
62. Henry C. Adams, "Relation of the State to Industrial Action," *Publications of the American Economic Association*, I (Jan. 1887), 12; Fine, *Laissez-Faire and the General-Welfare State*, 205–9; Ely, *Social Law of Service*, 161–75.
63. Albion Small, "The Meaning of the Social Movement," *American Journal of Sociology*, 3 (Nov. 1897), 340–54; Rauschenbusch, "Ideals of Social Reformers," 202; Blumin, *Emergence of the Middle Class*, 285–90.
64. Addams, *Twenty Years at Hull-House*, 196.
65. Ely, *Ground Under Our Feet*, 79–87.
66. William James, *Talks to Teachers on Psychology and to Students on Some of Life's Ideals* (1899; Cambridge, MA, 1983), 152–54, 182, 237; Fine, *Laissez-Faire and the General-Welfare State*, 283–84. Magazines for middle-class readers also served as a kind of model for new progressive values: See Matthew Schneirov, *The Dream of a New Social Order: Popular Magazines in America, 1893–1914* (New York, 1994).
67. Gorrell, *Age of Social Responsibility*, 29–30; Gladden, *New Idolatry*, 183.
68. Small, "Meaning of the Social Movement," 340.
69. Elizabeth Cady Stanton, "The Solitude of Self," in Susan B. Anthony and Ida Husted Harper, eds., *The History of Woman Suffrage*, 4 vols. (Rochester, NY, 1883–1900), IV, 189–90; Sklar, Schüler, and Strasser, eds., *Social Justice Feminists*, 79.

70. Aron, *Ladies and Gentlemen of the Civil Service*, 19, n. 12; John Bodnar, *The Transplanted: A History of Immigrants in Urban America* (Bloomington, IN, 1985), 117–43; William Toll, *The Making of an Ethnic Middle Class: Portland Jewry over Four Generations* (Albany, NY, 1982); Colleen McDannell, *The Christian Home in Victorian America, 1840–1900* (Bloomington, IN, 1986); David Katzman, *Before the Ghetto: Black Detroit in the Nineteenth Century* (Urbana, IL, 1973); Olivier Zunz, *The Changing Face of Inequality: Urbanization, Industrial Development, and Immigrants in Detroit, 1880–1920* (Chicago, 1982); Janette Thomas Greenwood, *Bittersweet Legacy: The Black and White 'Better Classes' in Charlotte, 1850–1910* (Chapel Hill, NC, 1994); Willard B. Gatewood, *Aristocrats of Color: The Black Elite, 1880–1920* (Bloomington, IN, 1990); Aron, *Working at Play*, 116, 118–19; Linda W. Rosenzweig, *The Anchor of My Life: Middle-Class American Mothers and Daughters, 1880–1920* (New York, 1993).
71. Bjelopera, "Lower Middle Class in Philadelphia," 1–179; Margery W. Davies, *Woman's Place Is at the Typewriter: Office Work and Office Workers, 1870–1930* (Philadelphia, 1982); Lisa M. Fine, *The Souls of the Skyscraper: Female Clerical Work in Chicago, 1870–1930* (Philadelphia, 1990); Sharon Hartman Strom, *Beyond the Typewriter: Gender, Class, and the Making of Modern Office Work* (Urbana, IL, 1992); Ileen A. DeVault, *Sons and Daughters of Labor: Class and Clerical Work in Turn-of-the-Century Pittsburgh* (Ithaca, NY, 1990); Jurgen Kocka, *White Collar Workers in America, 1890–1940*, trans. Maura Kealey (London, 1980); Melanie Archer, "Small Capitalism and Middle-Class Formation in Industrializing Detroit, 1880–1900," *Journal of Urban History*, 21 (Jan. 1995), 218–55; Zunz, *Making America Corporate*, 125–48.
72. Lewis Corey, *The Crisis of the Middle Class* (New York, 1935), esp. 112–50; Robert H. Wiebe, *The Search for Order, 1877–1920* (New York, 1967), 111–32; Stern, *Society and Family Strategy*, 72; Bledstein, "Introduction," 19–20; Derby Applegate, "Henry Ward Beecher and the 'Great Middle Class': Mass-Marketed Intimacy and Middle-Class Identity," in Bledstein and Johnston, eds., *Middling Sorts*, 107–24; Sven Beckert, "Propertied of a Different Kind: Lower Bourgeoisie and Middle Class in the Nineteenth-Century United States," in ibid., 285–95.
73. William James, *Talks to Teachers*, 152–54, 184; Weir, "Methods of the Rioting Striker," 953; Henry Demarest Lloyd, *Newest England: Notes of a Democratic Traveller in New Zealand, With Some Australian Comparisons* (New York, 1903), 376; Gilkeson, *Middle-Class Providence*, 10; Wright, *Moralism and the Model Home*, 109. A number of scholars rightly point out that almost every social group—immigrants, workers, farmers, even the upper class—spurred or supported at least some progressive measures: J. Joseph Huthmacher, "Urban Liberalism and the Age of Reform," *Mississippi Valley Historical Review*, 49 (Sept. 1962), 231–41; Gabriel Kolko, *The Triumph of Conservatism: A Reinterpretation of American History, 1900–1916* (New York, 1963); James Weinstein, *The Corporate Ideal in the Liberal State* (Boston, 1968); Peter G. Filene, "An Obituary for 'The Progressive Movement,'" *American Quarterly*, 22

(Spring 1970), 20–34; Gary M. Fink, "The Rejection of Voluntarism," *Industrial and Labor Relations Review*, 26 (Jan. 1973), 805–19; John D. Buenker, *Urban Liberalism and Progressive Reform* (New York, 1973); Georg Leidenberger, "'The Public Is the Labor Union': Working-Class Progressivism in Turn-of-the-Century Chicago," *Labor History*, 36 (Spring 1995), 187–210; Elizabeth Sanders, *Roots of Reform: Farmers, Workers, and the American State* (Chicago, 1999). Yet none of these groups advocated the full range of progressive positions as consistently as the middle class did. As I argue in this and succeeding chapters, progressive ideology emerged in part out of middle-class alienation from working-class and upper-class culture. Moreover, progressivism sprang from a level of discontent among middle-class women unequalled among the women of other classes.

Chapter Three

1. Rose Cohen, *Out of the Shadow* (New York, 1918), 230–31.
2. Ibid., 233, 246.
3. Ibid., 236, 238–42, 261, 300.
4. Ibid., 245–46, 273.
5. David Graham Phillips, *The Reign of Gilt* (New York, 1905), 141; Washington Gladden, *The New Idolatry and Other Discussions* (New York, 1905), 210–11; Walter Rauschenbusch, *Christianity and the Social Crisis*, ed., Robert D. Cross (1907; New York, 1964), 351–52; Theodore Roosevelt, *The Works of Theodore Roosevelt*, "National Edition," 20 vols. (New York, 1926), XX, 165.
6. Paul Boyer, *Urban Masses and Moral Order in America, 1820–1920* (Cambridge, MA, 1978), 175–87, 221–32; Simon N. Patten, *The New Basis of Civilization*, ed. Daniel M. Fox (1907; Cambridge, MA, 1968), 204–5; Josiah Strong, *Religious Movements for Social Betterment* (New York, 1900), 16–17; Robert M. La Follette, *La Follette's Auobiography: A Personal Narrative of Political Experiences* (Madison, WI, 1913), 40–41.
7. Carry A. Nation, *The Use and Need of the Life of Carry A. Nation* (Topeka, KS, 1905), 69–72; Robert Smith Bader, *Prohibition in Kansas: A History* (Lawrence, KS, 1986), 106–32.
8. Nation, *Use and Need*, 40, 56; Fran Grace, *Carry A. Nation: Retelling the Life* (Bloomington, IN, 2001), 18–136.
9. Ibid., 150–201; Nation, *Use and Need*, 76.
10. Ibid., 66; Bader, *Prohibition in Kansas*, 133–55; Grace, *Carry A. Nation*, 201–61; Norman H. Clark, *Deliver Us From Evil: An Interpretation of American Prohibition* (New York, 1976), 81–84.
11. Jacob Riis, *The Peril and the Preservation of the Home* (Philadelphia, 1903), 24; Strong, *Religious Movements for Social Betterment*, 49; Eric Rauchway, *The Refuge of Affections: Family and American Reform Politics, 1900–1920* (New York, 2001), 1–29, argues the centrality of the idea of the family for progressives.

12. Bader, *Prohibition in Kansas,* 140.
13. Clark, *Deliver Us From Evil,* 4, 57–59, 66; Boyer, *Urban Masses and Moral Order,* 191–204; Dewey W. Grantham, *Southern Progressivism: The Reconciliation of Progress and Tradition* (Knoxville, TN, 1983), 14–75; Paul S. Boyer, *Purity in Print: The Vice-Society Movement and Book Censorship in America* (New York, 1968), 23–52.
14. Ernest H. Cherrington, *The Evolution of Prohibition in the United States: A Chronological History* (Westerville, OH, 1920), 163–276; William D. P. Bliss, ed., *The New Encyclopedia of Social Reform* (New York, 1908), 716, 720; Clark, *Deliver Us From Evil,* 50.
15. Prince A. Morrow, "The Relations of Social Diseases to the Family," in American Sociological Society, *Papers and Proceedings, Third Annual Meeting* (Chicago, 1909), 53; David J. Pivar, *Purity Crusade: Sexual Morality and Social Control, 1868–1900* (Westport, CT, 1973); Boyer, *Urban Masses and Moral Order,* 192; Mark Connelly, *The Response to Prostitution in the Progressive Era* (Chapel Hill, NC, 1980), 3–4, 67–90.
16. Glenda Riley, *Divorce: An American Tradition* (New York, 1991), 78–107; Elaine Tyler May, *Great Expectations: Marriage and Divorce in Post-Victorian America* (Chicago, 1980), esp. 167.
17. Clark, *Deliver Us From Evil,* 11; Bader, *Prohibition in Kansas* 129–30; Grantham, *Southern Progressivism,* 176–77.
18. Anna B. Rogers, *Why American Marriages Fail* (Boston, 1909), 6–7 and 16, quoted in Riley, *Divorce,* 128; William L. O'Neill, *Divorce in the Progressive Era* (New Haven, CT, 1967), 33–88; Grantham, *Southern Progressivism,* 173.
19. Nation, *Use and Need,* 30, 76; Prof. A. B. Wolfe, in American Sociological Society, *Papers and Proceedings, Third Annual Meeting,* 59; Morrow, "Relations of Social Diseases to the Family," 57; Bader, *Prohibition in Kansas,* 141; Catherine Gilbert Murdock, *Domesticating Drink: Men, Women, and Alcohol in America, 1870–1940* (Baltimore, MD, 1999); Jeffrey P. Moran, "'Modernism Gone Mad': Sex Education Comes to Chicago, 1913," *Journal of American History,* 83 (Sept. 1996), 488–89.
20. This paragraph and the previous one draw on Roy Rosenzweig, *Eight Hours for What We Will: Workers and Leisure in an Industrial City, 1870–1920* (Cambridge, 1983), 93–126; Boyer, *Urban Masses and Moral Order,* 211–16; Norton Juster, *So Sweet to Labor: Rural Women in America, 1865–1895* (New York, 1979), 133–212; Sally McMurry, *Families and Farmhouses in Nineteenth-Century America: Vernacular Design and Social Change* (New York, 1988), 89–102; Jack Temple Kirby, *Rural Worlds Lost: The American South, 1920–1960* (Baton Rouge, 1987), 173–74.
21. Clark, *Deliver Us From Evil,* 69–79, 84–88, 92–117; Bader, *Prohibition in Kansas,* 129, 131–32, 160–61.
22. Ibid., 154; Clark, *Deliver Us From Evil,* 96–98; Grantham, *Southern Progressivism,* 160–77; Rosenzweig, *Eight Hours for What We Will,* 94, 100, 117–22.
23. Theodore Roosevelt, *The Letters of Theodore Roosevelt,* eds. Elting E. Morison et al., 8 vols. (Cambridge, MA, 1951–54), VI, 1131; Arthur S. Link, *Wilson: The Road to the*

White House (Princeton, NJ, 1947), 151–52; Arthur S. Link, *Wilson: The New Freedom* (Princeton, NJ, 1956), 259–60 and 389, n. 179.

24. Grantham, *Southern Progressivism*, 160–61; Clark, *Deliver Us From Evil*, 101–2; Bader, *Prohibition in Kansas*, 165–66; Paul E. Isaac, *Prohibition and Politics: Turbulent Decades in Tennessee, 1885–1920* (Knoxville, TN, 1965), 81–169; Jimmie Lewis Franklin, *Born Sober: Prohibition in Oklahoma, 1907–1959* (Norman, OK, 1971), 3–35; Paolo E. Coletta, *The Presidency of William Howard Taft* (Lawrence, KS, 1973), 254.
25. Willoughby C. Waterman, *Prostitution and Its Repression in New York City, 1900–1931* (New York, 1932), 80–116; Connelly, *Response to Prostitution*, 5–15; Boyer, *Urban Masses and Moral Order*, 193.
26. Connelly, *Response to Prostitution*, 49–54.
27. Morrow, "Relations of Social Diseases to the Family," 54; Connelly, *Response to Prostitution*, 16–19, 25–26.
28. Waterman, *Prostitution and Its Repression*, 16–25.
29. Riley, *Divorce*, 108–29; O'Neill, *Divorce in the Progressive Era*, 48–56.
30. Riley, *Divorce*, 99, 115–17; O'Neill, *Divorce in the Progressive Era*, 231–53.
31. Riley, *Divorce*, 111, 114–15; Roosevelt, *Works*, XV, 377.
32. O'Neill, *Divorce in the Progressive Era*, 71; Riley, *Divorce*, 118, 121–23; Nation, *Use and Need*, 102; Morrow, "Relations of Social Diseases to the Family," 59.
33. O'Neill, *Divorce in the Progressive Era*, 20; Riley, *Divorce*, 118–29; Samuel W. Dike in American Sociological Society, *Papers and Proceedings, Third Annual Meeting*, 163; George Elliot Howard, *A History of Matrimonial Institutions*, 3 vols. (Chicago, 1904), III, 160–223; George Elliott Howard, "Is the Freer Granting of Divorce an Evil?," in American Sociological Society, *Papers and Proceedings, Third Annual Meeting*, 158–60; Edward Alsworth Ross, *Changing America: Studies in Contemporary Society* (New York, 1912), 49–63; May, *Great Expectations*, 167.
34. Committee of Fifty, *The Liquor Problem: A Summary of Investigations, 1893–1903* (Boston, 1905), 143–83; Jane Addams, *The Spirit of Youth and the City Streets* (1909; Urbana, IL, 1972), 6, 29.
35. Washington Gladden, *Social Salvation* (Boston, 1902), 144–45.
36. Clark, *Deliver Us From Evil*, 87–88; Patten, *New Basis of Civilization*, 123, 213–14.
37. Anna Garlin Spencer in American Sociological Society, *Papers and Proceedings, Third Annual Meeting*, 62; Connelly, *Response to Prostitution*, 30–44.
38. Strong, *Religious Movements for Social Betterment*, 48; Albion Small in American Sociological Society, *Papers and Proceedings, Third Annual Meeting*, 192.
39. Louise de Koven Bowen, *Growing Up with a City*, ed. Maureen A. Flanagan (1926; Urbana, IL, 2002), 81–102.
40. Edith Wharton, *The House of Mirth* (1905; New York, 1985); Thorstein Veblen, *The Theory of the Leisure Class* (New York, 1899); Patten, *New Basis of Civilization*, 39–41, 210; Phillips, *Reign of Gilt*, 33, 37, 41–42, 48, 54.

41. Roosevelt, *Works,* XIII, 5, 9, 11, 21, 163, 172, 323, 357–58, 360; Roosevelt, *Letters,* III, 107–8, 535–36; William Henry Harbaugh, *Power and Responsibility: The Life and Times of Theodore Roosevelt* (New York, 1961), 52.
42. Lucius Beebe, *The Big Spenders* (Garden City, NY, 1966), 283–86; *New York Times,* April 3, 1908.
43. Roosevelt, *Works,* XV, 377–378; Roosevelt, *Letters,* III, 355–56; Marion Talbot in American Sociological Society, *Papers and Proceedings, Third Annual Meeting,* 45; Linda Gordon, *Woman's Body, Woman's Right: A Social History of Birth Control in America* (1976; New York, 1977), 136–58.
44. Roosevelt, *Letters,* IV, 1298–99; Roosevelt, *Works,* XV, 368–70, 500; John D. Buenker, *The Income Tax and the Progressive Era* (New York, 1985); Morton Keller, *Regulating a New Economy: Public Policy and Economic Change in America, 1900–1933* (Cambridge, MA, 1990), 208–18; Sidney Ratner, *Taxation and Democracy in America* (New York, 1967), 168–320; Edwin R. A. Seligman, *Essays in Taxation,* 10th ed. (New York, 1925), 126–44; R. Rudy Higgens-Evenson, *The Price of Progress: Public Services, Taxation, and the American Corporate State, 1877–1929* (Baltimore, MD, 2003), 77–91.
45. Frederick Townsend Martin, *The Passing of the Idle Rich* (London, 1911), 109–11, 260; Andrew Carnegie, *The Gospel of Wealth and Other Timely Essays,* ed. Edward C. Kirkland (1900; Cambridge, MA, 1962), 22, n. 3.
46. Martin, *Passing of the Idle Rich,* 128, 169–94, 220.
47. Boyer, *Urban Masses and Moral Order,* 127, 143–61, 155–58; Allen F. Davis, *Spearheads of Reform: The Social Settlements and the Progressive Movement, 1880–1914* (New Brunswick, NJ, 1984), 18–22; Grantham, *Southern Progressivism,* 224–30; Patten, *New Basis of Civilization,* 43, 51–52, 56.
48. Davis, *Spearheads for Reform,* 8–15, 23, 40–56, 66, and 268, n. 59; Grantham, *Southern Progressivism,* 222–23; Mina Carson, *Settlement Folk: Social Thought and the American Settlement Movement, 1885–1930* (Chicago, 1990), 101–21.
49. Gladden, *Social Salvation,* 32–33; Strong, *Religious Movements for Social Betterment,* 27–28, 33–34, 46–47, 50; Boyer, *Urban Masses and Moral Order,* 132–42; Donald K. Gorrell, *The Age of Social Responsibility: The Social Gospel in the Progressive Era, 1900–1920* (Macon, GA, 1988), 1–114.
50. Riis, *Peril and the Preservation of the Home,* 34–35; Boyer, *Urban Masses and Moral Order,* 179–87, 233–35; Davis, *Spearheads for Reform,* 65–74; Roy Lubove, *The Progressives and the Slums: Tenement House Reform in New York City, 1890–1917* (Pittsburgh, 1962), 49–184.
51. Boyer, *Urban Masses and Moral Order,* 235–42; Rosenzweig, *Eight Hours for What We Will,* 127–40; Davis, *Spearheads for Reform,* 70–83; Lubove, *Progressives and the Slums,* 231–38.
52. Cohen, *Out of the Shadow,* 249; Davis, *Spearheads for Reform,* 47–48; Carson, *Settlement*

Folk, 101–21; Rivka Shpak Lissak, *Pluralism and Progressives: Hull House and the New Immigrants, 1890–1919* (Chicago, 1989).

53. Cohen, *Out of the Shadow*, 249.
54. Ibid., 246–48, 256.
55. Ibid., 247, 273–75.
56. Ibid., 246, 305.
57. Rose Gollup Cohen, "To the Friends of 'Out of the Shadow,'" *Bookman*, 55 (March 1922), 36–40; Davis, *Spearheads for Reform*, 86–90; Lissak, *Pluralism and Progressives*, esp. 108–22; Carson, *Settlement Folk*, 101–21; Hilda Satt Polacheck, *I Came a Stranger: The Story of a Hull-House Girl*, ed. Dena J. Polacheck Epstein (Urbana, IL, 1989); Kathy Peiss, *Cheap Amusements: Working Women and Leisure in Turn-of-the-Century New York* (Philadelphia, 1986), 163–78.
58. Riis, *Peril and Preservation of the Home*, 24; David E. Shi, *The Simple Life: Plain Living and High Thinking in American Culture* (New York, 1985), 175–214.
59. Kenyon L. Butterfield, *Chapters in Rural Progress* (Chicago, 1909), 5, 69; William L. Bowers, *The Country Life Movement in America, 1900–1920* (Port Washington, NY, 1974), 3–5, 15–29, 40–61, 91–95; David B. Danbom, *The Resisted Revolution: Urban America and the Industrialization of Agriculture, 1900–1930* (Ames, IA, 1979), 23–50.
60. Kenyon L. Butterfield, "Rural Life and the Family," in American Sociological Society, *Papers and Proceedings, Third Annual Meeting*, 106–10; Butterfield, *Chapters in Rural Progress*, 17–22; Danbom, *Resisted Revolution*, 47–49; Bowers, *Country Life Movement*, 53, 77–89.
61. *Report of the Country Life Commission* (New York, 1911); Danbom, *Resisted Revolution*, 51–61; Bowers, *Country Life Movement*, 15–16, 38–39, 58, 64, 80–84.
62. Hal S. Barron, *Mixed Harvest: The Second Great Transformation in the Rural North, 1870–1930* (Chapel Hill, NC, 1997), 19–37; Rodney O. Davis, "Iowa Farm Opinion and the Good Roads Movement, 1903–1904," *Annals of Iowa*, 37 (Summer 1964), 333–34.
63. Grantham, *Southern Progressivism*, 336; Bowers, *Country Life Movement*, 22, 103; Barron, *Mixed Harvest*, 32–33.
64. Edward Alsworth Ross, *Social Control: A Survey of the Foundations of Order* (1901; Cleveland, 1969), 428.
65. Grantham, *Southern Progressivism*, 178–79; Riis, *Peril and Preservation of the Home*, 27–28; Patten, *New Basis of Civilization*, 35; David I. Macleod, *Building Character in the American Boy: The Boy Scouts, YMCA, and Their Forerunners, 1870–1920* (Madison, WI, 1983); Peiss, *Cheap Amusements*, 178–84; Addams, *Spirit of Youth and the City Streets*.
66. Phillips, *Reign of Gilt*, 50–71, 157; Woodrow Wilson, *The Papers of Woodrow Wilson*, ed. Arthur S. Link et al., 69 vols. (Princeton, NJ, 1966–94), XIX, 30, 227.
67. Anna Garlin Spencer in American Sociological Society, *Papers and Proceedings*,

Third Annual Meeting, 198; Juvenile Court of the City and County of Denver, *The Problem of the Children and How Colorado Cares for Them* (Denver, 1904), 22; Joseph F. Kett, *Rites of Passage: Adolescence in America: 1790 to the Present* (New York, 1977), 215–44; Macleod, *Building Character in the American Boy*, xv–xvi, 19–27, 37–38, 50–52, 98–99; Christopher Lasch, *Haven in a Heartless World: The Family Besieged* (New York, 1977), 3–21.

68. Grantham, *Southern Progressivism*, 178–99; Davis, *Spearheads for Reform*, 123–33; Keller, *Regulating a New Society: Public Policy and Social Change in America, 1900–1933* (Cambridge, MA, 1994), 197–208.
69. Cohen, *Out of the Shadow*, 246; Ross, *Social Control*, 166.
70. This paragraph and the next draw on Lawrence Cremin, *The Transformation of the School: Progressivism in American Education, 1876–1957* (New York, 1961), 3–176; Lawrence Cremin, *American Education: The Metropolitan Experience, 1876–1980* (New York, 1988); David B. Tyack, *The One Best System: A History of American Urban Education* (Cambridge, MA, 1974), 126–268; Grantham, *Southern Progressivism*, 246–57; John Bodnar, *The Transplanted: A History of Immigrants in Urban America* (Bloomington, IN, 1985), 189–97; David B. Danbom, "Rural Education and the Country Life Movement, 1900–1920," *Agricultural History*, 53: 2 (1979), 462–74; Barron, *Mixed Harvest*, 43–77; U.S. Bureau of the Census, *Historical Statistics of the United States. Colonial Times to 1970*, Bicentennial ed., 2 vols. (Washington, D.C., 1975), I, 370, 374–76.
71. Quotation from Barron, *Mixed Harvest*, 71.
72. Addams, *Spirit of Youth and the City Streets*, 8; Robert B. Westbrook, *John Dewey and American Democracy* (Ithaca, NY, 1991), 93–113, 167–82.
73. John Dewey, *The Child and the Curriculum and The School and Society* (Chicago, 1956), 15; Wilson, *Papers*, XIX, 30; Edgar Gardner Murphy, *Problems of the Present South: A Discussion of Certain of the Educational, Industrial and Political Issues in the Southern States* (New York, 1904), 72–74.
74. Addams, *Spirit of Youth and the City Streets*, 4, 102–3; Macleod, *Building Character in the American Boy;* Grantham, *Southern Progressivism*, 266; Rosenzweig, *Eight Hours for What We Will*, 143–48; Davis, *Spearheads for Reform*, 60–65; Harold Seymour, *Baseball: The People's Game* (New York, 1990), 46–48, 50–66.
75. Boyer, *Urban Masses and Moral Order*, 242–51; Seymour, *Baseball*, 48; Macleod, *Building Character in the American Boy;* Dominick Cavallo, *Muscles and Morals: Organized Playgrounds and Urban Reform, 1880–1920* (Philadelphia, 1981); Eric C. Schneider, *In the Web of Class: Delinquents and Reformers in Boston, 1810s–1930s* (New York, 1992), 132–38.
76. Sophonisba P. Breckinridge and Edith Abbott, *The Delinquent Child and the Home* (New York, 1912); Kenneth Cmiel, *A Home of Another Kind: One Chicago Orphanage and the Tangle of Child Welfare* (Chicago, 1995), 1–92; Timothy A. Hacsi, *Second Home: Orphan Asylums and Poor Families in America* (Cambridge, MA, 1997); Reena

Sigman Friedman, *These Are Our Children: Jewish Orphanages in the United States, 1880–1925* (Hanover, NH, 1994); Nurith Zmora, *Orphanages Reconsidered: Child Care Institutions in Progressive Era Baltimore* (Philadelphia, 1994), 1–179; Hyman Bogen, *The Luckiest Orphans: A History of the Hebrew Orphan Asylum of New York* (Urbana, IL, 1992), 137–212.

77. Juvenile Court of the City and County of Denver, *Problem of the Children*, 18; Schneider, *In the Web of Class*, 145–69; Steven Schlossman and Stephanie Wallach, "The Crime of Precocious Sexuality: Female Juvenile Delinquency in the Progressive Era," *Harvard Educational Review*, 48 (Feb. 1978), 71–75; Elizabeth J. Clapp, "Welfare and the Role of Women: The Juvenile Court Movement," *Journal of American Studies*, 28 (Dec. 1994), 359–83; Mary E. Odem, *Delinquent Daughters: Protecting and Policing Adolescent Female Sexuality in the United States, 1885–1920* (Chapel Hill, NC, 1995), 95–156; Elizabeth J. Clapp, *Mothers of All Children: Women Reformers and the Rise of Juvenile Courts in Progressive Era America* (University Park, PA, 1998).
78. Roosevelt, *Works*, XV, 530–31; Roosevelt, *Letters*, VI, 1899–1909; Davis, *Spearheads for Reform*, 132; Molly Ladd-Taylor, *Mother-Work: Women, Child Welfare, and the State, 1890–1930* (Urbana, IL, 1994); Kriste Lindenmeyer, *"A Right to Childhood": The U.S. Children's Bureau and Child Welfare, 1912–46* (Urbana, IL, 1997), 9–75.
79. Rosenzweig, *Eight Hours for What We Will*, 149–52; Seymour, *Baseball*, 49.
80. Strong, *Religious Movements for Social Betterment*, 47–48.
81. Gladden, *Social Salvation*, 136–37.
82. Ross, *Social Control*, 162, 422–24.
83. Patten, *New Basis of Civilization*, 150, 153–54, 156.
84. Ross, *Social Control*, 53; Gladden, *Social Salvation*, 5–6; George K. Holmes, "How Far Should Family Wealth Be Encouraged and Conserved?" in American Sociological Society, *Papers and Proceedings, Third Annual Meeting*, 217.
85. Cohen, *Out of the Shadow*, 300–301.

Chapter Four

1. Frank Julian Warne, "John Mitchell: The Labor Leader and the Man," *American Monthly Review of Reviews*, 26 (Nov. 1902), 556–60; *Washington Post*, May 13, 1902.
2. Robert J. Cornell, *The Anthracite Coal Strike of 1902* (New York, 1957), 12–94; Bruno Ramirez, *When Workers Fight: The Politics of Industrial Relations in the Progressive Era, 1898–1916* (Westport, CT, 1978), 30–48; Peter Roberts, *Anthracite Coal Communities: A Study of the Demography, the Social, Educational and Moral Life of the Anthracite Regions* (New York, 1904); Victor R. Greene, *The Slavic Community on Strike: Immigrant Labor in Pennsylvania Anthracite* (Notre Dame, IN, 1968), 1–12, 33–176.
3. Frederic William Unger, "George F. Baer: Master-Spirit of the Anthracite Industry," *American Monthly Review of Reviews*, 33 (May 1906), 545–48; Cornell, *Anthracite Coal Strike*, 1–35, 40–59, 72–73, 76–78, 83.

4. Ibid., 91, 97.
5. U.S. Bureau of the Census, *Historical Statistics of the United States,* Bicentennial ed., 2 vols. (Washington, D.C., 1975), I, 179; P. K. Edwards, *Strikes in the United States, 1881–1974* (New York, 1981).
6. Thomas Beer, *Hanna* (New York, 1929), 132–33; Ramirez, *When Workers Fight,* 4–13, 65–84; Marguerite Green, *The National Civic Federation and the American Labor Movement, 1900–1925* (Washington, D.C., 1956), 1–89; James Weinstein, *The Corporate Ideal in the Liberal State, 1900–1918* (Boston, 1968), 3–39.
7. Cornell, *Anthracite Coal Strike,* 91.
8. Warne, "John Mitchell," 556–60; Cornell, *Anthracite Coal Strike,* 49, 62; Elsie Gluck, *John Mitchell: Labor's Bargain with the Gilded Age* (New York, 1929); Ramirez, *When Workers Fight,* 49–64, 73–79; James O. Morris, "The Acquisitive Spirit of John Mitchell, UMW President (1899–1908)," *Labor History,* 20 (Winter 1979), 5–43; Craig Phelan, *Divided Loyalties: The Public and Private Life of Labor Leader John Mitchell* (Albany, NY, 1994), 1–166.
9. Cornell, *Anthracite Coal Strike,* 64–65, 72–74, 76–78, 81–90, 100–103, 123–24, 127, 132–33, 165–66; Phelan, *Divided Loyalties,* 166–75.
10. Ibid., 145–46, 151–53, 159–60, 168; Greene, *Slavic Community on Strike,* 181–205.
11. Unger, "George F. Baer," 546–48; Cornell, *Anthracite Coal Strike,* 143–45, 165–66, 170–71.
12. Walter Rauschenbusch, *Christianity and the Social Crisis,* ed. Robert D. Cross (1907; New York, 1964), 255; Cornell, *Anthracite Coal Strike,* 173–74.
13. Theodore Roosevelt, *The Letters of Theodore Roosevelt,* eds. Elting E. Morison et al., 8 vols. (Cambridge, MA, 1951–54), III, 515; Cornell, *Anthracite Coal Strike,* 103–10, 174–78; Washington Gladden, *Recollections* (Columbus, OH, 1909), 396–97; Jacob Henry Dorn, *Washington Gladden: Prophet of the Social Gospel* (Columbus, OH, 1967), 223–24.
14. Roosevelt, *Letters,* III, 338, 340–41, 349, 360–61, 365–66; Cornell, *Anthracite Coal Strike,* 178–88.
15. Roosevelt, *Letters,* III, 366; Cornell, *Anthracite Coal Strike,* 189–235.
16. Walter Wellman, "The Settlement of the Coal Strike," *American Monthly Review of Reviews,* 26 (Nov. 1902), 552, 555; Cornell, *Anthracite Coal Strike,* 236–59; Ramirez, *When Workers Fight,* 42–45.
17. Cornell, *Anthracite Coal Strike,* 169.
18. David Montgomery, *Workers' Control in America: Studies in the History of Work, Technology, and Labor Struggles* (Cambridge, MA, 1979), 9–31; David Montgomery, *The Fall of the House of Labor: The Workplace, the State, and American Labor Activism, 1865–1925* (Cambridge, MA, 1987), 171–213; Michael Kazin, *Barons of Labor: The San Francisco Building Trade and Union Power in the Progressive Era* (Urbana, IL, 1987), 46–53,

83–107; Eric Arnesen, *Waterfront Workers of New Orleans: Race, Class, and Politics, 1863–1923* (New York, 1991), 160–203.

19. Morton Keller, *Regulating a New Economy: Public Policy and Economic Change in America, 1900–1933* (Cambridge, MA, 1990), 123–24; Ramirez, *When Workers Fight*, 44, 67–71, 88–103; Clarence E. Bonnett, *Employers' Associations in the United States: A Study of Typical Associations* (New York, 1922); Roosevelt, *Letters*, III, 514–16; Selig Perlman, *A History of Trade Unionism in the United States* (New York, 1922), 190–98; Montgomery, *Fall of the House of Labor*, 269–75; Montgomery, *Workers' Control in America*, 47–90; David Brody, *Workers in Industrial America: Essays on the 20th Century Struggle* (New York, 1980), 26; David Brody, *Steelworkers in America: The Nonunion Era* (Cambridge, MA, 1960, 62–68; Daniel Nelson, "The New Factory System and the Unions: The National Cash Register Dispute of 1901," *Labor History*, 15 (Spring 1974), 163–78.
20. Stuart Brandes, *American Welfare Capitalism 1880–1940* (Chicago, 1976), 33; John R. Commons et al., *History of Labour in the United States, 1896–1932* (New York, 1935), 385–96; Ramirez, *When Workers Fight*, 147–59; Daniel Nelson, *Frederick W. Taylor and the Rise of Scientific Management* (Madison, WI, 1980), 6–19; Daniel Nelson, *Managers and Workers: Origins of the New Factory System in the United States, 1880–1920* (Madison, WI, 1975), 101–21.
21. Montgomery, *Fall of the House of Labor*, 207–13; Nelson, *Managers and Workers*, 3–54; Christopher Tomlins, *The State and the Unions: Labor Relations, Law, and the Organized Labor Movement in America, 1880–1960* (Cambridge, MA, 1985), 16–20.
22. Nelson, *Frederick W. Taylor and the Rise of Scientific Management*, 48.
23. Ibid., 29.
24. Nelson, *Frederick W. Taylor and the Rise of Scientific Management*, 44–45; Frederick Winslow Taylor, *Shop Management* (1903; New York, 1911), 168, 199–200; Montgomery, *Fall of the House of Labor*, 214–36.
25. Taylor, *Shop Management*, 130–31, 133, 146; Hugh G. J. Aitken, *Scientific Management in Action: Taylorism at Watertown Arsenal, 1908–1915* (Princeton, NJ, 1985); Montgomery, *Fall of the House of Labor*, 252; Nelson, *Frederick W. Taylor and the Rise of Scientific Management*, 92–94.
26. Gwendolyn Mink, *Old Labor and New Immigrants in American Political Development: Union, Party, and State, 1875–1920* (Ithaca, NY, 1986), 45–112; William E. Forbath, *Law and the Shaping of the American Labor Movement* (Cambridge, MA, 1991), 12–25.
27. Philip S. Foner, *Organized Labor and the Black Worker, 1619–1981*, 2nd ed. (New York, 1982), 64–79; Montgomery, *Fall of the House of Labor*, 198–201.
28. Foner, *Organized Labor and the Black Worker*, 80–100; Arnesen, *Waterfront Workers of New Orleans*, 149–203; Daniel Rosenberg, *New Orleans Dock Workers: Race, Labor, and Unionism, 1892–1923* (Albany, NY, 1988), 1–141.

29. Alice Kessler-Harris, *Out to Work: A History of Wage-Earning Women in the United States* (New York, 1982), 153–59; Nancy Schrom Dye, *As Equals and As Sisters: Feminism, the Labor Movement, and the Women's Trade Union League of New York* (Columbia, MO, 1980), 13–14, 29–30; Montgomery, *Fall of the House of Labor,* 201–3.
30. Foner, *Organized Labor and the Black Worker,* 92–93; Ramirez, *When Workers Fight,* 104–14; Kazin, *Barons of Labor,* esp. 105.
31. Allen F. Davis, *Spearheads for Reform: The Social Settlements and the Progressive Movement, 1880–1914* (New Brunswick, NJ, 1984), 103–22; John R. Commons, *Myself: The Autobiography of John R. Commons* (Madison, WI, 1963).
32. James B. Gilbert, *Work without Salvation: America's Intellectuals and Industrial Alienation, 1880–1910* (Baltimore, 1977), 83–96; T. J. Jackson Lears, *No Place of Grace: Antimodernism and the Transformation of American Culture, 1880–1920* (New York, 1981), 59–96; Susan Curtis, *A Consuming Faith: The Social Gospel and Modern American Culture* (Baltimore, 1991), 16–71; Daniel T. Rodgers, *The Work Ethic in Industrial America, 1850–1920* (Chicago, 1978), 78–82.
33. Jane Addams, "The Settlement as a Factor in the Labor Movement," in Residents of Hull-House, *Hull-House Maps and Papers* (New York, 1895), 183–204.
34. Ibid., 188; Keller, *Regulating a New Economy,* 122.
35. Dye, *As Equals and As Sisters,* 41–42; Elizabeth Anne Payne, *Reform, Labor, and Feminism: Margaret Dreier Robins and the Women's Trade Union League* (Chicago, 1988).
36. Kessler-Harris, *Out to Work,* 153; Dye, *As Equals and As Sisters,* 52–53, 55.
37. Kessler-Harris, *Out to Work,* 152; Dye, *As Equals and As Sisters.*
38. This paragraph and the following draw on Judith A. Baer, *The Chains of Protection: The Judicial Response to Women's Labor Legislation* (Westport, CT, 1978), 42–69; Melvin I. Urofsky, "State Courts and Protective Legislation during the Progressive Era: A Reevaluation," *Journal of American History,* 72 (June 1985), 63–91; Kessler-Harris, *Out to Work,* 166–214; Commons et al., *History of Labor in the United States,* 457–74; Forbath, *Law and the Shaping of the American Labor Movement,* 49–58.
39. Baer, *Chains of Protection,* 49–50; Commons et al., *History of Labor in the United States,* 540–61, 672–73.
40. Ibid., 564–75.
41. Arthur S. Link, *Wilson: The New Freedom* (Princeton, NJ, 1956), 255, n. 52, 264–74.
42. Melvyn Dubofsky, *We Shall Be All: A History of the Industrial Workers of the World* (Chicago, 1969), 38–51, 67; *A Report on Labor Disturbances in the State of Colorado, from 1880 to 1904, Inclusive, with Correspondence Relating Thereto,* 58th Cong., 1st Sess., 46–50, 112–62, 170–88.
43. Dubofsky, *We Shall Be All,* 51–55; *Report on Labor Disturbances in the State of Colorado,* 166–69, 189–329.
44. Dubofsky, *We Shall Be All,* 53, 55; Roosevelt, *Letters,* IV, 882–83, 900–901, 903, 905.

45. Dubofsky, *We Shall Be All*, 57–80; Joyce L. Kornbluh, ed., *Rebel Voices: An I.W.W. Anthology* (Ann Arbor, 1964), 7–9.
46. Ibid., v, 1–2, 12; Dubofsky, *We Shall Be All*, 81–83.
47. Ibid., 96–105; Payne, *Reform, Labor, and Feminism*, 77–78.
48. Dubofsky, *We Shall Be All*, 120–45; Foner, *Organized Labor and the Black Worker*, 107–8.
49. Dubofsky, *We Shall Be All*, 132–70; Kornbluh, *Rebel Voices*, 13.
50. Paolo Coletta, *The Presidency of William Howard Taft* (Lawrence, KS, 1973), 18–19, 24–25; George W. Alger, "Taft and Labor," *McClure's Magazine*, 31 (Sept. 1908), 597–602.
51. Robert Franklin Hoxie, *Trade Unionism in the United States* (New York, 1917), 211–53; Victoria Hattam, "Economic Visions and Political Strategies: American Labor and the State, 1865–1896," *Studies in American Political Development*, 4 (1990), 82–129; Tomlins, *State and the Unions*, 32–59. For a different view of the courts' individualism, see Karen Orren, *Belated Feudalism: Labor, the Law, and Liberal Development in the United States* (Cambridge, MA, 1991).
52. Forbath, *Law and the Shaping of the American Labor Movement*, 25–127; John Mitchell, *Organized Labor: Its Problems, Purposes and Ideals and the Present and Future of American Wage Earners* (Philadelphia, 1903), 324; Hattam, "Economic Visions and Political Strategies," 106–19; Tomlins, *State and the Unions*, 60–91; Keller, *Regulating a New Economy*, 125–33.
53. Leo Wolman, *The Boycott in American Trade Unions* (Baltimore, 1916), esp. 18–19, 22, 39–41, 131–34; Forbath, *Law and the Shaping of the American Labor Movement*, 90–94; David Bensman, *The Practice of Solidarity: American Hat Finishers in the Nineteenth Century* (Urbana, IL, 1985), 201–6.
54. Mitchell, *Organized Labor*, 336; Tomlins, *State and the Unions*, 65–67; Forbath, *Law and the Shaping of the American Labor Movement*, 141–47; Wolman, *Boycott in American Trade Unions*, 80–82.
55. Dubofsky, *We Shall Be All*, 173–79.
56. Link, *Wilson: The New Freedom*, 427–33.
57. U.S. Bureau of the Census, *Historical Statistics of the United States*, I, 179.

Chapter Five

1. Ann Bassett Willis, "'Queen Ann' of Brown's Park," [part one], *Colorado Magazine*, 29 (April, 1952), 81–98; Ann Bassett Willis, "'Queen Ann' of Brown's Park," [part four], *Colorado Magazine*, 30 (Jan. 1953), 58–76.
2. Ibid., 69–70, 75; G. Michael McCarthy, *Hour of Trial: The Conservation Conflict in Colorado and the West, 1891–1907* (Norman, OK, 1977), 143, 163.
3. Willis, "'Queen Ann' of Brown's Park," [part four] 70–75; McCarthy, *Hour of Trial*, 173–75.

4. Alfred D. Chandler, Jr., *The Visible Hand: The Managerial Revolution in American Business* (Cambridge, MA, 1977), 1–376; Thomas C. Cochran, *The Pabst Brewing Company: The History of an American Business* (New York, 1948).
5. Naomi R. Lamoreaux, *The Great Merger Movement in American Business, 1895–1904* (Cambridge, MA, 1985).
6. Lewis L. Gould, *The Presidency of Theodore Roosevelt* (Lawrence, KS, 1991), 28; Louis Galambos, *The Public Image of Big Business in America, 1880–1940: A Quantitative Study in Social Change* (Baltimore, 1975), 3–156; Dewey W. Grantham, *Southern Progressivism: The Reconciliation of Progress and Tradition* (Knoxville, 1983), 145–47; Lamoreaux, *Great Merger Movement,* 149–58; G. Warren Nutter and Henry Adler Einhorn, *Enterprise Monopoly in the United States: 1899–1958* (New York, 1969), 1–54.
7. Grantham, *Southern Progressivism,* 158.
8. Tom Sitton, *John Randolph Haynes: California Progressive* (Stanford, 1992), 19–33, 52–55; David P. Thelen, *Paths of Resistance: Tradition and Dignity in Industrializing Missouri* (New York, 1986), 220–21, 223–26; Sidney Fine, *Laissez-Faire and the General-Welfare State: A Study of Conflict in American Thought, 1865–1901* (Ann Arbor, 1956), 339–46; Frank Parsons, "Municipal Ownership" and "Public Ownership," in W. D. P. Bliss, ed., *New Encyclopedia of Social Reform* (New York, 1908), 788–95, 1001–10.
9. Grantham, *Southern Progressivism,* 143–44; Steven L. Piott, *The Anti-Monopoly Persuasion: Popular Resistance to the Rise of Big Business in the Midwest* (Westport, CT, 1985), 3–71; Hans B. Thorelli, *The Federal Antitrust Policy: Origination of an American Tradition* (Baltimore, 1954), 1–232, 610–11; Martin Sklar, *The Corporate Reconstruction of American Capitalism, 1880–1916* (Cambridge, MA, 1988), 86–145.
10. Stanley P. Caine, *The Myth of a Progressive Reform: Railroad Regulation in Wisconsin, 1903–1910* (Madison, WI, 1970); Gabriel Kolko, *Railroads and Regulation, 1877–1916* (Princeton, NJ, 1965); Grantham, *Southern Progressivism,* 143, 147; Stephen Skowronek, *Building a New American State: The Expansion of National Administrative Capacities, 1877–1920* (Cambridge, MA, 1982), 121–62.
11. David P. Thelen, *Robert M. La Follette and the Insurgent Spirit* (Boston, 1976), 23–24; H. Roger Grant, *Insurance Reform: Consumer Action in the Progressive Era* (Ames, IA, 1979), 15–22; Edwin R. A. Seligman, *Essays in Taxation,* 10th ed. (New York, 1925); R. Rudy Higgens-Evenson, *The Price of Progress: Public Services, Taxation, and the American Corporate State, 1877–1929* (Baltimore, MD, 2003), 39–51.
12. Robert H. Wiebe, *Businessmen and Reform: A Study of the Progressive Movement* (Cambridge, MA, 1962); Gabriel Kolko, *The Triumph of Conservatism: A Reinterpretation of American History, 1900–1916* (New York, 1963); Samuel P. Hays, *Conservation and the Gospel of Efficiency: The Progressive Conservation Movement, 1890–1920* (1959; New York, 1975); McCarthy, *Hour of Trial,* 26, 68; Mansel G. Blackford, *The Politics of Business in California, 1890–1920* (Columbus, OH, 1977).
13. Charles McCurdy, "The *Knight* Sugar Decision of 1895 and the Modernization

of American Corporation Law, 1869–1903," *Business History Review*, 53 (Autumn 1979), 304–42; Thorelli, *Federal Antitrust Policy*, 445–48; Lamoreaux, *Great Merger Movement*, 164–66.

14. Theodore Roosevelt, *The Works of Theodore Roosevelt*, "National Edition," 20 vols. (New York, 1926), XV, 222, 272, and XVI, 63.
15. Anna Robeson Burr, *The Portrait of a Banker: James Stillman, 1850–1918* (New York, 1927), 176; Gould, *Presidency of Theodore Roosevelt*, 40, 47–51; Thorelli, *Federal Antitrust Policy*, 421–25.
16. Gould, *Presidency of Theodore Roosevelt*, 51–53; Joseph Bucklin Bishop, *Theodore Roosevelt and His Time*, 2 vols. (New York, 1920), I, 183.
17. Thorelli, *Federal Antitrust Policy*, 425–28, 470–75; Gould, *Presidency of Theodore Roosevelt*, 53, 134; Lamoreaux, *Great Merger Movement*, 166–69.
18. Piott, *Anti-Monopoly Persuasion*, 105–130; Bruce Bringhurst, *Antitrust and the Oil Monopoly: The Standard Oil Cases, 1890–1911* (Westport, CT, 1979), 69–107; Allan Nevins, *John D. Rockefeller: The Heroic Age of American Enterprise*, 2 vols. (New York, 1940), II, 563–64, 571–74; Louis Filler, *The Muckrakers* (University Park, PA, 1976), 102–9; Ron Chernow, *Titan: The Life of John D. Rockefeller, Sr.* (New York, 1998), 523–24.
19. Roosevelt, *Works*, XV, 273–74; Bringhurst, *Antitrust and the Oil Monopoly*, 108–41; Gould, *Presidency of Theodore Roosevelt*, 212–18; Nevins, *John D. Rockefeller*, II, 555–63, 568–71; Chernow, *Titan*, 544–47, 553–55.
20. Paolo E. Coletta, *The Presidency of William Howard Taft* (Lawrence, KS, 1973), 153–64; Sklar, *Corporate Reconstruction.*
21. Chernow, *Titan*, 547, 556–59; Arthur S. Link, *Wilson: The Road to the White House* (Princeton, NJ, 1947), 514–55; Arthur S. Link, *Wilson: The New Freedom* (Princeton, NJ, 1956), 425–44.
22. James Harvey Young, *Pure Food: Securing the Federal Food and Drugs Act of 1906* (Princeton, NJ, 1989), 3–157; Gould, *Presidency of Theodore Roosevelt*, 165–69.
23. Young, *Pure Food*, 197–203; Filler, *Muckrakers*, 142–56.
24. Young, *Pure Food*, 204, 221–29; Upton Sinclair, *The Jungle*, ed. James R. Barrett (1906; Urbana, IL, 1988), 73, 94–96, 130; Filler, *Muckrakers*, 157–70; Thorelli, *Federal Antitrust Policy*, 475–77; Piott, *Anti-Monopoly Persuasion*, 72–88.
25. Young, *Pure Food*, 192, 221–52.
26. Roosevelt, *Works*, XV, 221, 272–73.
27. John Braeman, "The Square Deal in Action: A Case Study in the Growth of the 'National Police Power,'" in John Braeman et al., eds. *Change and Continuity in Twentieth-Century America* (Columbus, OH, 1964), 53–75; Gould, *Presidency of Theodore Roosevelt*, 166–67; Young, *Pure Food*, 174–93, 230–36, 287, 292.
28. Braeman, "Square Deal in Action," 57; Young, *Pure Food*, 262–72.
29. The battle over railroad policy, especially the enactment of the Hepburn Act of

1906, suggested similar lessons. Gould, *Presidency of Theodore Roosevelt,* 149–52, 158–65; John M. Blum, *The Republican Roosevelt,* 2nd ed. (Cambridge, MA, 1977), 87–105.

30. Link, *Wilson: The New Freedom,* 178–240
31. Ibid., 424–26, 435–42.
32. John Muir, *Our National Parks* (Boston, 1901), 1; McCarthy, *Hour of Trial,* 12–15, 76–79; Stephen R. Fox, *John Muir and His Legacy: The American Conservation Movement* (Boston, 1981).
33. McCarthy, *Hour of Trial,* 19–21; Hays, *Conservation and the Gospel of Efficiency.*
34. McCarthy, *Hour of Trial,* 19, 121.
35. Ibid., 15–16, 21–28.
36. Gould, *Presidency of Theodore Roosevelt,* 40, 111; Roosevelt, *Works,* XV, 102–4; McCarthy, *Hour of Trial,* 79–82; Paul Russell Cutwright, *Theodore Roosevelt: The Making of a Conservationist* (Urbana, IL, 1985).
37. Roosevelt, *Works,* XV, 102–9, 161; Gould, *Presidency of Theodore Roosevelt,* 40–42, 111–12.
38. Ibid., 61–62, 111–13; McCarthy, *Hour of Trial,* 94–128.
39. Gould, *Presidency of Theodore Roosevelt,* 199–202; McCarthy, *Hour of Trial,* 129–71.
40. Gould, *Presidency of Theodore Roosevelt,* 201–2; McCarthy, *Hour of Trial,* 83–87, 141, 221–22.
41. Gould, *Presidency of Theodore Roosevelt,* 169, 203–7; McCarthy, *Hour of Trial,* 171–235; Hays, *Conservation and the Gospel of Efficiency,* 49–146; Braeman, "Square Deal in Action," 75.
42. James Penick, Jr., *Progressive Politics and Conservation: The Ballinger-Pinchot Affair* (Chicago, 1968); Coletta, *Presidency of William Howard Taft,* 83–98; Link, *Wilson: The New Freedom,* 16–8, 125–35.
43. Morton Keller, *The Life Insurance Enterprise, 1885–1910: A Study in the Limits of Corporate Power* (Cambridge, MA, 1963), 12–14, 27–28, 38.
44. Grant, *Insurance Reform,* 28–33; Keller, *Life Insurance Enterprise,* 246; Filler, *Muckrakers,* 171–92.
45. Keller, *Life Insurance Enterprise,* 23, 47–48, 248–49; Lucius Beebe, *The Big Spenders* (New York, 1966), 121–29; R. Carlyle Buley, *The Equitable Life Assurance Society of the United States* (New York, 1959), 108–119.
46. Keller, *Life Insurance Enterprise,* 49–50, 249; Buley, *Equitable Life Assurance Society,* 118–25.
47. Keller, *Life Insurance Enterprise,* 214–26, 228–31, 246, 251–54; Buley, *Equitable Life Assurance Society,* 125–28; Richard L. McCormick, *From Realignment to Reform: Political Change in New York State, 1893–1910* (Ithaca, NY, 1981), 197–99.
48. Keller, *Life Insurance Enterprise,* 32, 228–34, 246, 249–50, 254; McCormick, *From Realignment to Reform,* 199–205.

49. Roosevelt, *Works,* XV, 225, 289–90; Keller, *Life Insurance Enterprise,* 194–213, 223, 235–42, 256–57.
50. Ibid., 240, 250–51.
51. Ibid., 241–42, 254–59; Grantham, *Southern Progressivism,* 153; Grant, *Insurance Reform,* 43–70.
52. Keller, *Life Insurance Enterprise,* 259–92; Buley, *Equitable Life Assurance Society,* 128–55.
53. McCormick, *From Realignment to Reform,* 205–72.
54. David Graham Phillips, *The Treason of the Senate,* eds. George E. Mowry and Judson A. Grenier (New York, 1964), 59, 215; Filler, *Muckrakers,* 245–59.
55. Roosevelt, *Works,* XVI, 415–21.
56. William Jennings Bryan, *Speeches of William Jennings Bryan,* 2 vols. (New York, 1911), II, 63–99.
57. Gould, *Presidency of Theodore Roosevelt,* 246.
58. Roosevelt, *Works,* XVI, 74–75, 84; Nevins, *John D. Rockefeller,* II, 574–78.
59. Roosevelt, *Works,* XV, 365–66, 414, and XVI, 75.
60. Frank Vanderlip, *From Farm Boy to Financier* (New York, 1935), 160, 166; Gould, *Presidency of Theodore Roosevelt,* 247–48; Theodore Roosevelt, *The Letters of Theodore Roosevelt,* Elting E. Morison et al., eds., 8 vols. (Cambridge, MA, 1951–54), V, 747; Chernow, *Titan,* 543.
61. Gould, *Presidency of Theodore Roosevelt,* 248–49.
62. Ibid., 249; Burr, *Portrait of a Banker,* 239.
63. Lamoreaux, *Great Merger Movement,* 118–37.
64. Roosevelt, *Works,* XV, 422, 491, 495–96; Gould, *Presidency of Theodore Roosevelt,* 274–77; Sklar, *Corporate Reconstruction,* 203–85; Arthur M. Johnson, "Antitrust Policy in Transition, 1908: Ideal and Reality," *Mississippi Valley Historical Review,* 48 (Dec. 1961), 415–34.
65. Ibid., 276–81; Lamoreaux, *Great Merger Movement,* 169–73; Roosevelt, *Letters,* V, 746–49; Grantham, *Southern Progressivism,* 157; Nevins, *John D. Rockefeller,* II, 558.
66. Bryan, *Speeches,* II, 102.

Chapter Six

1. William Allen White, *The Autobiography of William Allen White* (New York, 1946), 404–5; John Kasson, *Rudeness and Civility: Manners in Nineteenth-Century Urban America* (New York, 1990), 142.
2. John W. Cell, *The Highest Stage of White Supremacy: The Origins of Segregation in South Africa and the American South* (Cambridge, MA, 1982), 3; Frederick E. Hoxie, *A Final Promise: The Campaign to Assimilate the Indians, 1880–1920* (Lincoln, NE, 1984), xii.
3. Grace Elizabeth Hale, *Making Whiteness: The Culture of Segregation in the South, 1890–1940* (New York, 1998) emphasizes segregation as a means of uniting whites and establishing the ideology and practice of "whiteness." Important as

"whiteness" is to the history of the modern United States, I believe progressivism was an essentially different project.

4. This paragraph and the following two draw on William Ivy Hair, *Carnival of Fury: Robert Charles and the New Orleans Race Riot of 1900* (Baton Rouge, 1976) and Joel Williamson, *The Crucible of Race: Black-White Relations in the American South Since Emancipation* (New York, 1984), 201–9.
5. U.S. Bureau of the Census, *Historical Statistics of the United States: Colonial Times to 1970*, Bicentennial ed., 2 vols. (Washington, D.C., 1975), I, 14 and 22; C. Vann Woodward, *Origins of the New South, 1877–1913*, rev. ed. (Baton Rouge, 1971).
6. Edward Ayers, *The Promise of the New South: Life After Reconstruction* (New York, 1993), 132–59; Woodward, *Origins of the New South;* Williamson, *Crucible of Race,* 111–15, 180–81; Cell, *Highest Stage of White Supremacy,* 103–70.
7. Williamson, *Crucible of Race,* 116–17, 119–24, 140–79, 308; George M. Fredrickson, *The Black Image in the White Mind: The Debate on Afro-American Character and Destiny, 1817–1914* (New York, 1971), 228–82; I. A. Newby, *Jim Crow's Defense: Anti-Negro Thought in America, 1900–1930* (Baton Rouge, 1965); Thomas F. Gossett, *Race: The History of an Idea in America* (New York, 1997), 280–83.
8. Woodward, *Origins of the New South,* 353; Williamson, *Crucible of Race,* 128, 180–223; Neil R. McMillen, *Dark Journey: Black Mississippians in the Age of Jim Crow* (Urbana, IL, 1989), 224; U.S. Bureau of the Census, *Historical Statistics of the United States,* I, 422; Edward L. Ayers, *Vengeance and Justice: Crime and Punishment in the Nineteenth-Century American South* (New York, 1984), 223–65; George C. Wright, *Racial Violence in Kentucky, 1865–1940: Lynchings, Mob Rule, and 'Legal Lynchings'* (Baton Rouge, 1990); W. Fitzhugh Brundage, *Lynching in the New South: Georgia and Virginia, 1880–1930* (Urbana, IL, 1993), 1–160.
9. Williamson, *Crucible of Race,* 259–60.
10. Ibid., 418–19; Edgar Gardner Murphy, *Problems of the Present South: A Discussion of Certain of the Educational, Industrial and Political Issues in the Southern States* (New York, 1904), 34. The following account draws on Woodward, *Origins of the New South,* 354; Fredrickson, *Black Image in the White Mind,* 283–97; C. Vann Woodward, *The Strange Career of Jim Crow,* 3rd rev. ed. (New York, 1974); Howard N. Rabinowitz, *Race Relations in the Urban South, 1865–1890* (New York, 1978); Howard N. Rabinowitz, "More Than the Woodward Thesis: Assessing *The Strange Career of Jim Crow,*" *Journal of American History,* 75 (Dec. 1988), 842–56; McMillen, *Dark Journey;* George C. Wright, *Life Behind a Veil: Blacks in Louisville, Kentucky, 1865–1930* (Baton Rouge, 1985); John Dittmer, *Black Georgia in the Progressive Era, 1900–1920* (Urbana, IL, 1977); Leon F. Litwack, *Trouble in Mind: Black Southerners in the Age of Jim Crow* (New York, 1998), 179–279.
11. McMillen, *Dark Journey,* 41; Woodward, *Origins of the New South,* 321–49; J. Morgan

Kousser, *The Shaping of Southern Politics: Suffrage Restriction and the Establishment of the One-Party South, 1880–1910* (New Haven, CT, 1974); Michael Perman, *Struggle for Mastery: Disfranchisement in the South, 1888–1908* (Chapel Hill, NC, 2001).

12. Cell, *Highest Stage of White Supremacy*, 171–91; McMillen, *Dark Journey*, 8; U.S. Bureau of the Census, *Historical Statistics of the United States*, I, 422.
13. This and the following paragraphs draw on Gilbert Osofsky, *Harlem: The Making of a Ghetto*, 2nd ed. (New York, 1971); Kenneth L. Kusmer, *A Ghetto Takes Shape: Black Cleveland, 1870–1930* (Urbana, IL, 1976); David A. Gerber, *Black Ohio and the Color Line 1860–1915* (Urbana, IL, 1976); Allan H. Spear, *Black Chicago: The Making of a Negro Ghetto, 1890–1920* (Chicago, 1967), 11–49; Thomas Lee Philpott, *The Slum and the Ghetto: Neighborhood Deterioration and Middle-Class Reform, Chicago, 1880–1930* (New York, 1978), 115–45; James E. DeVries, *Race and Kinship in a Midwestern Town: The Black Experience in Monroe, Michigan, 1900–1915* (Urbana, IL, 1984), 7–106; Ray Stannard Baker, *Following the Color Line: American Negro Citizenship in the Progressive Era*, ed. Dewey Grantham, Jr. (1908; New York, 1964), 108–47.
14. As Osofsky, *Harlem*, and Kusmer, *Ghetto Takes Shape*, make clear, early twentieth-century black residential enclaves were not yet ghettoes.
15. Williamson, *Crucible of Race*, 339.
16. Gossett, *Race*, 144–227, 253–86; David Levering Lewis, *W. E. B. Du Bois: Biography of a Race, 1868–1919* (New York, 1993), 388–89; Ralph E. Luker, *The Social Gospel in Black and White: American Racial Reform, 1885–1912* (Chapel Hill, NC, 1991); Elisabeth Lasch-Quinn, *Black Neighbors: Race and the Limits of Reform in the American Settlement House Movement, 1890–1945* (Chapel Hill, NC, 1993), 1–46; Philpott, *Slum and the Ghetto*; David Southern, *The Malignant Heritage: Yankee Progressives and the Negro Question, 1901–1914* (Chicago, 1968); Gilbert Osofsky, "Progressivism and the Negro: New York, 1900–1915," *American Quarterly*, 16 (Summer 1964), 153–68; Jack Temple Kirby, *Darkness at the Dawning: Race and Reform in the Progressive South* (Philadelphia, 1972); Fredrickson, *Black Image in the White Mind*, 302–4; Dewey W. Grantham, Jr., "The Progressive Movement and the Negro," *South Atlantic Quarterly*, 54 (1955), 461–77. Although discussing England rather than the United States, Michael Freeden, "Eugenics and Progressive Thought: A Study in Ideological Affinity," *Historical Journal*, 22 (Sept. 1979), 645–71, is suggestive about the fundamental compatibility between environmentalist and race thought for progressives. But issues of class were most important.
17. Murphy, *Present South*, 7, 34–35; Edgar Gardner Murphy, *The Basis of Ascendancy: A Discussion of Certain Principles of Public Policy Involved in the Development of the Southern States* (New York, 1909), xv; Ralph Luker, *A Southern Tradition in Theology and Social Criticism, 1830–1930* (New York, 1984), 287–378; Hugh C. Bailey, *Edgar Gardner Murphy: Gentle Progressive* (Coral Gables, FL, 1968).

18. Cell, *Highest Stage of White Supremacy*, 177.
19. Theodore Roosevelt, *The Letters of Theodore Roosevelt*, eds. Elting E. Morison et al., 8 vols. (Cambridge, MA, 1951–54), V, 226; Thomas G. Dyer, *Theodore Roosevelt and the Idea of Race* (Baton Rouge, 1980), 1–68, 89–122; Lewis L. Gould, *The Presidency of Theodore Roosevelt* (Lawrence, KS, 1991), 22–24, 118–22, 236–44; Seth M. Scheiner, "President Theodore Roosevelt and the Negro, 1901–1908," *Journal of Negro History*, 47 (July 1962), 169–82; Woodward, *Origins of the New South*, 462–67; Williamson, *Crucible of Race*, 345–55; Willard B. Gatewood, Jr., *Theodore Roosevelt and the Art of Controversy: Episodes of the White House Years* (Baton Rouge, 1970), 32–134.
20. Roosevelt, *Letters*, III, 190; Frederick E. Hoxie, *A Final Promise: The Campaign to Assimilate the Indians, 1880–1920* (Lincoln, NE, 1984), 105.
21. Gould, *Presidency of Theodore Roosevelt*, 23, 119; Williamson, *Crucible of Race*, 351; Roosevelt, *Letters* III, 383–85.
22. Woodward, *Origins of the New South*, 466; Gould, *Presidency of Theodore Roosevelt*, 238.
23. Ann J. Lane, *The Brownsville Affair: National Crisis and Black Reaction* (Port Washington, NY, 1971); Gould, *Presidency of Theodore Roosevelt*, 241–43.
24. Paolo E. Coletta, *The Presidency of William Howard Taft* (Lawrence, KS, 1973), 75, 264; John Milton Cooper, Jr., *The Warrior and the Priest: Woodrow Wilson and Theodore Roosevelt* (Cambridge, MA, 1983), 210–11, 273–74; Richard B. Sherman, *The Republican Party and Black America from McKinley to Hoover, 1896–1933* (Charlottesville, VA, 1973), 83–112; Arthur S. Link, *Wilson: The New Freedom* (Princeton, NJ, 1956), 246–52.
25. Lasch-Quinn, *Black Neighbors*, 14–15; Stephen Diner, "Chicago Social Workers and Blacks in the Progressive Era," *Social Service Review*, 44 (Dec. 1970), 393–410.
26. Hair, *Carnival of Fury*, 178–79; Alan Lomax, *Mister Jelly Roll: The Fortunes of Jelly Morton, New Orleans Creole and "Inventor of Jazz,"* 2nd ed. (Berkeley, CA, 1973), 57. This and the following paragraphs also draw on August Meier, *Negro Thought in America, 1880–1915: Racial Ideologies in the Age of Booker T. Washington* (Ann Arbor, MI, 1963); Louis Harlan, *Booker T. Washington: The Making of a Black Leader, 1856–1901* (New York, 1972); Louis Harlan, *Booker T. Washington: The Wizard of Tuskegee, 1901–1915* (New York, 1983); Cell, *Highest Stage of White Supremacy*, 14–15, 230–75; Williamson, *Crucible of Race;* McMillen, *Dark Journey;* Wright, *Life Behind a Veil;* Spear, *Black Chicago*, 71–89; Dittmer, *Black Georgia in the Progressive Era*, 163–80.
27. Litwack, *Trouble in Mind*, 3–51.
28. Benjamin E. Mays, *Born to Rebel: An Autobiography* (1971; Athens, GA, 1987), 1, 17, 22–26.
29. Meier, *Negro Thought in America*, 103, 105–7.
30. "The Boycott Movement against Jim Crow Streetcars in the South, 1900–1906," in August Meier and Elliott Rudwick, *Along the Color Line: Explorations in the Black Experience* (Urbana, IL, 1976), 267–89; Dittmer, *Black Georgia in the Progressive Era*, 16–19.

31. Meier, *Negro Thought in America*, 174; Harlan, *The Wizard of Tuskegee.*
32. W. E. B. Du Bois, *The Souls of Black Folk* (1903; New York, 1989), 5, 43; Lewis, *W. E. B. Du Bois*, 11–296.
33. Ibid., 297–434.
34. Dittmer, *Black Georgia*, 173–74.
35. Kevin K. Gaines, *Uplifting the Race: Black Leadership, Politics, and Culture in the Twentieth Century* (Chapel Hill, NC, 1996); Glenda Elizabeth Gilmore, *Gender and Jim Crow: Women and the Politics of White Supremacy in North Carolina, 1896–1920* (Chapel Hill, NC, 1996); Gail Bederman, "'Civilization,' the Decline of Middle-Class Manliness, and Ida B. Wells's Antilynching Campaign (1892–94)," *Radical History Review*, 52 (Winter 1992), 5–32; Lasch-Quinn, *Black Neighbors;* Ruth Hutchinson Crocker, *Social Work and Social Order: The Settlement Movement in Two Industrial Cities, 1889–1930* (Urbana, IL, 1992), 68–93; Mary Church Terrell, *A Colored Woman in a White World* (Salem, NH, 1992); Patricia Ann Schechter, *Ida B. Wells-Barnett and American Reform, 1880–1930* (Chapel Hill, NC, 2001); Linda O. McMurry, *To Keep the Waters Troubled: The Life of Ida B. Wells* (New York, 1998); Evelyn Brooks Higginbotham, *Righteous Discontent: The Women's Movement in the Black Baptist Church, 1880–1920* (Cambridge, MA, 1993); Cynthia Neverdon-Morton, *Afro-American Women of the South and the Advancement of the Race, 1895–1925* (Knoxville, TN, 1989).
36. U.S. Bureau of the Census, *Historical Statistics of the United States*, I, 14; Williamson, *Crucible of Race*, 209–23; Roberta Senechal, *The Sociogenesis of a Race Riot: Springfield, Illinois, in 1908* (Urbana, IL, 1990), 2 and 191.
37. U.S. Bureau of the Census, *Historical Statistics of the United States*, I, 14; Francis Paul Prucha, *Atlas of American Indian Affairs* (Lincoln, NE, 1990), 4–7, 142–43. This section draws mainly on Hoxie, *Final Promise;* Francis Paul Prucha, *The Great Father: The United States Government and the American Indians*, 2 vols. (Lincoln, NE, 1984), II, 609–916; John F. Berens, "Old Campaigners, New Realities: Indian Policy Reform in the Progressive Era, 1900–1912," *Mid-America*, 59 (Jan. 1977), 51–64; Dyer, *Theodore Roosevelt and the Idea of Race*, 69–88; Gould, *Presidency of Theodore Roosevelt*, 207–9; Donald J. Berthrong, *The Cheyenne and Arapaho Ordeal: Reservation and Agency Life in the Indian Territory, 1875–1907* (Norman, OK, 1976); Janet A. McDonnell, *The Dispossession of the American Indian, 1887–1934* (Bloomington, IN 1991).
38. Berthrong, *Cheyenne and Arapaho Ordeal*, 266; Hoxie, *Final Promise*, 95.
39. Ibid., 118, 122.
40. Hamlin Garland, *Hamlin Garland's Observations on the American Indian, 1895–1905*, Lonnie E. Underhill and Daniel F. Littlefield, Jr., eds. (Tucson, AZ, 1976), 169–170, 177; Roy W. Meyer, "Hamlin Garland and the American Indian," *Western American Literature*, 2 (Summer 1967), 109–25.
41. Dyer, *Theodore Roosevelt and the Idea of Race*, 86; Hoxie, *Final Promise*, 107.

42. Theodore Roosevelt, *The Works of Theodore Roosevelt,* "National Edition," 20 vols. (New York, 1926), XV, 163–64.
43. Hoxie, *Final Promise,* 163.
44. Ibid., 220; also Daniel McCool, "Indian Voting," in Vine Deloria, Jr., ed., *American Indian Policy in the Twentieth Century* (Norman, OK, 1985), 105–34.
45. Donald L. Parman, "The 'Big Stick' in Indian Affairs: The Bai-a-Lil-Le Incident in 1909," *Arizona and the West,* 20 (Winter 1978), 343–60; Roosevelt, *Letters* VI, 1448–53.
46. Hoxie, *Final Promise,* 107–8.
47. Kasson, *Rudeness and Civility,* 80, 116–17; John Kasson, *Amusing the Million: Coney Island at the Turn of the Century* (New York, 1978), 12. See also David Harvey, *Consciousness and the Urban Experience* (Baltimore, 1985).
48. Sam Bass Warner, Jr., *The Private City: Philadelphia in Three Periods of Its Growth* (Philadelphia, 1968), 169–73; Kathleen Neils Conzen, "Immigrants, Immigrant Neighborhoods, and Ethnic Identity: Historical Issues," *Journal of American History,* 66 (Dec. 1979), 603–15; John Bodnar, *The Transplanted: A History of Immigrants in Urban America* (Bloomington, IN, 1985), 175–79; Olivier Zunz, *The Changing Face of Inequality: Urbanization, Industrial Development, and Immigrants in Detroit, 1880–1920* (Chicago, 1982), esp. 3–8, 340–42; Humbert Nelli, *The Italians in Chicago, 1880–1930: A Study in Ethnic Mobility* (New York, 1970), 22–54; Philpott, *Slum and the Ghetto,* 130–45; Howard P. Chudacoff, *Mobile Americans: Residential and Social Mobility in Omaha, 1880–1920* (New York, 1972), 35–83; Kusmer, *Ghetto Takes Shape,* 35–38, 43–45; Wright, *Life Behind a Veil,* 51–52; David Ward, *Cities and Immigrants: A Geography of Change in Nineteenth-Century America* (New York, 1971), 105–45.
49. The following account draws on Higham, *Strangers in the Land,* 68–182; Dyer, *Theodore Roosevelt and the Idea of Race,* 123–42; Gould, *Presidency of Theodore Roosevelt,* 36–37, 87–88, 257–62; Gossett, *Race,* 287–309; Gwendolyn Mink, *Old Labor and New Immigrants in American Political Development: Union, Party, and State, 1875–1920* (Ithaca, NY, 1986).
50. Jacob Riis, *The Battle with the Slum* (New York, 1902), 203–4.
51. Roosevelt, *Works,* XV, 161–62.
52. William Henry Harbaugh, *Power and Responsibility: The Life and Times of Theodore Roosevelt* (New York, 1961), 295.
53. U.S. Department of Commerce, *Historical Statistics of the United States,* I, 107; Gould, *Presidency of Theodore Roosevelt,* 257–62.
54. Higham, *Strangers in the Land,* 109, 164–65; Link, *Wilson: The New Freedom,* 274–76.
55. Mark Haller, *Eugenics: Hereditarian Attitudes in American Thought* (1963; New Brunswick, NJ, 1984), 3–143; Donald K. Pickens, "The Sterilization Movement: The Search for Purity in Mind and State," *Phylon,* 28 (1st Qtr. 1967), 78–94.
56. Riis, *Battle with the Slum,* 405.

57. Murphy, *Present South*, 89. "Progressivism for Whites Only" is a chapter title in Woodward, *Origins of the New South*, 369.
58. Michael E. McGerr, *The Decline of Popular Politics: The American North, 1865–1928* (New York, 1986); Thomas Goebel, *A Government by the People: Direct Democracy in America, 1890–1940* (Chapel Hill, NC, 2002). For works emphasizing more democratic aspects of progressivism, see: James T. Kloppenberg, *Uncertain Victory: Social Democracy and Progressivism in European and American Thought, 1870–1920* (New York, 1986); Gilmore, *Gender and Jim Crow;* Leon Fink. *Progressive Intellectuals and the Dilemmas of Democratic Commitment* (Cambridge, MA, 1997); Kevin Mattson, *Creating a Democratic Public: The Struggle for Urban Participatory Democracy During the Progressive Era* (University Park, PA, 1998); Robert D. Johnston, *The Radical Middle Class: Populist Democracy and the Question of Capitalism in Progressive Era Portland, Oregon* (Princeton, NJ, 2003).
59. Kousser, *Shaping of Southern Politics*, 250–61; McGerr, *Decline of Popular Politics*, 45–52; and Washington Gladden, *The New Idolatry: and Other Discussions* (New York, 1905), 168, 171, 198.
60. Michael McGerr, "Political Style and Women's Power, 1830–1930," *Journal of American History*, 77 (Dec. 1990), 864–85; Kasson, *Rudeness and Civility*, 117–18, 131–32; William R. Leach, "Transformations in a Culture of Consumption: Women and Department Stores, 1890–1925," *Journal of American History*, 71 (Sept. 1984), 319–42.

Chapter Seven

1. Sherwood Anderson, *Sherwood Anderson's Memoirs: A Critical Edition*, ed. Ray Lewis White (Chapel Hill, NC, 1969), 198; T. J. Jackson Lears, "Sherwood Anderson: Looking for the White Spot," in Richard Wightman Fox and T. J. Jackson Lears, eds., *The Power of Culture: Critical Essays in American History* (Chicago, 1993), 13–37; William A. Sutton, *The Road to Winesburg: A Mosaic of the Imaginative Life of Sherwood Anderson* (Metuchen, NJ, 1972).
2. Anderson, *Sherwood Anderson's Memoirs*, 235–311; Lears, "Sherwood Anderson," 22–23.
3. Anderson, *Sherwood Anderson's Memoirs*, 249, 258, 266; Sutton, *Road to Winesburg*, 162–205.
4. Stephen Kern, *The Culture of Time and Space, 1880–1918* (Cambridge, MA, 1983), 13–14.
5. Sherwood Anderson, *A Story Teller's Story: A Critical Text*, ed. Ray Lewis White (Cleveland, 1968), 218–26; Sutton, *Road to Winesburg*, 187–88, 552–65.
6. Ibid., 196–97.
7. Donald K. Gorrell, *The Age of Social Responsibility: The Social Gospel in the Progressive Era, 1900–1920* (Macon, GA, 1988), 7–8; Woodrow Wilson, *The Papers of Woodrow Wilson*, ed. Arthur S. Link et al., 69 vols. (Princeton, NJ, 1966–1994), XXIV, 105–6.

8. H. Allen Brooks, *The Prairie School: Frank Lloyd Wright and His Midwestern Contemporaries* (Toronto, 1972); Robert C. Twombly, "Saving the Family: Middle Class Attraction to Wright's Prairie House, 1901–1909," *American Quarterly*, 27 (Mar. 1975), 57–72.
9. Frank Lloyd Wright, *Writings and Buildings*, ed. Edgar Kaufmann and Ben Raeburn (n.p., 1960); Frank Lloyd Wright, *Autobiography* (New York, 1943), 80.
10. Ibid., 111–13, 162, 164, 167; Meryle Secrest, *Frank Lloyd Wright* (New York, 1992), 187–216.
11. Wright, *Writings and Buildings*, 85–106; Wright, *Autobiography*, 166–67.
12. Wright, *Writings and Buildings*, 43, 314; Wright, *Autobiography*, 138–39.
13. Wright, *Writings and Buildings*, 41, 44, 284, 313; Kern, *Culture of Time and Space*, 154–58; Secrest, *Frank Lloyd Wright*, 152–53, 169–71, 177–78.
14. Wright, *Writings and Buildings*, 43–44, 104, 313; Kern, *Culture of Time and Space*, 186–87; Secrest, *Frank Lloyd Wright*, 153.
15. Joseph J. Corn, *The Winged Gospel: America's Romance with Aviation, 1900–1950* (New York, 1983), 3–11, 29–50; Tom D. Crouch, *A Dream of Wings: Americans and the Airplane, 1875–1905* (New York, 1981).
16. Corn, *Winged Gospel*, 10.
17. Kern, *Culture of Time and Space*, 111–14; Clay McShane, *Down the Asphalt Path: The Automobile and the American City* (New York, 1994), 27–29, 54–56.
18. James J. Flink, *America Adopts the Automobile, 1895–1910* (Cambridge, MA, 1970), 1–52, 202–331; McShane, *Down the Asphalt Path;* Howard L. Preston, *Automobile Age Atlanta: The Making of a Southern Metropolis, 1900–1935* (Athens, GA, 1979), 11–16.
19. Virginia Scharf, *Taking the Wheel: Women and the Coming of the Motor Age* (New York, 1991), 23–24; Flink, *America Adopts the Automobile*, 100–102.
20. McShane, *Down the Asphalt Path*, 21–40, 122–24, 136, 184; Flink, *America Adopts the Automobile*, 106–9; Preston, *Automobile Age Atlanta*, 18, 76–89; Reynold M. Wik, *Henry Ford and Grass-Roots America* (Ann Arbor, 1972), 27, 39–40; Wright, *Autobiography*, 163; Secrest, *Frank Lloyd Wright*, 147.
21. Kern, *Culture of Time and Space*, 110; Wik, *Henry Ford and Grass-Roots America*, 14–33; McShane, *Down the Asphalt Path*, 179.
22. Ibid., 30, 127–31, 133, 178–79, 183; Michael L. Berger, *The Devil Wagon in God's Country: The Automobile and Social Change in Rural America, 1893–1929* (Hamden, CT, 1979), Flink, *America Adopts the Automobile*, 70–71.
23. Wik, *Henry Ford and Grass-Roots America*, 17; McShane, *Down the Asphalt Path*, 177–78; Flink, *America Adopts the Automobile*, 66–69; Berger, *Devil Wagon in God's Country*, 68; 13–31.
24. U.S. Bureau of the Census, *Historical Statistics of the United States: Colonial Times to 1970*, Bicentennial ed., 2 vols. (Washington, D.C., 1975), II, 716; McShane, *Down*

the Asphalt Path, 103–8, 135; Scott L. Bottles, *Los Angeles and the Automobile: The Making of the Modern City* (Berkeley, CA, 1987), 55; Flink, *America Adopts the Automobile*, 55–60, 72–86, 268–78.

25. Ibid., 69–70, 83–85.
26. Berger, *Devil Wagon in God's Country*, 35–44, 51, 55–74, 80–86; Wik, *Henry Ford and Grass-Roots America*, 24, 26, 34–37; Flink, *America Adopts the Automobile*, 109–12; Joseph Interrante, "You Can't Go to Town in a Bathtub: Automobile Movement and the Reorganization of Rural Space, 1900–1930," *Radical History Review*, 21 (Fall 1979), 151–68.
27. Scharf, *Taking the Wheel*, 21, 27–28.
28. McShane, *Down the Asphalt Path*, 151–58, 167.
29. Ibid., 157–59; Scharf, *Taking the Wheel*, 21, 32.
30. Ibid., 25, 29; McShane, *Down the Asphalt Path*, 149–51.
31. Scharf, *Taking the Wheel*, 35–50, 53–54.
32. McShane, *Down the Asphalt Path*, 29–30, 62–66, 188–89; David Nasaw, *Children of the City: At Work and at Play* (New York, 1986); Flick, *America Adopts the Automobile*, 65–66.
33. McShane, *Down the Asphalt Path*, 118–19, 175–76, 179–88, 197–201; Flink, *America Adopts the Automobile*, 166–99.
34. McShane, *Down the Asphalt Path*, 190–94, 200–201.
35. Kern, *Culture of Time and Space*, 65–69, 79–80, 115; U.S. Bureau of the Census, *Historical Statistics of the United States*, II, 783.
36. David Nasaw, *Going Out: The Rise and Fall of Public Amusements* (New York, 1993), 120–29; Roland Gelatt, *The Fabulous Phonograph: From Edison to Stereo*, rev. ed. (New York, 1965), 72.
37. Charles Musser, *The Emergence of Cinema: The American Screen to 1907* (New York, 1990), 1–336; Nasaw, *Going Out*, 120–53, 173; George C. Hall, "The First Moving Picture in Arizona—or Was It?: The Tragic Tale of C. L. White's Marvelous Projectoscope Show in Arizona and New Mexico Territories, 1897–98," *Film History*, 3:1 (1989), 1–9; Kathryn H. Fuller, *At the Picture Show: Small-Town Audiences and the Creation of Movie Fan Culture* (Washington, D.C., 1996), 1–27; Charles Musser, with Carol Nelson, *"High-Class Moving Pictures: Lyman H. Howe and the Forgotten Era of Traveling Exhibition, 1888–1920* (Princeton, NJ, 1991); Burnes St. Patrick Hollyman, "The First Picture Shows: Austin, Texas, 1894–1913," in John L. Fell, ed., *Film Before Griffith* (Berkeley, CA, 1983), 188–95.
38. Daniel Joseph Singal, "Towards a Definition of American Modernism," in Singal, ed., *Modernist Culture in America* (New York, 1991), 1–27; Henry F. May, *The End of American Innocence: A Study of the First Years of Our Own Time, 1912–1917* (New York, 1959), 219–23.

39. Kern, *Culture of Time and Space,* 131–38.
40. Ibid., 138–48.
41. Ibid., 16–20.
42. Ibid., 183–85.
43. Ibid., 182.
44. May, *End of American Innocence,* 143–47; Robert M. Crunden, *American Salons: Encounters with European Modernism, 1885–1917* (New York, 1993), 30–55.
45. Singal, "Towards a Definition of American Modernism," 15–16 and 26, n. 22; Wright, *Writings and Buildings,* 91; Morton F. White, *Social Thought in America: The Revolt Against Formalism* (New York, 1949).
46. Crunden, *American Salons;* Kern, *Culture of Time and Space,* 18, 29–31, 118, 184.
47. Mabel Dodge Luhan, *Intimate Memories,* 4 vols. (New York, 1933–1937), I, 265.
48. Lois Palken Rudnick, *Mabel Dodge Luhan: New Woman, New Worlds* (Albuquerque, 1984), 1–57.
49. Mabel Dodge Luhan, *Intimate Memories,* III, 39, 307; Rudnick, *Mabel Dodge Luhan,* 59–120; Crunden, *American Salons,* 383–409.
50. Luhan, *Intimate Memories,* III, 81.
51. Ibid., 83.
52. Ibid., 25–26.
53. Milton W. Brown, *The Story of the Armory Show* (New York, 1963), 42, 152; Crunden, *American Salons,* 363–73.
54. Rudnick, *Mabel Dodge Luhan,* 68; Crunden, *American Salons,* 394.
55. Rudnick, *Mabel Dodge Luhan,* 66–71.
56. Brown, *Story of the Armory Show,* 28, 87, 110, 114, 118, 135–36.
57. Ibid., 87, 133, 139–40.
58. Ibid., 118; Theodore Roosevelt, *The Letters of Theodore Roosevelt,* Elting Morison et al., eds., 8 vols. (Cambridge, MA, 1951–54), III, 8.
59. Brown, *Story of the Armory Show,* 160–61.
60. Nathan G. Hale, Jr., *Freud and the Americans: The Beginnings of Psychoanalysis in the United States, 1876–1917* (New York, 1971), 3–16, 47–173.
61. Max Eastman, "Exploring the Soul and Healing the Body," *Everybody's Magazine,* 32 (June 1915), 741–50; John C. Burnham, "The New Psychology," in Adele Heller and Lois Rudnick, eds., *1915, the Cultural Moment: The New Politics, the New Woman, the New Psychology, the New Art, and the New Theatre in America* (New Brunswick, NJ, 1991), 117–27; Sanford Gifford, "The American Reception of Psychoanalysis, 1908–1922," in ibid., 128–45.
62. Hale, *Freud and the Americans,* 13; Max Eastman, "Mr.-er-er—Oh! What's His Name?" *Everybody's Magazine,* 33 (July 1915), 95–103.
63. Luhan, *Intimate Memories,* III, 43, 307; Rudnick, *Mabel Dodge Luhan,* 121–42.

64. Luhan, *Intimate Memories,* III, 439–67; Gifford, "American Reception of Psychoanalysis," 133–34.
65. Luhan, *Intimate Memories,* III, 505–12; Gifford, "American Reception of Psychoanalysis," 134–35.
66. Luhan, *Intimate Memories,* III, 534; Gifford, "American Reception of Psychoanalysis," 135–36.
67. Franz Boas, *The Mind of Primitive Man* (New York, 1911); George W. Stocking, Jr., *Race, Culture, and Evolution: Essays in the History of Anthropology* (New York, 1968); Marshall Hyatt, "Franz Boas and the Struggle for Black Equality: The Dynamics of Ethnicity," *Perspectives in American History,* 2 (1985), 269–95.
68. Madison Grant, *The Passing of the Great Race, or, the Racial Basis of European History* (New York, 1916), 228.
69. Musser, *Emergence of Cinema,* 130–31, 148–50, 380; Nasaw, *Going Out,* 167.
70. U.S. Bureau of the Census, *Historical Statistics of the United States,* I, 95; James R. Grossman, *Land of Hope: Chicago, Black Southerners, and the Great Migration* (Chicago, 1989), 1.
71. Anderson, *Storyteller's Tale,* 224; Gertrude Stein, "Portraits and Repetition," in *Writings and Lectures, 1911–1945,* ed. Patricia Meyerowitz (London, 1967), 98–99, 103; Rudnick, *Mabel Dodge Luhan,* 47; Luhan, *Intimate Memories,* III, 64.

Chapter Eight

1. *New York Times,* Oct. 15, 1911; Ray Robinson, *Matty, An American Hero: Christy Mathewson of the New York Giants* (New York, 1993), 127.
2. Ibid.; "'Matty's' Boyhood," *Literary Digest,* 48 (June 6, 1914), 1383–84, 1386.
3. *New York Times,* Oct. 15, 1911, Oct. 27, 1911.
4. Robinson, *Matty,* 114, 152–53; *New York Times,* Oct. 22, 1911; Andy McCue, *Baseball by the Books* (Dubuque, IA, 1991), 67–69.
5. Kathy Peiss, *Cheap Amusements: Working Women and Leisure in Turn-of-the-Century New York* (Philadelphia, 1986), 34–45; U.S. Bureau of the Census, *Historical Statistics of the United States,* Bicentennial ed., 2 vols. (Washington, D.C., 1975), I, 168–72; Daniel T. Rodgers, *The Work Ethic in Industrial America, 1850–1920* (Chicago, 1978), 106–7; Roy Rosenzweig, *Eight Hours for What We Will: Workers and Leisure in an Industrial City, 1870–1920* (Cambridge, MA, 1983), 179–80; David Nasaw, *Going Out: The Rise and Fall of Public Amusements* (New York, 1993), 62–65; Joseph Zeisel, "The Workweek in American Industry, 1850–1956," in Eric Larrabee and Rolf Meyersohn, eds., *Mass Leisure* (Glencoe, IL, 1958), 145–53.
6. U.S. Bureau of the Census, *Historical Statistics of the United States,* I, 164–72; Rosenzweig, *Eight Hours for What We Will,* 179–81; Peter R. Shergold, *Working-Class Life: The 'American' Standard in Comparative Perspective, 1899–1913* (Pittsburgh, 1982).

7. Rodgers, *Work Ethic in Industrial America,* 102, 105; Nasaw, *Going Out,* 4; Andrew R. Heinze, *Adapting to Abundance: Jewish Immigrants, Mass Consumption, and the Search for American Identity* (New York, 1990), 130; Richard Wightman Fox, "The Discipline of Amusement," in William R. Taylor, ed., *Inventing Times Square: Commerce and Culture at the Crossroads of the World* (New York, 1991), 83–98; Gregory A. Waller, *Main Street Amusements: Movies and Commercial Entertainment in a Southern City, 1896–1930* (Washington, D.C., 1995), 39.
8. Peiss, *Cheap Amusements,* 115–38; Nasaw, *Going Out,* 65–95; Judith A. Adams, *The Amusement Park Industry: A History of Technology and Thrills* (Boston, 1991).
9. John Kasson, *Amusing the Million: Coney Island at the Turn of the Century* (New York, 1978); Gary Kyriazi, *The Great American Amusement Parks: A Pictorial History* (Secaucus, NJ, 1976); Woody Register, *The Kid of Coney Island: Fred Thompson and the Rise of American Amusements* (New York, 2001), 85–144.
10. Nasaw, *Going Out,* 19–46; Peiss, *Cheap Amusements,* 142–45; Waller, *Main Street Amusements,* 78–83; Robert W. Snyder, "Vaudeville and the Transformation of Popular Culture," in Taylor, ed., *Inventing Times Square,* 133–46.
11. Lewis Erenberg, *Steppin' Out: New York Nightlife and the Transformation of American Culture, 1890–1930* (Chicago, 1984), 113–75; Edward A. Berlin, *King of Ragtime: Scott Joplin and His Era* (New York, 1994), 153; Nasaw, *Going Out,* 104–19; Lary May, *Screening Out the Past: The Birth of Mass Culture and the Motion Picture Industry* (Chicago, 1983), 33–34; Susan Curtis, *Dancing to a Black Man's Tune: A Life of Scott Joplin* (Columbia, MO, 1994), 87; Peiss, *Cheap Amusements,* 88–114; William Howland Kenney, *Chicago Jazz: A Cultural History, 1904–1930* (New York, 1993), 62–64.
12. Russell Sanjek, *American Popular Music and Its Business: The First Four Hundred Years,* 3 vols. (New York, 1988), II, 401–20; U.S. Bureau of the Census, *Historical Statistics of the United States,* II, 696–97.
13. Berlin, *King of Ragtime;* Stephen Kern, *Culture of Time and Space, 1880–1918* (Cambridge, MA, 1983), 123–24; Reid Badger, *James Reese Europe: A Life in Ragtime* (New York, 1995); Philip Furia, "Irving Berlin: Troubadour of Tin Pan Alley," in Taylor, ed., *Inventing Times Square,* 191–211.
14. George S. Kanahele, ed., *Hawaiian Music and Musicians: An Illustrated History* (Honolulu, 1979), 45–46, 325–26.
15. Kenney, *Chicago Jazz,* 3–116; Kern, *Culture of Time and Space,* 124; May, *Screening Out the Past,* 33; Gunther Schuller, *Early Jazz: Its Roots and Musical Development* (New York, 1967); Kathy J. Ogren, *The Jazz Revolution: Twenties America and the Meaning of Jazz* (New York, 1989); Burton W. Peretti, *Jazz in American Culture* (New York, 1997), 10–60.
16. Elliott J. Gorn and Warren Goldstein, *A Brief History of American Sports* (New York, 1993), 98–177; G. Edward White, *Creating the National Pastime: Baseball Transforms Itself, 1903–1953* (Princeton, 1996), 10–46; Nasaw, *Going Out,* 96–103; Robert

F. Burk, *Never Just a Game: Players, Owners, and American Baseball to 1920* (Chapel Hill, NC, 1994), 179; Michael Gershman, *Diamonds: The Evolution of the Ballpark from Elysian Fields to Camden Yards* (New York, 1993), 84–121; Harold Seymour, *Baseball: The Golden Age* (New York, 1971), 3–165; John Thorn and Peter Palmer, with Michael Gershman, eds., *Total Baseball*, 4th ed. (New York, 1995), 106.

17. May, *Screening Out the Past*, 35–36, 63–64; Russell Merritt, "Nickelodeon Theaters, 1905–1914," in Tino Balio, ed., *The American Film Industry* (Madison, WI, 1976), 59–79; Charles Musser, *The Emergence of Cinema: The American Screen to 1907* (New York, 1990), 297–495; Eileen Bowser, *The Transformation of Cinema, 1907–1915* (New York, 1990), 4–8; Nasaw, *Going Out*, 161; Rosenzweig, *Eight Hours for What We Will*, 192–93; Waller, *Main Street Amusements*, 65–71; "The Nickelodeon," in Gerald Mast, ed., *The Movies in Our Midst: Documents in the Cultural History of Film in America* (Urbana, IL, 1982), 43–45; Robert C. Allen, "Motion Picture Exhibition in Manhattan, 1906–1912," in John L. Fell, ed., *Film Before Griffith* (Berkeley, CA, 1983), 162–75; Burnes St. Patrick Hollyman, "The First Picture Shows: Austin, Texas, 1894–1913," in ibid., 188–95; Kathryn H. Fuller, *At the Picture Show: Small-Town Audiences and the Creation of Movie Fan Culture* (Washington, D.C., 1996), 23–46.
18. Bowser, *Transformation of Cinema*, 13, 15.
19. Waller, *Main Street Amusements*, 76–78, 86–121; Nasaw, *Going Out*, 205; Bowser, *Transformation of Cinema*, 53–72, 121–36, 167–215, 235–72; May, *Screening Out the Past*, 63–66, 147–66; Merritt, "Nickelodeon Theaters," 73–75; Rosenzweig, *Eight Hours for What We Will*, 208–15.
20. White, *Creating the National Pastime*, 22–23; Steven A. Riess, *Touching Base: Professional Baseball and American Culture in the Progressive Era*, rev. ed. (Urbana, IL, 1999), 49–84; Sanjek, *American Popular Music and Its Business*, II, 342; *National Cyclopedia of American Biography*, 63 vols. (New York, 1893–), XXVII, 474; May, *Screening Out the Past*, 152, 169–76, 253–54; Bowser, *Transformation of Cinema*, 10, 12; Rosenzweig, *Eight Hours for What We Will*, 172–79; Neil Gabler, *An Empire of Their Own: How the Jews Invented Hollywood* (New York, 1988).
21. Kenney, *Chicago Jazz*, xiii, 123.
22. Nasaw, *Going Out*, 168–69; Elizabeth Ewen, "City Lights: Immigrant Women and the Rise of the Movies," in Stuart Ewen and Elizabeth Ewen, eds., *Channels of Desire: Mass Images and the Shaping of American Consciousness* (New York, 1982), 81–105; Rosenzweig, *Eight Hours for What We Will*, 197–98; May, *Screening Out the Past*, 38; Merritt, "Nickelodeon Theaters," 73; Peiss, *Cheap Amusements*, 142–45, 148–53.
23. Nasaw, *Going Out*, 169–70; Bowser, *Transformation of Cinema*, 203; Rosenzweig, *Eight Hours for What We Will*, 197; Peiss, *Cheap Amusements*, 150.
24. Nasaw, *Going Out*, 71, 105; Kasson, *Amusing the Million*, 41, 95; Jane Addams, *The Spirit of Youth and the City Streets* (New York, 1909), 96.

25. May, *Screening Out the Past,* 152–53; Bowser, *Transformation of Cinema,* 1–3, 8–9, 122–23; Garth S. Jowett, "The First Motion Picture Audiences," in Fell, ed., *Film Before Griffith,* 196–206; Waller, *Main Street Amusements,* 70–71; Nasaw, *Going Out,* 170–71; Merritt, "Nickelodeon Theaters," 63–64; Rosenzweig, *Eight Hours for What We Will,* 193–204; Fuller, *At the Picture Show,* 38.
26. Peiss, *Cheap Amusements,* 151.
27. Nasaw, *Going Out,* 86–87, 99–100, 164–65; Rosenzweig, *Eight Hours for What We Will,* 212–13.
28. Bowser, *Transformation of Cinema,* 103–19; Richard deCordova, *Picture Personalities: The Emergence of the Star System in America* (Urbana, IL, 1990); Norma Talmadge, "Close-Ups," in Balio, ed., *American Film Industry,* 95.
29. Bowser, *Transformation of Cinema,* 93–102.
30. May, *Screening Out the Past,* 106, 108, 120, 125.
31. John F. Kasson, *Amusing the Million;* Nasaw, *Going Out,* 85–86, 91; Peiss, *Cheap Amusements,* 10–114, 132–34; George Kibbe, "The Puzzle of the Under-World," *McClure's,* 41 (July 1913), 99–111; May, *Screening Out the Past,* 33.
32. Clay McShane, *Down the Asphalt Path: The Automobile and the American City* (New York, 1994), 142, 169–70; Musser, *Emergence of Cinema,* 118; Peiss, *Cheap Amusements,* 155–57; May, *Screening Out the Past,* 104–6.
33. Ibid., 49; John D'Emilio and Estelle Freedman, *Intimate Matters: A History of Sexuality in America* (New York, 1988), 171–235; Janet Staiger, *Bad Women: Regulating Sexuality in Early American Cinema* (Minneapolis, 1995), 1–53; Jeffrey P. Moran, "'Modernism Gone Mad': Sex Education Comes to Chicago, 1913," *Journal of American History,* 83 (Sept. 1996), 481–513.
34. Nathan G. Hale, Jr., *Freud and the Americans: The Beginnings of Psychoanalysis in the United States, 1876–1917* (New York, 1971), 3–16, 265–66, 342, 405; D'Emilio and Freedman, *Intimate Matters,* 223; Paul Robinson, *The Modernization of Sex: Havelock Ellis, Alfred Kinsey, William Masters, and Virginia Johnson* (New York, 1976), 27.
35. Morton Keller, *Regulating a New Society: Public Policy and Social Change in America, 1900–1933* (Cambridge, MA, 1994), 30–33.
36. Mari Jo Buhle, *Women and American Socialism, 1870–1920* (Urbana, IL, 1981), 268–80; Linda Gordon, *Woman's Body, Woman's Right: A Social History of Birth Control in America* (1976; New York, 1977), 206–30.
37. Mabel Dodge Luhan, *Intimate Memories,* 4 vols. (New York, 1933–1937), III, 69–71; Gordon, *Woman's Body, Woman's Right,* 186–245; David M. Kennedy, *Birth Control in America: The Career of Margaret Sanger* (New Haven, CT, 1970), 108–35.
38. Margaret Sanger, *The Pivot of Civilization* (New York, 1922), 22–23, 231–32, 238–39.
39. Luhan, *Intimate Memories,* III, 168–70.
40. George Chauncey, *Gay New York: Gender, Urban Culture, and the Making of the Gay Male World, 1890–1940* (New York, 1994).

41. Alice B. Stockham, *The Lover's World: A Wheel of Life* (Chicago, 1903), 63.
42. Lauren Rabinowitz, "'Temptations of Pleasure': Nickelodeons, Amusement Parks, and the Sights of Female Sexuality," *Camera Obscura*, 23 (May 1990), 70–89; Marjorie Rosen, *Popcorn Venus: Women, Movies and the American Dream* (New York, 1973), 59–61; Eve Golden, *Vamp: The Rise and Fall of Theda Bara* (Vestal, NY, 1996); May, *Screening Out the Past*, 106; Staiger, *Bad Women*, 147–62.
43. June Sochen, *The New Woman: Feminism in Greenwich Village, 1910–1920* (New York, 1972); Christine Stansell, *American Moderns: Bohemian New York and the Creation of a New Century* (New York, 2000).
44. Lillian Symes, "Still a Man's Game: Reflections of a Slightly Tired Feminist," *Harper's*, 158 (May 1929), 678–86; Nancy F. Cott, *The Grounding of Modern Feminism* (New Haven, CT, 1987), 41–42, 151; Sochen, *New Woman*, 38.
45. Judith Schwarz, *Radical Feminists of Heterodoxy: Greenwich Village, 1912–1940*, 2nd ed. (Norwich, VT, 1986), 35–39, 75–95; Cott, *Grounding of Modern Feminism*, 48; Sochen, *New Woman*, 41, 43–44, 61–66.
46. Cott, *Grounding of Modern Feminism*, 150–51; Gordon, *Woman's Body, Woman's Right*; Beryl Satter, *Each Mind a Kingdom: American Women, Sexual Purity, and the New Thought Movement, 1875–1920* (Berkeley, CA, 1999), 21–56, 111–49; Winifred Harper Cooley, "The Younger Suffragists," *Harper's Weekly*, LVIII (Sept. 27, 1913), 7–8; Gordon, *Woman's Body, Woman's Right*, 183–85, 238.
47. Cooley, "Younger Suffragists," 8.
48. Cott, *Grounding of Modern Feminism*, 39; Sochen, *New Woman*, 47; Schwartz, *Radical Feminists of Heterodoxy*, 25, 43–45.
49. Sochen, *New Woman*, 21; Crystal Eastman, *Crystal Eastman on Women and Revolution*, ed. Blanche Wiesen Cook (New York, 1978), 47; Cott, *Grounding of Modern Feminism*, 152; Symes, "Still a Man's Game," 679; Allen F. Davis, *American Heroine: The Life and Legend of Jane Addams* (New York, 1973), 60–62.
50. Sochen, *New Woman*, 26.
51. Peiss, *Cheap Amusements*, 54, 106–14.
52. Luhan, *Intimate Memories*, III, 527.
53. Floyd Dell, "Feminism for Men," in *Looking at Life* (New York, 1924), 14–24.
54. Lears, "Sherwood Anderson," 29; Schwartz, *Radical Feminists of Heterodoxy*, 83; Ellen Kay Trimberger, ed., *Intimate Warriors: Portraits of a Modern Marriage, 1899–1944: Selected Works by Neith Boyce and Hutchins Hapgood* (New York, 1991), 207; Dell, "Feminism for Men," 16.
55. Trimberger, ed., *Intimate Warriors*, 205; Hutchins Hapgood, *A Victorian in the Modern World* (1939; Seattle, 1972), 159, 395.
56. May, *Screening Out the Past*, 106; Golden, *Vamp*, 105–6; Lois W. Banner, *American Beauty* (1983; Chicago, 1984), 45–65, 154–74; "The Revolt of the Women," *Century*, 87 (April 1914), 964–65.

57. Nasaw, *Going Out,* 174.
58. Bowser, *Transformation of Cinema,* 37–38; May, *Screening Out the Past,* 40–41, 50; Nasaw, *Going Out,* 174–75; Rosenzweig, *Eight Hours for What We Will,* 204–8; Kathleen D. McCarthy, "Nickel Vice and Virtue: Movie Censorship in Chicago, 1907–1915," *Journal of Popular Film,* 5:1 (1976), 40–42; Mast, ed., *Movies in Our Midst,* 47, 61–63; Fuller, *At the Picture Show,* 34–36, 41–42; Ted Ownby, *Subduing Satan: Religion, Recreation, and Manhood in the Rural South, 1865–1920* (Chapel Hill, NC, 1990).
59. Elisabeth Israels Perry, *Belle Moskowitz: Feminine Politics and the Exercise of Power in the Age of Alfred E. Smith* (New York, 1987), 41–57.
60. Kevin Brownlow, *Behind the Mask of Innocence: Sex, Violence, Prejudice, Crime: Films of Social Conscience in the Silent Era* (Berkeley, CA, 1990), 4–12; Paul Boyer, *Urban Masses and Moral Order in America, 1820–1920* (Cambridge, MA, 1978); Daniel Czitrom, "The Politics of Performance: From Theater Licensing to Movie Censorship in Turn-of-the-Century New York," *American Quarterly,* 44 (Dec. 1992), 525–53; McCarthy, "Nickel Vice and Virtue," 37–55; Nancy J. Rosenbloom, "Between Reform and Regulation: The Struggle over Film Censorship in Progressive America, 1909–1922," *Film History,* 1:4 (1987), 307–25; Daniel Czitrom, "The Redemption of Leisure: The National Board of Censorship and the Rise of Motion Pictures in New York City, 1900–1920," *Studies in Visual Communication,* 10 (Fall 1984), ca. 3–4.
61. Richard A. Armour, "Effects of Censorship Pressure on the New York Nickelodeon Market, 1907–1909," *Film History,* 4:2 (1990), 113–21; May, *Screening Out the Past,* 43–44; Bowser, *Transformation of Cinema,* 39, 48.
62. Kennedy, *Birth Control in America,* 21–34.
63. David J. Langum, *Crossing Over the Line: Legislating Morality and the Mann Act* (Chicago, 1994), 1–76; Mark Thomas Connelly, *The Reponse to Prostitution in the Progressive Era* (Chapel Hill, NC, 1980); Francesco Cordasco, *The White Slave Trade and the Immigrant* (Detroit, 1981).
64. Nasaw, *Going Out,* 105–14; Peiss, *Cheap Amusements,* 102–8; Perry, *Belle Moskowitz,* 54–56.
65. Rosenbloom, "Between Reform and Regulation," 307–25; May, *Screening Out the Past,* 53–59; Bowser, *Transformation of Cinema,* 48–52; Nancy J. Rosenbloom, "In Defense of the Moving Pictures: The People's Institute, the National Board of Censorship, and the Problem of Leisure in Urban America," *American Studies,* 33 (Fall 1992), 41–60; Robert Fisher, "Film Censorship and Progressive Reform: The National Board of Censorship and Motion Pictures, 1909–1922," *Journal of Popular Film,* 4 (1975), 145–46; Staiger, *Bad Women,* esp. 1–28, 86–115, 118–19; Mast, ed., *Movies in Our Midst,* 63–72, 144–53.

66. Rosenbloom, "Between Reform and Regulation," 312–13, 316–17; Nasaw, *Going Out*, 203–4; Mast, ed., *Movies in Our Midst*, 136–43; Golden, *Vamp*, 59. For a different assessment, see McCarthy, "Nickel Vice and Virtue," 37–55.
67. Kennedy, *Birth Control in America*, 72–107.
68. Perry, *Belle Moskowitz*, 57; Allen Sangree, "'Fans' and Their Frenzies: The Wholesome Madness of Baseball," *Everybody's*, 17 (Sept. 1907), 378–87.
69. Brownlow, *Behind the Mask of Innocence*, 4; May, *Screening Out the Past*, 53; Staiger, *Bad Women*, 96; Rosenzweig, *Eight Hours for What We Will*, 183–91, 213–14; Vachel Lindsay, *The Art of the Moving Picture* (New York, 1915), 207, 214; McCarthy, "Nickel Vice and Virtue," 47; Bowser, *Transformation of Cinema*, 2; Peiss, *Cheap Amusements*, 150.
70. Mast, ed., *Movies in Our Midst*, 45, 48, 52–53, 60–61; Fuller, *At the Picture Show*, 85–93; Rosenbloom, "In Defense of the Moving Pictures," 50; May, *Screening Out the Past*, 52–53; Bowser, *Transformation of Cinema*, 38–39.
71. Donald Wilhelm, "Our Uncensorious Censor," *Independent*, 93 (Jan. 15, 1918), 43.
72. Nasaw, *Going Out*, 31–32, 47–49, 91–92, 100–101, 115–16; Waller, *Main Street Amusements*, 111; Fuller, *At the Picture Show*, 30–34, 42; Mary Carbine, "'The Finest Outside the Loop': Motion Picture Exhibition in Chicago's Black Metropolis, 1905–1928," *Camera Obscura*, 23 (May 1990), 18.
73. Nasaw, *Going Out*, 51–61, 74–78, 93.
74. Carbine, "'Finest Outside the Loop,'" 8–41; Nasaw, *Going Out*, 49–51, 59–60, 171–73, 202–4; Thomas Cripps, *Slow Fade to Black: The Negro in American Film, 1900–1942* (New York, 1977), 41–69; Mast, ed., *Movies in Our Midst*, 123–32.
75. Randy Roberts, *Papa Jack: Jack Johnson and the Era of White Hopes* (New York, 1983), 18, 21, 28.
76. *New York Times*, July 5, 1910; *St. Louis Post-Dispatch*, July 4, 1910; Roberts, *Papa Jack*, 61, 91, 97; Al-Tony Gilmore, *Bad Nigger!: The National Impact of Jack Johnson* (Port Washington, NY, 1975), 39–40, 42.
77. Roberts, *Papa Jack*, 109–110; Gilmore, *Bad Nigger!*, 42–44, 47–49, 59–74; Benjamin E. Mays, *Born to Rebel: An Autobiography* (1971; Athens, GA, 1987), 19; *New York Times*, July 5, 1910.
78. *New York Times*, Dec. 22, 1912, Dec. 24, 1912, Dec. 25, 1912; Roberts, *Papa Jack*, 28, 75, 81; Gilmore, *Bad Nigger!*, 14, 18.
79. Dan Streible, "A History of the Boxing Film, 1894–1915: Social Control and Social Reform in the Progressive Era," *Film History*, 3:3 (1989), 235–57; Gilmore, *Bad Nigger!*, 18, 75–93; Roberts, *Papa Jack*, 146; *New York Times*, Oct. 20, 1912.
80. Roberts, *Papa Jack*, 146–47; Gilmore, *Bad Nigger!*, 21, 95–116.
81. *New York Times*, June 5, 1913; Gilmore, *Bad Nigger!*, 123.
82. Gilmore, *Bad Nigger!*, 20–21; William H. Wiggins, "Jack Johnson as Bad Nigger: The Folklore of His Life," *Black Scholar*, 2 (Jan. 1971), 34–46.

Chapter Nine

1. Woodrow Wilson, *The Papers of Woodrow Wilson,* ed., Arthur Link et al., 69 vols. (Princeton, NJ, 1966–1994), XLI, 519–29; David M. Kennedy, *Over Here: The First World War and American Society* (New York, 1980), 10–14.
2. Herbert Croly, *The Promise of American Life* (1909; Boston, 1989); Walter Lippmann, *Drift and Mastery* (1914; Englewood Cliffs, NJ, 1961), 167; Walter Weyl, *The New Democracy: An Essay on Certain Political and Economic Tendencies in the United States* (New York, 1912); Wilson, *Papers,* XXIV, 324; Jane Addams, *The Second Twenty Years at Hull-House* (New York, 1930), 32.
3. John Morton Blum, *V Was for Victory: Politics and American Culture during World War II* (New York, 1976), xii.
4. William E. Leuchtenburg, "Progressivism and Imperialism: The Progressive Movement and American Foreign Policy, 1898–1916," *Mississippi Valley Historical Review,* 39 (Dec. 1952), 483–504; Walter I. Trattner, "Progressivism and World War I: A Reappraisal," *Mid-America,* 44 (July 1962), 131–45; John Milton Cooper, Jr., "Progressivism and American Foreign Policy: A Reconsideration," *Mid-America,* 51 (Oct. 1969), 260–77; J. A. Thompson, "American Progressive Publicists and the First World War, 1914–1917," *Journal of American History,* 58 (Sept. 1971), 364–83.
5. Donald Richberg, *Tents of the Mighty* (Chicago, 1930), 96; Kennedy, *Over Here,* 7, 20–22, 33–34, 40–41.
6. Ibid., 38–40; Walter Lippmann, "The World Conflict in Relation to American Democracy," *Annals of the American Academy of Political and Social Science,* 72 (1917), 1–10; Newton D. Baker, *Frontiers of Freedom* (New York, 1918), 96; Charles Hirschfeld, "Nationalist Progressivism and World War I," *Mid-America,* 45 (July 1963), 139–56.
7. Allen F. Davis, "Welfare, Reform and World War I," *American Quarterly,* 19 (Autumn 1967), 520; Kennedy, *Over Here,* 43–44, 49–53; F. L. Allen, "The American Tradition and the War," *Nation,* 104 (April 26, 1917), 484–85; Sidney Kaplan, "Social Engineers as Saviors: Effects of World War I on Some American Liberals," *Journal of the History of Ideas,* 17 (1956), 347–69; Robert B. Westbrook, *John Dewey and American Democracy* (Ithaca, NY, 1991), 195–227; Mark Meigs, *Optimism at Armageddon: Voices of American Participants in the First World War* (New York, 1997), 36–68.
8. Thompson, "American Progressive Publicists," 381.
9. Robert E. Park, "What May Sociologists Do Toward Solving the Problems of the Present War Situation?" *American Journal of Sociology,* 23 (July 1917), 15–16, 20, 33–34, 40–41; Harriott Stanton-Blatch, *Mobilizing Woman-Power* (New York, 1918), 90; Stuart I. Rochester, *American Liberal Disillusionment in the Wake of World War I* (University Park, PA, 1977), 41.

10. Randolph Bourne, *War and the Intellectuals: Essays by Randolph S. Bourne,* ed. Carl Resek (New York, 1964), 5, 60; Casey Nelson Blake, *Beloved Community: The Cultural Criticism of Randolph Bourne, Van Wyck Brooks, Waldo Frank, and Lewis Mumford* (Chapel Hill, 1990), 157–80.
11. Robert H. Ferrell, *Woodrow Wilson and World War I, 1917–1921* (New York, 1985), 14, 24–30; Grosvenor B. Clarkson, *Industrial America in the World War: The Strategy Behind the Line, 1917–1918* (Boston, 1923), 78.
12. Ferrell, *Woodrow Wilson and World War I,* 99–100; Daniel R. Beaver, *Newton D. Baker and the American War Effort, 1917–1919* (Lincoln, NE, 1966); Joseph L. Morison, *Josephus Daniels: The Small-d Democrat* (Chapel Hill, NC, 1966); Robert D. Cuff, "We Band of Brothers—Woodrow Wilson's War Managers," *Canadian Review of American Studies,* V (Fall 1974), 135–48.
13. Burl Noggle, *Into the Twenties: The United States from Armistice to Normalcy* (Urbana, IL, 1974), 55–56; Frederic L. Paxson, "The American War Government, 1917–1918," *American Historical Review,* 26 (Oct. 1920), 54–76, which provides an early but still useful overview of the wartime state.
14. Jordan A. Schwartz, *The Speculator: Bernard M. Baruch in Washington, 1917–1965* (Chapel Hill, NC, 1981); Clarkson, *Industrial America in the War,* 66.
15. Robert D. Cuff, *The War Industries Board: Business-Government Relations During World War I* (Baltimore, 1973); Clarkson, *Industrial America in the World War,* 9, 154, 292.
16. George H. Nash, *The Life of Herbert Hoover: Master of Emergencies, 1917–1918* (New York, 1996), 154; Robert D. Cuff, "Herbert Hoover, the Ideology of Voluntarism and War Organization during the Great War," *Journal of American History,* 64 (Sept. 1977), 358–72.
17. Robert D. Cuff, "Harry Garfield, the Fuel Administration, and the Search for a Cooperative Order during World War I," *American Quarterly,* 30 (Spring 1978), 39–53.
18. Kennedy, *Over Here,* 252–55; K. Austin Kerr, *American Railroad Politics, 1914–1920* (Pittsburgh, 1968).
19. John Whiteclay Chambers, II, *To Raise an Army: The Draft Comes to Modern America* (New York, 1987), 125–204; Ferrell, *Woodrow Wilson and World War I,* 16–18.
20. Valerie Jean Connor, *The National War Labor Board: Stability, Social Justice, and the Voluntary State in World War I* (Chapel Hill, NC, 1983); Joseph Anthony McCartin, *Labor's Great War: The Struggle for Industrial Democracy and the Origins of Modern American Labor Relations, 1912–1921* (Chapel Hill, NC, 1997).
21. Gerald D. Nash, "Herbert Hoover and the Origins of the Reconstruction Finance Corporation," *Mississippi Valley Historical Review,* 46 (Dec. 1959), 456–57.
22. Ferrell, *Woodrow Wilson and World War I,* 196–97; Kennedy, *Over Here,* 16–17.
23. Clarkson, *Industrial America in the War,* 229; Mark Sullivan, *Our Times: The United States, 1900–1925,* 6 vols. (New York, 1926–1935), V, 380.

24. George Creel, *How We Advertised America* (New York, 1920), 3, 5.
25. Donald Wilhelm, "Our Uncensorious Censor," *Independent*, 93 (Jan. 15, 1918), 43; Thompson, "American Progressive Publicists," 377.
26. Wilson, *Papers*, XLII, 504. This paragraph and the following draw on Kennedy, *Over Here*, 25–27, 66–86; H. C. Peterson and Gilbert Fite, *Opponents of War, 1917–1918* (Seattle, 1968); Ferrell, *Woodrow Wilson and World War I*, 204–10.
27. Peterson and Fite, *Opponents of War*, 202–7.
28. Creel, *How We Advertised America*, 105; George Creel, "Propaganda and Morale," *American Journal of Sociology*, 47 (Nov. 1941), 350; George Creel, *Rebel at Large: Recollections of Fifty Crowded Years* (New York, 1947), 24.
29. Stephen Vaughn, *Holding Fast the Inner Lines: Democracy, Nationalism, and the Committee on Public Information* (Chapel Hill, NC, 1980); John R. Mock and Cedric Larson, *Words That Won the War: The Story of the Committee on Public Information, 1917–1929* (Princeton, NJ, 1939); Donald Wilhelm, "The Government's Own Publicity Work," *American Review of Reviews*, 56 (Nov. 1917), 507–11; Wilhelm, "Our Uncensorious Censor," 21.
30. Creel, *How We Advertised America*, 5, 16–17, 24.
31. Alexander Whiteside, "Our New Americans and War Activities," *Survey*, 40 (June 15, 1918), 309–12; Kennedy, *Over Here*, 63–66; Mock and Larson, *Words That Won the War*, 213–32.
32. John Higham, *Strangers in the Land: Patterns of American Nativism, 1860–1925* (1955; New York, 1973), 194–263; Frederick C. Luebke, *Bonds of Loyalty: German-Americans and World War I* (DeKalb, IL, 1974); Vaughn, *Holding Fast the Inner Lines*, 62–65, 273–75.
33. Kennedy, *Over Here*, 53–56; Carol S. Gruber, *Mars and Minerva: World War I and the Uses of the Higher Learning in America* (Baton Rouge, 1975); George T. Blakey, *Historians on the Homefront: American Propagandists for the Great War* (Lexington, KY, 1970).
34. Frank A. Vanderlip, "National Thrift," in Elisha M. Friedman, ed., *American Problems of Reconstruction: A National Symposium on the Economic and Financial Aspects* (New York, 1918), pp. 415–25; Clarkson, *Industrial America in the World War*, 217–21, 331–43.
35. Herbert Hoover, *The Memoirs of Herbert Hoover: Years of Adventure, 1874–1920*, 244; Kennedy, *Over Here*, 118.
36. William Clinton Mullendore, *History of the United States Food Administration, 1917–1919* (Stanford, CA, 1941); Nash, *Life of Herbert Hoover: Master of Emergencies*, 31–32, 158–59; Kennedy, *Over Here*, 118–19.
37. David E. Kyvig, *Repealing National Prohibition*, 2nd ed. (Kent, OH, 2000), 5–19.
38. Clarkson, *Industrial America in the World War*, 332–33.
39. Davis, "Welfare, Reform and World War I," 521–22; Robert A. Woods, "The Regimentation of the Free," *Survey*, 40 (July 6, 1918), 397.
40. Maurine Weiner Greenwald, *Women, War, and Work: The Impact of World War I on*

Women Workers in the United States (Westport, CT, 1980), 3–34; Robert Zieger, *America's Great War: World War I and the American Experience* (Lanham, MD, 2000), 142–49; Davis, "Welfare, Reform and World War I," 525–26.

41. Eleanor Flexner and Ellen Fitzpatrick, *Century of Struggle: The Woman's Rights Movement in the United States,* enlarged ed. (Cambridge, MA, 1996), 241–317; Sara Hunter Graham, *Woman Suffrage and the New Democracy* (New Haven, CT 1996); Christine A. Lunardini, *From Equal Suffrage to Equal Rights: Alice Paul and the National Woman's Party, 1910–1928* (New York, 1986); Christine Lunardini and Thomas J. Knock, "Woodrow Wilson and Woman Suffrage: A New Look," *Political Science Quarterly,* 95 (Winter 1980–81), 655–71.
42. Kennedy, *Over Here,* 17–18; Wilson, *Papers,* XLI: 527–28; Newton D. Baker, *Frontiers of Freedom* (New York, 1918), 94; Nancy Gentile Ford, *Americans All!: Foreign-Born Soldiers in World War I* (College Station, TX, 2001).
43. Nancy K. Bristow, *Making Men Moral: Social Engineering during the Great War* (New York, 1996), 82; Raymond D. Fosdick, *Chronicle of a Generation: An Autobiography* (New York, 1958), 142–86; Fred Davis Baldwin, "The American Enlisted Man in World War I" (Ph.D. diss., Princeton University, 1964), 31–142.
44. Bristow, *Making Men Moral,* 221–24; Davis, "Welfare, Reform and World War I," 528–30; Baker, *Frontiers of Freedom,* 96.
45. Ferrell, *Woodrow Wilson and World War I,* 31–32.
46. Davis, "Welfare, Reform and World War I," 523.
47. Ibid., 519; Woods, "Regimentation of the Free," 396.
48. Josephus Daniels, "Labor's Golden Age Here," in Edwin Wildman, ed., *Reconstructing America: Our Next Big Job* (Boston, 1919), 228–29; George W. Perkins, "The American of To-morrow" in Elisha M. Freidman, ed., *American Problems of Reconstruction* (New York, 1918), 51–52; Clarkson, *Industrial America in the World War,* 3–4. See also Paxson, "American War Government," 76.
49. Woods, "Regimentation of the Free," 398; Robert A. Woods "A New Purpose," *Survey,* 41 (Dec. 7, 1918), 288–89; Clarkson, *Industrial America in the World War,* 218–19.
50. Bristow, *Making Men Moral,* 179–206.
51. George Walker, *Venereal Disease in the American Expeditionary Forces* (Baltimore, MD, 1922), 39, 224–25; James H. Hallas, *Doughboy War: The American Expeditionary Force in World War I* (Boulder, CO, 2000), 204–5. For a different view, see Fred D. Baldwin, "The Invisible Armor," *American Quarterly,* 16 (Autumn, 1964), 432–44.
52. Ross L. Finney, *Causes and Cures for the Social Unrest: An Appeal to the Middle Class* (New York, 1922), 106, 187, 221.
53. Clarkson, *Industrial America in the World War,* 183, 186, 218, 229.
54. Paul Klapper, "New Demands in Education," in Elisha M. Friedman, ed., *America and the New Era* (New York, 1920), 324.

55. John Dickinson, "The War and American Ideals," in Friedman, ed., *America and the New Era*, 256–57.
56. Sullivan, *Our Times*, V, 489–90. See also Warner Fite, "Individualism in the New Social Order," in Friedman, ed., *America and the New Era*, 95.
57. Chambers, *To Raise an Army*, 211–14.
58. Finney, *Causes and Cures for the Social Unrest*, 82–83.
59. Kennedy, *Over Here*, 255–56.
60. Robert K. Murray, *Red Scare: A Study of National Hysteria, 1919–1920* (Minneapolis, 1955); Robert L. Friedham, *The Seattle General Strike* (Seattle, 1964); Greenwald, *Women, War, and Work*, 216–23; Stephen H. Norwood, *Labor's Flaming Youth: Telephone Operators and Worker Militancy, 1878–1923* (Urbana, IL, 1990); Ronald L. Filipelli, ed., *Labor Conflict in the United States: An Encyclopedia* (New York, 1990), 3–5; David Brody, *Labor in Crisis: The Steel Strike of 1919* (Philadelphia, 1965).
61. Elliott M. Rudwick, *Race Riot at East St. Louis* (Carbondale, IL, 1964); Alex Swan, "When Whites Riot—The East St. Louis Massacre," *International Socialist Review*, 34 (Oct. 1973), 12–24; Ferrell, *Woodrow Wilson and World War I*, 213–18.
62. Kennedy, *Over Here*, 66–69; Higham, *Strangers in the Land*, 234–311.
63. Murray, *Red Scare*, 36. This and the following paragraphs draw on Murray, and also Stanley A. Coben, "A Study in Nativism: The American Red Scare of 1919–1920," *Political Science Quarterly*, 79 (March 1964), 52–75.
64. Finney, *Causes and Cures for the Social Unrest*, 1.
65. Woods, "Regimentation of the Free," 398.
66. Murray, *Red Scare*, 169.
67. Davis, *American Heroine*, 245, 252, 254, 261, 269.
68. Ibid., 269.
69. Richberg, *Tents of the Mighty*, 91–93.
70. Wilson, *Papers*, LIII, 61.
71. Noggle, *Into the Twenties*, 49–52; Wilson, *Papers*, LIII, 279. Wilson's own attraction to conservative values may have played a role, too. With some frustration, Walter Lippmann had earlier pointed to "the inner contradiction of Woodrow Wilson," seemingly drawn simultaneously to an individualistic, competitive past and a progressive, regulated future. "He knows that there is a new world demanding new methods, but he dreams of an older world," Lippmann observed. "He is torn between the two." Lippmann, *Drift and Mastery*, 82
72. David Burner, "1919: Prelude to Normalcy," in John Braeman et al., *Change and Continuity in Twentieth-Century America: The 1920s* (Columbus, OH, 1968), 5.
73. H. W. Brands, *T. R.: The Last Romantic* (New York, 1997), 773–816; Richberg, *Tents of the Mighty*, 97; James Oliver Robertson, *No Third Choice: Progressives in Republican Politics, 1916–1921* (New York, 1983).

74. Bourne, *War and the Intellectuals*, 50; Henry Bruére, "The Federal Employment Service," in Wildman, ed., *Reconstructing America*, 237–38.
75. This paragraph and the following draw on Wesley M. Bagby, *Road to Normalcy: The Presidential Campaign and Election of 1920* (Baltimore, 1962); and Robert K. Murray, *The Harding Era: Warren G. Harding and His Administration* (Minneapolis, 1969), 43–70.
76. *Official Report of the Proceedings of the Seventeenth Republican National Convention* (New York, 1920), 15–16, 117, 258, 263–65, 277.
77. Robert Bacon and James Brown Scott eds., *Men and Policies: Addresses by Elihu Root* (Cambridge, MA, 1925), 204–5; *Official Report of the Proceedings of the Seventeenth Republican National Convention*, 264, 276.
78. Ibid., 279; Davis, "Progressives and the Business Culture of the 1920s," 80–81; Ellis W. Hawley, *The Great War and the Search for a Modern Order: A History of the American People and Their Institutions, 1917–1933*, 2nd ed. (New York, 1992), 42–44; Herbert Hoover, *American Individualism* (Garden City, NY, 1922), 7–8.
79. Paul W. Glad, "Progressives and the Business Culture of the 1920s," *Journal of American History*, 53 (June 1966), 78.
80. Calvin Coolidge, *The Autobiography of Calvin Coolidge* (New York, 1929), 136–37, 158.

Conclusion

1. Jane Addams, *The Second Twenty Years at Hull-House* (New York, 1930), 192; Arthur S. Link, "What Happened to the Progressive Movement in the 1920's?" *American Historical Review*, 74 (April 1959), 1205–20; Herbert Margulies, "Recent Opinion on the Decline of the Progressive Movement," *Mid-America*, 45 (Oct. 1963), 250–68; Jackson K. Putnam, "The Persistence of Progressivism in the 1920's: The Case of California," *Pacific Historical Review*, 35 (Nov. 1966), 395–411; J. Stanley Lemons, "The Sheppard-Towner Act: Progressivism in the 1920's," *Journal of American History*, 55 (March 1969), 776–86; Clarke A. Chambers, *Seedtime of Reform: American Social Service and Social Action, 1918–1933* (Minneapolis, 1963); Robert F. Himmelberg, ed., *Business-Government Cooperation, 1917–1932: The Rise of Corporatist Policies* (New York, 1994); William J. Barber, *From New Era to New Deal: Herbert Hoover, the Economists, and American Economic Policy, 1921–1933* (Cambridge, MA, 1985); Robert K. Murray, *The Politics of Normalcy: Governmental Theory and Practice in the Harding-Coolidge Era* (New York, 1973); Robert H. Ferrell, *The Presidency of Calvin Coolidge* (Lawrence, KS, 1998); Marc Allen Eisner, *From Warfare State to Welfare State: World War I, Compensatory State Building, and the Limits of the Modern Order* (University Park, PA, 2000); Eugene M. Tobin, *Organize or Perish: America's Independent Progressives, 1913–1933* (New York, 1986), 131–244.
2. Charlotte Perkins Gilman, *The Living of Charlotte Perkins Gilman: An Autobiography* (New York, 1935), 62, 323; George Creel, *Rebel at Large: Recollections of Fifty Crowded Years* (New York, 1947), 367; Addams, *Second Twenty Years at Hull-House*, 188–96.

3. Donald Richberg, *Tents of the Mighty* (Chicago 1930), 59.
4. Creel, *Rebel at Large*, 289; Otis L. Graham, Jr., *An Encore for Reform: The Old Progressives and the New Deal* (New York, 1967), 101–28, 167–72; Gary Dean Best, *The Retreat from Liberalism: Collectivists versus Progressives in the New Deal Years* (Westport, CT, 2002).
5. James Weber Linn, *Jane Addams: A Biography* (New York, 1935), 283; Creel, *Rebel at Large*, 326, 370; Graham, *Encore for Reform*, 24–100, 129–65, 172–86.
6. Ibid., 173; Creel, *Rebel at Large*, 337, 370.
7. Alan Brinkley, *The End of Reform: New Deal Liberalism in Recession and War* (New York, 1995); John Morton Blum, *V Was for Victory: Politics and American Culture during World War II* (New York, 1976).
8. Franklin D. Roosevelt, *The Public Papers and Addresses of Franklin D. Roosevelt, Vol. One: The Genesis of the New Deal, 1928–1932* (New York, 1938), 680, 740, 755.
9. Allen J. Matusow, *The Unraveling of America: A History of Liberalism in the 1960s* (New York, 1984); Steve Fraser and Gary Gerstle, eds., *The Rise and Fall of the New Deal Order, 1930–1980* (Princeton, NJ, 1989); Robert Dallek, *Flawed Giant: Lyndon Johnson and His Times, 1961–1973* (New York, 1998).
10. Godfrey Hodgson, *The World Turned Right Side Up: A History of the Conservative Ascendancy in America* (Boston, 1996); Rick Perlstein, *Before the Storm: Barry Goldwater and the Unmaking of the American Consensus* (New York, 2001); Robert Dallek, *Ronald Reagan: The Politics of Symbolism* (Cambridge, MA, 1999); Paul Boyer, ed., *Reagan as President: Contemporary Views of the Man, the President, and His Policies* (Chicago, 2002).

INDEX

About the Author

Michael McGerr is Professor of History and Associate Dean of the College of Arts and Sciences at Indiana University—Bloomington. The winner of a fellowship from the National Endowment for the Humanities and of outstanding teaching awards, he is in regular demand as a speaker on various topics in American history, politics, and culture.